Every Word You Write . . .
Vichy Will Be Watching You

For Gino,

Our very welcome guest for the New Year, who travels to lots of interesting places. Perhaps this book will pique your interest in France and some of its history!

Robert W. Parson
January 1, 2014

Every Word You Write ... Vichy Will Be Watching You*

Surveillance of Public Opinion in the Gard Department 1940–1944: The Postal Control System During Vichy France

Robert W. Parson

* Lyric borrowed (but altered) from: "Every Breath You Take," *Synchronicity* (1983) by The Police. The album takes its title from Arthur Koestler's *The Roots of Coincidence*. Speaking nonphilosophically, by coincidence Koestler, a German Jewish refugee in France, was interned in a French concentration camp, Le Vernet, for four months in 1939–1940. Camps like this actually were initiated under the Third Republic but were run mostly under Vichy. He later compared his treatment there to that handed out in camps run by the Nazis in Germany, in *Scum of the Earth*.

—Robert O. Paxton, *Vichy France: Old Guard and New Order, 1940–1944* (New York: Knopf, 1972), 170.
—Michael R. Marrus and Robert O. Paxton, *Vichy France and the Jews* (Stanford: Stanford University Press, 1995), 175.

Every Word You Write… Vichy Will Be Watching You: Surveillance of Public Opinion in the Gard Department 1940–1944: The Postal Control System During Vichy France

Published by Wheatmark®
1760 East River Road, Suite 145
Tucson, Arizona 85718 U.S.A.
www.wheatmark.com

ISBN: 978-1-60494-883-7 (paperback)
ISBN: 978-1-60494-927-8 (ebook)
LCCN: 2012953727

Contents

Introduction

I retired early in 1998, after having spent more than thirty-seven years in various sales, marketing, and management positions with General Electric, the Dutch Philips Company, and Panasonic Corporation of America. My wife and I moved to Tucson, Arizona, from New York City and Connecticut, after researching a variety of media that considered various criteria for retirement places. An important element on our wish list for such a penultimate move was the presence in our new location of a major public or private institution of higher learning. The University of Arizona's presence in Tucson was a major determinant in our choice to reside in the high Sonoran Desert of Tucson.

Being able to hike, golf, and play tennis whenever I wanted to was fun, but the truth is that after a year or two, I was looking to do something more intellectually stimulating. My wife, Teruko, had done her undergraduate studies in Spanish literature at the National University in Mexico City, but as a *passante,* meaning that she—like most students there—did not technically graduate, as she had not taken the necessary oral exam or written the required thesis. Through faculty friends at National University, she managed to obtain her transcript records, and she was accepted as a member of the junior class in 2001 at the University of Arizona with a double major in French and Spanish. In December 2005, at age sixty-two, she graduated summa cum laude with a BA degree. Inspired by her example, I decided to renew my educational path, and my Connecticut Yankee upbringing aided me: knowing that two could park in the university garage system on one pass doubly inspired me to follow her!

My major at Brown University in the mid- to late fifties had been US history. Some online research revealed that the professor specializing in the colonial United States and American Revolution period at the University of Arizona had attended Phillips Exeter Academy while I was there, although he was three years my junior. I introduced myself to Professor Jack Marietta, and he pointed me in the right direction to apply to the master's graduate program in history, into which I was formally accepted in the winter semester of 2002. I remained an Americanist en route to earning my MA degree in May 2006 at a riper age than my wife: sixty-nine. Two of my committee advisors spoke about me at the departmental graduation ceremony. One of them, Associate Professor Kathleen Morrissey, amusingly summed up my thesis as being "about the stream of white yeoman farmers—mostly non-slave holders—from western North Carolina who volunteered to join the Confederacy in 1861, and two years later—if they hadn't died of disease or been killed in battle—streamed right back home as deserters." Professor Marietta related how he recently had had a student who was the child of one of his students from thirty-odd years before. The fact that I, three years his senior, had managed to obtain my master's degree that day inspired him to teach a bit longer. So went the trail west in my pursuit of my favorite subject: history.

But that trail took a turn back eastward, and I mean *really* way back, as in all the way to France and the Dark Years of its World War II plight. This was thanks to another teacher I also was fortunate enough to encounter, as with Jack and Kathy, Associate Professor David Ortiz. David taught the obligatory historiography seminar in which I and thirteen other master's and PhD candidates participated. He had the exceptional ability to explain complicated theories or philosophies so that students could easily comprehend them. Now that was a teaching attribute we all appreciated after reading one or two rather lengthy monographs on diverse subjects such as fascism, Marxism, or totalitarianism, for example, each week. Well, how did David change the life—or at least, the historical subject matter—of one hard-of-hearing old codger Parson?

One day in fall 2004, while the class was comparing the differences in fascist movements led by Mussolini in Italy and Hitler in Germany, Professor Ortiz broadened the discussion to include some aspects of Vichy France. He referred to the American historian, Robert O. Paxton, as the author of a path-breaking book published in the early 1970s, first in English and later in French, which caused major consternation and widespread debate among the French people who had lived through the Occupation, as well as among French scholars.[1] Paxton's arguments refuted the generally accepted wisdom: that Marshall Pétain and his Vichy government had protected a defeated and supplicant France after 1940 from a worse fate at the hands of Hitler by acting as a shield wielded by Pétain and his government to attenuate Nazi actions in France through a policy of collaboration in the hope of regaining French sovereignty. It was a dream—and many would later call it a shameful one—and Hitler would have essentially none of it. Paxton's thesis, after several years of very intense discussion in private and public venues that included the French press, prevailed, especially with historians of France[2] who were of the same generation as Paxton, who was forty years old when his book was first published. I remember that class moment distinctly, as I said to myself, somewhat incredulously, "What? An American who changed the minds of French men or women on a controversial subject matter 100 percent French?" I had just spent six weeks in Paris living with a French family while attending the summer session of "Arizona in Paris," so personal experience made me wonder. But the Paxtonian Revolution did take place,[3] and its message is widely respected and accepted to this day.

---

1 Robert O. Paxton, *Vichy France: Old Guard and New Order, 1940-1944* (New York: Knopf, 1972), xxxv–xxxvi. It is interesting to note that Dr. Paxton, due to French law existent at the time he was researching his book, could not gain access to the French archives for his needs. The law loosened up to some degree in 1979 (see page xxi in the Introduction to Paxton's 2001 paperback edition issued by Columbia University Press, which this author has used and prevailed upon Dr. Paxton to autograph). Therefore his original research documentation had to be based upon American and *German* archival materials. The French translation of his book followed the next year, generating press reviews and the subsequent controversy. *La France de Vichy, 1940–1944* (Paris: Seuil, 1973).

2 See multiple chapters in *France at War: Vichy France and the Historians* (New York: Berg, 2000), eds. Fishman, Downs, Sinanoglou, Smith, and Zaretsky.

3 See chapter 1, "The Paxtonian Revolution," by Jean-Pierre Azéma, in *France at War: Vichy France and the Historians*. Ibid., 13–20. See also Henry Rousso, *The*

Nearly two years passed, with my interest in Paxton filed away in the back of my mind while I finished class work and then prepared for my oral exam and defense of my thesis. Every summer my wife and I returned for a few months to Nîmes in southern France, where we had bought an apartment in 2005. During those summers, we began to break down the social barriers and gained several local French friends. In summer 2006, on a stopover in Paris, chance brought me to an English-language bookshop on the rue de Rivoli where I came across Professor Paxton's *Vichy France,* which I purchased and started to read on the TGV train bound for Nîmes. Between the dedication page and the first page of the new 2001 introduction, I experienced something akin to what the French call a *coup de foudre,* but in the sense of coincidence. The first person Bob Paxton had chosen for dedication was a history instructor at Phillips Exeter Academy, Henry W. Bragdon, by whom I had also been taught. I later found out that Bob had graduated five years before me, in 1950. In his updated introduction, Bob mentioned the continued high public interest in our American Civil War, and that in 1960 he had expected to experience similar levels of open discussion in France on his doctoral thesis subject: "the officer corps of the French army during the Vichy regime."[4] It was not to be.

A further coincidence of sorts was that Paxton was the great-grandson of Brigadier General Elisha Franklin Paxton, who died leading the remnants of the Stonewall Brigade on the second day of battle at Chancellorsville on May 3, 1863. I had spent much time walking Civil War battlefields in Virginia, which included Chancellorsville and the approximate location where that general fell. I also had visited Lexington, Bob's hometown, and the burial locations of two of the Confederacy's greatest military heroes, Robert E. Lee and Thomas J. "Stonewall" Jackson. Bob Paxton's great-grandfather is interred near Jackson's gravesite.[5] I own an

---

Vichy Syndrome: History and Memory in France since 1944 (Cambridge: Harvard University Press, 1994), 251–271.

4   Robert O. Paxton, *Vichy France: Old Guard and New Order, 1940–1944* (New York: Columbia University Press, 2001), ix–x. In future, I will refer only to this edition.

5   Ernest B. Furgurson, *Chancellorsville 1863: The Souls of the Brave* (New York: Vintage Books, 1993), 227–229, 234, 244, 362. Douglas Southall Freeman, *Lee's Lieutenants: A Study in Command* (New York: Charles Scribner's Sons, 1943), volume two, 648 n. Both Freeman and Furgurson relate the alleged story of how

autographed letter of Robert E. Lee's from 1866 when he was president of Washington College (now Washington and Lee, where Bob did his undergraduate work). Later on I learned that another relative of Bob Paxton's, Judge John White Brockenbrough, had been the trustee of Washington College's board chosen to offer Lee its presidency. The reflection from so many coincidences certainly did shine—for me, at least. After reading *Vichy France* and appreciating how Bob Paxton's impeccable research opened many minds in a foreign nation to a new interpretation of one of the most contentious issues in their long history, I was hooked on learning more about the Vichy period. I decided to attempt to contact Bob Paxton after my return home to Tucson at some point before going back to Nîmes in early 2007.

Back in Arizona, I came across Robert Zaretsky's regional study on the Gard department,[6] *Nîmes at War*.[7] While reading it, I was intrigued with how Vichy tried to keep close tabs on what their citizens were thinking through the mechanism of the *contrôle postal technique*, or surveillance system, which went far beyond normal wartime censorship efforts. The Gard archives were situated 1.5 kilometers down the hill from our apartment, so I began to think about writing a regional study concerning the system, how it functioned in the Gard, and what it attempted to discern about local public opinion in 1940–1944. Of course, I would need to visit the archives and see what records they had upon my return to Nîmes. In the meantime, Zaretsky's bibliography was a fertile source for further period reading, including other regional studies on what ordinary French people were thinking under the Occu-

---

Paxton had a premonition of his death the night before, May 2, after hearing of the tragic wounding of Stonewall Jackson. Just before Jackson died, he spoke highly of E. F. Paxton, and R. E. Lee mentioned Paxton for "conspicuous courage" in his post-battle report (Official Records, 25, pt. 1, p. 803).

6   Departments are the administrative divisions of France, of which there currently are ninety-six within continental France and the island of Corsica. Other departments exist for France's overseas possessions.

7   Robert Zaretsky, *Nîmes at War: Religion, Politics, and Public Opinion in the Gard, 1938–1944* (University Park: Pennsylvania State University Press, 1995), 1–6. I should note that sometime after Professor Zaretsky completed his research in the early 1990s and before I started in 2007, the archives changed their numeric/ alpha dossier marking system. All the dossiers I consulted started with the number/ letter 1 W (then additional following numbers) to indicate the contemporary history period starting with 1940, or so I was told.

pation in different French departments. As Paxton mentioned in his new foreword, "It is with respect to French public opinion that more recent scholars have found my work lacking." He admitted that his public opinion sections could have stood a more nuanced approach. However, as footnoted, he had very little access to French archives that housed, for example, the prefects' monthly syntheses, when he was writing his book thirty years earlier. He went on to state his reasons for not backing away from his original approach.[8]

With the advent of 2007, it was time to contact Bob Paxton. I sent him an e-mail describing my background and listing some of our areas of mutual interest: Exeter, history of the American Civil War, France in the twentieth century. I also mentioned my personal chagrin at having the same birthday as Hitler. I followed up with a phone call and caught him at home near Columbia University, where he is professor emeritus of French history. During our chat, he mentioned that he was recuperating from a nasty fall on the icy sidewalks of Manhattan, and he was therefore somewhat laid up. I asked him if he would be willing to autograph my copy of his book if I FedEx'd it to him, and he graciously said that he would. A week or two later, after I had received the book back with his most kind and too-flattering dedication words, I contacted him again and suggested that it would be nice to meet each other, if possible, over the summer in France. He agreed, and I said I would contact him in France to see how, when, and where we could get together.

In late March, my wife and I flew in different directions. She flew west to Tokyo to help her mother, who had been diagnosed with early to mid-stage Alzheimer's, settle into a medical facility that could attend to her with appropriate care. My wife stayed about three months, handling all the intricate paperwork and arrangements. I flew east to France, knowing that I had plenty of bachelor time on my hands to get started with my Gard archival research and see where it might lead me. I arrived in Nîmes around mid-April and soon thereafter made my first visit to the archives, housed in a pre-WWII multistory masonry building with a courtyard full of trees and taking up a square block on 20 rue des Chassaintes.

Although my French is far from grammatically correct, I have been able to meet French people and make myself and my needs and wants

---

8 *Vichy France.* Ibid, xiv–xxv.

understood, politely enough. I know that the French, certainly in the Midi and in many other places, do appreciate the effort to speak their language. So I managed to cope with the necessary first step, which was to get my *carte de lecteur* (card reader) for the archives départementales that first morning. The next major step—getting my gentle and clean hands on dossiers of interest to my research subject—turned out to be a bit more daunting. A codicil in the French law of 1979 that controlled archival material for the Occupation period guaranteed protection for sixty years for documents "that call into question private life or concern state security or national defense."[9] That law, though, had the flexibility to allow, upon proper approval, an exemption (*dérogation*) normally granted to research historians. The files I was interested in definitely fell into the category of "private life." These particular files contained letters, telegrams, and telephone conversations of countless thousands of people inside and outside the Gard, including many Jews, whose mail, phone calls, or telegrams were intercepted surreptitiously, read, transcribed in multiple typewritten copies if they were of interest, and then carefully resealed and sent on to their final destination in most cases.

Thus, I was shortly led to the office of the directrice of the Gard archives, Mademoiselle Marie-Claire Pontier, on the morning of April 19. Mlle. Pontier listened politely as I explained the archival materials needed for my research. I wrote down her reply verbatim in French. In short, she would have to contact the Minister of Culture in Paris to seek permission (the famous *dérogation*), because the letters intercepted by the contrôle postal were personal ones covered by French privacy laws. Therefore, the normal sixty-year holding period mentioned above applied. She also wanted to determine whether or not this specific type of letter was communicable, due to the fact that the vast majority of writers and recipients never knew that their letters had been opened. (In chapter 1, I will explain how the system worked.)

Six days later, Mlle. Pontier came looking for me in the main document-reading room. She informed me that my exemption had been approved. I would like to thank her and all the staff members who were so kind, cooperative, and understanding over the past four years. I especially want to express my appreciation to Mr. Christian Limantour, who always has been so friendly and helpful. Initially, I caused him lots of

---

9 Ibid, xxi.

headaches and extra work. I used their copying service before I started making digital photos of documents of interest to my research. I wish all the staff the very best of luck in the move they will make to new, modern quarters in Nîmes early in 2013.

Thus, I began to inspect a variety of documents that I selected from a catalog with the unsurprising current title employed for the Vichy period: "Provisional State." The documents were copies that had been retained in the office of the prefect from 1940–1945. My wife was expected to arrive in France from Japan toward the middle of June, so I spent day after day in the archives reviewing many old and dusty paper documents. I learned about French holidays, especially in the month of May, when there are several and the state functionary offices close, allowing the staff to *faire le pont*—literally, to make the bridge—and turn a three-day holiday into a four-day weekend.

I contacted Bob Paxton, and he and his wife, Sarah Plimpton, graciously invited us to lunch at their converted farmhouse in southern Burgundy on August 18. I arranged for us to stay at a B&B for a couple of nights not far from their location, which gave us the flexibility to taste wines in the Macon area on the way back to Nîmes. Bachelor days were soon over—thank goodness—and finally my wife and I headed north of Lyon toward Cluny. On the arranged day, we headed across the beautiful rolling hills of southern Burgundy to meet the Paxtons at long last. Getting to their house, even with Bob's very detailed directions, was a challenge beyond my capabilities—this was in the days before we owned a GPS. Happily, in the village, we asked a woman about *les Américains,* and she turned out to be the person who watched over the Paxtons' house in their absence. She led us right to the driveway where Bob was waiting—and worrying that we would never find the place! We thoroughly enjoyed their company and generous hospitality, including a fine French luncheon of first course, main meal, salad, cheese, and dessert, accompanied by excellent Burgundy wines. Bob and Sarah have no pretensions, and the conversation was fun and interesting and not just French history-centric. Teruko called Bob *sensei,* the mark of Japanese respect for a learned teacher. I now call him friend and teacher. Sarah is a serious painter of modern art and complements Bob perfectly. She has lived far longer in France than all of us put together. For five years, we have made these luncheons an annual event: in 2008, we met at our place in Nîmes; in 2009, at a restaurant in Lyon; and for the last three years, at the Paxtons' Burgundy retreat. Both Teruko and I say that Bob swings a mean *panier à salade* (salad shaker) in the backyard near the frog pond!

Not surprisingly, I would like to dedicate my work to Robert O. Paxton, my friend, mentor, and inspiration. He has managed to take the Americanist and turn him into a student of twentieth-century French history, concentrating on the tumultuous events in France of the 1930s that had so much to do with what happened to France during 1939–1945 and beyond. Of course, any errors or acts of commission or omission in the work that follows are totally mine. I hope they are few and far between.

I mentioned earlier that I have walked many American Civil War battlefields: Gettysburg in Pennsylvania; Antietam in Maryland; the Seven Days battlefield around Richmond, Fredericksburg, Chancellorsville, the Wilderness, Spotsylvania, Jackson's Valley Campaign, New Market, Cedar Creek, Petersburg, the Crater—all in Virginia; as well as Chickamauga in Georgia, Sumter in South Carolina; Stones River in Tennessee; and Pea Ridge in Arkansas. In the war between our divided nation, which at the time had a population of some 31,400,000 Americans, including the slaves—more than 620,000* men and boys died—two-thirds from disease and one-third from battle-related incidents. The war allegedly began as a fight to preserve states rights but evolved, as Abraham Lincoln's mind and purpose did, into *A Battle Cry for Freedom* for the slaves.[10] I have always felt one could learn much about our nation, then and now, by walking the grounds where so many men and boys fell in defense of such different causes.[11]

Recently, I was in the French village of Thines, the population of

10 Eric Foner. *The Fiery Trial: Abraham Lincoln and American Slavery* (New York: W.W. Norton, 2010). Kindle Edition locations 4676–86, 6796–6812.
11 E. B. Long with Barbara Long. *The Civil War Day by Day: An Almanac 1861–1865* (Garden City: Doubleday & Company, Inc., 1971), 700–702. Also, James M. McPherson, *Ordeal by Fire: The Civil War and Reconstruction* (New York: McGraw-Hill Companies Inc., 2001), 163–164. *On April 3, 2012. the *New York Times* published an article by reporter Guy Gugliotta, titled "New Estimate Raises Civil War Death Toll," on page D1 in the science section. Using newly digitalized census data, historian J. David Hacker has recalculated the death toll and his new estimate of 750,000, a 20 percent increase, is being well received by other prominent Civil War historians.

which is just over two hundred and which occupies a Cévennes mountaintop aerie in the Ardèche *département*. As historian Steven Kaplan wrote,[12] one of the wonderful attributes of the French countryside is that you can drive fifty kilometers (thirty miles) over the mountains and across the rivers and valleys to discover exhilarating changes in topography, climate, architecture, and light, as well as in food, drink, accent, and more. That is part of the wonderful spice of life that is France. In Thines, I took a photo of the roster of men from the area who died *pour la France* in the Great War of 1914–1918. Their *monument aux morts* is a plaque within Thines's twelfth-century church, Notre Dame de Thines, which historian and author Prosper Mérimée classified as a historic monument in 1848, when he was in charge of that effort to unify France. On the list were twenty-one men from the environs, including the church's curate. Think of this fact for a moment and ponder that in a nation of about 40,000,000 in 1914, approximately 1,400,000 Frenchmen, mostly from rural communities, died on the battlefields of France, in addition to some 300,000 civilians. Compare it to America in 1861–1865 and the indelible impression our Civil War left on our nation's psyche, kept alive by the multitude of books that continue to be written on that subject. I sent the photo to Bob Paxton, who wrote in reply: "The sheer numbers of the war dead, 1914–1918, are always shocking. I used to tell my students in the French history course to look at war memorials if they visited France—then they would understand a lot of things about France."[13] He was and still is right in this assessment and advice.

A couple of last acknowledgements are most certainly in order. I would like to acknowledge retired general Louis Danton and his lovely wife, Marie-Thérèse, for their interest in my project and for the introduction to a real local resistance hero, Pierre-Albert Clement, who, at age twenty, lost his right arm in a skirmish with some Germans retreating through the Gard in late August 1944. M. Clement has been so kind in sharing his memories, still fresh, of that time and of the choice he made as a young man from the Lozère. He and his charming wife, Cécile, hosted a lovely luncheon in her family's six-hundred-year-old mas, a stone farmhouse, in Saint Frézal de Ventalon, which is in a remote area in the Lozère, situated on a slope in the Cévennes. Before lunch on

---

12   *Le Figaro* magazine, week of July 24, 2010, 36.
13   Personal communication to author of July 3, 2010.

this memorable day, we had visited the site of the Maquis camp he had joined sixty-six years earlier.

On the American side, I would like to thank a cousin who is a professional writer, Matthew Bradley, for his close reading of an earlier version of the manuscript.

Finally, this work would never have been undertaken without the encouragement, support, and example-setting of my wife of more than thirty-five years, Teruko Izumita Parson. Instead of just dedicating this work to her, I'll continue to try to dedicate myself to her, a work-in-progress happily still!

Every Word You Write . . .
Vichy Will Be Watching You

Prologue: Investigations

Choices

"Sometimes (Sartre was right) choices were made by not making them."[1] —Robert Paxton, 2001

"Qu'on rende justice à notre souvenir âpres la guerre, cela suffit." "So long as justice is rendered to our memory after the war is over, that will be sufficient."[2] —Boris Vildé, circa February 23, 1942

---

1   *Vichy France.* Ibid, xxxii.
2   Pierre Laborie, *L'Opinion Française Sous Vichy* (Paris : Seuil, 1990), 334, 332. See B. Vildé, *Journal et Lettres de prison, 1941–1942* (Paris : Cahiers de l'IHTP/ CNRS, no. 7, février 1988), présentation de François Bédarida et Dominique Veillon. The quotation is from Vildé's last letter to his wife, Irène, before he and six other imprisoned associates were executed by firing squad at Fort-Mont Valérien on February 23, 1942. Vildé, born in Russia in 1908, came to France from Estonia via Germany in 1932 and became a naturalized French citizen four years later. He was a linguist and ethnographer at the Musée de l'homme in Paris. After the fall of France in June 1940, he made the choice to help form an intellectual resistance network with some of his colleagues. They used their connections throughout France to collect intelligence on the German occupiers, helped various people escape to Britain, and started a clandestine newspaper called *Résistance.* He was arrested March 26, 1941, when his group was betrayed by a Vichy sympathizer. See also: Julian Jackson, *France: The Dark Years 1940–1944* (Oxford, UK: Oxford University Press, 2001), 403.

The despair engendered by the devastating military defeat France suffered in May–June 1940 was so enormous among the people and the government that after the acceptance on June 22 of the armistice that Marshal Pétain supported and sought, the existing Third Republic's parliament was convinced by Pétain's horse trader, Pierre Laval, to commit *hara-kiri*. They accomplished this by approving a constitutional revision (624 yea votes to 4 nays) and then granting to Pétain full powers (569 yeas to 80 nays and 17 abstentions) to alter that document, which he drastically accomplished on July 11. Thus was born, quite legally, the wherewithal that allowed Pétain and his Vichy government to pursue aggressively a dual policy of external collaboration and internal renewal.[3] This latter effort was called the National Revolution, and it was meant, in part, to reverse the decadence blamed for France's decline in the twentieth century, which Vichy supporters gave as the fundamental reason for the debacle France had just suffered on the battlefield. One of its central pillars was to revolve around the family, rooted in traditional workplaces and communities. A new moral notion of family was born of the failure of France to increase its population, which was blamed on the liberalities of the Third Republic. Critical to Vichy's effort to strengthen the family was finding a way to toughen up its young men, morally and physically.[4]

To accomplish this mission, Marshal Pétain and his Vichy regime chose to alter and expand the role of the military censorship organization that the Reynaud government had set up as war was declared in 1939. A vast surveillance system, *le service du contrôle technique* (SCT), based within the postal distribution system, was created not only to watch society but also to monitor public opinion in areas of key interest to Vichy. Pétain's ministers employed the strong prefect and police organizations to control this surveillance structure. Vichy facilitated this effort by introducing the identity card and placing policing under prefect control in all towns with more than ten thousand inhabitants. About 350,000 private letters were inspected each week within Vichy, and their findings formed the basis for surveying public opinion.[5] Angelo Chiappe, the Gard's prefect during 1940–44, was very active in super-

---

3   *France: The Dark Years.* Ibid, 132–134.
4   *Vichy France.* Ibid, 165–168; *France: The Dark Years.* Ibid, 149–150.
5   Ibid, 259–260.

vising the repressive and opinion-sampling efforts of his SCT sections. Chiappe, a committed Collaborationist, was tried and executed for his crimes in January 1945 by de Gaulle's interim government. The English historian Roger Austin has written a cogent analysis of the SCT's evolution and its importance to Vichy, which has revealed how far some senior military intelligence officers went in redefining who the enemy within France was. They included Communists, foreign Jews, and Freemasons at the start. Also of significance was the method by which suspect private communications were to be pursued, which exposed Vichy's insecurity and demonstrated the key role the SCT played in policing. Finally and importantly, Austin's analysis disclosed how policy decisions were influenced by the regime's knowledge and/or interpretation of public opinion.[6]

Let us now fast-forward eight to twelve months to 1941 to examine an actual investigative case, for which a little context is in order. Hitler's loss of the air war, known as the Battle of Britain, in late summer/fall 1940 caused his military ambitions to turn elsewhere. First, in March 1941, the Nazis invaded North Africa to support the Italians against the British; then they entered the Balkans, where Hitler's forces blitzed Yugoslavia; and finally, they pulled Mussolini's fat out of the fire in Albania and Greece. All this was preparatory to Hitler's main objective: to invade the Soviet Union, which he did in an advance on a wide front on June 22 that took Stalin by complete surprise. By July 16, Smolensk had fallen to the Wehrmacht.[7]

In France, the National Revolution was in trouble in the unoccupied southern third of the country, which was Vichy's domain. Pétain was still

---

6   Roger Austin. *Surveillance and Intelligence under the Vichy Regime: The Service of contrôle technique 1939–45. Intelligence and National Security*, volume 1, issue 1, 1986, 123–124. Austin concludes that "the development of the SCT under Vichy can best be understood in three stages: the first, July 1940–March 1941, was an intermediate period during which the organizational structure of military censorship was taken over and its purpose radically altered; the second, March 1941–May 1942, marks under Admiral François Darlan a particularly important stage when the SCT activities were a clearly coordinated arm of government; and finally between May 1942 and August 1944, Pierre Laval's reorganization of the SCT to be directly dependent on his own office, represents a period when the SCT was of vital importance to government policies of persuasion and coercion."
7   Jean-Pierre Azéma, *De Munich a la Libération 1938–1944* (Paris : Seuil, 2002 and 1979), 378–380.

extremely popular as a person and a symbol. However, the vicissitudes of daily life were exacting a toll on the French people, and the collaboration efforts in foreign policy with Germany, the occupier of the northern and western two-thirds of France, were not popular. Moreover, on October 3, 1940, Pétain's Vichy government had adopted the first "Statute on the Jews," aimed primarily at French Jews. It was very exclusionary in nature and was followed on June 2, 1941, by a second statute that imposed further restrictions. By no means were these the only anti-Semitic laws inflicted by Vichy on French Jews.[8] We will discuss this policy later in more detail, but suffice it to say that although it was a very French variant of anti-Semitism, it anticipated and facilitated in France some of the steps implemented by Hitler as a result of the infamous Wannsee Conference of January 1942 (the "Final Solution"). This French-Jewish policy was the most damning legacy of the whole Vichy experiment. As Michael Marrus and Robert Paxton wrote, "Without any possible doubt, Vichy had begun its own anti-Semitic career before the first German text appeared, and without direct German order."[9]

Shortly after August 5, 1941, the prefect of the Gard in Nîmes, Angelo Chiappe, received a letter with attachments on behalf of his counterpart in the Savoie department in Chambéry, about one hundred kilometers east of Lyon, both of which were located within the Vichy zone. The cover letter was marked "Very Secret," and its subject was "Interception of surveillance materials" (*Interception des contrôles techniques*), and its attachments were listed as "two copies of postal interceptions and one copy of a police report." After the typical French polite salutations, the prefect went on to say that his police commissioner had conducted an inquiry into the actions of a certain Mlle. Liliane Fourny of Chambéry, who had made a reference in one of the letters to a certain M. Jean Champeyrache, who was a resident of Alès, the second largest city in the Gard department.

Both letters, from two different men, were addressed to Mlle. Liliane Fourny, Poste Restante (General Delivery) in Chambéry and were dated, respectively, June 14 and June 15. The Vichy surveillance organization

8   Ibid. 90-92. *Vichy France.* Ibid. 173–174.
9   Michael R. Marrus and Robert O. Paxton, *Vichy France and the Jews.* (Stanford: Stanford University Press, 1995.) 7. Originally published in 1981 in France and the USA.

in Chambéry (contrôle technique—whose organization and operational method I will describe in chapter 1) made typewritten extract copies of these two letters, and the decision was made to forward on the letter, written by a "Maurice" in Lyon, after resealing it. It was very evident that Maurice's letter was redolent in sexual overtones and double entendres. It also was sent to the prefect of the Rhône department, as Maurice lived in Lyon. The letter dated the fifteenth and intercepted in Chambéry on the sixteenth was sent by someone who signed off as "M. Y." of Alès and was singled out for investigation, as it suggested methods for abortion, offering the most detailed and rudimentary instruction. One suggestion was that Mlle. Fourny should obtain a long, narrow tube for insertion into her vagina through which she should force a warm, soapy solution into the womb, which would trigger an abortion a few hours later. The writer told her "not to exaggerate" the depth or amount of liquid and to try a dry test run first. The second suggestion, which was the primary suggestion, was to obtain some German eau-de-vie (a fruit brandy, prepared by a pharmacist) as the solution.

Now we come to the face-to-face interview with Liliane Fourny, conducted by Police Commissioner Roquain, probably sometime in July 1941. The one-page report to the prefect of the Savoie was dated August 5, It stated Mlle. Fourny's age as eighteen years and listed her address as 55 route de Bassens, Chambéry. Mlle. Fourny denied knowing anyone by the name of Blanchet in Lyon; she was asked this question because Maurice had used Blanchet's name and pharmacy in Lyon as a return address on his letter. She admitted that she was an acquaintance of Maurice Hamelin, a shoe salesman, whom she had met three years before at Thonon-les-Bains when she was fifteen. She had taken a ride with him in his car that day and when she asked to take the wheel, he had given her a spanking, apparently on her buttocks, in response. She said she did continue to write to him in Lyon, but she had never had sexual relations with him.

She admitted to having had sexual relations with M. Jean Champeyrache, of 18 or 28 rue de Baudeville, Alès, Gard. He had been in a Chantiers de la Jeunesse camp (more on these "youth" work projects of Vichy in a later chapter) at Entremont-le-Vieux in the Savoie when this liaison had occurred. She had tried to trick him into believing she was pregnant and asked about his intentions to marry her. His letter revealed his level of concern. He said her news was upsetting and that he was going to ask a friend to supply him with information on how to abort the child. However, she testified that she never heard further from him, which might indicate that the original letter marked *"proposition de saisie"* by the contrôle technique in Chambéry was never forwarded to her. She swore that she had never been pregnant and had experienced her regular periods, to which her parents could attest. Commissioner Roquain ended his report by saying that no contrary information had been received to bring her testimony into question. However, he affirmed that his services would maintain a continuing surveillance of her activities. He ended his report with this sentence: "Furthermore, her moral standards are considered to be very low."[10]

This can be interpreted as an example of functionaries working for the state who are simply continuing to perform their duties as ordered. Or perhaps they are also trying to follow the tenets of Pétain's national reform endeavor (his preferred reference was *redressement français*) while employing traditional and Catholic mores to investigate and comment on youth who do not meet those regenerative standards and seem to represent the worst, in their minds, of the decadence seen behind the fall of France. Decades later and an ocean apart, it is difficult to place oneself in the shoes of those state officials and understand the choices they made. But considering all the paperwork and legwork that went into this investigation, it is reasonable to ask the question: was this making a mountain out of a molehill? And was this a case of making a choice by not making one at all?

Our second investigation involves allegations that some Israelites (as Jews, especially foreign ones, were called in France) were up to nefarious schemes. The Jews in question lived in Remoulins, a commune some twenty-five kilometers from Nîmes on the route to the Roman aqueduct, the Pont du Gard. The accusation surfaced at the end of March 1941, and the investigation was concluded essentially by the end of May. It occurred in the midst of Vichy's campaign for settling scores from the 1930s and before, and was part of not only the "France for the French"

---

10 Archives Départementales du Gard (henceforth ADG), 1 W 35, four documents marked 926–929. On document no. 928 one can see a box at the top of the photographed page marked "Confidential" and indicating that it is forbidden to show or discuss these intercepts with outside third parties in order to protect its source, meaning where and how the intercepted document was obtained.

xenophobic thrust against foreigners who had fled to France but also of Vichy's overt anti-Semitic actions. These actions, as mentioned earlier, statutorily started on October 3, 1940, and were also applicable to French Jews, specifically excluding them from service as public functionaries, public school instructors, media jobs, and cultural influencers like film directors. The next day prefects were authorized to intern foreign Jews in *camps de concentration*. We will hear of an infamous one at Gurs in our investigative narrative. On October 7, 1940, the Crémieux decree of 1871, which had granted native Algerian Jews French citizenship, was repealed. This is ironical as famous Crémieux family members came from Remoulins. Just after this case was concluded, a new Jewish statute was enacted (July 22, 1941), which allowed for any Jewish enterprise to be confiscated and managed by non-Jewish Frenchmen, so-called provisional administrators, appointed by the Commissariat-General for Jewish Affairs (CGQJ), which was created as the administrative entity for all Jewish matters by Vichy in March 1941.[11]

On April 4, 1941, the office of the prefect of the Gard received a letter marked urgent from Vichy's Ministry of the Interior, written by its secretary-general of the police. A note dated March 22 at Vichy was attached: "Subject: the monopolization of fabrics in the Gard." It went on to say "*the normal well-informed sources* [author's italics] have reported that some Israelite speculators are looking to purchase some farms or buildings around Remoulins (Gard) to warehouse fabrics, principally draperies, before practicing illicit pricing on the black market." The cover letter, dated March 31 on Etat Français stationery, summarized the contents of the letter and politely ordered the prefect to have an investigation undertaken at once and to transmit its results back with "urgency." Prefect Chiappe sent a copy to his special commissioner, who handwrote an instruction to Inspector of Special Police Boyer to conduct said investigation. Boyer, who was temporarily assigned to an office in Uzès, prepared himself for his work in Remoulins sixteen kilometers to the east. By April 13 he had completed his investigation and reported that day his findings from Uzès back to his police superior in Nîmes, who forwarded a copy to the prefect on the sixteenth.

The typewritten report's subject was entered as "information on potential schemes by Israelites who reside in the Remoulins area." A

---

11 *De Munich a la Libération.* Ibid, 91–92; *Vichy France.* Ibid, 74.

handwritten annotation by the chief assistant in the prefect's office indicated that another division, the 1st, should be consulted before finalization of the matter. Inspector Boyer indicated up front that he had also gathered information from the chief notary of Remoulins as well as the recorder concerning recent property transactions for that commune, which had a population of around four hundred inhabitants within its limits. This research showed that no real estate transactions had been recorded for the period between 1940 and 1941 to date by or for any Israelites living in Remoulins or its surrounding region. All these transactions were typewritten on six wide ledger sheets and submitted with Boyer's complete report. More on this later, but it vividly speaks to the level of administrative minutiae called upon in these types of investigations.

Boyer then listed the Jewish families living there, which included members of the family of Leopold Rothschild, who had been born in Randegg, Baden, in Germany, north of the Swiss city of Zurich, in 1864. He and his family most likely fled as refugees from the Saar area to France in the late 1930s and were interred in the camp at Gurs (Basses-Pyrénées), where his wife died. His son, Issy, age forty-four, and his wife, Lotte (Levy), lived with him, as did his daughter, Marthe, age thirty-nine, whose husband, Berthold Oppenheimer, "would be still in Germany." Another child, Betty Rothschild, age thirty-seven, was listed but with the comment "at present in America" by her name. Another son was listed with no name or age and only the comment "currently in Tel Aviv, Palestine." Leopold's occupation in Germany was noted as being related to real estate and Boyer's report mentioned that it had been a significant business enterprise.

The other Jewish family in residence since the hostilities broke out was the Levy family, who also were refugees from the Saar region of Germany. Jules Levy, the father, was listed as a stateless (*apatride*) person. His wife lived with him, along with their four children. Raymond, age thirty-two, had volunteered for the French army in August 1938, and the other son, Simon, was called up in 1940 and later assigned to a stateless person camp. Two young daughters completed the Levy family in Remoulins. Boyer concluded that the Levys only engaged in run-of-the-mill business, lived quietly, didn't go out much, and never drew attention to their activities. Charles Hirsch, another Saar refugee, age thirty-six, lived with them and had been in the hosiery manufacturing business. He held a pass that allowed him to travel widely on business within ten departments of the Unoccupied Zone, which were enumerated.

A certain M. Peupion, a sales representative of fabrics for the Muller Company of Nîmes, lived near Remoulins and made sales calls there. Nothing abnormal had ever been noted in his sales activities. Boyer concluded his report by commenting that although he found no criminal activities during his investigation, on his next routine visit to Remoulins, he would follow up and report any criminal or abnormal findings he might observe concerning these Jewish individuals. The formal investigative report was thus ended.

On April 30 the prefect drafted a confidential handwritten instruction to the Gard's Director for Records of Property Administration (*L'Enregistrement des Domaines et du Timbre*) containing the speculation about nefarious Israelite schemes in Remoulins and ordered him to research all property transfers for 1940–1941, and report back to him with supporting documentation. The director reported back on May 14 that after reviewing the material he received from his associate in Remoulins concerning all land transfers therein between June 1, 1940, and May 1, 1941, nothing untoward in actions or property transfers had occurred by the Jews that the prefect's note had set its sights on. He did add, though, that his inspector had found paperwork whereby Leopold Rothschild had empowered his son, Issy Rothschild, in February 1941, to be a real estate agent for him in Remoulins. The director stated that the two Rothschilds had lived in the locality for a few months, and his sources told him that they didn't seem to have any property in the canton. He included the typewritten ledger-style transactional summary report mentioned by Inspector Boyer and explained what its columns meant. It contained seventy-one transactions completed by the legal affairs notary of Remoulins and nineteen more conducted by various notaries for properties outside the town. The report contained no purchases by either the Rothschild or Levy clans. But five choice acquisitions were recorded for M. Louis Guin in the village of Collias on the Gardon River, not far west from the Roman-constructed Pont du Gard. M. Guin, a non-Jew and owner of the Chateau de Vendargues in Caissargues, apparently had plenty of ready cash.

Functionary follow-through was ended on this investigation in the Gard on May 24 with the prefect's report to the Secretary-General for the Police (General Direction for National Security-General Direction for Police Criminal Services) at Vichy on the subject of "Israelite Refugee Families at Remoulins." The prefect summarized the particulars concerning the Rothschild and Levy families and stated that their respective activities were benign: "no transactions have been undertaken [by them] in the last months to warehouse fabrics for illegal speculation." He stressed that the surveillance continued. "I will not be remiss in keeping you informed of any relevant fact observed later on."[12]

We have witnessed, through the documentation I have seen, photographed, and now written about, two rather different investigations made by agents of the Vichy administration and ordered by the Vichy state, for which the prefect was the all-powerful representative in a French department. One could be labeled rather innocuous (the morals charge) and the other one, the Jewish surveillance, serious in nature, as in a way it anticipated in the Unoccupied Zone a census of Jewish people's locations that was imposed first in the Occupied Zone and in July 1942 in Vichy, by Pierre Laval's government. As indicated, Leopold Rothschild and his wife had been confined by Vichy in the Gurs concentration camp. Perhaps they were part of the 6,504 Jews expulsed from Baden and Saarpflaz in Germany by Gauleiters Burckel and Wagner and sent unannounced in sealed trains to Lyon on October 22, 1940. The Vichy authorities protested in vain to the German Armistice authorities, so the cattle-car train was sent on to Gurs in the Pyrénées where, upon opening, some dead bodies were found. We know Mme. Rothschild died there at some point under very disgusting conditions.[13] Whether insignificant or serious, how was this intrusive information about all these individuals—one, a young female citizen of suspect morals and the others, stateless Jews—obtained from those "normal well-informed sources"? This is a subject we will pursue in subsequent chapters.

---

12   ADG, 1 W 140. internal folder marked *Juifs 706*. This thin dossier contains all the documents referenced by date in these investigations used in the prologue.
13   *Vichy France and the Jews*. Ibid, 10–11.

The Functioning of Vichy's Contrôle Postal Surveillance Service

Collaboration in the form of "structural accommodation had been by far the most important from the point of view of the occupier."[1]

When Hitler's army invaded Poland on September 1, 1939, the French army mobilized immediately. Some three months later on December 12, 1939, the Third Republic's secretariat of state for war issued a secret prefectural circular, which set up an innocent-sounding organization, *le service de contrôle technique* (SCT), to handle a special wartime censorship operation throughout France. One would think this meant reading mail the troops sent home (or vice versa) and redacting sentences deemed sensitive by intelligence authorities.

That was not the case. Various commissions, run initially by military personnel but supervised by an interior ministry official often from the police were set up in major cities to operate within the *Postes-Téléphone-Télégraphe* (PTT) organization and its sorting facilities (*centres de tri*). The commissions listened to and transcribed telephone conversations they intercepted. They opened and read ordinary citizens' private or

---

1 Philippe Burrin, *La France à l'Heure Allemande 1940–1944* (Paris: Seuil, 1995), 469–470. Burrin's separation of collaboration into three categories, structural, opportunistic (or voluntary), and political/ideological is a helpful nuance, but perhaps as Julian Jackson points out, it is not necessarily definitive. The interpretations of collaboration, at least in France, tend to shift over time. Jackson writes of the need for fluidity in the concept but also appreciates the Italian school of thought pioneered by Primo Levi, who introduced the term "grey zone." *France: The Dark Years.* Ibid., 242–244.

commercial mail and telegrams. They steamed open these letters, scrutinized them for subject matters of interest, and if they deemed them innocuous, resealed and sent them on to their final destination. Anything they deemed of interest for reasons of security or public opinion they extracted and typed out in multiple onionskin copies marked "Secret" for distribution to designated governmental entities, like the departmental prefect's office, the interior ministry's police sections, the intelligence service (*Rensignements-généraux*), and the archives. The military or police official in charge of a commission had great latitude in judging the seriousness of a security breach; if they deemed a private communication too great a threat, it might never be sent on to the final addressee.

The organization really got going under the Vichy regime. A circular dated October 12, 1940, prescribed that summary reports of the information garnered should be sent to the affected prefect on a prearranged basis, at least monthly. This was the commencement of rudimentary efforts to canvas public opinion. We saw in the examples cited in the prologue that certain cases selected for investigative follow-up could result in dissemination of the information to several affected prefects in different departments. An additional circular of November 15, 1941, formalized a procedure for prefects to send syntheses regularly up the line to the Vichy government, as well as empowering them to request surveillance of certain individuals' correspondence. Finally, after Pierre Laval returned to power under Pétain in 1942, the SCT moved under his office, the *chef du gouvernement*. Laval placed Gaston Edmond Brun in charge of that operation.

After the war, Brun wrote an apologist's comment about Laval's efforts to protect him from the Gestapo, which had found that Brun had tapped the telephones of German journalists in Vichy. Brun's comments appeared as part of the voluminous papers assembled by Laval's son-in-law, René de Chambrun, in his revisionist effort to resurrect Laval's reputation in the early 1950s. In his three-page paper, Brun rather gratuitously summarized his function in 1950: "My duty was to present to the government a picture of public opinion through the aid of a 'Gallup-style' system, based on surveillance of communications by post, telephone, and telegraph."[2] His description was correct, except for his comparison to a Gallup poll.

What was most impressive about the SCT was the average number of

---

2   Gaston Edmond Brun. (Stanford University: inventory of René de Chambrun Papers, 1914–1995), 1297–1298, document no. 121.

letters steamed open and read each week in the departments Vichy controlled, which ran to something on the order of four hundred thousand, once the system was fully operational during 1941. Although these communications were supposed to be kept secret and were designated for information, not police purposes, it did not prevent the findings from circulating within police organizations, economic control areas, the Commissariat for Jewish Questions, etc.[3]

The need for complete confidentiality was often stressed:

Vichy, 14 October 1941

The Minister, Secretary of State for the Interior, to all Prefects of the Free Zone. Subject: Secret nature of communications received from the Civil Service for Control Technique.

By a circular dated 13 October 1940, my predecessor had especially drawn to your attention the absolute need to keep secret all communications received from the Postal Surveillance Control System. In effect, as soon as the existence of such an organization should become known, its sources of information would be dried up. ...

I ask you to be vigilant that in no case the actual interceptions be sent to the service charged with making use of the information, and original documents of this nature ought to stay in your office. The information's content should be sent for follow-up after being copied, in a form of <u>an informational note received of anonymous origin</u>, issued by <u>a reliable source</u>."[4]

Historians Marrus and Paxton have offered a concrete example

---

3   Denis Peschanski, *"L'Opinion publique,"* in *Vichy 1940–1944, Archives de guerre d'Angelo Tasca,* ed. by Denis Peschanski. (Milan-Paris, Feltrinelli-CNRS, 1986), 42. *La France a l'Heure Allemande.* Ibid., 190. *L'Opinion Française Sous Vichy.* Ibid., 334–336. Jacques Poujol, *"Une arme secrète de gouvernement de Vichy: le contrôle postal,"* in *L'Œil et l'Oreille de la Résistance.* Ibid., 127–131.

4   ADG, 1 W 35, marked 129. This document was issued by Joseph Rivalland, secretary general for the police, for the minister of the interior, Pierre Pucheu. Pucheu was the first collaborationist Vichy minister to be tried by de Gaulle's French Committee of National Liberation for treason and was executed by firing squad in Algiers in March 1944. In January 1943, when Rivalland was the regional prefect in Marseille, he did an about-face and refused to carry out a German order to furnish a list of hostages. He provided only one name—his—for which he was dismissed. *France: The Dark Years.* Ibid., 264.

COMMISSION MIXTE P. T. Tph.
de CONTROLE TECHNIQUE de NIMES
– – – – – – – – – – – – –

No 135 /A

RAPPORT STATISTIQUE
DES RENSEIGNEMENTS RECUEILLIS DANS LES
INTERCEPTIONS POSTALES, TELEGRAPHIQUES ET
TELEPHONIQUES PENDANT LE MOIS DE JANVIER 1944

–o – o – o – o – o – o –

Ce rapport a été établi à l'aide de

15.164 opinions recueillies dans 34.213 lettres lues
   782 opinions recueillies dans 47.367 télégrammes lus
 1.263 opinions recueillies dans 7.945 communications
        téléphonique écoutées .

    Les chiffres qui accompagnent les titres des
différents paragraphes représentent le nombre d'allusions
relatives au sujet traité.
    Les opinions citées entre guillemets sont des
extraits littéraux des correspondances .

DESTINATAIRES

Monsieur l'Inspecteur Général
   Chef du SERVICE des CONTROLES TECHNIQUES
   Hôtel Thermal = VICHY - . . . . EX. No 1

Monsieur le Préfet du GARD - NIMES - . . . . EX. No 2
Monsieur l'Inspecteur Principal de 1ère Classe
   Inspecteur Régional des CONTROLES
   TECHNIQUES de MARSEILLE - . . . . .EX. No 3

ARCHIVES 6 . . . . .EX. No 4

NIMES, le 31 JANVIER 1944

L'Inspecteur de 3ème Classe PIQUET
   Président de la Commission Mixte (P.T.T.)
   de Contrôle Technique de NIMES ;

"34,213 letters read, 47,367 telegrams read, 7,945 telephone conversations listened in on." What the Gard Department contributed to the Vichy Government's SCT efforts in January 1944, one month after the figures quoted by Marrus and Paxton.

of how challenging such an effort would be: "Vichy officials themselves, however, kept close tabs on public opinion. Prefects submitted monthly reports, plus additional reports on special occasions. The office of the Minister of War prepared for Marshal Pétain weekly and monthly evaluations of public opinion based on extensive sampling of letters, telegrams, and telephone calls. During the month of December 1943—the figures are scarcely believable—this service read 2,448,554 letters, intercepted 20,811 telephone calls, and inspected 1,771,330 telegrams."[5]

When I first read the statistics quoted by Marrus and Paxton, I was struck by the enormity of the quantity. Through my own research in the Gard archives, however, I came to realize how diligently the numerous agents assigned to this service toiled away in the Gard's section of the Service du Contrôle Technique (SCT). In November 1984, at a conference held in Paris by the Institute of Modern French History (*Institut d'histoire du temps present*) concerning resistance efforts within the PTT (postal-telephone-telegraph communications services), historian Jacques Poujol gave a presentation on the workings of the SCT. Another participant, Jacques Delarue, an ex-police official from Limoges and ex-member of Combat (one of the southern zone early resistance organizations), said the following about M. Poujol's paper: "I add, M. Poujol, that the numbers you have revealed have stupefied me for I was not thinking they would reach such importance. It means then there was a fantastic quantity of personnel engaged in this absolutely secret work."[6] It is time to examine how this organization came into being.

Pétain and his ministers were necessarily interested in what the people within the Vichy zone were thinking. Vichy's dictatorship had eliminated the usual means to gauge public opinion: a free press, elections, and open parliamentary debate. Pétain also wanted to reform public morals, so he had another motive for watching public opinion closely. Therefore, the reports evolved beyond event narrative and investigations to statistical

---

5   *Vichy France and the Jews*. Ibid., 181. The reference is (AN: AGii 461 CCXXXVI-G), «*Rapport statistique des renseignements recueillis dans les interceptions postales, télégraphiques, et téléphoniques pendant le mois de décembre 1943*.» As I will cover later on, I have good statistical reasons to believe the number of telephone interceptions was underestimated by Vichy in this report.

6   IHTP, *L'oeil et l'oreille de la Résistance* (Toulouse: Eres, 1986), 139.

grids tabulated on indexed subjects of interest to the Vichy state, based on the raw correspondence. General subjects of interest were food supplies and cost of living, the black market, Jewish matters, the resistance, and youth organizations. They also documented the public's impressions of Marshal Pétain, his government, and its National Revolution policies, as well as feelings about the Germans in the Occupied Zones. Although the Germans controlled mail to and from the Unoccupied Zone, it did grow in volume after Germany occupied all of France in November 1942. Vichy kept track of those letters too. The fact that private communications among citizens were being surreptitiously opened, read, or listened to did not seem to bother Vichy officials, morally or ethically. The choice made to carry out this policy so thoroughly by members of the police adds an additional element to the overt actions Vichy policemen countenanced; for example in the most dastardly case, their cooperation in rounding up the Jews in France to hand over to the Nazis in 1942.

Pétain's government appointed a new but experienced prefect to the Gard department on September 25, 1940—one Angelo Chiappe. Born in Ajaccio, Corsica, he was the younger brother of Jean Chiappe, former prefect of the Paris police, and a right-wing conservative deputy who had voted with the majority in June to give Marshal Pétain full constitutional powers. The marshal later appointed Jean Chiappe to the post of high commissioner for the French Levant, but he died en route to his new post, shot down (mistakenly, perhaps) by the Italian air force over Sardinia on November 27, 1940. Both brothers had been members of Charles Maurras's anti-Republican movement, *Action française.*

Angelo Chiappe's appointment as the head functionary of the *Etat français* in the Gard was part of Pétain's effort to select men loyal to him and his governmental policies. The office of prefect was a key link in the French administrative system. High state functionaries like Jean Moulin, deemed disloyal by their actions, were dismissed. Prefect Chiappe proved so loyal and enthusiastic in performing his Collaborationist Vichy duties that he was tried and condemned in Nîmes for collaboration and sharing intelligence with the enemy during the post-Liberation purges. He was executed near the Roman arena in January 1945. Ironically, he had most likely witnessed in that same location the guillotining of two Faita family members, who were affiliated with the resistance movement Franc-Tireurs et partisans (FTP). They were sen-

O P I N I O N

SYNTHESE

Les renseignements interceptes sur l'opinion
du pays se montrent assez pessimistes sur l'avenir de la
France et souhaitent en general la victoire de l'Angleterre
Les Juifs semblent etre de plus en plus indesirables.
Le pays semble faire confiance au Marechal Petain et a
l'oeuvre qu'il accomplit.
L'opinion pense que la presse et la radio sont asservies
par l'Allemagne et que la guerre sera longue.
Les causes de notre defaite militaire semblent etre
expliquees par le Front populaire.
Une lettre de Montfrin (Gard) denote chez une institutrice
un etat d'esprit assez lamentable.

In September 1940, opinions secretly surveyed by the Gard's SCT reflected a pessimistic outlook for France, but the hope for an English victory. However, the presence of Jews was becoming more and more undesirable. Generally great faith was placed in the person of Marshal Petain and his policies.

tenced to death for blowing up the "Maison Caro" in February 1943, killing five German troops and two French prostitutes. Today, a plaque honoring the Faitas marks the spot where they were executed. There is no mention of Angelo Chiappe.[7]

Before Chiappe arrived at his new post in Nîmes from Pau, where he had been the prefect of the Basses-Pyrénées (now the Pyrénées-Atlantiques), the SCT in Nîmes was administered by a M. Laguerre, representative for the Control Commissions during the initial stages of summary reporting to the prefect. A military captain Felip was the sub-commissioner in charge of all the telephone conversations and transcriptions at that time (July 1940). Laguerre's weekly report of July 21 indicated that due to the restrictions placed on the size of the Vichy French army by the armistice conditions set by Germany, he was moving to reduce military personnel on the three commissions (telephone, telegrams, and mail) involved in the Gard's local SCT efforts and to replace them with civilians. He also mentioned that one of the commissions could now screen mail dispatched by train for Paris, Toulouse, Rennes, Nantes, Bordeaux, and Belgium. Telegram supervision was speeding up, and the traffic had increased significantly due to the large number of refugee families who had fled to the Gard and had been separated by the huge exodus of May through June. Telephone traffic control was in a rather chaotic state, as too many individuals or businesses were requesting connection and phone numbers. He set forth some recommendations that gave the SCT control over the priority for authorizing which organizations received telephone service. He placed private individuals at the bottom of the totem pole.

It was too early to judge the veracity of themes in public opinion from such reports, but the fact that distribution of food supply was limited by lack of truck transport and gasoline was very predictive for its future importance, as was the comment on the lack of primary materials for factories in the Gard to be able to resume their economic output. On September 9, Laguerre reported that "the replacement of military personnel on the commission by civil personnel had been definitely achieved by September 3." However, a Captain E. Cordonnier was the replacement for Captain Felix. Laguerre went on to indicate that his SCT also dealt with letters coming from the Occupied Zone of France

7   *Nîmes at War.* Ibid., 235, 245–246.

The plaque honoring the Faitas, near the Roman Arena in Nimes. A new plaque was added in 2010 to honor the lawyer who defended them, Charles Bedos, who was deported to Mauthausen concentration camp for his efforts on their behalf.

and that they were informative. Again, one must be careful not to draw too many firm conclusions from his brief opinion section, but it did mention that people seemed to want an English victory, that the presence of foreign Jews was "more or less undesirable and that the country seems to have confidence in Marshal Pétain and in what he has accomplished." He went on to state that the people thought the press and radio in Paris were "enslaved by Germany and that the war will be long." Some writers blamed the cause of France's military defeat on the Popular Front movement of the mid-1930s. Lastly, a female primary school teacher in Montfrin was criticized for having expressed herself in a deplorable, mean-spirited fashion![8] That commune was at the confluence of the Gardon and Rhone Rivers, and its 3,500-square-meter chateau had been purchased in the mid-1920s by Robert Schreiber, whose wealthy Jewish family will be the primary subject of a later chapter.

Back in Nîmes, Captains Felix and Cordonnier kept their minions busy listening covertly to telephone conversations of wide variety. On July 18, the fact that gasoline was in short supply was featured in two transcribed conversations in Nîmes and Le Vigan. In both conversations the people inferred that certain people had connections that allowed them to drive around showing off. The individual in Le Vigan castigated members of the military who drove around on outings with their wives while he was unable to obtain any gas supplies. The black market was just a germ of an idea at this time. Cordonnier had transcripts of higher interest, perhaps. On September 4, an operator overheard a conversation in German between the German Control Commission in Nîmes and his counterpart in Roanne near Lyon. The transcribing operator did not comprehend German very well but did understand that the Germans were attempting to locate some people from Permasens in the Saar. The Commission of French Control in Lyon must have been listening in too, as they asked Captain Cordonnier's office for the phone number contacted in Roanne. On September 14, a conversation between an anonymous caller and M. Lufiacre, the supervisor in the Gard for the purchase and distribution of potatoes, was overheard. The Gard was largely dependent on viticulture and therefore had to seek outside sources for large quantities of food staples like potatoes, vegetables, and fruits. Phrases naming seed varieties and areas for potato production, like Limoges in

---

8   ADG, 1 W 40, marked 379 (21 juillet 1940) and 442 (9 septembre 1940).

S'est soumis aux disposi-
tions de la loi du 11/12/1942

JUIF : Autrichien

Nom *Aronoff* Ep^x

Prénoms *Gilbert*

Né le 21.12.1942 à *Calvisson*

de *Lazar* et de *Hirsch Minna*

Français par

Situation de famille *Célibataire*

Religion Juive

Profession *S.P.*

Adresse *Calvisson depuis Mai 1941*

Autres renseignements

Date d'entrée en France
né en France

The Vichy Government inaugurated in France the mandatory personal identity card system. The photo shows how they refined the process to better single out the Jews in their efforts to collaborate with Hitler's Germany.

the Limousin region, were mentioned, but the secret listener was suspicious. It turned out to be food for later thought and surveillance.

Five days earlier, a heated argument was overheard between the director of the upscale Hotel Imperator in Nîmes and his counterpart at Nîmes' Information Center. Apparently, the hotel housed the German Commission, and various civilian and military refugees seeking some permission from the Germans presented themselves to the hotel staff as being sent there by the Information Center. This was probably a case of frayed nerves and therefore much ado about nothing. On September 7, a mother called her son from the Hotel Imperator and spoke about a "Mr. Combat" and her son's need to be careful about going out. She also warned her son to speak guardedly on the telephone. The investigative antennas went up. On September 4, someone in Bagnols-sur-Cèze telephoned Montpellier to say that he had observed the contents of seventeen railway freight cars being unloaded hurriedly, for fear that the goods might otherwise be confiscated. The empty cars were needed most likely by the Germans for shipping war materials to Romania. His correspondent suggested that he complain to Vichy but the originator said that if he had no access to rail transport within two weeks he would have to close down his business anyway. He was so upset that he expressed the fear that the Germans would soon move the demarcation line farther south by fifty kilometers.

Telegrams were inspected to keep the SCT current in many areas. In July the Red Cross in Nîmes begged Berne for food supplies to feed 20,000 young Belgian refugees in Béziers and Montpellier, in the adjoining Hérault department. Other municipalities sought gasoline or transport in order to be able to plant crops for winter or obtain shipment of produce from outside the Gard. The Sussman Ehrlieh relief organization in Nîmes begged the general commanding the Marseille region for an interview, to explain the urgent situation of stateless Jews from the Saar and elsewhere in Germany. Another telegram implored the president of the German military commission in Vichy to provide an extra railway car for the wives and children of demobilized Belgian officers at Pont St. Esprit, so they could accompany their husbands back to Belgium. August telegrams went to America, including one to Dominick and Dominick on Wall Street from a Nîmois entrepreneur, seeking fabrication rights for American fruit-juice processing.

In the SCT report for the week ending August 24 it was noted that a factory that manufactured explosives had received the authorization to expand their production capacity to meet the needs of the important Alès and La Grande-Combe coal mines, whose coal output was critical to the Gard and German economies. Future public opinion sections will stress the importance the vast majority of people in the Gard attributed to their personal survival needs and the selfish protective shell they would draw down around themselves to block out other concerns they considered nonessential. But events soon demonstrated the need to hunker down for a long, tough haul as part of Germany's "New Europe" in a worldwide war enveloping France and her empire.[9]

The Hotel Imperator seemed to be a focal point for business opportunities that various citizens saw as opening the door to riches. The wine industry was dominant in the Gard's agricultural output, and the German market inside and outside France was seen to need large quantities of inexpensive French wines, which made local wine production a subject of endless speculation efforts. In the armistice terms, more imposed than negotiated by Germany with supplicant France, article 18 stated "the cost of maintaining German occupation troops on French territory will be borne by the French (i.e., Vichy) government."[10] This form of tribute, which amounted to four hundred million francs a day, converted from marks at the unfavorable rate of 1 to 20, mockingly served as a potential fountain of plenty for Germans to purchase the local needs of their occupation troops as well as export purchases of French commodities and military equipment.

One outraged hotel guest on August 26 cried out that several wine *négociants* he named had combined to take wine production from the likes of him so that he could not honor local valid orders, in order to serve the German market. Captain Cordonnier duly received the transcribed report and names. On August 29 Cordonnier obtained a single-spaced full-page report with far more detail on the same subject as a result of a call from the same M. Richard at the Imperator to another contact down the coast in Béziers. The deal described called for 1,200 to

---

9   ADG, 1 W 40, August 27 and 29, 1940; weekly report August 18–24, marked 89; August 11, August 16, marked 99; August 17, July 6, July 26, marked 145; July 21, July 18, marked 23 and 26; September 4, marked 23–24; September 14, marked 45; September 9, marked 33; September 8, marked 31.

10   *De Munich a la Libération*, Ibid., 72 ; *Vichy France*, Ibid., 53.

1,500 truckloads per month of wine. It indicated that a former Hérault center-left deputy, Paul Barthe, with influence in Vichy, was behind the business monopoly, whose initial transaction was valued at fifty million francs. The outsiders hoped to become insiders and planned to go to Paris to meet with the German officials and return via Vichy to meet with the appropriate French authorities. The challenges to get in on the action were significant as the potential transactions were financially complicated, requiring banking contacts across borders. However, the *négociants* seemed to have no problems getting to Paris at this early date when so many ordinary people complained about difficulties in being able to cross the demarcation line.

At this early stage of the SCT, when things were just getting organized in Vichy, the reporting and investigation was most likely controlled by and intended for local departmental analysis. However, as the hotel rooms and bathtubs in Vichy filled up with files of papers for daytime consumption, they included volumes churned out from the interior ministry, designed to turn SCT's evolving decentralized information system into a standardized reporting format for Vichy's benefit. Administratively speaking, due attention within Vichy had to be paid to procedures demanded by the German liaison authorities. When Marcel Peyrouton was promoted from second in command of the interior to first in command in September 1940, he issued an instruction to all Vichy prefects on September 23 that was meant to reinforce his and his predecessor's requirements for the handling of official mail between the Occupied Zone and the Free Zone. To it was attached a copy of his circular No. 120, spelling out those details. All letters had to be typewritten, and no handwritten annotations were admissible, either on the letter or the envelope.

The attachments included the original German instructions that had been issued by the German military authority in Paris in July, under the signature of General Walter von Brauchitsch.[11] They were duly translated into French by Vichy's transmissions section. The purpose of this instruction was to make clear the agreement reached on the German order conditioning the exchange of official mail going from and to the Vichy government between the Free and Occupied Zones. The Germans were to control the exchanges at a guarded crossing point

---

11   ADG, 1 W 35, marked 261–263.

on the demarcation line near Moulins, the departmental seat for the Allier, in which the spa city of Vichy was located. A grand total of three hundred official governmental correspondences, submitted in open envelopes, could pass the line per day, going north or south. The letters coming from Paris for Vichy had to be submitted to the German control operation in Moulins. It was obvious that they had time to peruse whatever they wished to examine before passing them on to a sealed transport for travel to Vichy. Official Paris-bound correspondence was to be received by German employees at the demarcation line for carrying to the German control commission in Paris, where they would be handed over to the French PTT for final delivery. Initially, each Vichy-based ministry could select twenty official correspondences per day in their marked, unsealed envelope. Not surprisingly, the German authorities approved inclusion of a limited amount of additional correspondence of particular economic importance from private commercial organizations. The instructions were extremely precise and urgently warned the ministerial distribution list of German sanctions, potentially including prison and even the death penalty, for transgressions of procedure. French sovereignty, an issue of supreme importance to Marshal Pétain and his close advisers, had the thinnest of veneers in this exchange process.

On August 3, these instructions were passed down the administrative functional line by Vichy. The Ministry of Public Works communications section wrote the correspondence in question. The letter was addressed to the Minister of the Interior (*à Monsieur le Ministre Secrétaire d'état à l'Intérieur*), who was in command of the prefects and the police. It outlined the new regulations, effective August 1, and included van Brauchitsh's (sic) French text as well. It also stressed the severity of possible sanctions for breaking the rules. Additionally, the letter emphasized the German requirement that no leaks to the public would be countenanced. It also noted that official departmental correspondence bound for the Occupied Zone had to be sent to Vichy for consolidation. The writer, Minister Piétri, further noted on August 28 that the Germans had agreed to double the amount of official correspondence per day (to six hundred total or forty per ministry). The prefects were thus informed about the increase in the daily numbers of allowable correspondence for the Ministry of the Interior bound for the Occupied Zone.[12]

For the average French citizen, especially those in proximity to either side of it, the demarcation line represented a real hardship for both personal and commercial matters. People could cross the line, as schoolteacher Jean Guéhenno, returning to Paris, did on September 1, 1940, at Moulins, after waiting his turn for some hours at St-Pourçain. His offered his impressions on the way home: "Nowhere did I see any traces of battle but everywhere evidence of panic [and] abandoned and looted cars. There had been no war. Fear had rendered it impossible."[13] Yet while Vichy remained unoccupied through November 1942, only about a couple of thousand German troops were devoted to duty along that rather lengthy and winding line separating the various zones. Wherever they resided, however, most French citizens expressed their wish for the line to disappear, and it was especially disliked due to the limitations imposed by the German authorities on how many written communications would be allowed to pass through it each day. If one thought that the official governmental correspondence limitations were draconian for Vichy, it was nothing compared to what the nearly forty million French people had to suffer in such restrictions. At first, only three hundred private letters a day were allowed, which grew later to five hundred and then a thousand. In September 1940, "domestic post-cards" were introduced, whereon a correspondent could indicate with an X their state of health or such mundane things. Many families had been separated by the exodus, so they lived often in limbo, without news of missing family members. Additionally, with over 1,500,000 French prisoners of war in German stalags, their families back home agonized over the fate of their sons and husbands. The doubt and distress exacted on wives and mothers in the rural communities was especially challenging as the peasantry had formed the backbone of those called to the colors in 1939–1940.[14]

As Vichy coped with what Germany dictated under the armistice terms, Vichy officials also organized the relationship of the most

---

12   ADG. Ibid., marked 257–260.
13   Jean Guéhenno, *Journal des Années Noires 1940-1944* (Paris: Gallimard, 1947, édition 2002), 41–42.
14   *L'OEil e l'Oreille de la Résistance*. Ibid., 28 ; *Vichy France*. Ibid., 53.

powerful representative of the *Etat Français* in each of their departments, the prefect, with the SCT organizations already in operation. On
October 13, 1940, Interior Minister Peyrouton issued a secret order to
all prefects in the Unoccupied Zone. He affirmed that after the armistice was signed, the control of communications was ongoing because
of the exceptional circumstances that existed since formal hostilities had
ceased. He ordered the prefects to organize a close, direct liaison, if they
hadn't already, with the various control commissions and their prefecture. This was to entail the placement of one of his staff, chosen carefully
by each prefect, on each commission. This person had to be a current,
experienced functionary, in whom the prefect had full confidence, and
be of equal rank to the various SCT commissions' officers. The prefect's
agent would have to swear a special oath of professional secrecy, which
the presidents of the surveillance commissions would furnish him. This
representative need not sit in every commission meeting, but he ought
to be very unflagging in his collaborative effort. The prefect's appointee
had the power to instruct the presidents which groups or individuals
should have their mail and/or telephone calls under close surveillance,
and they in turn had to report back information of interest that could
be of use.

Peyrouton underlined the importance of the absolute necessity
to keep information gleaned from the SCT's commissions top secret,
warning that should the existence of the SCT become publicly known,
its ability to function efficiently would cease. He admonished the prefects
never to employ original, confidential intercepts in their communications, as they should never be mentioned. Only anonymous extracts
should be used, with the functionaries assigned to follow-up investigations. He instructed the prefects to report back to him quickly on how
they had organized their departments to accomplish this goal, including
the names and backgrounds of the personnel they had selected to liaise
with the SCT commissions. "Lastly, every fifteen days, you will submit
to me a synthesis, stamped to the attention of the Director General of
Criminal Investigation, containing representative interceptions of that
time frame."[15] The quotation that appears on this chapter's first page
from Joseph Rivalland indicated that many prefects were remiss in following Peyrouton's instructions.

---

15   ADG. Ibid., marked 153–154.

Peyrouton himself was dismissed from his job by Admiral Darlan when he assumed his function among several others while forming his government in February 1941. This pleased the Germans in Paris and Vichy as Peyrouton had been among the plotters in Vichy who had prevailed upon Marshal Pétain to rid himself of Germany's close connection, Pierre Laval, on December 13, 1940. Fundamentally, though, Peyrouton was an administrator turned minister. He used this fact as his defense in his postwar trial for collaboration, where he testified, "I did not pose any questions. I repeat: I am not a Republican, I am not anti-Republican, I am an agent, a functionary. If I had to pose such questions to myself in thirty-five years of service, I would have to pose them thirty-five times."[16] His prefects, as well as other senior officials, had had to swear a personal oath of loyalty to Marshal Pétain during 1941. Peyrouton did not mention this fact in his statement, which basically implied that he was even-handed in doing his job to keep the state functioning under a nonchaotic, safe state of law and order. It is ironic that Pétain ordered his prefects to take an oath to him while they administered the basic violation of a citizen's privacy in clandestinely opening personal mail or listening to their phone conversations.

René Bousquet, secretary general in charge of the police, refined the reporting policy for prefectural reports based on SCT intercepts, on January 6, 1943. He issued this directive on behalf of the head of the government, Pierre Laval, who had returned to power in April 1942. Bousquet had been the key go-between for Laval in committing the French police to cooperate actively with German orders for the roundup of Jews for deportation in both the Occupied and Free Zones in the summer of 1942. (I will cover this later in depth, relative to public opinion.) Bousquet negotiated the key terms of this secret accord with SS officer Carl Oberg, agent in charge of German police actions in France, which he and Oberg signed on August 8, 1942. Vichy's quid pro quo was the recognition by the Germans that the French police were independent. This Faustian Vichy bargain with the Nazi devil over French sovereignty resulted in the collaborative efforts of the French police forces in the arrest of the vast majority of the nearly seventy-six

---

16 *France: The Dark Years.* Ibid., 147, 263. Jackson's primary source for the quotation is M. O. Baruch, *Servir l'Etat*, 309–314.

thousand Jews, who were then deported, mostly to the death camp of Auschwitz.

The intercept-related document's subject was "bi-weekly synthesis of telephone, telegram, and postal interceptions and a monthly report concerning the utilization of the SCT data."[17] It referenced Peyrou-tan's circular of October 13, 1940, and four additional police circulars from April 26, 1941, through March 4, 1942. It simply stated that as of January 1, 1943, the format for prefectural reports would be on a monthly basis. It was to arrive before the fifth of the following month, on time and limited to only a single copy. The police circulars were again mentioned, as they apparently had tightened up the parameters of the bi-weekly syntheses. Bousquet reemphasized in the final paragraph that lateness in reporting would not be tolerated, employing typical French administrative form. Angelo Chiappe, prefect of the Gard, handwrote instructions to copy his delegate-general to the SCT commission. In the context of the time, early winter 1943, the Americans had posses-sion of French North Africa after the November invasion, shortly after which Admiral Darlan had been assassinated in Algiers. In response, Hitler had occupied almost all of Vichy, and things looked bleak for Paulus's German Sixth Army around Stalingrad as well as for Rommel in Tunisia. The winter conditions were harsh on the vast majority of the French people who were hunkered down within their protective shells. Resistance groups, however, had improved their organization and had begun limited activity against the occupier. So Bousquet's effort to bring more cohesion and efficacy to these reports was not surprising. After all, he was another expert in administration, having risen also through the prefectural ranks.

After the war, Bousquet followed a trajectory, like much of France. First, he would be tried as a collaborator, but later on he would rejoin society and manage to blend in successfully for a long time. Under de Gaulle, most Frenchmen were glorified as resisters, but the pendulum swung back during the upheavals of the late 1960s, greatly influenced by Marcel Ophüls's film *The Sorrow and the Pity*. This film shattered that image of total resistance within both Europe and France, and subse-quently Paxton's thesis generated widespread debate within France about the true meaning of Vichy's policies. Then followed the period of memory

---

17   ADG. Ibid., marked 185 CAB.

searching given impetus by the documented exposure by Serge Klarsfeld of how the Jews were rounded up and deported by Vichy and its functionaries, thereby actively aiding Germany's Final Solution. Bousquet, who had been in Germany under house arrest at war's end, was put on trial in 1949 but received a slap on the wrist, a five-year minimum sentence of *Dégradation nationale*, which was immediately rescinded for what were called his resistance activities. He had friendships with people in high places, including President François Mitterrand right into the early 1980s. Mitterrand was exposed for slowing down the preparation of the 1997 crimes-against-humanity trial of Maurice Papon, another functionary, who had followed Bousquet's orders in deporting more than one thousand Jews from Bordeaux. It was highly likely that Papon never would have gone to trial if Bousquet had not been shot dead by a mentally unbalanced man in a Paris flat in 1993.[18]

Charles de Gaulle was not one to relinquish hard-earned power, at least not in 1945. De Gaulle instructed Adrien Tixier, his interior minister since September 1944, to issue a circular from Paris to every regional and departmental prefect, every secretary general of the police, every chief official for the Regional Intelligence Service, and every regional chief official for the SCT about the future functioning of the SCT. Dated October 13, 1945, the memo laid out the general instructions that the SCT was to follow, effective November 1, 1945. Particular attention was drawn to paragraphs X and XI, "relative to the relationships between external authorities and the SCT, for circulation of information and requests for surveillance."[19] Therefore, the new French government made the choice to continue for some period the Vichy policy for intercepting private communications and telephone calls in order to make further investigations and attempt to read what was on the public's mind. Some of what they interpreted as the feelings of Frenchmen toward the British and Americans was communicated to the

---

18   *Vichy Syndrome.* Ibid., 149–150; *France: The Dark Years.* Ibid., 621–624. Robert O. Paxton had testified for the prosecution at the trial of Maurice Papon. On July 23, 2009, during lunch with our wives in Lyon, I asked him if it was a major regret that Bousquet's assassination prevented him from testifying in such a trial for Bousquet, and his answer was most affirmative.

19   ADG. Ibid., 1 W 35, marked 13. I should note that the paragraphs mentioned were not in the archival folder, and therefore the document quoted is only the cover letter, Circ. Min. No. 786.

Allies. A year earlier, in August 1944, the prefect of the Maine-et-Loire in Angers summed up his citizens' attitude: "Lord, liberate us from our protectors and protect us from our liberators." The Americans had liberated Angers on August 11, but they certainly didn't know what the local French citizenry were praying for on that day.[20]

---

20   Richard Vinen, *The Unfree French: Life under the Occupation* (New Haven: Yale University Press, 2006), 330–331. The quotation is attributed to Marc Bergère. *Une société en épuration: Épuration vécue et perçue en Maine-et-Loire. De la libération au début des années 50 (Rennes 2003)*, 31.

Opinion in Summer/Fall 1940

Dazed, Indifferent, and Confused but in Flux

"The thing we must get across above all in our first issues, with evidence to back up our arguments, is that the shortages of food and other essential supplies that we are suffering are due not to the British blockade but rather to wholesale looting by the Germans in all sectors of our economy." —Agnès Humbert, Paris, December 1940[1]

"The great sorrows for the country aren't felt very much by the French people. What they feel, rather, are their own private pains. [...] If the German domination could assure us abundance, nine Frenchmen out of ten would accept it; of which three or four with a smile." —André Gide, July 9, 1940[2]

"Mme. Aubouin told me the day after the armistice she had received a letter from a French friend who held extremely reactionary political views, who wrote: 'Finally victory is ours!' She

---

1 Agnès Humbert. *Résistance: A Woman's Journal of Struggle and Defiance in Occupied France* (New York: Bloomsbury, 2008), 24–25, 306. One of the original founders in summer 1940 of the *Musée de l'homme* network, Humbert was arrested by the Gestapo in April 1941, along with most originators of the group. Tried with them in 1942, she was convicted and sentenced to five years imprisonment. She was sent to Germany as a slave laborer and rescued by the Americans in April 1945, when her first thoughts turned to her *Musée de l'homme* comrades: "My thoughts turn to Vildé, Lewitsky, Walter and the others. This is what they died for, so that Nazism should perish. And now, before my very eyes, the beast is slowly dying."
2 *L'Opinion Française sous Vichy.* Ibid., 16 n2.

said it took her a few moments to understand." —Charles Rist, July 1940[3]

"Yesterday I waited in line five hours to receive a food ration card. I was listening to the other people in line. Their heads were as empty as their stomachs. The confusion of their minds is appalling. The crowd is resigned, without hope. One would expect to wish for an English victory. But some among the demobilized feel that such a victory would add to their shame. Their hurt pride wants the English to suffer defeat like they did. No one mentions the Germans. [...] The main issue is not to die of hunger this winter. [...] This country has lost its soul." —Jean Guéhenno, September 19, 1940[4]

"Met [François] Mauriac full of despair. What to do? What to do? , he kept repeating." —Jean Guéhenno, September 20, 1940[5]

As a result of the debacle to which the French nation succumbed in May–June 1940, the despair was collectively so great that the vast majority of French people, except for those of extreme ideological persuasion, like Mme. Aubouin's friend, suffered a crisis of national identity. The armistice achieved by Marshal Pétain led, in July, to his Vichy regime's implementation of its twin Collaborationist and National Revolutionary agendas. Those goals filled a void that came about less from military disaster than from divisions within the social and political fabric of the country, which went back to the late nineteenth century. However, many events of the 1930s aggravated those root and branch schisms in France, and a moral malaise of enormous proportions erupted. France, like all other Western industrialized nations, had to be viewed in the context of the world's financial crisis, brought on by the Depression, and the impact of the foreign policy ambitions of the European fascist and Communist states. France's defeat in 1940 was caused by mistakes made by its generals.[6] Vichy propaganda capitalized

---

3 *L'Opinion Française sous Vichy.* Ibid., 58–59 n3.

4 *Journal des Années Noires.* Ibid., 45.

5 Ibid., 46.

6 Alistar Horne. *To Lose a Battle: France 1940* (New York: Penguin Books, 1979), 655–658.

on its magnitude to shift the blame to the ills and divisions of the 1930s, which, although real, were not fatal. Pétain thereby could focus on his claims that French society had been corrupt and in moral decay. This in turn was linked to the crisis of national identity.

The dysfunctional and corrupt parliamentary system and the hateful relationship between the Left and the Right were accompanied by an uncertain national leadership, whose changes and divisions prolonged and accelerated the breakdown in national solidarity and identity. Under these circumstances, straws were grasped at in the form of xenophobia and anti-Semitism, or calls for a government with special powers. The targets were the Spanish refugees fleeing Franco, the Jews fleeing Hitler, or the workers' movement in France, which was hated by the bourgeoisie. To these blinding aberrations were added myopic pacifism from most all political spectrums, a poor appreciation of the real threat of fascism, and exaggerated fears of Communism. Were the real threats within or without? The burden of ignorance was there for all classes and all political parties to bear. Therefore, as war with Germany drew near after the Munich fiasco, it is fair to conclude that the national and political unity necessary for France to support the Daladier government's war preparation plans were extremely challenging. Vichy could not and would not be "Four Years to Erase from Our History," no matter how hard many people tried.[7] It was no knee-jerk abnormality, and its naissance must be searched for in the context of the weighty broad crisis that existed in the collective mind-set within France in the decade leading up to the war.

Pierre Laborie offers a comprehensive list of the multiple, complex circumstances that weighed upon France's behavior in the late 1930s:

1.   An aging demography haunted by the memory of the hemorrhaging of blood expended during the Great War of 1914–1918, where the men who died had not been replaced as a result of the low birth rates in France in the war's aftermath.

2.   An ongoing economic crisis of major proportions.

3.   The fears of and confrontations with a reinvigorated activist

---

7   *France: The Dark Years.* Ibid., 1–2. This is the title of the memoirs of André Mornet, who was the prosecutor at the postwar trial of Marshal Pétain. Mornet served Vichy as well, when he offered his services to the state at the Riom trial fiasco of Daladier and Blum, *et al.*, in February 1942.

labor force in the summer of 1936, aggravated by the mirror effect with the Spanish Civil War.

4.   The divisions that developed in labor's ranks in the face of bourgeois society's revenge-seeking after the Popular Front government had fallen and split apart in 1938–1939.

5.   The ideological conflicts supported on the anti-labor, anti-Communist, anti-secular side by the Catholic Church.

6.   The broad-based support of strange bedfellows for pacifism, whose ambiguities complicated the obstinate effects of anti-Communism.

7.   A symptomatic deterioration of national unity as indicated by the total absence of an unambiguous consensus for action. This was largely caused by the failure of Daladier and Reynaud governments to define clearly for the French people the exterior existential threat that Hitler's Nazi state represented to the French state and nation.[8]

Not having a firm moral compass in troubled and confusing times made it difficult to discern what public opinion really was and therefore to make sense of it. A well-put question concerns what continuities might have existed under this unstable situation that anticipated Vichy and were carried over into its fabric. An example of how hindsight was necessary, even for established historians to fathom such baffling times, was offered by Marc Bloch. He wrote in May 1940 to Lucien Febvre, his cofounder of the historical *Annales* journal, that he had vastly underestimated the impact of the Popular Front on the French propertied middle class. "We have not fully realized ... the unbelievably strong, tenacious and unanimous reaction which the Popular Front provoked among such people. One must retain this date almost equal to June [1848] as one of the great moments of the history of France."[9]

In Marcel Pagnol's 1940 film *La Fille du puisatier*, the most famous scene is near its end, when the two reconciled families—the well-finders, representing the peasantry, and the wealthy shop owners, the bourgeoi-

---

8   *L'Opinion Française sous Vichy.* Ibid., 70–71.
9   *France: The Dark Years.* Ibid., 77.

sie—gather around the radio on June 17 to listen to Marshal Pétain explain to the French people why he was desirous of suspending hostilities in seeking an armistice with the victorious German army. As a result of this speech and its phraseology, most of the subsequent 1.5 million French POWs surrendered. The film, quintessential Pagnol, was neither pro-Vichy nor anti-Third Republic. However, the eyes of the listeners seemed to reflect disbelief, quickly followed by relief and acceptance, even though they were far from any battlefields in their Provence countryside locale. This was the real beginning point of the French people's trust in the marshal, a faith in his person that was borne out far longer than for his future policies.[10] They were willing to accept what he said at face value, although Pétain was not above being selective in how he darkened his interpretation of the prewar period's malaise.

Four days later, Hitler's representatives presented his armistice terms to France's chief negotiator, General Charles Huntziger, in the same railway car near Compiègne where General Foch had presented the Allies' terms to the Germans in November 1918. Hitler, planning for an early invasion of England, wanted a supine but cooperative France at his beck and call. Therefore his terms were quite reasonable, considering how devastating had been France's defeat. He called for France to be divided into two zones, an Occupied one in the north and an Unoccupied one in the south; after demobilization, a small French army would be permitted to maintain internal order in the southern zone; French prisoners of war would remain in prison camps in Germany until the war was over; the French fleet would be disarmed and remain in their home ports, but the Germans promised not to touch them; the French nation would bear the costs relating to any German troops in France. The French negotiators accepted the terms the next day, June 22, as none of them violated Petain's three red lines for refusal: full occupation of France; take-over of any part of the French fleet; German demands to encroach upon France's overseas empire. Hitler made Mussolini temper his demands, as the French had to sign an armistice also with the Italians, so both documents were signed on June 24, going into effect the next day. The Italians would administer only a small area around Menton on the French Riviera, adjacent to the Italian border. Hitler's lenient negotiating tactics had secured him what he wanted: no part of the French fleet

---

10   Ibid., 27–28.

would join the British to help resist invasion, and administering France would be cheap in both money and manpower.[11]

Vercors's *Le Silence de la mer* (1942) and Irène Némirovsky's "Dolce" from *Suite Française*, published posthumously in 2004, have several things in common. They were both written during the Occupation, and both featured cultured and correctly mannered German officers billeted in homes they shared with the main French characters. German officers and troops had been ordered to comport themselves correctly vis-à-vis the French citizenry with whom they came in contact in Occupied France, mostly until later in 1941 when some assassinations of German troops started to occur. Although living conditions were not easy for the average Frenchman in Paris or Rennes or Bordeaux, life in mid- to late 1940 was very different from the harsh treatment meted out to the French in areas controlled by the German military during 1914–1918. This is not to say that the Germans were (or even felt they were) popular with the French. But anti-German incidents were minimal at this time of triumph, and the Germans in command in Paris were pragmatic. General Otto von Stulpnagel, head authority of the German military administration in the Occupied Zone, famously said, "If one wants the cow to give milk, it must be fed."[12] Correctness and good behavior by the Occupation troops were noted by the French, and most acts of violent resistance that resulted in more brutal reprisals were about a year away.

Winston Churchill made his most famous speeches when they were most needed, the summer of 1940, quite in contrast to those of Daladier or even Reynaud in France, whose rhetoric could not match reality on the ground. Just after the miracle of Dunkirk, which Churchill noted was not how one won a war, he rallied the British people with

---

11   *De Munich a la Libération.* Ibid., 71–73.
12   *France: The Dark Years.* Ibid., 171, 275. Von Stulpnagel made his remark in September 1940. The first Frenchman executed, Jacques Bonsergent, was arrested and shot on December 23, 1940. He had been in a group of young Parisians who had jostled some German soldiers on the street, and in the ensuing altercation he had raised his fist against one of the Occupiers. German posters were placed around Paris announcing the incident. Agnès Humbert, *Résistance: A Woman's Journal of Struggle and Defiance in Occupied France* (New York: Bloomsbury, 2008), 60. Arrested on April 15, 1941, Agnès Humbert overheard her prisonmates praying that two of their comrades be saved from execution. In this way, she confirmed in her mind the earlier execution of Bonsergent. Humbert was an associate of Boris Vildé's group.

this famous rhetoric: "We shall go on to the end. We shall fight on the seas and the oceans; we shall fight with growing confidence in the air; we shall defend our island whatever the cost may be; we shall fight on the beaches; we shall fight on the landing grounds; we shall fight in the fields and in the streets; we shall fight in the hills; we shall never surrender."[13] In June 1940, he was Great Britain's prime minister, but as a former First Lord of the Admiralty, he and his admirals were especially worried by a subclause in article 8 of the French armistice with Germany that allowed for elements of the French fleet in North Africa to be recalled to French mainland ports, 80 percent of which were in the Occupied zone. Churchill and his naval commanders did not trust Hitler. The British prime minister gave an order to launch a fleet action, codenamed Catapult, which he knew would not go down well in France. That action took place on July 3, 1940, in the roads of Mers el-Kébir near Oran, where Admiral Marcel Gensoul commanded an important flotilla of the French Atlantic fleet stationed there. An ultimatum was issued by the British fleet commander that was rejected, so the maneuvering British commenced firing, which the French foolhardily answered at anchor, as their ships could not get up steam right away. The unequal sea engagement resulted in the deaths of 1,297 French sailors, and the French nation was once again infuriated with perfidious Albion. On July 4, the Vichy government broke off diplomatic relations with Great Britain.[14]

German troop levels in northern France had remained high in the summer of 1940, as Hitler was planning on invading England. But first he had to gain air superiority over the Channel, and that involved destroying the British Royal Air Force's fighter wings. Goering had boasted that the Luftwaffe could achieve this goal and launched his attacks on August 8. Thus the Battle of Britain commenced. The British Spitfires and Hurricanes, aided by the secret weapon of radar, which allowed their limited resources to concentrate against superior numbers, heroically prevailed against the German efforts to knock them from the skies. Next Goering tried to bomb the English into submission via the Blitz, aimed at population centers like London. The British civilians steadfastly persevered

---

13   *The New Yorker*, August 30, 2010, "Finest Hours" by Adam Gopnik, 75.
14   *L'Opinion Française sous Vichy.* Ibid., 239; *France: The Dark Years.* Ibid., 128–129.

while the German bombers were decimated by the RAF, and by the end of September, a furiously disappointed Hitler turned his attention and ambitions eastward to Stalin's Russia. He canceled permanently any invasion plans for England early in October.

Until his plans for England were dashed, Hitler had no interest whatsoever in changing the status quo in France, which to Hitler meant a weak and quiet Vichy. However, Pétain's uncomfortably ambitious and independent second-in-command, Pierre Laval, established a close relationship with Otto Abetz, who became very important when Hitler appointed him ambassador to France on August 3. Abetz and Laval shared the desire for German and French cooperation within a New Europe dominated by Hitler's Germany. What opened Hitler's mind to collaboration with France was the demonstration by Vichy that it would resist English-backed Free French efforts to gain a foothold in various French African colonies. In September, Vichy forces at Dakar in West Africa had rebuffed an Anglo-Gaullist sea invasion, and French aviation elements had bombed Gibraltar in retaliation.

Hitler saw some advantage to be gained in cooperating with France and Italy in the Mediterranean and North Africa and thereby keeping Great Britain off balance. France would keep Hitler's western flank secure while he planned to conquer Russia. As a gesture of his interest in working together, Hitler approved Vichy's wish to increase the size and armament levels of its army and air force in North Africa. On October 10, Pétain made a speech with broad foreign-policy implications, especially concerning Franco-German relations. France, he said, foresaw how new friendships could be developed if the "victor chose a new peace of collaboration."[15] Hitler saw enough potential to upset England in its long-established Mediterranean sandbox that he decided to meet individually with the leaders of Italy, Spain, and Vichy France, traditional rivals with coastlines and colonies abutting that sea, in order to cajole, beg, or entice them to employ a coordinated strategy.

He met first with Mussolini and got his agreement to a deal to be kept secret from the French for a while. Next, he traveled on his train through France to Spain, where he met Franco, whom Hitler could not persuade to forsake neutrality, mainly because Hitler refused to force France to cede some of its Moroccan territory to Spain as compensation

---

15 *Vichy France.* Ibid., 72; *France: The Dark Years.* Ibid., 172–173.

for Franco's cooperation. On his return from his disappointing meeting at Hendaye, he met with Pétain and Laval at Montoire-sur-Loir near Tours on October 24. In spite of numerous Vichy entreaties for high-level discussions with Germany, these meetings at Montoire were on very short notice and somewhat of a surprise. Therefore preparations were limited and the discussions were very general in nature. The result was largely symbolic for the Vichy government and perhaps mostly remembered by the French for photographs of Laval and Pétain in Hitler's company. The French people were interested in domestic issues that could lead to improvements in their harsh living conditions and, of course, in the fate of the million-plus French POWs in Germany.

Pétain made specific promises to the nation on October 31 when he opened with the famous preface: "I enter into the way of collaboration. In the near future, the weight of suffering of our country could be lightened, the fate of our prisoners ameliorated, occupation costs reduced, the demarcation line made more flexible, and the administration and supply of our territory easier."[16] The French people would remember these words, as none of these promises were kept except further collaboration. The disappointment in expectations from Montoire resulted in an uneasiness that would form the first small dent in the shield of the marshal's person, to whom the emotionally drained French had ascribed, in desperation, veneration and even the ability to work miracles. The surprise dismissal of Laval by the marshal on December 13 shifted the national conversation, but the common people's malaise remained very much alive in their subconscious.

As the first winter under Vichy approached, Marshal Pétain, who had made a gift of himself to France, was idolized by a huge majority of Frenchmen, who clung to his persona like shipwrecked people embraced an overturned, drifting lifeboat. They saw no alternative, so they consented to go with the flow toward a new national purpose, based on their faith in his infallibility. The Catholic clergy, pleased with the overthrow of the Third Republic and Pétain's rejection of its secular policies, gave the marshal its active support from the pulpit, as it felt his policies would lead the way to national redemption. The rural-centric people of Vichy, overwhelmingly of the Catholic faith, were unhappy with vivid memories of the divisiveness they associated with the debacle of

---

16   *Vichy France.* Ibid., 74–77.

the spring, so they followed the marshal in hopes of finding unity and reconciliation. The public at large was so dazed and demoralized from that disaster that it adopted a wait-and-see mind-set and had no great reaction to the collaboration inherent in the Montoire conference or the innate injustice of the First Jewish Statute. Prudent inertia, not enthusiastic support, was the true frame of mind, except for the right-wingers. The real risk for Vichy, of course, was that these policies might fail to achieve national unity. Then that government and its initiatives could prove ephemeral. Angelo Tasca, who worked for Vichy, foresaw this in his journals, where he noted that both zones referred to "the government of Vichy" and not "the French government," which indicated to him that the public's consideration of Vichy's National Revolution might be temporary.[17]

The onset of winter in December 1940 witnessed further withdrawal by the average French citizens into each of their own little worlds, beset by the daily privations they encountered in life. Finding food and home heating supplies and being able to afford to pay for them became obsessions for the French, each and every day. It was less advantageous to live in a city than on a farm, as food distribution was a huge bottleneck. Yet farmers faced challenges, as many of the peasant heads of household were prisoners of war in Germany. So life was tough everywhere, and the winter's extreme cold would make it incrementally worse. This obsession with finding the necessities of life was a phenomenon that started at this time and lasted until the Allied forces liberated France in 1944, and we will see multitudinous examples of it throughout the Gard in that same period. As Pierre Laborie rightly noted: "Despite small-scale variations, the attention paid to these problems [of food resupply, lack of home heating materials and transportation] was a foundation for public opinion formation, and constitutes for 1940–1944 a good barometer by which to measure feelings and the eventual impact of events."[18]

By the end of December, some valid generalizations were apparent. In spite of the slaughter of French sailors at Mers el-Kébir and the attack by the Anglo-Gaullists on Dakar, Senegal, the majority of Frenchmen in all zones wished for an English victory and a German defeat. These feelings were aspirations, as most French did recognize that the

---

17 *L'Opinion Française sous Vichy.* Ibid., 237 n2.
18 Ibid., 237

war was far from over and that it would be a long, drawn-out struggle. People listened to the BBC for their news if they could, as they intuitively realized there was more biased propaganda found in Parisian radio broadcasts or newspapers, which were controlled by the Germans by and large, or in Vichy's official pronouncements, often pro-German. Pro-British feelings were more conditioned by the anti-Germans ones, but neither was at the love or hate stage yet. On the other hand, Vichy soon comprehended how unpopular the meeting with Hitler had been.

Some damage control was required as evidenced by the instructions to the prefects, issued by Interior Minister Peyrouton, to stress clearly that the marshal "has only accepted the principle of collaboration" and that he and his government are "alone capable to judge the real situation born of the defeat." He continued, "Solicitous of national honor, they are following the only course capable to assure winning back national health and prosperity."[19] Two days later, Peyrouton ordered all prefects, mayors, and police to forbid listening to the BBC to mitigate its reported impact. The marshal himself publicly toured the five largest cities in Vichy, starting in Toulouse on November 5. Pétain was widely seen and applauded, but it was perhaps a small beginning of what historian Jean-Pierre Azéma categorized as *maréchalisme*, wherein people could maintain their attachment and affection for the old man, the hero of Verdun, who gave his person to France in 1940, but start to disassociate themselves gradually from the course of events, associated with terms like pétainisme or vichyism.[20]

---

19   Ibid., 241
20   *L'Œil et l'oreille de la Résistance*. Ibid., 92. At the conference, Azéma explained why historians had to distinguish between maréchaliste and pétainiste. "We have the proof from prefects who closely monitored the subject, and from the contrôle postal syntheses, that the great majority of the French were possibly always maréchalistes; but in 1941 they were no longer pétainistes. After Montoire, from which point Pétain chose the path of political collaboration, a majority of those who supported the man, Pétain, and his Vichy policies could still stay maréchalistes in evaluating Pétain, but they were no longer pétainistes in the sense that they had rejected the politics of collaboration. In 1941 the great majority of French became attentiste-wait-and-see-ers. The marshal's loyal prefects confirmed that, informing Peyrouton, their minister of the interior, "Look out, the population has just swung away; be careful; they are not following our lead any longer." We will witness numerous manifestations of this dichotomy between the man and his government's policies and the ministers who implemented them in the Gard department.

German actions in what were called the annexed territories of Alsace and Lorraine did much to damage the uncoordinated efforts to enhance their reputation with the French population. November 11, 1940, marked the start of the compulsory expulsion of one hundred thousand Lorrainers who would not give up their French citizenship. They were followed by four thousand Alsatians.[21] Both forced evacuations were preceded by the surprise arrival of seven thousand Jews, whom the Nazis shipped from Germany into France. Even Marshall Pétain was agitated over these nonnegotiated events and spoke out against these peremptory expulsions, which outraged the French people. Collaboration seemed a one-way street marked with German signposts. In November on Armistice Day, there occurred a spontaneous anti-German demonstration on the Champs-Elysées by students, which saw German troops being called to reinforce the French police. Anti-German slogans were shouted, which resulted in some arrests.

These occurrences strengthened the pro-British, anti-Collaborationist and anti-German trends that were growing nascent among the populace. Laval was viewed by the French as the poster boy for cooperation with the Germans, so when he was sacked in early December in a Vichy palace coup orchestrated by some ministers close to the marshal, the veneration level for Marshal Pétain was further elevated, perhaps to its highest level ever. The expelled Alsatians proudly spread the story of Sainte Odile, their patron saint, who in CE 690 prophesized that the "Germans would become the most warlike nation on earth," and the "Antichrist" conqueror from the Danube would be initially victorious but would reach his apogee in the sixth month of the war's second year. Defeat, however, would follow in a second period that would reflect diminishing fortunes for the conqueror. These statements made the Germans very uneasy, and as it turned out in early 1943, they proved to be not without reason.[22]

---

21   *De Munich a la Libération.* Ibid., 172, n3. Azéma notes that it required sixty-three railway convoys to pour out these refugees into the Free Zone. The vast majority had just one hour to pack up to fifty kilos of luggage, maximum, to take with them, along with two thousand francs. Re: foreign events, 1 W 40 undated synthesis, undoubtedly for late November, references the same two thousand francs allowed but mentions twenty minutes only for preparation, which could be true for certain refugees' experiences.

22   *L'Opinion Française sous Vichy.* Ibid., 242–246 ; *Vichy France.* Ibid., 55;

Now we shall look at opinion in the Gard for this early time frame to see whether or not it closely mirrored public reactions to the events we have discussed above. One disclaimer must be stated at the onset: the local departmental records in the archives for 1940 were the sparsest I found for the overall period of 1940–1944. Robert Zaretsky conducted his research about the Gard in Nîmes' archives during 1987–1988. He found similar constraints and wrote that "the monthly reports on public morale for April or May [1940] have been either lost or destroyed," while discussing the mood of the people during the debacle that began on May 10. Further on in his book *Nîmes at War*, while discussing local reactions to the Pétain-Laval meetings with Hitler at Montoire, he revealed another gap in 1940 concerning "the paucity of police reports for the months of October and November."[23]

Mme. Péricand is a character in Irène Némirovsky's *Suite Française*, who flees Paris in the wild exodus with her children, nursemaid, and wheelchair-bound father-in-law. She is a bourgeois matriarch who is a Catholic and an anti-Republican. She and her family undergo German strafing attacks and bombings in their panicky voyage south, but she manages to escape again while keeping her jewelry close to her body and her youngest children in hand. She forces a peasant, whose mule is pulling a car, to take her to a train station, where connection can be made for Nîmes, where her mother has a finely appointed house. She longs for the comfortable beds with clean linen sheets there. She is proud that her efforts alone have saved her possessions and family. But suddenly she realizes something, lets loose a choked scream, and cries tearfully to the nanny, "We have forgotten my father-in-law!"[24] Ultimately, Mme. Péricand and her brood get to Nîmes. They are fictional joiners of the more than 150,000 actual refugees who fled the German invasion to that city of 93,000 inhabitants and its Gard environs. There, the last Third Republic's prefect, Auguste Martin, had to cope with the impact of this huge influx of French and Belgians on the Gard's 400,000 people. That was, until he was replaced on September 25 by Pétain with the Vichy loyalist prefect, Angelo Chiappe.[25]

France: The Dark Years. Ibid., 174.

23   *Nîmes at War.* Ibid., 49, 81.

24   *Suite Française.* Ibid., 179–181.

25   *Nîmes at War.* Ibid., 51.

Only five (mostly incomplete) weekly reports exist covering the period from July 21 through October 4, 1940, so their value for gauging public opinion is quite limited. However, during the week of July 21–28, Commissioner Laguerre's SCT communications surveillance agents intercepted local mail that flagged problems in distributing food supplies, whose root cause was insufficient transport and fuel.[26] The interconnection of these issues would be root and branch for continuous problems in food replenishment over the entire war period in the Gard. We must keep in mind that the Gard, agriculturally speaking, had been for a long time a monoculture. Its sun-drenched fields produced large quantities of wine for export, mostly intended for table-wine consumption. As a result, the vast majority of food staples had to be imported, which would cause great problems in the times of penury that quickly descended upon the Gardois. Chestnuts grew in abundance in the rough Cévennes mountain area in the north of the department, along with some potatoes. Some cereal products, such as wheat and rye, grew in the plains. Other than chestnuts, none was enough for self-sufficiency.

Industrially, the Gard's economy carried over some vestiges of its textile business from the late nineteenth century when it had been very important. Nîmes was famous for its blue dye used in clothing, like in today's blue jeans. Hosiery production continued to maintain a minor importance, but the coal-mining output of the Alès-La Grande-Combe basin was what contributed the largest economic impact in the Gard after viticulture; coal fostered other industries to grow in the area that needed to operate large furnaces in their production process. Alès, with nearly 42,000 inhabitants, and nearby La Grande-Combe's 12,400 people were the second and third largest cities after Nîmes, according to the 1936 census. Their combined coal output, the third largest in all of France, would be highly valued by the Germans as long as they controlled France.[27] Speaking of industrial output, Laguerre reported that the lack of primary raw materials used in their industrial production was also a problem for reestablishing what had been the normal level of economic activity in those factories.[28]

Laguerre indicated that some letters had been intercepted from the

---

26   ADG. 1 W 40.,dated July 21, 1940, marked 379, 380.
27   *Nimes at War.* Ibid., 3–4.
28   ADG 1 W 40. Ibid.

Occupied Zone en route to various Gardois. A Parisian complained about the rising cost of the French staple, bread, to 3 franc 15 centimes a kilo, and added that the restaurants were also taking advantage of the situation by raising prices too. An individual from Rouen in Normandy wrote, "Can't find any foodstuffs; all bought up by the German troops who are numerous but correct." Someone in Angers on the Loire River complained that no coffee was available and again blamed the Germans for snapping it all up.[29]

The commissioner's report for August 18–24 references the departures of numerous Belgian and French refugees from the Gard, bound for their original homes from which they had fled. It states that this fact should spell relief from constraints on available food supplies, at least in theory. However, local people continuously complained in letters that the irregular availability of truck transport continued to have a deleterious effect on the delivery of the large orders for food supplies that were placed. Unsurprisingly, wine was abundantly plentiful. Local summertime production of fruits and vegetables eased things, but potatoes were scarce, and large orders had been placed, one even to Brittany for one thousand tons. Large cheese, meat, and chicken orders were placed with other areas in France. Cooking oils, fat, butter, and products made from them, such as soap, were in constant short supply. People were reported as adjusting to scarcities like gasoline and starting to try to convert their cars to alternative fuel sources like gazogene.[30] Many urgent orders for coal had been placed with the mining basin producers, but rail transportation was still somewhat disorganized as a result of the war. It was reported that the Germans had given permission for a chemical explosive factory in the Gard to expand their production capacity to meet the needs of the mines for their product. Finally, two tanneries in Nîmes were to be investigated, as they both had placed large orders with firms in other departments, one for as much as 1,700 tons of leather hides.

---

29   ADG. 1 W 40. Ibid.

30   Gazogene or producer gas systems were sometimes retrofitted to cars or trucks with internal-combustion engines, as gasoline was so difficult to obtain. In these systems an on-board digester produced a combustible (if weak) gas from charcoal, wood, manure, or other biodegradable matter. The challenges in 1940–44 were undoubtedly significant to making such a retrofit in France. http://www.oldcarsweekly.com/features/retromobile_2009_salutes_alternative_energy

Those raw materials fell into the suspicious category for some reason in the commission's mind.[31]

The report for September 1–7 was very brief and showed the impact annual wine harvest output could have on availability. Two weeks earlier, wine had been "abundant," but now it was in short supply, so prices had increased 10–15 francs per hundred liters. The harvest in the Gard was estimated to start on September 9 or 10, and sulfur anhydride, a chemical used in the distillation process of wine whose by-product is sulfites, was in short supply in both France and their North African colonies. Gard wine producers were still worried by Algerian competition as they shared the same low price-point segment of the overall market. Evidently, the vintners in the Gard were thinking that France's neutrality would still protect their shipping on the Mediterranean. Many prices of foodstuffs were cited, but the brief report ominously ended with negative comments on the inability to ship anything in a timely fashion due to the lack of transport.[32]

The report for September 7–13, 1940, mentions five subjects covered but only one, a short opinion synthesis, remains. It does start off by noting the interception of several letters expressing opinions favorable to the likelihood and desire for an English victory. Then Laguerre mentions that, according to letters opened, the presence of foreign Jews is becoming more and more undesirable. Not surprisingly, the comment is made that the populace seems confident in Marshal Pétain and what he has accomplished so far at this pre-Montoire point in time. People are suspicious about German control over the newspapers and radio in the Occupied Zone and believe the war will be a long one. Finally, the opinion is expressed that France's military defeat was caused by Blum's Popular Front government and its policies. One should not read too much into this last statement, as it should be noted that politically in 1936, there existed in the Gard a strong alliance between the Socialist and Communist parties, which combined for 59 percent of the local vote and which combination was supportive of the Popular Front movement.[33]

The final synthesis available for 1940 was for the week of September

---

31   ADG. Ibid. 1 W 40 for August 18–24, 1940, marked 88–89.
32   Ibid., September 1–7, 1940, marked 442.
33   *Nimes at War.* Ibid., 5.

28–October 4, and it would have been prepared for Prefect Chiappe just after his arrival in Nîmes from his prior prefectural post in Pau, near the Basque area of southwestern France. It is limited to remarks concerning the outlook for economic activity in the Gard. Half of the reported information concerned the local wine trade, which was very active. New wines were starting to be shipped, and the 1940 harvest was superior in its alcoholic strength and equal in quantity to a good average year's crop. It was reported that the Algerian producers of inexpensive wine were nervous about their competiveness with mainland France areas like the Midi. The fact that a good wine harvest had occurred in France caused some of these Algerian producers to offer to pay for the return shipment of empty wine casks, an item in short supply.

The local Pechiney chemical plant was making daily deliveries of sulfur anhydride, used for treating the unfermented juice from the pressing of the grapes, but there was contention over the price demanded by Pechiney. A telegram from a local wine organization, the National Import and Concentration Group of Nîmes, to Vichy's finance ministry demanded immediate action for fiscal modification of price supports for the wine "must," which they say had been promised by the Minister of Food Supply (*Ravitaillement*), or the concentrators wouldn't start the work process. This would gravely compromise the production of sugar substitutes. In the future, Vichy was to attempt to control the economy through state planning, managed by young expert technocrats, as part of its National Revolution. At this early date, there most likely was more confusion than organization.

Fruits and vegetables were given cursory mention, as supplies were generally available from summer/early fall local produce. Farmers in Bagnols-sur-Cèze reported that manure was in short supply for fall seeding. Meat was the single food concern mentioned in this report. Hosiery production was hurt by lack of material. The metallurgy industry received orders for twenty tons of zinc, mostly from forges in Alès. Railroad cars to transport manufactured goods were impossible to obtain, and the French Cement Society telegraphed "still no freight cars since September 10," and therefore an order for one hundred tons of steel rebar rods to reinforce concrete for the Grande-Combe mines was backordered.

Truckers had attempted to adapt their vehicles to gazogene converters as a fuel source. These trucks would try to burn coal or wood as the combustion source to drive their power trains. Cars proved more adaptable to being jury-rigged in this fashion as they were much lighter in weight, and a Nîmes garage owner's letter to the Vichy consul general in Madrid was intercepted, in which he asked for help in promoting him as an export source for five thousand gazogene converters sought by Franco's government. Finally, the Nîmes Chamber of Commerce petitioned and received from Vichy's Ministry of Industrial Production a loan of seventy thousand francs for its Institute of Scientific and Industrial Research. It was too early for any comments on the First Jewish Statute, even if the pages on opinion could have been found, as it was only instituted by Vichy on October 3 and did not appear in the *Journal officiel* until the eighteenth of that month.[34]

On August 28 and September 12, two gentlemen from the Gard, Roger Chabaud of Pont-St Esprit and Louis Recolin of Nîmes, wrote separate letters to Marcel Déat in Clermont Ferrand. Déat, an ex-reformist socialist deputy who had migrated to fascism, had tried to convince Pétain since France's defeat to form a single party as Vichy's political instrument going forward. He wrote in the newspaper *L'Œuvre* on July 8, "We need, like other peoples who have carried out their revolution, whether Italy, Germany or Russia, a party, a single party, which establishes and orients the shared aspirations of the people."[35] Pétain did not want this and chose to concentrate on forming all war veterans into a single Legion of Veterans as its alternative. Déat threw in the towel and left Clermont on September 12 for Paris, where he joined other disgruntled fascists.

The Chabaud and Recolin letters are revealing for how much sympathy for Great Britain they reveal, in spite of the writers' adherence to Déat and his support for collaboration with Germany in a New Europe. Chabaut had promised to write Déat of reactions to events by the Gardois. "Here we are patriotic (proud of the flag). This defeat has profoundly humiliated our people. Here they hate Nazism. They all wish for an English victory, and people listen to de Gaulle on the radio from London, not to the French radio. People hold Mr. Churchill in admiration. People do not bite their lips over the tragic farce of Mers

34 ADG. Ibid., 1 W 40. September 28–October 4, 1940, marked 449–450.
35 *France: The Dark Years*. Ibid. 143–144 and n6.

el-Kébir. ...The English people are also admired. ...The acute perception, and there is cause for it, is that the failure of our General Staff is the reason for our defeat. I personally witnessed its incompetence up close. In brief, the people here are for England."[36]

M. Recolin blamed the French Republic, not England, for the war, through France's shortsightedness in not encouraging England to join France and Germany in a triumvirate against Bolshevism. He credited England, not France, as having worked for peace (through appeasement of which he, Recolin, evidently approved). He wrote, "As for reproaching their attitude since the armistice, it must be noted we abandoned our alliance with them (as we both had been by Belgium) but some resentment has manifested itself (I do say they were not justified in the bombardment at Mers el-Kébir or the blockade of our coasts). But one cannot accuse the English of having harmed or badly served us all during the war, for without their air force where would we have been?"

These statements and others in the two lengthy intercepted letters are remarkable because both men were more pro-fascist-minded than pro-Pétain, and these letters were written in 1940 when the marshal was at the absolute apogee of his popularity. Recolin compliments Déat's courage in supporting Gaston Bergery's July declaration at Vichy by quoting something he attributes to André Gide: "If it is beautiful to perish or wish to perish in order to maintain one's virtue, it is absurd not to understand that one is going to die."[37]

Another letter intercepted on September 11 was signed by eleven Nîmois who lamented the fact that radio emissions were officially censured and limited to French stations. These people rather naively desired to be able to make up their own minds by listening to a variety of different radio sources, be they English, French, or German. It went on to say, "It is not in the least a question of sentimental friendship for England. But why does it appear that we should take joy in British

---

36 ADG. Ibid., 1 W 40.

37 Ibid., marked 433–434. Julian Jackson relates how much maneuvering went on in Vichy between factions hoping to influence Pétain's way forward. Weygand, Laval, Bergery, and more all lobbied for Pétain's favor. Bergery, an ex-radical now enamored with fascism, issued a declaration on July 7 that called for close cooperation with Germany and was supported by ninety-seven deputies at Vichy, including Déat.

defeats and German victories, when the one defeated us and the other was our ally? It is a fact: an English victory is not so precious for France. However, doesn't a total German victory represent for us the worst disaster?" These Nîmois' honest call for truth was just a cry in the wilderness. It resulted in the SCT investigating all the signatories.[38]

False rumors could lead to a favoring of British chances in the war, even from devoted Pétain and Vichy supporters. M. de Denechin's letter of September 9 to a Nîmoise was intercepted, in which he stated: "It is certain that Germans have failed in an invasion of England and have left more than 45,000 men at the bottom of the English Channel. Those who survived were horribly burned and invalided out of the army. All over the Occupied Zone they say the German morale is bad, very bad, and you can believe that this information is very serious for the Germans." He goes on to tell Mme. Fabre of his faith in Pétain, who must be obeyed and has much more to accomplish and must have the support of men like Henriot and Briand, in his opinion. He ends by expressing his hatred for the Third Republic politicians: "If one could shoot immediately the 83 bastards who voted against him [Pétain] it would be best; and begin with Blum, Zay, Cot, Herriot, Jeanneney, and Daladier."[39]

A letter of August 28 was intercepted from a Nîmois who felt that the English, in fighting on, were twisting Hitler's tail. He knew a French captain on Lord Gort's staff who corroborated that the French general staff had done a poor job of coordinating things with the British expeditionary forces. Material and personnel deficiencies had also been noted, and the writer felt most sympathetic to the British over any arguments that broke out between the Allies in the heat of battle against the Germans. He wrote: "The English viewed our troops as cowardly [incorrectly] and our aviation as non existent [true in quality of fighters and personnel versus the RAF, generally speaking], so they decided to retreat home to fight. There was nothing glorious about our efforts. I believe unfortunately that is the truth." A letter from Sagries near Uzès to an acquaintance in Vichy was opened by the SCT on September 6, and the writer thought that all that was going on in Vichy and the two zones was destroying French civilization. He felt like quitting France (if

38 Ibid. Letter September 1940, marked 13.
39 Ibid., letter of September 9, 1940, marked 428.

he could) and wrote: "The best that we can hope for is that England wins the war, and that they give us back what has been taken from us. ... It is not a question of us adapting, as you cannot adapt and stay either free or French. Moreover there is no proof that this letter will not draw the attention of a police lightning blow." He was correct to worry about this.

On November 30, a letter was intercepted from Vergèze, home to the economically important Source Perrier bottling works. The writer explained she was knitting for the unfortunate Lorrainers: "That those very correct Germans, to use the journalistic phrase, chased from their hearths so that they could steal their homes!!! How horrible! I prefer not to broach this subject with you as I cannot be calm about it. In any case my opinion is unchanged and I admire, approve of and firmly hope in the cause of the English which will result in conquering these dirty people. ... I can no longer admire Pétain. He cannot be forgiven for overturning the Republic." Another individual in Moussac, the Gard, expressed similar feelings on December 23, 1940: "Of course, like 95 percent of the French, we are heart and soul for the English and we listen to London and Boston when they are not jammed. Personally, I have full confidence in the English who are a tenacious people who above all have leaders, unlike us, who have spiritual and moral values."[40]

Perhaps some of the Germans did not comport themselves so "correctly," whether they were in uniform or in mufti. Earlier mention had been made about German Control Commission members making inquiries about certain Saar refugees in Nîmes on September 4 and German officials asking about industrial output in the Alès mining basin in late August. But it was in Nîmes that a citizen witnessed a rude insult to a French military officer by a visiting German officer. He wrote to a lady in the Allier, home to Vichy: "All these Germans here, it's incredible. They are at the Hotels Imperator and Lisita, [they both still exist today] near the Roman Arena. The other day there was a discussion between a French and German officer. The Frenchman rose from his table to go to the bathroom and when he returned, a German officer had taken his place. Politely the French officer addressed

---

40   Ibid., letter of September 5, 1940; letter of November 28, 1940, marked 797; letter of December 23, 1940, marked 781.

him … Sir… The German answered that there were no places for the vanquished. The poor French officer had forgotten that we had lost. Naturally the discussion led to the arrival of the police and then the 'loser' yielded his seat to the 'winner.'"[41]

The availability of food supplies was already a subject of growing concern in the Gard, which needed to obtain staples from other French departments. The lack of means of transportation and the splitting up of France into different zones further complicated obtaining provisions. People knew in their bones that the approach of winter would only worsen these conditions. The Gardois welcomed efforts made to return refugees to their homes in the north, including all the Belgians who had fled south to the Gard. They represented 5 percent of the normal population in the department and had to be fed and housed. An official Red Cross wire to its Berne, Switzerland, headquarters was intercepted in Nîmes on July 26. The communication elaborated on the situation: "The extreme undernourishment of 20,000 Belgians … and the urgent need for train shipments of cheese, powdered and condensed milk." By August 17, evidently the decision to provision the returning Belgians was effected. An intercepted telegram of that day noted there were trains loaded with refugees returning to Belgium with "1,550 kilos of cheese, 3,000 pairs of sandals, 21,500 eggs, and 2,500 kilos of fruit, 650 kilos of jam, 100 kilos of biscuits, and some pharmacy products." The request was made to replace 95,000 francs that had been provided the travelers. The same day a group of Belgian officers' wives petitioned the German Military Commission in Vichy to allow fifteen of them and their thirty children to accompany their demobilized husbands on a train leaving Pont-Saint-Esprit for Brussels on August 19.[42]

Other refugees who were not going anywhere were the Jews, whom the Germans had dumped in the Unoccupied Zone from the Saar, some of whom ended up in the Gard. A telegram of July 6 was intercepted in Nîmes, addressed to the French commandant of the 15th Region in Marseille, which said: "Please study urgently the situation of stateless refugees coming from Germany and the Saar–stop–request authorization to come to Marseille to explain personally the situation."[43] Some

---

41   Ibid., letter of September 9, 1940, marked 409.
42   Ibid., telexes of July 26 and August 17, 1940.
43   Ibid., telex of July 6, 1940.

foreign Jews were taking steps to get out of neutral Vichy. An American in Nîmes, L. A. Nutter, sent a telegram to Chase Bank in New York City on behalf of a Jewish mother and child on August 16, which was read by the SCT. It said: "Please pay American Export Lines, New York, five hundred dollars passage expenses Mrs. Szekely and child. Reservation steamer Exchorda leaving Lisbon September nineteenth. Have them confirm their agent Lisbon–stop–Also cable American consul Barcelona one hundred dollars for Mrs. Szekely cable reply Hotel Imperator Nîmes." Hopefully, they had left France already for Barcelona and then Lisbon, as intended. If they did, they were among the relatively few Jewish refugees lucky enough to get out of Vichy France and avoid being future candidates for the crematoria of Auschwitz.[44] As noted earlier, on September 4, an intercepted telephone call from the German Control Commission in Nîmes to its counterpart in Roanne indicated that there was renewed interest by the Germans in the names and addresses of Jewish refugees from the Saar.[45]

Vichy's First Jewish Statute of October 3 definitely caused anxiety among prescient elements of the Jewish community in the Gard. If they felt safe, the prominent Jews of means could help other less fortunate Jews emigrate. HICEM, the well-recognized Jewish emigration society founded in Paris in 1927, had a branch in Marseille.[46] A telegram was intercepted on December 25 to General André Boris, a Jewish Reserve Army officer, who came to Nîmes during the exodus and assumed a leadership position for Jews who wished to emigrate. It outlined the complicated preparation steps necessary for emigration to the Americas, which allowed only people from neutral countries, nonmobilized belligerents, or women and children from Germany, Austria, and Czechoslovakia to qualify for potential emigration. They needed funds and addresses of relatives who would accept them at their destination.

HICEM stated: "We must underline that only candidates possessing valid visas for the destination indicated were acceptable–stop–we advise candidates to register at the prefecture." What those candidates only learned later was that the visas had expiration dates set by Vichy,

---

44   Ibid., telegram of August 16, 1940, marked 99.
45   Ibid., telephone intercept of September 4, 1940, marked 74.
46   *Vichy France and the Jews*. Ibid., 113–114.

and they had to board a ship that sailed by that date, or they would be denied permission to leave. The normal French bureaucratic steps were made even more complicated for the Jews, especially foreign ones in concentration camps. The telegram from a Jewish relative in Lakewood, New Jersey, to a certain Marxsohn family in Nîmes exposed an even more difficult situation and was intercepted on December 30, 1940. It said: "It is Marguerite cabling to free my mother from camp Gurs; 7,000 francs necessary; it is Marguerite asking for her mother's bank account number so she can send this advance immediately–stop–Tomorrow 50 dollars will leave as will the same amount each succeeding month." Gurs was in the department that Angelo Chiappe was responsible for in 1939 and whose most famous survivor was the historian Hannah Arendt.[47]

That new prefect, Angelo Chiappe, whose brother had once been the prefect in charge of the Paris police, was well aware that the Vichy government was wary of Communist intrigues, in spite of the seemingly friendly relations between Hitler's Germany and Stalin's Soviet Union. During the Phony War, a Third Republic decree dissolved the French Communist Party.[48] A large portion of the laborers working in the mines around Alès and La Grande-Combe remained Communist sympathizers. So it comes as no surprise that Prefect Chiappe asked his sub-prefect in Alès to look into the current situation. On November 6, 1940, the police commissioner of La Grande-Combe reported back to both his direct boss and Prefect Chiappe the results of his inquiry into the Volpillère Company, "where a certain number of workers constituted a veritable Communist nucleus." He reported that the owner of the two workshops, Mr. Fernand Volpillère, was above suspicion.

Although his surveillance of the ex-Communist workers resulted in nothing remarkable or abnormal, he judged that certain workers had been and still were "fervent proponents of Stalin's causes." He then enumerated ten individuals, half of whom were classified as "very suspect" and the other half as "Communists but less dangerous." Their factory work seemed normal, but the suspects could gather outside to plot if they so desired. He then put in a plug for more police and trans-

---

47   ADG. Ibid., 1 W 40. telegram of December 25, 1940, marked 765 and telegram of December 30, 1940, marked 785; *Nimes at War.* Ibid., 136–137.
48   *France: The Dark Years.* Ibid.,113–115.

portation to help continue his surveillance efforts as the distance to La Grande-Combe and the Volpillère shops was not negligible. It would be nearly seven and one half months more before France would be surprised, as Stalin would be shocked, with Hitler's assault on Mother Russia.[49]

On November 27, 1940, Jean Chiappe perished, as we know, shot down over the Mediterranean en route to assuming his new position as high commissioner for Vichy in the Levant. The following telephone conversation was transcribed on December 3 in Nîmes between the proprietor of the Prisunic retail store there and his counterpart in Lyon. The Nîmois said he had decided to send a condolence letter to Prefect Chiappe concerning the death of his brother, Jean. The transcribing agent wrote: "One of the speakers read the letter over the phone and the upshot seemed to be of a manner too blatant concerning 'national sentiments,' and all the remarks they exchanged were ironically nuanced, interspersed often with mocking snickers. It seemed to come out again that the sender of this letter is expressing feelings quite different from all those that are written." The agent or his supervisor hand wrote below the transcription: "Reported and for the edification of the prefect's office manager." Undoubtedly the boss himself would get to see the condolence letter, which was to be put in his hands, and then judge it in light of this interpretive report from the SCT.[50]

As winter set in, the people of the Gard were adjusting to a new prefect who was Corsican, Catholic, and a fervent supporter of collaboration, based ideologically on intolerance toward Communists, Jews, and Freemasons.[51] Chiappe's endorsement of Pétain's, Darlan's, and Laval's policies for cooperation with Germany will be examined more closely as we go forward. His Corsican birth did not help him in the Gard, and the close working relationship he developed with the head of the Catholic Church in Nîmes, Bishop Jean Girbeau, would cause future problems with the strong Protestant minority that existed in the department. Even though the evidence might be limited, we have seen examples that strongly indicate that the Gardois, although most concerned about their individual well-being for survival under toughening

---

49   ADG 1 W 40. Ibid., report dated November 6, 1940 #2, 501.
50   Ibid. Telephone interception of December 3, 1940, marked 845.
51   *France: The Dark Years.* Ibid., 266.

conditions, were pro-English and anti-German. It was not total love for the one and hate for the other, but the hate side would start taking a continuous upward path later in 1941, and true Anglophobia would never come into being.

Opinion in 1941

The First Winter/Spring of Discontent, the Summer Solstice Surprise, and the Winds of Collaboration's Fall from Grace

"Yesterday evening I turned on Vichy radio just at the moment where Marshal Pétain was reading a new message to the French people …M. Flandin was replacing M. Laval …who was no longer 'the dauphin.' The marshal furthermore assured France …and M. Hitler that he had dismissed M. Laval for domestic political reasons; foreign policy would not be modified. So Laval was dropped by Pétain. Had he promised too much to the Germans and forced a 'cornered' Pétain to fight back? Or was the affair purely 'domestic'?" —Jean Guéhenno, December 15, 1940[1]

"Cold and hunger for so many people. It's misery.... Material life is becoming more and more difficult, potatoes are rarely found."
—Jean Guéhenno, December 23, 1940[2]

"Life in Paris has become very difficult. We have ration books, but they are good for nothing as the shops are empty. We have managed to live at home the past fifteen days thanks to food packages we have received from friends and cousins in Brittany."
—Jean Guéhenno, January 3, 1941[3]

---

1   *Journal des Années Noires.* Ibid., 79–80.
2   Ibid., 82–83.
3   Ibid., 89.

"France, France, do you hear? Will you let yourself be sold by Darlan? (Sung to the air of Frère Jacques on the BBC)." —Jean Guéhenno, May 6, 1941[4]

"Yesterday in the name of French law, 5,000 Jews were taken to concentration camps. Poor Jews come from Poland, Austria, Czechoslovakia, miserable people of little means put in great peril by the state. It's called a purge. On rue Compans several men had been led away. Their wives, their children begged tearfully to the police but in vain. The average Parisian who witnessed these heartrending scenes was revolted and full of shame." —Jean Guéhenno, May 16, 1941[5]

Pierre Laval had been busy traveling between Vichy and Paris in early December in his attempt to implement the "New Policy" of collaboration with German authorities in France that had come out of the Montoire meetings. The problem was that he had very minimal results to show for his efforts, and his overt taking of the reins in hand in these negotiations had created jealous enemies for him within Vichy's inner circle, enemies who included Marshal Pétain himself. On the evening of December 13, Marshal Pétain called a surprise meeting of every member of the Council of Ministers and asked each member to write out a letter of resignation. An oblivious Laval added his to the pile and was shocked when Pétain accepted it. This was immediately followed by Interior Minister Peyrouton's special security police taking Laval off to his country home at nearby Chateldon and placing him under house arrest. This bizarre cabinet shuffling was unannounced to the Germans, and its news created an angry uproar in Paris from Laval's friend, Ambassador Otto Abetz, which came near to shattering relations between the two countries.

Abetz considered Laval of key importance to his efforts to wrest control of Franco-German relations from the German military in

---

4   Ibid., 137.
5   Ibid. ,139. According to Marrus and Paxton, the majority of the 3,700 Jewish males (the actual number) who received police summonses on May 14 to report to the Paris Prefecture of Police did just that and were arrested and sent off to the camps at Pithiviers and Beaune-la-Rolande, which would become infamous as final deportation assembly points for Auschwitz. *Vichy France and the Jews.* Ibid., 223.

France, so he had his own agenda to protect when he informed Hitler of Laval's dismissal. Hitler had a long revanchist memory over the humiliating defeat of 1918, along with many other reasons not to trust the French. Pétain's lightning-bolt action ruined the ceremony Hitler had prepared on December 15 for the reburial at the Invalides of Napoleon's son, the Duc de Reichstadt, which added fuel to the fire. Hitler always suspected, mistakenly so, that Pétain was a closet revanchist. However, beyond any reason for anger, the Führer was really not very interested in French collaboration except for keeping France quiescent, as a source of wartime supply for Germany's benefit. This was especially so, as in late September, Hitler already had turned his military ambitions to the east and Mother Russia after Goering's failure in the Battle of Britain. On December 18, Hitler issued orders to delay Operation Barbarossa, the operational plan for the invasion of Russia, until June 1941. Two days earlier, a furious Abetz arrived in Vichy and took Laval away to Paris at gunpoint. But the "New Policy," from Germany's point of view, was put into abeyance founded on loss of interest.

The Paris-based *lycée* professor Jean Guéhenno had no idea how prescient his journal comment on Laval's dismissal was. The quotation had ended: "So Laval was dropped by Pétain. Had he promised too much to the Germans and forced a 'cornered' Pétain to fight back? Or was the affair purely 'domestic'?" From the French side the reasons behind the shock of December 13 had both domestic and exterior relation causes, but the weight was balanced on the domestic side. Laval had some personal habits that grated on the austere octogenarian Pétain. Laval's slovenly unkemptness was an irritant to Pétain, but the fact that Laval, a chain-smoker, continuously blew cigarette smoke in the marshal's face was especially exasperating to the dour old man. Yet mannerisms like these were minor compared to how Pétain was affronted by what he felt was disrespect for the Marshal's position by Laval, "*le maquignon*" (the horse-trader) who sought the spotlight alone to negotiate the desired post-armistice settlement with Germany. Laval thereby needed to deliver on his promises to improve living conditions in France under the armistice. However, there was a trend in Vichy to rid former parliamentarians from its ministries. Laval was the last parliamentarian to go.

The fact remains that Laval failed in extracting the minimum that Pétain wanted post-Montoire: significant releases of French POWs;

reduction of Occupation costs; easing of the demarcation line; improved living conditions for the French people. But the domestic issue that put the nail in Laval's coffin was the humiliating fiasco suffered over Pétain's desire to rule Vichy from Paris, a move that Laval opposed. Vichy made an outlandish maneuver, which had to have Pétain's tacit approval, when it announced unilaterally that Vichy would have two alternating capitals, Versailles and Vichy. Germany was not consulted at all, and Hitler's predictable reaction on November 29 was to countermand the order on technical grounds. Laval had been in Paris on this date, and he was viewed with suspicion by his many rival ministers, including Peyrouton, Bouthillier, and Alibert.[6] Pétain was upset by being denied the right given in the armistice agreement to have the seat of French government in Paris, and Laval was doomed. But the main Vichy foreign-policy tenet remained: to continue to collaborate with Germany in order to regain sovereignty over their internal affairs and operate as an equal partner along with Hitler and his invincible army in his New Europe.

Three ironies were apparent—one right away in December and the other two during winter 1941. Pétain, as a result of these events, only increased his personal popularity among the French people. His firing of Laval was viewed initially at least as a defense of France and a slap in the face of Germany. Laval, whom the French considered a rank advocate of collaboration, was replaced briefly by Flandin and then on February 9 by Admiral François Darlan, whose appointment was accepted by Abetz and Berlin. The second irony is that Darlan ended up pushing for more intensive collaboration than Laval or Pétain had even envisaged up to that point in time. The third paradox is that Hitler, who had eschewed cooperation with France in Africa, was forced to prop up his Italian ally, Mussolini, in Libya by dispatching Rommel's Africa Corps there on February 22 in order to counter English advances. A sign appeared in Cahors in January 1941 concerning the Italian cross Hitler had to bear, first in Greece and now in North Africa: "If you wish to visit Italy, join the Greek army."[7]

Whatever the basis for Pétain's decision to fire Laval—and he could very well have had some ulterior motives for so doing—his image as the

---

6 *France: The Dark Years.* Ibid., 175.
7 *Vichy France.* Ibid., 102–109.
L'Opinion Française sous Vichy. Ibid., 240 n2.

father protector definitely benefited from the event, as Laval was the poster boy figure for active partnership with Germany. People saw the marshal as a super patriot, courageously protecting France's sovereignty and ferociously resisting the occupier. This fact strengthened his reputation and the confidence the French felt in him. This was a strong feeling widely espoused by the populace that grew right into the late spring of 1941, despite the great physical hardships of the winter.

More subconsciously felt—but ripe for reaction to the proper events—were a couple of other germinating seeds of public opinion. The majority of French stomachs were queasy about a state policy of collaboration with Hitler. It fed on the marshal's ambivalence toward such policies, some pro, some con, which led to confusion concerning Laval's efforts for realpolitik under a Germany, whom many Frenchmen felt would win the war. This aversion to collaboration had nothing to do with the formation of any resistance in France, which was just a speck in the eye of the beholder at this time. For example, Captain Henri Frenay left the army to start the Combat resistance group in the Unoccupied Zone early in 1941. Combat and its competitors entered the organizational phase for resistance movements springing up in the south. However, the majority of Frenchmen adhered to a wait-and-see frame of mind; this mind-set had on its flanks strong loyalty to the marshal and suspicion, if not dislike, of collaboration. At first these trends were subordinated to the immediate problems of daily living under the vicissitudes posed by harsh winter conditions. But the dislike for the Germans and collaboration with them was a trend that would resurface later in 1941, which resulted in divorcing the majority of the French people, over time, from being married to Vichy state policies. This separation would begin to be revealed during 1941, but not in a linear, upward path; there would be ups and downs, yet the road to the tumultuous break in public opinion with Vichy and its policies in 1942–1943 would be irreversible.[8]

Admiral Darlan, the head of France's most visible and moveable asset, its fleet, was a powerful figure whose support Pétain appreciated. In contrast to Laval, his military orderliness was another asset in Pétain's eyes, as well as the vision they shared that Germany would win the war—Pétain, probably; Darlan, highly likely—and that collaboration with Germany was necessary (Pétain, for allowing domestic reforma-

---

8 Ibid., 247.

tion; Darlan, for economic competitiveness in a New Europe along with military cooperation with Germany to protect France's colonies). As a personality, Darlan could be scheming and opportunistic. Upon being appointed Pétain's dauphin as vice-president of the council, he kept his portfolio as naval minister and sought to protect his flanks from rival ministers, which Laval had failed to do. He obtained Pétain's permission to head up several other ministries, including Foreign Affairs, Information, Interior, and later, Defense. These multiple positions suited his extravagant tastes and gave him great bargaining power, along with which came the onus to produce results for Pétain and Vichy.

To further French collaboration efforts, Darlan had to counter the cold shoulder that Laval's dismissal had created among the Occupation agencies. To accomplish this he saw as crucial the need to find a way to interest Hitler again in France. Darlan and the French had been impressed by Hitler's lightning victory over the Yugoslavs in April. Around the same time, Darlan saw two anti-British events in North Africa and the Middle East that might renew Hitler's interest in cooperating with France, which could gain some quid pro quos. These were Rommel's counter-offensive, aimed at Egypt, and the Arab revolt in Baghdad, where permission to overfly Syria and use French airfields to refuel would aid German efforts in Iraq. Both seemed to indicate Hitler's renewed interest in the Mediterranean. Darlan sensed a thaw in the wind when Ambassador Abetz informed him that he would be welcomed at Berchtesgaden in early May. He was ready to offer French support for a strategic design that he felt could gain concessions for France from Hitler.

In preparation for his Hitler summit, Darlan met early in May with Abetz in Paris, where Darlan approved German usage of French airbases in Syria in support of the anti-British revolt in Iraq. He asked for German concessions in exchange, relative to reducing occupation costs, easing of demarcation line restrictions, and further returns home of French POWs from Germany. Abetz did not have the authority to approve such special considerations and other than promising further talks on Occupation costs, he basically delayed any discussion of these issues until the Hitler meeting scheduled for May 11. On the surface, the meeting went well, with Hitler saying that Germany was winning the war but that cooperation from France could hasten the victory over

England. He said that each dispensation made by France would be met by one of equal significance by Germany. Darlan returned to Vichy to report that state collaboration in domestic production for German needs and military cooperation in appropriate colonies was the way for France to gain bargaining power.

Pétain spoke to the nation on the radio on May 15: "Frenchmen: You have learned that Admiral Darlan recently conferred with Chancellor Hitler. I had approved this meeting in principle. The new interview permits us to light up the road into the future and to continue the conversations that had begun with the German government. It is no longer a question today of public opinion, often uneasy and badly informed, being able to estimate the chances we are taking or measure the risks we take or judge our acts. For you, the French people, it is simply a question of following me without mental reservation along the path of honor and national interest. If through our close discipline and our public spirit we can conduct the negotiations in progress, France will surmount her defeat and preserve in the world her rank as a European and colonial power. That, my dear friends, is all that I have to say to you today."[9]

This strategy became the basis on May 27 of the Protocols of Paris, which Darlan signed for Vichy, and Abetz and other military officials signed for Germany. The military concessions made by Darlan on behalf of Vichy were striking, especially in light of Vichy France's existing policy of neutrality: 1) formal acceptance by the French of German usage of its airbases in Syria; 2) permission for Germany to resupply Rommel's army via the French Tunisian port of Bizerte; 3) permission for German submarines to operate eventually out of a special facility in Dakar, Senegal. These contrasted greatly with the minor concessions made by the Germans in return: a slight reduction in the monthly Occupation costs; the return home of about 100,000 aged POWs; a small moderation in the demarcation line procedures; and allowance of some minor enhancements for Vichy's military.[10] A fourth protocol was signed semi-secretly by Abetz and Darlan but was not announced to the public. It promised eventual publicity by the German government "to justify

---

9   *New York Times*. Reported on May 16, 1941. http://www.ibiblio.org/pha/policy/1941/410515b.html

10   *Vichy France*. Ibid., 117–118; *France: The Dark Years*. Ibid., 179–180.

before French public opinion the eventuality of an armed conflict with England and the United States."[11]

All was for naught, as events in the colonies very quickly were to take control over the bargaining process. There is much historical debate over why the French side did not approve all the protocols, but it certainly stemmed from the lack of Germans concessions. The French turndown was heavily influenced by the objections raised by Delegate-General Maxime Weygand, who rushed back from Algeria to Vichy on June 3. He argued angrily that military cooperation in his North African command with Germany would be self-defeating and ease the path of the Gaullist dissidents to gain traction in France's overseas colonies. The British had watched with dismay the arrival of the first Luftwaffe planes in France's Syrian airfields in early May. The chicken that Weygand warned against came home to roost only four days later when the English aided a Free French invasion of Syria on June 7, 1941. The Vichy troops put up stiff resistance, but after a month they surrendered, and Syria was lost to Vichy and thereby neutralized by the Gaullists for their British allies. This protocol concession to Germany proved most embarrassing to Darlan and Pétain.

When Vichy's Council of Ministers turned down the protocols on June 6, this unexpected event caused Hitler (or perhaps gave him the excuse) to break off the negotiations, as his full attention was focused elsewhere. "Elsewhere" was a 1,200-mile-wide front on the Russian border, along which two million German troops were unleashed in a surprise invasion on the day after the summer solstice, June 22. This was another unanticipated event that upset Darlan's strategic design. Perhaps in order to save face with Pétain, Darlan on July 14 chose to raise the ante with Hitler and put in a demand that called for an equal partnership with Germany through complete restoration of French sovereignty. Under the circumstances, his demand was ridiculous, and his timing could not have been worse. A month later, the Germans answered that they were too tied up on the Eastern Front to continue talks about French collaborative efforts. Darlan continued in vain to pursue talks of French military cooperation with Abetz. A German freeze came into effect, and when the promised release of prisoners of war was announced proudly in the French press, the Germans promptly reneged upon it.

---

11 *De Munich a la Libération.* Ibid., 116.

Hitler and Darlan shared one concrete goal: to get rid of Weygand, who was retired by Pétain in November. Additionally, the swift advance by the German Wehrmacht deep into Russia, which swept up hundreds of thousands of Russian prisoners of war, pleased both Pétain and Darlan for its anti-Bolshevist success. The idea of a New Europe without Stalin and his Communist cohorts had an appeal for Vichy's heads of state. The aspiration for a sovereign France at the side of a triumphant Germany increased the appetite of both Pétain and Darlan to end the impasse with Hitler for achieving Vichy's collaboration with the Third Reich. The two top French leaders were not about to give up.

One final note on a somewhat under-the-radar event of June: the Second Jewish Statute was enacted by Vichy on June 2, 1941. Earlier, a new organization, the Commissariat-General for Jewish Questions (CGQJ), had been set up in March to handle such laws and their implementation. Pétain and Darlan were content to leave Jewish affairs up to their appointee, Xavier Vallat, and refrain from making public comments on that subject. The general public was aware of these discriminatory laws against Jews, both foreign and domestic, as they were published in detail in Vichy's official journal, which was duplicated in the local newspapers so that the Jewish people affected could act in accordance with such laws.[12]

What were the issues and attitudes present in the Gard during the first six months of 1941, and how were they affected by the events that had transpired? The interpretive reports by SCT officials are again limited, and none was found for the first four months of the year. The harsh winter conditions Jean Guéhenno had recorded about living in Paris in January had continued and worsened throughout France in both its rural and urban areas, including the unoccupied south. The individual daily ration of that French staple, bread, had been reduced to 275 grams per adult, or about 10 ounces, by April.[13] In the Gard the report to the prefect for May 16–30, 1941, mentioned that the same problems as in early May still persisted: inadequate food supplies, high cost of living, and inadequate wages. There was a thriving black market in wine, as the supplies were short. People in the mining area of Grande-Combe

---

12   *L'Opinion Française sous Vichy.* Ibid., 249; *Vichy France.* Ibid., 120–125; *France: The Dark Years.* Ibid., 181.
13   *De Munich a la Libération.* Ibid., 378.

received insufficient wine allocations. The hard-working miners protested vociferously over this fact. When supplies were short, no matter what the commodity, the administering entities, in this case, the Committee of Food Distribution, was the butt of many citizens' complaints. Government price-setting was liked by the populace when goods were adequate but avoided when there were scarcities. This report was issued on June 3, so there was a comment about the new Jewish Statute, which was reported as being widely and openly commented upon, especially in foreign Jews' intercepted correspondence. They were said to be very concerned and hoped to be able to leave for America but feared that visa issuance might be suspended. Refugees from Alsace-Lorraine still wanted to return home but were doubtful, and they said "the boches are still the same, they don't change at all."

A survey report later in June from Uzès indicated that 662 letters out of 670 were opened, read, and then resealed and sent on to their final destination. The high cost of living and food shortages were mentioned. But morale was satisfactory and confidence in Marshal Pétain was high in his effort to put France on a new path. People wanted an end to war, as well as a peace treaty with Germany. Private vegetable gardens helped the local situation, but fish and meat were rarely available, as was fertilizer. In Le Vigan conditions were worse, or so said the 303 letters read in secret. The spinning-mill industry was hard hit with many unemployed workers. Food, including meat and vegetables, was scarce. The high cost of living was a constant complaint and grain for animal feed and fertilizer for the wine fields was lacking. People were generally pessimistic, yet some expressed hopes for better days. The German success in Crete against the English was mentioned in passing, as was the Iraq rebellion. Darlan's speech of June 10 was favorably commented upon, especially concerning the promised repatriation of French POWs. In this broadcast speech, Darlan twice warned of the threat to rebuilding France from Communism and its local leadership, who he said were influenced by money and propaganda coming out of Russia. Darlan clearly outlined the purposes of his German talks: "This task of the government is triple: to ameliorate the French people's situation, to prepare for peace in that measure a conquered nation can, and to prepare France's future in a New Europe."[14]

---

14 *New York Times*. Reported on June 11, 1941. http://www.ibiblio.org/pha/

The report appended more surveys in Uzès and Bessèges, the former being more agricultural and the later more industrial. Both areas had experienced high cost of living and food shortages, toughest on the poor working class found primarily in Bessèges. The special commissioner crossed out a section about Jews who were protesting their treatment, so perhaps Prefect Chiappe never saw this sentence about the synod in Alès deciding in closed session to write a protest letter to Admiral Darlan about the statute and its inherent anti-Semitism. They also indicated Jewish worries about their ability to get accepted by the United States. A final addendum from Bessèges of May 28, from 389 letters read, repeated the comments about the high cost of living, inadequate salaries, and the lack of foodstuffs that caused people to steal from home gardens. Nine out of ten letters stressed these tough conditions. Morale and confidence were both influenced deleteriously by the fear, in this month of May, of the next winter.

A report from Youth Camp No.18 at Le Vigan for the month of June mentioned that of 2,475 letters opened, 9 percent indicated morale was good, 2 percent that it was bad, and 89 percent indicated that the writers were apathetic. This was not good news for the success of Pétain's National Revolution, which had made extensive efforts to inspire a youth movement to supplement its veteran's organization. This camp had many complaints over poor food and hard, meaningless work. Barracks or tents leaked from the heavy rains. In Alès on June 11, there was a lack of bread, and the miners "work like galley slaves." Some men feared the conflict in Syria would get them called up, but one reported that the visit of General Emile Laure, Pétain's chief of military staff and future biographer, was greeted enthusiastically. There was an internment camp in Saint-Hippolyte du Fort for English citizens whose mail was scrutinized. The severe bombing of London was noted, as was the high English confidence in their ultimate victory. The comment was made that in both France and England, the challenges of daily life were severe.

English correspondents observed that Americans could not fathom collaboration by France with Germany and only wanted France to be free again. People heard American rearmament was a slow process. Some Belgians were still in the Gard who were all for an English victory and freedom for their country and France. Some felt the German occupation

timeline/410610awp.html

troops' morale was worse than in 1940, as they were worried about England's continued resistance. POW letters from German stalags indicated that life was easier there than at home. Correspondence intercepted from Alsace-Lorraine indicated continuing ongoing expulsions and hard living conditions in that region. One individual said 50 percent of the first-communion girls in Altkirch had become pregnant and promptly blamed it on the German troops. "An Alsatian girl must not refuse a German Reich son!" The departure of German troops to the east was noted, and the comment was made that local German supply requisitions made life worse. A late June survey in Alès noted many observations about poor food supplies and high living costs. Wages were too low, and the lines were long to obtain food and wine, whose limit was half a liter per day, which was not enough for the mine workers. Activity was intense in the coal mines, but transport to deliver timber for shaft reinforcement was lacking. People showed a lack of interest in everything except familial survival, so their opinions were restricted to that basic concern.[15]

June's ten-page synthesis report was based on telegraph and telephone intercepts that indicated that people were disappointed that the promised easing of passage of the demarcation line had failed to materialize. Therefore, people still were trying to smuggle goods across or sneak over with a guide, who would charge about 120 francs per person. Feelings were highly emotional over the military events in Syria and Russia, and public opinion was perplexed with each succeeding event's report. Because they could not figure out what was happening, people were very troubled. This uneasiness led to questions about why the Germans were in France's colony, Syria. The Gaullist-English intervention caused worries over French casualties and the possible cut-off of supplies from the colonies, should the conflict spread to North Africa. On the invasion of Russia by Hitler, people envisaged some advantages for France, from the wear and tear on both belligerents, and the fall of Bolshevism, and should that happen, the problems coping with it that would fall into Germany's lap. One Gardois wrote: "It is like consecrated bread: my first good day since May 10, 1940."

The economic topic of the day was salary levels. The employers

---

15 ADG. Ibid., 1 W 42. Report No. 27, May 16–30, 1941, marked 3090J; Survey May 28, 1941, marked No. 1034; various town surveys of June 11, 1941.

admitted that higher wages must be paid but couldn't find the profit margins to afford paying them. They looked to the state for an answer but complained vociferously over administrative red tape bringing all things to a halt. "It is a mess everywhere with all these groups and dirty functionaries." The government was criticized in spite of the National Revolution. "It's the same old personnel. Favoritism continues, and contacts are more useful than ever. Nothing has changed." The same old complaints were heard about lack of adequate food supplies and prices that were too high. But the prices set by the agencies kept fresh vegetables off the market, and peasant attitudes were criticized. "Now one must be rich or influential to get food." This section ended with this contrasting remark: "The legion [the Legion of Veterans] sends telegrams to Marshal Pétain and Admiral Darlan expressing their admiration, confidence, and devotion, as do special delegations and numerous families."

The bulk of the report was devoted to economic and commercial news. Horses, which cost more than forty thousand francs each, were very scarce, as were piglets and goats. Heavy rains and the Rhône overflowing its banks hurt the wine and grain crops. Industrial production was harmed by a general lack of key materials, such as cement, sand, aluminum, metal pipes and panels, raw cotton, leather, and accessories. Lack of iron meant little or no activity in metallurgy, especially tinplate. "The Germans had promised 1,000 tons of iron, but their needs in Russia will reduce that by 85 percent next month." The Gard coal mines (the third most important in France) were very active; however, local suppliers were hard pressed to provide mining maintenance items like timber and dynamite due to poor truck transport availability. In general, no work meant more unemployment. The wine business was at a standstill with no availability, and the wine commission was criticized for misguided policies that would benefit only the black marketers. State ration orders were turned down and ex-Third Republic wine commissioner Paul Barthe was widely disparaged. There were lots of threats and recriminations, but the basic reality was that no wine was available, making it particularly hard on consumers, especially miners and laborers. People looked to North Africa's colonies as an alternative source of supply, but the war made shipping via the Mediterranean very risky, and scarcity raised prices.

Transportation was another huge problem. Lack of railroad freight cars caused producers to store goods and/or stop production. Trucks lacked lubricants, and their gazogene combustion engines often broke down, and the charcoal they required was hard to find. River traffic had been hurt by the Rhône's inundations. Food distribution problems were a frequent subject of discussion. Some people thought the government should tax foodstuffs to stabilize food prices, but local small producers hoarded their production, and the black market thrived from people with the means to pay the prices demanded. The ability to stockpile goods in anticipation of the next winter was poor, as there was no charcoal for heating or cooking, and preserving supplies were limited and vegetables were too expensive to acquire in quantity. Everybody complained about the official governmental organizations and their failure to improve circumstances.

Under foreign news, the stateless Israelites were very nervous, as they heard from their American relatives that their US visas could be suspended by Washington, which was rethinking its immigration policy in light of the current European situation. The British in the camp at St-Hippolyte du Fort were anxious over their lack of money to pay for prepaid telegrams for dispatch to England.[16] A later June report intercepted letters with in-depth comments on political events. The report summarized June as a month of important events that "stirred up" public opinion: the speeches of Admiral Darlan and Marshal Pétain; the British-Gaullist invasion of Syria; the new Jewish Statute; the German victory in Crete; and the most unexpected German invasion of Russia. The writer of the report admitted that the reactions were difficult to define.

The Gardois had been generally disappointed by the Darlan-Hitler talks at Berchtesgaden, as nothing had been gained from what was promised: "No improvement at the demarcation line; the slow return of prisoners of war, which has added to food provision troubles as the majority of prisoners are farmers, and no relief to the weariness engendered by the harsh war economy." Darlan's speech received mixed reactions and one local citizen called him "a good Hitler gauliter [sic]." Others were for his agreements but the majority accepted the fact that Germany "is in the driver's seat." Pétain's speech, on the first anniver-

---

16 Ibid. Report No. 28 for June 1941, by Mixed Control Commission for Telegraph and Telephone, marked 10, and 12–20.

sary of the armistice, evoked wishes for his long-term success. Others commented on his deep love of France and sincere desire to reestablish France's glory. He was not criticized personally but his government was for its poor organization, which involved too many functionaries, and a central state-controlled economy, which was called poorly adapted to the French character.

The fact that three cars were used to transport ex-prime minister Paul Reynaud to exile in Digne-les-Bains upset people, due to the general lack of transport. The Second Jewish Statute surprised no one and caused few comments, except for the foreign Jews hoping to emigrate to America. In summation, the report noted that opinion was divided. Many hoped for an English victory, especially the refugees, while the proponents of collaboration were undecided in light of the conflicting events of June. The unquestioning devotion of the French to the personage of the marshal was very evident, as was the recognition, for the moment, that Darlan's distasteful collaboration policy was merely evidence that there was no other choice. Toward the English, one had to maintain a "French attitude." These last comments might have appealed to Prefect Chiappe and his Vichy state superiors if they had the occasion to read them.

The attack on the French Empire in Syria elicited a conditioned reflex for the need to fight back in spite of the odds, but at the same time it revealed the fear of deeper military involvement with Germany's war aims. Mussolini's announcement on June 10 concerning Greece was greeted with indifference in the Gard. However, the invasion of Russia by Germany was commented upon passionately both by French Communists hoping for a directed purpose, now that the confusion engendered by the Nazi-Soviet Pact of 1939 was over, and the "objective majority" of the French, who feared that Bolshevism would come to France in the event of a German defeat. The main belief, however, was that although Germany would defeat Russia, it would become so weak in the process that France could gain a relative advantage that would allow it to reassume its proper place in the world. Apparently, the Gardois who remembered Napoleon's experience in Russia were holding their tongues for the moment. The paucity of news from the Occupied Zone did mention the continued departure of German troops from France bound for the Russian front, and their low morale was commented upon. The growing preference for Britain over Germany in the area was noted, along with the fact that the Vichy government could not alter the general opinion held that an English victory was desirable. One mention was made that Vichy was very active in trying to convince their citizens to "think French." However, the people commented little on this subject, as they were mostly preoccupied with daily living concerns.[17]

The bi-weekly report for July 20–August 5, 1941, continued the litany of observations on general malaise, concerning difficulties in obtaining sufficient food supplies along with other daily life exigencies. Comments were made about limited Gaullist and Communist activities, with the latter's propaganda considered secretive and discreet. Intercepts from Communists indicated they wanted revenge on the Germans, which would cause trouble for Vichy. The Gaullist Anglophiles were inspired by events in Syria and Russia and foresaw a Grand Alliance against Germany, composed of Britain, Russia, and Roosevelt's United States of America. The Pétain and Darlan hardcore collaboration loyalists cited the continued German advances in Russia, including the fall of Smolensk on July 16, as a positive indicator of Russia's imminent collapse.

The Jewish Statutes were mentioned again concerning the worries of foreign Jews trying to get to the USA. A letter from Pastor Marc Boegner of Nîmes, who was not only the top Protestant figure in the Gard but also in all of France, was intercepted. In it, he expressed his organization's dismay over the racial injustices the Jews were suffering and the sympathy felt for a local Jewish community so persecuted. Boegner bravely went public with his comments, and one letter intercepted from the Creuse area accused the pastor of being "unpatriotic in criticizing a law of Marshal Pétain, who is so French and whose dictates must be followed." The synthesis does not mention any details behind Pastor Boegner's statement about Jewish suffering. But an intercepted telegram of July 21 from a Mr. Bluwstein to a François Lew at the Hotel Imperator did detail the atrocious conditions at the Jewish internment camp at St-Maurice Dibie in the Gard's northeastern area. It spoke of barbarous mistreatment and severe corporal punishment for twenty-five Jews who would perish in conditions worse than Dachau unless someone intervened with Vichy.

---

17 Ibid. Report No. 29 for June 1941, from the Commission of Postal Control of Nimes, marked 342–347.

The danger inherent in taking at face value all such reports is illustrated by its emphasis on the word "remarkable," contained in an intercepted letter that described the screening in Nîmes of two German films, *La Fille au Vautour* and the virulently anti-Semitic propaganda film *The Jew Süss*. The actual letter had a more nuanced meaning. This July 18, 1941, letter to a friend in Algeria referred to several *"pas mal films boches"* [not bad German films] being shown in Nîmes and singled out these two as quite remarkable, going on to describe the audience's reaction to *The Jew Süss*: "It was, moreover, curious and a bit paradoxical to hear the crowd of spectators scream at the Jews. There have already been three years of that [xenophobia concerning foreign Jews] going on. Human fickleness is infinite!" The writer mentioned that the Veterans' Legion seemed to be taking root locally but went on to criticize the ultra right-wing Action Française movement as being counterproductive. His comments on the heroic resistance by French troops in Syria were not really anti-English, as he only wished for the Brits to take on the Germans directly. He feared [incorrectly] that Moscow would fall in a fortnight but saw a place for France after the demise of Bolshevism and the resultant exhaustion of Germany. He stated that the dismissal of Admiral Abrial, governor general in Algeria, by General Weygand in North Africa ought to be explained to the people of Vichy. Weygand was Vichy's delegate-general to the North African colonies.[18]

The report ended by returning to the number-one topic all over the Gard: food supply. Prices were driven up by short supplies in vegetables, fruits, and even wine, which was the Gard's main crop. All things were driven by fears of a worsening of conditions by winter. A Mme. Collin of Remoulins bemoaned on June 20 that she could no longer obtain good wines like Gigondas or even jug wine. Her source for Gauloise cigarettes was a neighbor's one package allocation per week, and all smokers were complaining about it. The SCT took note of how she ended her letter: "the deplorable France of Pétain."[19] People were even killing pets for meat, and in Saint-Chapres the meat ration was down to 50 grams per week, per person. There were no potatoes available and dairies would soon have to close, as there was no fodder for the cows. People were

---

18   ADG 1 W 40 letter of July 18, 1941, marked No. 365. Telegram of July 21, 1941, marked No. 955.
19   Ibid. Letter of June 20, 1940, marked No. 1512.

lining up at the garbage dumps with pails in hand to sift through the refuse.[20]

A late July survey of 389 letters read in Beaucaire, an industrial town on the Rhône River canal, mentioned that the lack of coal for powering production had caused some factories to shut down. Food shortages were highlighted, especially in green vegetables and wine. Bad weather and an insect infestation would affect the coming wine harvest negatively. In spite of these difficulties the people maintained faith in Marshal Pétain being able to raise France up again, as he was giving his all to achieve that goal. A survey of agricultural-based Uzès stated that it did not suffer like Beaucaire for produce, but meat, wine, and tobacco were in poor supply. The farmers hoped that Marshal Pétain would save the nation. On August 4, a phone conversation between a construction firm in Nîmes and a major cement supplier in Marseille was transcribed by the SCT. The Nîmois was the president of the construction syndicate, and he said failure to supply the long-ordered cement would shut down all construction within two weeks. The point made was that work for the state therefore would be shut down and more than two thousand workers would be put out of work. The man in Marseille listened sympathetically but he had heard the same story before from other communes. He advised the Nîmois to be patient and suggested complaining to the proper minister in Vichy.

On July 29, M. Albert Drode of Nîmes wrote a letter in which he passed on news of what he had seen in Paris, likening it to famine-like times there. He said "our guests," the Germans, were hardly appreciated, and their presence was like propaganda for de Gaulle, but it was more talk than action. He commented that the women in Paris who openly cavorted with the Germans would get a close shave after the war was over, in payment for their actions. In Nîmes, the food supply was very bad, with little or no meat and only carrots and tomatoes available as vegetables. He asked himself how they were going to survive the winter. However, he was prudent in speaking unfavorably about his godfather's profiting from activities in the black market. A letter from Chicago to a marquise in the Gard was intercepted on August 9 that described the seizure of the Barclay Bank in Nice and Lindbergh's pro-German movement in the USA. The letter was marked for investigation

---

20 Ibid. Report for weeks of July 20–August 6, 1941, marked No. 4559.

because of a caricature appended to its end that showed Admiral Darlan, Laval, and Bonnet in a lifeboat, along with some rats. The inscription read "France's future liberty," along with the commentary "All these rats are going to the bottom." A Jewish man in Nîmes, originally from Salonika, wrote the Kahn family, who lived in Vichy, about the new Jewish Statute being rarely commented upon. However, for Jews like him, its publication caused increased worry and considerable talk among Jewish acquaintances who hoped to emigrate to America. Jewish merchants in Nîmes were forbidden to man their stalls in the outdoor public market. He observed that news had been slow to reach his sister that her son had been killed in action near Charleroi, Belgium, one year before.[21]

Marshal Pétain took some crucial measures in August 1941 that committed Vichy to a policy of more active partnership with Germany. He created a more fascist-like controlled state, buttressed by police and court action. This was announced to the French people on August 12, 1941, by Marshal Pétain in a lengthy (for him) five-page radio address, referred to in French as the "*Mauvais vent*" (Ill or Evil Wind) speech. It ended with the enumeration of twelve new repressive fiats. It started: "Frenchmen! I have grave things to tell you. For the last several weeks I have felt an ill wind rising in many regions of France. Disquiet is overtaking minds; doubt is gaining control of spirits. The authority of my government is made the subject of discussion; its orders are often poorly executed. … A real uneasiness afflicts the French people. … France cannot be governed without the assent of public opinion … an assent more necessary than ever *in the authoritarian regime* [author's italics]. This public opinion is today divided. France cannot be governed unless the initiative of her chief finds corresponding exactness and faithfulness in the bodies transmitting it. This exactness and faithfulness are still lacking. … Authority no longer emanates from below. The only authority is that which I entrust or delegate. I have delegated it to Admiral Darlan. … In 1917, I put an end to mutiny. In 1940, I put an end to rout. Today I wish to save you from yourselves."[22]

Among the twelve dictates he announced were the affirmation of

---

21   ADG 1 W 40. Telephone transcript No. 864 of August 4, 1941, and letter No. 597 of July 29, 1941; letter No. 860 of July 9, 1941, and letter No. 1534 of June 19, 1941.

22   *New York Times*, August 13, 1941. http://www.ibiblio.org/pha/policy/1941/410812a.html

suspension of all political parties and new anti-Masonic measures listing high Freemason officials; a doubling of the means of police action; more centralization of state powers over the entire economy; and ominous changes to the constitutional procedures for judging certain crimes against the state. Finally, all ministers and high officials had to swear a personal oath of fealty to Marshal Pétain. Jean Guéhenno characterized the speech thusly: "A vulgar, devious and threatening discourse. He must really comprehend that France is not behind him. The logic of treason obliges the government always to betray more. But the logic of suffering will increase each day the nation's resistance to that treason. …To sum up, he will double the means of the police in order to better defend the French against themselves."[23]

In his speech, Pétain had to recognize that any assistance the collaboration had gained from Germany's success in the east and its corollary of an anti-Bolshevik movement stood no chance of offsetting the shift in public opinion he had sensed, which was the reason for his speech of tough love. Pierre Laborie makes this salient point with great perspicacity. The undercurrent of erosion in public opinion's support for the National Revolution at home and a foreign policy based on collaboration was a harbinger of the ultimate failures that occurred.[24] The fact that Marshal Pétain touched on public opinion twice in his "ill wind" text denotes a new significance that his government now attached to this subject. Admiral Darlan's office issued a statistical note on August 20, 1941, drawing attention to the fact that on average 300,000 to 370,000 letters were read by the combined SCT organizations each week. In the attempt to gauge what the French were thinking, a moveable target subject to controlled and uncontrollable events and circumstances, SCT officials were to ask four more questions regularly:

Does the marshal have the people's approval?
Does the admiral have the people's approval?
Does the policy of collaboration have the approval of the people?
Will a German victory be the result of the war?[25]

---

23 *Journal des Années Noires.* Ibid., 176.
24 *L'Opinion Française sous Vichy.* Ibid., 250–251.
25 *Le Régime de Vichy a existé.* Ibid., 42.

Robert Paxton considers that "June–August 1941 should rank as a major turning point, perhaps more significant than the more standard December 13, 1940."[26] I agree with him. In spite of the problems Pétain and Darlan had in implementing their strategic plans with Germany, Darlan continued negotiations that committed Vichy ever more closely to repressive German ways within France. A major factor behind this was the shift by the French Communist party away from fettered neutrality, now that Hitler's invasion of Russia had unshackled them and their militants, to active support of all Hitler's enemies. July witnessed many acts of sabotage in the Occupied Zone, which the Germans and French quickly labeled as acts of terrorism, and the Communists were the nearly exclusive perpetrators. Germans swiftly and brutally reacted to counter these activities, and Vichy was bound to follow suit, as indicated by moves that occurred, set by the tone of Pétain's August 12 speech.

On August 21, 1941, a Young Communist, Pierre Georges, angered by the execution two days before of two of his Young Communist allies, shot and killed a young German naval cadet, Moser, in plain daylight in the middle of the busy Barbes-Rochechouart Paris metro station. This was the first German military person killed in post-armistice France. The French acted on August 27 to mitigate German countermeasures in a Special Section Court, which came into existence as a result of the constitutional changes announced in Pétain's August 12 speech. A tribunal d'état was formed on September 10, whose five judges sentenced to death, without the right of appeal, two Communists and a Jew who were being held on misdemeanor charges. These three men were guillotined the next day, but the Germans were not deterred in their vengeance over subsequent assassinations of German personnel, which followed in fairly rapid order in Paris, Bordeaux, and Nantes.

The ante was significantly raised by the Germans through hostage seizures and the subsequent executions of innocent men when the French failed to find and turn over any of the guilty assassins. On September 30, 1941, the sub-prefect of Brive in the Corrèze reported: "The great majority of the population is hostile to the Germans and to collaboration."[27] This hostility really pointed out a growing trend

---

26   *Vichy France.* Ibid., 223.
27   *L'Opinion Française sous Vichy.* Ibid., 253, n1.

toward hatred for the occupier amongst the general population, certainly at first in the Occupied Zones. At this time, the militant Communists had no relationship with de Gaulle's movement, which opposed the assassinations. The Communists acted for their own purposes as they sought retribution against the German occupiers. The fact was that any and all organized resistance movements were very fragile in the last trimester of 1941. Early fall 1941 witnessed the apogee of German military success in Russia, but the rise of Germanophobia in France at this time is unquestionable. However, the French rage at the hostage executions was more an expression of incredulous disapproval than any step toward organized opposition. The individual assassinations of Germans by Communist agitators were widely disapproved by the French citizenry, as they resulted in the Germans executing twenty-four hostages in September, along with ninety-eight more on October 22–23, of whom at least sixty-eight were Communists, including a teenager, Guy Moquet.[28]

Pétain, whose popularity had diminished somewhat as a result of his August pronouncements, resurrected his personal image by actions he took on the hostage issue late in October. On October 22, he appealed to the Germans to show mercy toward the hostages by saying: "I cry out to you in a broken voice to no longer allow bad things to happen to France." On October 25, he attempted to offer his person as a hostage at the demarcation line, but his bluff, if it was one, was not called by the Germans. They ignored him and continued their vindictive hostage-taking policy, which ultimately led to the French police doing much of the Germans' dirty work for them, through Vichy's desire to exert French sovereignty.[29] But with all Frenchmen faced now with the reality of harsh basic living conditions as a second winter of occupation approached, along with a new reality of German brutality, a subtle change was taking place in the general French attitude toward Philippe Pétain. Since July, the uneasiness Pétain sensed in the public was accompanied by its withdrawal into *attentisme*'s self-protective shell, accompanied by a heavy dose of skepticism about his government's policies. Amorphous public opinion was ready to move on a different trajectory. And Pétain himself was evolving in the unsettled public's mind into a living symbol, as sum-

---

28 *De Munich a la Libération*. Ibid., 236–237.
29 *L'Opinion Française sous Vichy*. Ibid., 224–227, 250, n1 and n2, 255.

marized again by Brive's SCT in November 1941: "We, who believe in him, pray for him and God will do the rest."[30]

Two events concerning Adolf Hitler dramatically affected French public opinion in December 1941. On December 11, Hitler addressed the Reichstag in an eighty-eight-minute harangue, which was coordinated with the delivery in Washington DC of a note from Germany to the United States government, which ended as follows:

"The government of the Reich consequently breaks off diplomatic relations with the United States of America and declares that under these circumstances brought about by President Roosevelt, Germany too, as from today, considers herself as being in a state of war with the United States of America."[31]

This declaration of war by Hitler was accompanied by the defeat of the seemingly invincible German Wehrmacht before Moscow on December 20, which added a totally new perspective to the World War that Japan's surprise attack on Pearl Harbor had expanded. France was split into three schools of opinion. The largest one was the undecided group of people whom the two smaller factions sought to influence. The first competitor seeking to influence opinion was composed of those committed to collaboration with Germany in an anti-Bolshevik crusade, some with a loyalty to Vichy, and others with their own fascist agendas but all utterly devoted to Marshal Pétain. The second emerging courter of public opinion was the Resistance, made up of many disparate organizations competing among themselves for power and membership, but all of whose ultimate aim was the same: to liberate France. The mainstream constituted the majority, a wait-and-see crowd that could be influenced by eventful winds that moved their emotions; for instance, like the hostage situation. But they, by now, did share some convictions to which appeals could be made. They were antagonistic toward collaboration. They were anti-Germany and would welcome its defeat. They were loyal to the marshal's person but not to his state or its policies. And they were fed up with the inefficient functioning of the state, which could not seem to improve food supplies or other conditions related to the challenges of daily living.[32]

---

30   *L'Opinion Française sous Vichy*. Ibid., 257.

31   *http://www.ihr.org/jhr/v08/v08p389_Hitler.html*

32   *L'Opinion Française sous Vichy*. Ibid., 258–259.

In the Gard, we have already seen the total preoccupation with daily living challenges: food supply and other critical shortages, criticism of the profiteering afforded by the black market, and frustrations with state bureaucratic inefficiencies. All these pragmatic issues for the formation of public opinion would continue and generally be aggravated by the actual situation. Let us delve into these and the other more elusive elements that would lay the fundamentals for substantial movement in public opinion come 1942 among the apprehensive but watchful people in the Gard in these last five months of 1941.

The report for the first two weeks of August started right off echoing the same general uneasiness about food supply, especially in its biggest city, Nîmes, where fears coalesced around the approaching winter. "Here in Nîmes, it's always the same; you can't find anything, and if something arrives you must stand in line for several hours, but when your turn arrives, there is nothing left. It's useless to grumble since it's only those who get preferential treatment who eat." People complained vociferously about the issuance of "priority" cards for food rations, and as fewer people had them, the majority without them blamed the state bureaucracies. Rural people, many of them farmers, were disliked by the urban dwellers because they had gardens to raise fruits and vegetables for themselves or their small communities. But meat was scarce everywhere, and fodder was difficult to obtain for farm animals, especially milk cows, which led to some counter-productive slaughtering.

A farmer took the government to task with a growing and disquieting complaint: "We are victims of a paper-procedure-crazy bureaucracy that wipes out all honest efforts." A telephone conversation not referenced in the report, from a business in Alès to an associate of the Director of Food Resupply in Nîmes, went into detail on this general objection: "Why all these duplicate certificates? It's absurd. In private business we'd kick such a director out the door." The associate agreed but said that he must follow the regulations. The response was, "They are cretins at Vichy. They speak of the National Revolution which is nothing but a complete screw-up. We have to redo these certificates two and three times, and then print them again. Now I have to recount the 36,000 of them."[33] War comments were diverse, and certain ones exhibited anger at the Communists and wanted Germany to prevail. Others call the Germans

---

33　ADN. 1 W 40 telephone call of August 6, 1941 No. 879.

"boche cows" but hoped the invasion of Russia would hasten the end of the war. One hard-liner wrote, "The truth is that the Russians (Stalin) are the source of all our misfortunes. If they had not signed the alliance treaty with the Germans in August 1939, we would never have had the war. They should have to regret being such rascals to us."

Marshal Pétain's speech was not disparaged in print and his highly elevated personal stature was still honored, as shown by this comment by a Nîmois: "Let us have great confidence in the one who has made a gift of his person to France, who has already obtained great results and who will lead us surely to the recovery and tranquility that we so desire. This is the most cherished vow that all the French wish him to accomplish." Unfavorable comments concerning Pétain's government were attributed to the usual suspects: Communists, political agitators, Jews, and Free-masons. A letter written by a noble to another member of the nobility, not referenced by the report, agreed in effect by saying that "should England win, we run the risk of the return of Jews and Freemasons, but the victory of Germany will put all Europe under the Hitlerian boot," so the writer hoped the two sides would wear each other out. He supported the marshal but noted the differing attitudes of the French in the two zones. He personally backed the government but felt the people in the Occupied Zone believed the government was overboard in its collaboration efforts with Germany.[34]

A Captain Reynaud, who wrote his mother in Nîmes, was of a far different mind: "It is all the fault of Marshal Pétain: no returned prisoners; no lessening of demarcation restrictions; the dead and wounded who arrive each week from Syria; the loss of Indochina;[35] the children who

---

34   ADN. 1 W 40 letter of August 4, 1941, No. 666.

35   *Vichy France.* Ibid., 82–83. In 1940 the Japanese military in south China wanted to establish operational bases in the Vichy French colony of Indochina. The French colonial administration was powerless to oppose the Japanese and on September 22, 1940, a formal base rights agreement was signed in exchange for Japanese recognition of French sovereignty. Japan started to establish some air, sea, and land bases right away. Subsequently, Japan launched air attacks from such bases in December 1941 against British naval and land forces. Outright takeover occurred on March 9, 1945. My neighbor in Nîmes, Mme. Arlette Felber, born Cavalin, lived in Cambodia during the war on a rubber plantation her father managed. She told me how she regularly played tennis at a country club near Phnom Penh, with Japanese officers. She and her family were later interred by the Japanese right after March 9, 1945.

croak from hunger; the absence of everything and prices which have increased 20 percent." He refused to mention his location, as he feared military censorship, but little did he know that other administrators would read his personal letter. He condemned the mentality of people around him whom he felt hadn't been crushed enough as they took too much pleasure in frivolous activities.[36] Opponents of the National Revolution blamed capitalistic profiteers for acting like wolves guarding sheep while the common people suffered harsh living conditions, or the Catholic Church's string-pulling to get Vichy to be the puppeteer of a clerical state. Concerning the local economy, the continued shortage of coal for factory use was noted. Two local wine négociants were arrested for speculation due to attempts to manipulate the sale of inadequate supplies of wine at prices over the levels set by the government.[37]

A few phone conversations intercepted in August were commented upon in a separate report, which started off by indicating that people were very reticent to comment on the phone about great issues of the time. The reason for this most likely was that the people who had phones, mostly businesses or well-to-do citizens, suspected they were tapped. The malaise over poor food supplies and the future of France was mentioned, as well as the problems in passing the demarcation line. One conversation touched on the POWs in Germany and their possible return, but it was rumor-based. Finally, one realist agreed that France must allow Japan the right to enter their Indochina colony as they wished, as the French forces were powerless to resist.[38]

A lengthy report for the same time frame, based on intercepted letters, commenced with a summary of anti-national activities of all forms. An Englishwoman who lived in Nîmes would be investigated because her sister wrote her a letter from Bath, in which she said Vichy should be ashamed over their treatment of interned English citizens. "It seems Vichy cares not at all what will become of France, they leave it all up to the Germans." But a letter from the British internment camp at St-Hippolyte du Fort from a prisoner to his wife in Cumberland seemed to indicate poor treatment. He wrote, "Here the authorities appear to want to put us on an accentuated starvation diet. I had a surprise yester-

---

36   ADG. 1 W 40 letter of August 5, 1941.
37   ADG. 1 W 42. Report dated August 19, 1941, marked No. 4912J.
38   Ibid. Monthly Telephone and Telegraph report No. 30 of August 1941.

day. The jailer gave me fifteen extra days of detention for no reason. I do not object to being punished should I do something wrong, but I will object to being punished for no reason whatsoever."[39] Another intercepted letter pinpointed a clandestine Communist meeting location in Marseille. No doubt a copy of this report went to the prefect for the Bouches-du-Rhône department in Marseille, as the Communist party had been dissolved in September 1939. Their militants were described as tramway and construction workers, who were "violence prone," and had become active again in light of the German invasion of Russia. Their actions were defined as distributing Communist propaganda tracts by inserting them in mailboxes and affixing wall posters.

Many letters alluded to the hopes for an English victory. This Gaullist-attributed endeavor was blamed on the refugee population, which was seen to support England and de Gaulle as a way to recuperate "their assets," which if they were Jewish, might have been confiscated under Vichy's anti-Jewish laws by Xavier Vallat's CGQJ. Letters supported the English blockade of the continent and mentioned the massive requisitions made on France by Germany as the real reason for France's hard times. Writers deprecated the idea that an oppressed people would be willing to collaborate with their oppressor. A Jewish refugee from Alsace wrote from Nîmes, after a visit to Vergèze, that the Source Perrier Company was exporting large quantities of their bubbly spa water to Germany. He also mentioned that a merchant in Nîmes exported three thousand pairs of children's shoes to Germany as well. But in fact, most of the products taken by the Germans for their war use came from the Occupied Zone. The letter continued about activities in Mulhouse, where the Germans converted the synagogue into an auction house, where they sold the furniture confiscated from the Jews in Colmar, and in Colmar they sold the Jewish possessions from Mulhouse. He wrote more: "I was told that the marshal had granted an audience to Mr. Kolb." Jewish people did not usually get a good return-on-investment from such audiences with Pétain. Witness what happened to a Freemason acquaintance after meeting with Pétain: "I read that René Barade, a lawyer from Paris's 18th district, ex-deputy from Colmar and head of the Nancy Valley Masonic Lodge 'Fidelity,' was put on a list to be removed from committees he had

---

39   Ibid. Letter dated August 26, 1941, marked No. 1342. Letter dated August 31, 1941, marked No. 1505.

served on in Nîmes and in the Alpes-Maritimes."[40] The report blamed the BBC for influencing the writers of these intercepted letters. Anti-Vichy sentiments were expressed in one letter: "Long live the Republic and down with the Tyrants." The "Israelites" were singled out as the most fervent Gaullist and Anglophile supporters.

Intercepts from the Occupied Zone indicated that the Germans were trying to use anti-Bolshevik French feelings to gain sympathy. Other letters stated that Gaullist propaganda was very active in using vexatious German actions to stir up the public, and one letter estimated the level of support for de Gaulle at 75 percent. Both of these estimates should be taken with a grain of salt, but this was the first Gard report to devote real attention to the Gaullist movement. It was dangerous to allude to de Gaulle in any fashion, as seen from a letter intercepted in Nîmes from an American who had asked his Nîmois friend if he could emigrate to New York. The naive New Yorker placed a large "V" in red ink near his signature, which led to an investigation of his pal in Nîmes.[41]

Several correspondents did discuss war weariness but tempered that effect with expressions of confidence in Marshal Pétain. That was not the case with opinions expressed about Darlan. One writer mentioned his collaboration with Hitler as "disgusting" and, touching upon the Germans, stated: "after all they had stolen from France along with their desire to take the little that remains, Darlan can really admire this handsome Hitler. May they both one day, along with others in the collaborating government, croak in the same sack." The remonstrations against the Jewish Statutes by Jews and Pastor Boegner were mentioned, along with the grand rabbi's personal protestation to Marshal Pétain. A Mr. Weill in Mexico wrote his brother in Nîmes that he had arranged his acceptance into Mexico as a political refugee, but he must still visit the Mexican consulate in Marseille to obtain his visa. Perhaps it was the brother in Mexico saying it was acceptable to give the consul a "gift" that this letter was copied to both prefects in the Gard and Bouches-du-Rhône.[42] The French press and radio broadcasts originating in Paris were mentioned as being controlled by German propaganda.

In summation, opinion was characterized as being divided, with

---

40 Ibid. August 1941 letter, marked 57–58.
41 Ibid. Letter of August 8, 1941, marked 13236.
42 Ibid. Letter of August 14, 1941, marked 13253.

many adherents desirous of an English victory; they outnumbered the partisans of collaboration. Yet an overall current of thought persisted to serve the marshal and follow him without second thoughts. However, in commenting on interior events from the Occupied Zone, the summary noted that opinion did not rally around the government of Marshal Pétain. The section devoted to food supply highlighted many difficulties, including the high cost of commodities that middle-class wage earners could not afford. The statement was made that people thought only of themselves. One letter described "long lines and waits often result in no provisions, followed by disputes and fights." The biggest supply shortages were tobacco and especially wine. Many people asked the same question: "How can one explain to us that in an area essentially devoted to wine production, there can be a shortage of wine?"[43]

The September report described Communist propaganda in the Unoccupied Zone as "doubling" in activity since the invasion of Russia, but that was obviously a guess, as the SCT described suspect comments as "veiled" or "insinuated." Yet examples ran the gamut: "Do you believe in a Nazi victory, or do you see the possibility of one favorable to our cause?" and "Communism is working strong and the ground is favorable." People did comment that Communist graffiti appearing on walls and doors was fairly common. The working class was mentioned, not surprisingly, as a bastion of Communist support. Jews who opposed the National Revolution were also accused of having Communist affiliation. "Gaullism had numerous adherents" is the lead-off comment about its propaganda. The report noted that its adherents listened faithfully to de Gaulle's speeches on the BBC.

Many refugees supported Gaullism's victory because it would allow them to return home, so the conclusion was that they were from Alsace-Lorraine. One refugee in Marseille asked another in the Gard if he could receive BBC transmissions. He found them very interesting because the local press and radio did not "tell the truth." He suggested that his friend ought to appreciate the English more if he wanted to return to a Strasbourg that was once again French. "Only an Anglo-Saxon victory will allow us to realize that dream." He refrained from sharing other confidences as he was afraid that his mail would be read. He closed by

---

43   Ibid. Monthly Commission de Contrôle Postal de Nimes report No. 30, August 1941, marked No. 550.

warning his friend "any local news about the English will only be propaganda signed by Goebbels, nothing more."[44] Many "V's" and Crosses of Lorraine symbols were noted as being seen, even on bank and police station walls. An intercepted letter equated collaboration with an enemy as being barbarous and unforgivable. In spite of all these comments, there seemed to be no trace of a Gaullist organization in the Gard, which was likely true at this point in time.

Under "other," the report had some comments on the local anti-Communist, fascist-oriented party of Jacques Doriot, the Parti Populaire Français (PPF). "Our section in Nîmes is becoming stronger and people speak of us as a force with which to be reckoned." The Jews were called Gaullist supporters who sought to regroup in order to resist their individual registration under the newly imposed Second Jewish Statute. However, for two Jewish haberdashers, it was a business-as-usual letter that got the attention of the SCT in Nîmes. Sam David wrote his customer at Maison Robert Couture in Nîmes that he had, in Perpignan, "some herringbone tweed jackets and silk Moroccan dresses in stock [he] ought to come and see." The SCT noted that these might be "non-declared goods."[45] Information was hard to come by from the Occupied Zone, but the report noted that with the passage of time the Communists had become more closely aligned with England, and that the Germans were on the trail of Communist militants. Gaullist propaganda in Paris was reported as being very active and "that 90 percent of the Parisians are for him and await the signal to march under the cross of Lorraine." This quote certainly exaggerated the support for the Gaullist organization anywhere in France in the fall of 1941.

Favorable comments lingered about Pétain's speeches of August and the hope was expressed that the French would rally closely around him. "Frenchmen must be moved by the words of a man such as Marshal Pétain, who has sacrificed all to save his country. We must follow him blindly. He is the miracle who has saved France." On September 10, a Nîmois devotee wrote that in Pétain's latest speech he and his government gave "a hard fist to the Communists, Freemasons, and black marketers." He went on to state that too many people were Gaullists and pro-English "who do not understand the blind obedience that we must

---

44   Ibid. Letter of September 18, 1941, marked No. 1579.
45   Ibid. Letter of September 17, 1941, marked No. 205.

have in our chief." Here was that common phrase again.[46] Pétain gave a second speech in August, this one to the Council of State, with the purpose of building up Darlan's stature. Darlan's speech of August 14 "received no comment" in intercepts analyzed for this report. Speaking of intercepted mail, one Nîmois seemed to be fully aware of that operation. He started his letter: "Long live the marshal. Long live the Legion. I open with these national rallying cries, which I support 100 percent, in case my letter will be opened by the Control. Yours was opened, as mine are frequently. As a Legion section chief I know enough nitwits, Communists, ex-SFIOs who never had their mail opened. There are many opportunists out there who cry Long Live the Marshal but at the bottom of their rotten hearts only want Leon Blum and his clique of Jews and Freemasons to return to power."[47] One could be troubled by the following comment about war weariness and collaboration with Germany: "It is better to collaborate than to struggle." Yet someone of a far different opinion wrote, "Is France going to yield its ports in Algeria, Tunisia, and Morocco to the collaborators as those same collabos have asked it to do in Indochina?" This comment came from a Gardois worried over the fate of French nationals at the hands of the Japanese.

Bourgeois opinion in the Gard, which feared the strong Communist influence among the miners in the Alès basin, took solace in the strong German advances in Russia. However, the report, in referencing this feeling, also noted that some people saw in the mutual destruction or exhaustion for both countries a way for France to rise again. There was more news than last time from the Occupied Zone where Anglophile and Gaullist activity was increasing. "If Vichy people could visit Paris, they would understand and quit collaborating. The Bretons are Anglophiles and even welcome the British air raids." There was opinion expressed against the Vichy government of Marshal Pétain and all letter writers wished for an English victory.[48] There were some comments on the impending departure of French volunteers in Jacques Doriot's anti-Bolshevik Legion (LVF) to fight alongside the Nazis at the Russian front.[49] Finally, a letter from M. Rugier of Nîmes got the SCT's atten-

---

46   Ibid. Letter dated September 10, 1941, marked No. 2436.
47   Ibid. Letter dated September 10, 1941, marked No. 2409.
48   Ibid. Monthly Commission de Contrôle Postal report No. 31, September 1941, marked No. 1112.
49   Three battalions of the Légion de volontaires français arrived on the eastern

tion: "Monsieur Ecl...[?] comes to see us each evening. It seems that everyone he visits since his claim against M. Bibet at the Prefecture, has problems. He wants to strangle Angelo [a direct reference to M. Angelo Chiappe, prefect of the Gard]. Will it happen?"[50]

The report for October reflected the public's continued frustration with war weariness and harsh living conditions. "The outlook is bleak for the future" wrote one correspondent. Disappointment was voiced in the failure of the government to keep its promises to secure the release of significant numbers of POWs. Grievances were common about the lack of a well-functioning economy. Fingers were pointed in all directions at people putting sticks in the bicycle wheels of Marshal Pétain's reorganization efforts. The local Legion of Veterans was attacked for lacking spirit and for the old veterans' clashing with their cadre, whom they accused of being infiltrated by Communists. Their former president complained that there were too many legionnaires in name only. Bosses complained that their workers were slackers and the workers pointed the finger back at the bosses for not paying them a living wage. People cried out against fraud and speculators. Some people wrote "Down with Pétain" in the WC and others were for carting them off to prison. A letter from a son in the USA to his Nîmoise mother exhibited outrage at the execution of French hostages by the Germans in Nantes. He wrote that if he "had the misfortune to be a German, [he] would be horrified at the thought of all the hatred for them that is spreading around the world." He also mentioned the change evolving in American opinion that would lead to war with Hitler and the growing appreciation of de Gaulle's efforts to build resistance movements in France.[51]

Paul Barthe, the ex-Third Republic deputy from the adjacent department of the Hérault, had been placed on administrative internment stemming from accusations that he favored certain wineries over distrib-

---

front in October 1941, with Doriot in command. Neither wanted there by the Germans nor prepared for the fighting conditions in Russia—they had no winter uniforms—they were removed from frontline duty after two weeks, having suffered about 250 casualties. Julian Jackson states that no volunteers were sought by Vichy in its Free Zone and points out that Pétain's message to the volunteers thanking them for their support in defending "part of our military honor," was redolent with ambiguity. *France: The Dark Years.* Ibid., 194.

50   ADG. 1 W 42. Ibid. Letter dated September 6, 1941, marked No. 1380.
51   Ibid. Letter dated October 21, 1941, marked No. 14524.

utors. He was accused of administrative malfeasance, and his enemies took pride in making an example out of him as a pen-pusher who was out to sabotage the National Revolution. Behind this outcry was the fear of winter's onset: the high cost of living, deficiencies in food supplies caused by the black market, and the disproportionate gap between prices and salaries. One Nîmois wrote, "If you want to buy a liter of olive oil it is available for 100 francs on the black market, all you want, but not for us on my salary of 8 francs a day and Albert's of 6 francs. And here is the winter and I don't know what to do about coal for it is cold as a dog with a wicked wind, and all I can burn is briquettes which I kill myself to fetch 2 kilometers and pay 40 francs for 100 small pieces. I put 4 pieces in the stove which does not give off much heat but what do you expect when the monthly allocation is only 200 pieces."[52] Someone railed at monopolists, peasants, and price-setting offices. A woman complained about vegetable gardeners selling eggplants around Alès at black-market prices. This caused a police investigation, which reported back to officials in Nîmes that there was rigorous supervision of these gardeners and there was no black market. "And about the eggplants, they were sold at the beginning of the season when there was no tax at five francs each wholesale and at six francs each to retailers. Since the tax, they sell at eight francs a kilo."[53] The latter price sounded like a bargain.

The Parisians were reported as being upset over the assassinations of Germans due to the retaliations they caused. They accused the English radio broadcasts of stirring up the Communists. One such letter from a young French armistice army officer went on to say that in spite of all the German propaganda, the Parisians favored the English. It continued: "Gaullism is losing some points as their recruits are mostly Communists and Jews. And in spite of what you read the LVF has been lamentably checked in Russia." He mentioned witnessing, in September, German mechanized troops passing eastward through Paris "equipped with our French tank models Hotchkiss (H39) and Gomua [sic]." He was relieved to cross the demarcation line at Chalon-sur-Saône on October 1 and view in the Macon railway station "people who were singing the Marseillaise with all their heart upon the return of some

---

52   Ibid. Letter dated October 12, 1941, marked No. 9161.
53   Ibid. Letters dated October 15 and 17, 1941, marked 2160.

liberated prisoners of war."[54] There were favorable comments on trips taken by top Vichy officials: Marshal Pétain to Lyon; Admiral Darlan to Nice; General Dentz to Arles. The Marshal made remarks on the new court procedures for handling actions by people considered as enemies of the state. Other than the report commenting that these remarks were approved, there were no quotations from citizens on that controversial subject.

M. Caziot, the Minister of Agriculture, disapproved of peasants' hording for the winter, which angered city dwellers who accused them of encouraging the black market and the use of bartering. One city dweller in Nîmes mentioned they had to cope with food shortages there, as their aged grandmother could not be moved, so "they must suffer hunger just like the families with young children who go to sleep with their hunger." That hunger did not stop her from castigating the Germans for killing hostages in Paris, which she quantified at one hundred "for killing one of theirs."[55] Farmers in the Aveyron, the Lozère, and the Haute-Loire, who normally supplied farm needs for the Gard, were singled out for criticism in these regards. People complained there was little work available gathering chestnuts, beets, or making salted fish. Chestnuts were very plentiful in the Cévennes area of the Gard in the fall so something was amiss here. Two intercepts from St-Jean du Gard and Bessèges explained why: "I saw M. Fermaud this morning at the market, and the peasants were very unhappy because the government imposed a two franc tax on chestnuts, and these are the last ones seen on the market." The second letter explained what happened. "Each time a staple crop is taxed, a new black market is created. If you want some chestnuts, you have to go to the farmer's property and pay ten to fifteen francs a kilo."[56] Fruits were in short supply as were some vegetables. Differing price-control levels between the Gard and the Lozère paralyzed the exchange of some products and pointed up the government's ineffectiveness.[57]

November's synthesis concerning opinion noted people were still hesitant about talking confidentially on the phone. The same expressions of uneasiness and war weariness persisted as in October. One writer com-

---

54   Ibid. Letter dated October 12, 1941, marked No. 9157.
55   Ibid. Letter dated October 23, 1941, marked No. 2395.
56   Ibid. Letters dated October 20 and 23, 1941, marked No. 2348 and 2396.
57   Ibid. Monthly Commission de Contrôle Postal report No. 32, October 1941, marked No. 312, 316.

mented, "I've had enough! I'm disgusted, fatigued and without resources to cope with multiple difficulties." There were no comments on military events. However, the accidental death in an airplane crash in a remote area of the Gard on November 12 of General Charles Huntziger, the Vichy war minister, was regretted. People were dismayed by the forced retirement of General Weygand and suspected that the Germans were behind that decision, which indicated to them how much control the Germans were exerting over their Vichy puppets. An example of the public expression of growing anti-German opinion came from a letter describing what happened in a cinema in Toulouse. When a German delegation appeared in the newscast of General Huntziger's funeral, the audience emitted a "torrent of catcalls" and boos. This type of outcry led to an order that all newscasts in cinemas be shown with the houselights on.[58] Remarks were registered that shipments managed to enter into the Occupied Zone but nothing flowed back. The people understood that much of this consisted of supplies bound for Germany and reinforced the negative concerns about the long war ahead.

In economic news, horses were impossible to buy, and animal feed was practically nonexistent. The few horses available were too weak for hard work. Even feed for pigs and chickens was lacking, so an early slaughter of hogs was indicated in telegrams. The weather was not yet too cold, but the olive crop was poor. Farmers still held back goods for barter and the black market, and a lack of seed supply was blamed on the ineffectual administration. Natural or chemical fertilizers were also impossible to obtain. Many Gardois criticized the partiality of the French press, radio, and film industries. "Lots of us listen to the BBC; if ours were better [more truthful] it wouldn't be like that." With the approach of winter local thoughts turned to the plight of the POWs and veterans tried to organize aid for their unfortunate brethren in German stalags. No enthusiasm existed for collaboration. The latest Jewish laws had forbidden Jews to work in many additional fields of endeavor. One Jew in Nice wrote that he could no longer work as an insurance agent. Support for the English had not been eroded by the recent German military success in Russia. Debate continued among the Gardois over any potential benefits to France from the war in the east. A few saw France as a partner in Germany's New Europe but the majority

---

58   *L'Opinion Française sous Vichy.* Ibid., 254 n1.

thought that France could only count on herself, some said thanks to the marshal. "It is absurd to count on foreign salvation; one must believe in France rising back up under her estimable leader who aspires only to her deliverance."[59]

December's report repeated complaints about no relaxation of the demarcation line and no return of POWs. Again there were no comments on Marshal Pétain or his government, but there were many gripes concerning the overall poor administrative handling of policies and procedures affecting daily life. Excessive red tape was blamed for hindering the flow of goods and services, the result of which was the chaos suffered by the public. People refrained from talking on the phone due to concerns about being listened in on. Again, general malaise and despondency were widely commented upon and the attitude reflected that life's difficulties seemed insurmountable. The war in Russia, Libya, and now the Pacific elicited many comments about its global spread and fear for long duration, with consequences that would be felt for generations to come. The Gardois hoped that France's North African colonies wouldn't be drawn into the conflict and some local insurance companies expressed concern over their liabilities in Tunisia. Pétain had been granted a meeting with Marshal Hermann Goering at Saint-Florentin on December 1 after Weygand had been dismissed. His usual demands/requests for France had been met with this response from Goering: "Who won this war? You or us?"[60] Comments in this report about that meeting were mostly skeptical: "Who knows what they cooked up?"

German interference in all things French seemed to be growing, and French discontent with that fact was too. Local industry continued to suffer from the critical lack of raw materials needed to support the manufacturing process. Many factories had shut down due to the nondelivery of the essential commodity of coal and delays in receipt of other materials. These factories included a vegetaline manufacturer in Alès (no coal even there, which was the local center for coal production), an explosives factory in Saint Marcal (no paraffin), a chemical factory in Beaucaire (no paper sacks), and a tube factory in Bessèges (no metal for tubing). Commerce was slack due to the unavailability of merchandise to sell, even wine. "Nothing to sell, it's disgusting." There were numerous

---

59 ADG. 1 W 42. Ibid. November 1941 summary report No. 33 marked 380.
60 *France: The Dark Years*. Ibid., 183.

complaints about fraudulent actions as well as the black market. Typical comments of frustration were "If you want to survive it's better to be a *bad* Frenchman," and "No one can supply me with good information so how do you expect me to answer your question about delivery?" A December week's delivery of potatoes from outside the Gard totaled 927 tons for its 400,000 population, or five pounds a person. But there were many fruit and vegetable shortages reported including beets, citrus fruits, dates, salted fish, and even apples and chestnuts. One person wrote: "You know people come to Montfrin who pay more than the set price in order to get vegetables. It goes on all the time."[61]

As 1941 came to an end, the stage was being set for greater collaboration by the leaders of the Vichy government in their efforts to find a restored independent role for a sovereign France in the New Europe led by a seemingly triumphant Germany. The question to be answered, however, was whether a significant majority of the French people were willing to follow along where the Vichy government was aiming to take them. The people's mood was still one of ambiguity in spite of a discernable spirit of uneasiness, manifested in feelings of weariness and uncertainty associated now with a war of worldwide proportions. Marshal Pétain was still greatly venerated as a person and symbol, but a distinct separation was developing in the majority of the public between him personally and his Vichy government's collaborative policies. The challenges of daily living under occupation conditions were supreme in the public's mind. French public support for England's continued struggle against Hitler was unabated and strengthened to some degree by America joining the crusade against the Axis powers.

As January 1942 opened, French resistance to its occupier was increasing, but it did not yet approach anything that resembled coordinated organization. The Germans in France had now entered a stage where dislike for their presence had morphed into hatred, which only worsened as their repressive actions grew more obvious and violent in both the military and economic spheres. The Communist bugaboo existed in France among bourgeois and rightist cliques, but it did not significantly affect the anti-German and pro-Anglo-American French equations. What all these combined factors represented was that France, as the new year dawned, was becoming ripe for seeking a new internal

---

61   ADG. 1 W 42. Ibid. December 1941 summary report No. 34 marked 381.

path, which would later reject Vichy's active participation through "hard Pétainism"[62] in pursuing Collaborationist economic, social, and political war aims. The weight of shocking events in 1942 that would accumulate within and without metropolitan France would have a clarifying effect upon the French mind-set, even though the fog of war would shroud the battlefields of the world throughout the entire year, before finally clearing in 1943.

---

62   *De Munich a la Libération*. Ibid., 188. The transition from Pétainisme by persuasion to hard Pétainisme was only a glimmer in 1941, but it was definitely hinted at in Petain's "Bad Wind" speech.

Opinion in 1942

The Winds of Change

"Pétain also spoke on the radio last night and it was no less strange. A pitiful moment was when without realizing it he read twice a whole paragraph from his message. It was impossible not to feel a great pity. How would France be without this old man whose attention span weakens every moment. Naturally the Parisian papers did not mention a word of this speech this morning." —Jean Guéhenno, January 1, 1942[1]

"You get so cold you can't think of anything else." —Jean Guéhenno, January 21, 1942[2]

"Yesterday evening by moonlight, the English bombed the Renault factories in Boulogne-Billancourt. The people were not indignant and most were badly hiding their jubilation. Tomorrow morning, twenty more hostages will be shot." —Jean Guéhenno, March 4, 1942[3]

"It's done. At the wish of Hitler, Laval is the head of government in France. The old man has given him his powers and passes to

---

1 *Journal des Années Noires.* Ibid., 230 ; *France: The Dark Years.* Ibid., 184. Jackson mentions Pétain's growing frustration, after the St Florentin meeting with Goering, evident in this address where he referred to himself in such terms as "partial-exile" and "semi-liberty."
2 *Journal des Années Noires.* Ibid., 232.
3 Ibid., 244.

the phantom state before even dying." —Jean Guéhenno, April 20, 1942[4]

"For eight days now the Jews must wear a yellow star and call upon them the public's contempt. Never have people been so kind with them." —Jean Guéhenno, June 16, 1942[5]

"What joy we felt yesterday morning. The Americans have landed everywhere in North Africa." —Jean Guéhenno, November 9, 1942[6]

"You have only one duty: to obey. You have only one country that I embody: France." —Marshal Pétain as quoted by Jean Guéhenno, November 21, 1942[7]

The year 1942 was a watershed for the French, in the sense that while external events seemed to favor the Germans for most of the year, internally there were increasing undercurrents of connections that would burst forth into the open in the following year, which would be inimical to Vichy loyalists and the German occupiers. This did not mean that the resistance moments were at all strong in numbers of active adherents or even in organization, although since Jean Moulin had parachuted into unoccupied France in early 1942, cooperation between competing organizations had started to improve. For example, the increase in the different Resistance groups' clandestine newsletters at the end of 1942 was about three and a half times the number distributed at the end of 1941. That translated into about 145,000 underground press copies being distributed in a nation of forty million people.[8] The point is that the numbers of active resisters were still very small in this time frame, as was the number of core ideologues for the Vichy state. The huge majority of French men and women were *attentistes*, who did not have much hope for the future and struggled to live day to day. These people constituted the vast "silent majority" of

---

4   Ibid., 250.
5   Ibid., 260
6   Ibid., 298.
7   Ibid., 302.
8   *France: The Dark Years*. Ibid., 438–439.

France in 1942, who might be temporarily upset with British bombings and Communist-led assassinations of Germans but who were experiencing a growing hatred of the Germans for their reprisals and other vicious actions. This broad center of France largely rejected collaboration, and showed signs of an increase in their commitment to an Allied victory.

Two events occurred that would have tremendous impact upon Vichy and the French. One would have lasting consequences that would damn Vichy's reputation forever, and the other would give de Gaulle a boost while causing Hitler to occupy all of France. These two actions were Vichy's vigorous collaboration in rounding up the Jews, and the invasion of France's North African colonies by the Americans. But as 1942 opened, Jean Guéhenno's quote of January 21 spoke to the point of the hardships suffered by all the French that winter, the extreme coldness of which only worsened the hunger that the French people collectively felt constantly in the pit of their stomachs. It was evident to Pétain's citizenry that his policy of active collaboration with Germany was not resulting in improved delivery of basic food and heating supplies for the average French citizen. This letdown was a major source of disappointment.[9] And although Vichy's bureaucracy had grown in numbers by 38 percent, complains over its ineffectiveness in failing to deliver the promised essential living conditions were only growing louder.

We have read many complaints that blamed the functionaries for the chaos that frustrated people in their daily survival efforts, for which there were valid reasons too. A law passed by Vichy on March 15, 1942, which attempted to control the black market, was a failure. Peasants became objects of scorn for their reputed hoarding of food for sale on the black market, which had some justification, but the government's poor distribution set-up also deserved a good portion of the blame. Additionally, in the law just mentioned, the government excused past peasant infractions committed "in view of the direct satisfaction of personal or family needs." The following breakdown for total beef slaughtering shows where it all went: of 1,150,000 tons of beef butchered, the farmers kept 250,000, matched by another 250,000 tons that "evaporated" into

---

9 *Vichy France.* Ibid., 309–310. Paxton states that in Germany food rations were first reduced on April 6, 1942. A nervous Ambassador Abetz accepted "extraordinarily high" food deliveries from France in a plan that would extract high allocations from the Occupied Zone and let Vichy make the decision how to feed all of France from its own Free Zone's inadequate sources.

thin peasant air; the Germans took 240,000 for themselves and another 120,000 tons went to intermediaries; 100,000 tons went to people with priorities; and the last 190,000 went to ordinary consumers who queued up, which equated to about 14 grams each day, per person.[10]

The existence of the demarcation line was a real hindrance to food-supply distribution for the monoculture departments in the Midi like the Gard, because of where the production centers of important food staples were located in France. The Occupied Zone produced 70 percent of the wheat, the prime component for bread; 85 percent of the butter; 65 percent of the beef; and almost all of the sugar. We have read the torrent of intercepts that complained, since late 1940, about empty stomachs. The convoluted and complicated rationing system meant, in theory, that individuals aged twenty-one to seventy were to get (if available) 1,327 calories per day, down from 3,000 calories, prewar. However, the people with enough ready cash, which meant the middle-class urban bourgeois and the wealthy, used the "System D," a familiar term for improvising to adapt to the shortcomings of the rationing system that generally meant the black market or other equivalents, like barter. Jean-Pierre Azéma estimated "that from 1942, meat, milk, and eggs would cost two to five times the official taxed prices on the black market; potatoes four to five times; butter six to eight times." As average people went hungry, blame was liberally assigned to peasants, the rich, including any foreign Jews, and the Vichy administration, other than the austere Marshal Pétain. Families of modest means without country cousins, who could ship them "family care packages," suffered the most, and their anger was justifiably augmented and directed at a state that was failing to deliver both politically and administratively.[11]

By the end of 1941, Marshal Pétain was very much disappointed with Admiral Darlan, who, like his predecessor, had failed in his assigned mission to gain concessions from Hitler in return for France's efforts at collaboration. In January, a bizarre *pas-de-deux* took place in Paris between Ambassador Abetz and Jacques Benoist-Méchin, a young Vichy sub-minister for German relations, who both tried to resurrect Hitler's interest in offering concessions to Vichy. This dance of go-betweens went back and forth, arousing Darlan's hopes, while Pétain remained skepti-

---

10   *De Munich a la Libération.* Ibid., 160 n1.
11   Ibid., 158-162; *France: The Dark Years.* Ibid., 249–251.

cal. By the end of January it was a case of much ado about nothing, with the exception that it drove another nail in Darlan's coffin. Vichy also suffered an overt fiasco that resulted from its attempted show trial of Daladier, Blum et al., which had opened at Riom on February 19, 1942. Darlan looked ineffective when these two Third Republican ex-prime ministers made a mockery of Vichy's efforts to blame them for France's defeat. The Germans were angered as they had wanted these former leaders tried for causing the war. Laval, ever the opportunist, was alert to Darlan's vulnerability, and waited in the wings for the moment to strike. He was prepared to show a reluctant Pétain that he had changed his close-to-the-vest ways of maneuvering, and now could get the audiences necessary to obtain a far-reaching arrangement with Germany that would allow France a meaningful role within Germany's New Europe.

Disenchantment had not totally trumped dislike when Pétain met Laval secretly in the forest of Randan on March 26, 1942, to discuss new cabinet possibilities. However, Laval did not overreach and patiently awaited further developments from Pétain's desire to use continued French neutrality to maintain some ties with America, while not upsetting Germany. Pétain secretly sent a personal representative, René Fonck, to show the Germans in Paris his proposed list of new ministers. Then America's Ambassador Leahy was shown the list and the go-between, Pétain's *chef du cabinet* Du Moulin de Labarthète hinted at some German pressure in favor of Laval being included, as well as the fact that Darlan might be replaced. Leahy, in turn, objected to Laval, and Abetz heard of this, so a test of strength was engaged between the two belligerents. Darlan shot himself in the foot by the provocative self-preservation tactics he employed, and Berlin felt obliged to put their support behind America's *bête noire*, Laval. Darlan resigned his top position on April 17 but remained as commander in chief of the armed forces. Laval took over on April 26 as "head of government," thanks to passage of a new Constitutional Act 11 on April 18, whereby Pétain resigned that position while retaining his "head of state" title. France was about to enter a much more demanding and darker phase of collaboration.[12]

Two German decisions took place in late March that had direct influences on the new collaborative route Laval would undertake. He did keep Marshal Pétain informed of his intentions as they both tried

---

12   Ibid., 184–185; *Vichy France*. Ibid., 131–134.

to protect French autonomy under the hardening German occupation. The first decision was the appointment on March 21 of Fritz Sauckel as Germany's coordinator for acquisition of all foreign labor for work in the Reich's factories. His demanding labor negotiations with Laval would first develop two months after Laval's formal return to power. The other decision, the one that led to the most shameful period in Vichy history, grew out of the German adoption at the Wansee Conference of its "Final Solution," the first step for the eradication of the Jewish race. On March 27, 1942, the first trainload of 1,112 Jewish deportees left the French transit concentration camp at Drancy, bound for Auschwitz in Poland. According to Marrus and Paxton, these Jews were supposedly sent in reprisal for attacks on German servicemen in France and included some French Jews, while the majority was of foreign origin. They were the Jews first swept up in Paris during August and December 1941, and only nineteen would survive Nazi extermination.[13]

Julian Jackson points out a key difference in German attitudes toward French efforts at collaboration between Laval's first time in power and the second. In 1940, the Germans had no interest in what France had to offer, and in 1942, the French were in no position to offer enough to satisfy Germany's voracious appetite.[14] Laval maneuvered as best he could to lessen the impact of their demands while hoping the French would accept the result. He ended up pleasing neither while falling down a personal black hole of collaboration. On June 15, Sauckel, a tough Nazi bully, came to Paris to lay down the law to Laval concerning his numerical needs for skilled French labor in the homeland. He was empowered to force the conscription of French labor, of which Laval was aware. Therefore Laval proposed a scheme whereby he could show the French some return of French POWs in exchange for volunteers willing to go to work in Germany. This became the notorious Réleve system, which was announced in the French press in June and under which one French prisoner of war was be released for every three skilled French laborers who volunteered to go to work in Germany.

The number of volunteers would not satisfy German demands, so more draconian measures would be imposed later, and under the Réleve terms Germany could select which POWs would be returned—these

---

13   *Vichy France and the Jews.* Ibid., 227.
14   *France: The Dark Years.* Ibid., 215.

turned out to be the oldest and most infirm ones they held. It required a propaganda effort by Vichy to publicize it, which turned out to be the beginning of a disaster for Laval and Vichy, as the Réleve was highly unpopular with the average Frenchman. Yet Laval, the eternal optimist, viewed negotiations to implement this labor exchange arrangement as realistic opportunities, rather than disastrously disliked policies. He also was convinced by mid-year 1942 that Germany was winning the war, a fundamental reason behind his new efforts at collaboration. On June 22, 1942, he amazingly went so far as to announce the following in the newspapers: "I desire the victory of Germany, for without it, Bolshevism would tomorrow install itself everywhere." This remark would be a key instrument for the prosecution when they sought the death penalty for Laval at his trial for treason just after the war.[15]

At the time Laval uttered those unpardonable words, there were only about three thousand German military police in all the Occupied Zones of France.[16] That made it crucial for the German authorities to secure the complete cooperation of the powerful French police force of nearly one hundred thousand men, thirty thousand of whom were in Paris, if the key new Nazi aims in France were to be realized. These plans included the securing of French labor, the deportation of the Jews in France, and the tracking down of resistance forces and terrorists within France who represented a threat to the German occupation forces.[17] In May, Himmler's deputy, Reinhardt Heydrich, accompanied SS general Carl Oberg, the new head of German police in France, to Paris. The German police now were independent from the military, and Oberg needed to form a close bond with the minister in charge of the French police, René Bousquet, as French police support had become the fundamental backbone of collaboration. They first met in early May, and their give-and-take discussions went on for three months. Bousquet, an administrator and former prefect who prized order and detested the Communists, wanted above all else to keep the German police out of French police affairs. He believed that the maintenance of this as a guiding principle would reinforce the limited French sovereignty that

15   Ibid., 215.
16   *Vichy France and the Jews.* Ibid., 241.
17   Ibid., 242.

still existed for Vichy and strengthen it considerably in the occupied territories.

Bousquet assured Oberg that the French gendarmes would willingly do the dirty work on behalf of German policy, and in return, Oberg's men would back off from interfering with French police work within the Occupied Zones. The Bousquet-Oberg agreement was signed on August 8, 1942, but much dirty work had been done by the French police on behalf of the Germans in the interim. These two men were bound at the hip, and French complicity with German occupation aims was firmly anchored in French control of internal order "against anarchism, terrorism, and Communism, and generally against all foreign actions susceptible of troubling order within France."[18] Some sixteen thousand resistance suspects, mainly Communists, but including some followers of de Gaulle, were arrested by the French police, working in concert with Oberg's forces in the twelve-month period that began in May. The use of torture did not inhibit the French police, and they had no reticence in turning suspects directly over to the German authorities. But it was in their treatment of the Jews that the most ineradicable stain accrued to the French police, as a direct result of the orders they were given by the Vichy government.[19]

The subject of large-scale forced deportations of Jews from France to the east had been broached with Bousquet by Oberg on May 6, and the former had asked if foreign Jews in detention camps in the Unoccupied Zone could be included. Decisions were left pending German policy conclusions, and in June, the demand came for the deportation of forty thousand foreign and French Jews, three-quarters of them to come from the Occupied Zone but with more details to be worked out. On July 2, Oberg finalized the compromise negotiations with Bousquet, who did not protest the principle behind the arrests. The French police would arrest only foreign Jews in both zones, but Laval prevailed in obtaining a German concession for arresting children under age sixteen so they could accompany their parents on "humanitarian" grounds. The ever-pragmatic Laval really didn't want Vichy to have to babysit any children left behind.

The operation was scheduled to kick off in Paris on July 16–17,

---

18 *Vichy France.* Ibid., 296.
19 *France: The Dark Years.* Ibid., 216.

utilizing some nine thousand French police officers.[20] The roundup part of the operation, named *Vent printanier*, was facilitated by the existence of a French police card-file system that had already cataloged the names, addresses, professions, and nationalities of 150,000 Jews in the department of the Seine. French Jews were color-coded differently from foreign ones. The German target was the arrest of twenty-eight thousand Jews in two days, with the majority to be incarcerated in the *Vélodrome d'Hiver*, an outdoor sports arena in Paris's fifteenth *arrondisement*, and the balance in the camp at Drancy, which became the primary departure point for Poland. The result was disappointing to the Germans but heartrending for the 12,884 Jews actually swept up in the two days. Conditions in the *Vél' d'Hiv* were barbaric: only two doctors were allowed for seven thousand people, of whom four thousand were children. It was hot during the day and cold at night, and there was insufficient water, blankets, and sanitation facilities for the five days people were kept under such foul conditions. The French people who witnessed this roundup had shown sympathy for the detainees, and many Jews had slipped though the wide cordon.

By the time deportations from France were suspended in September (except for four convoys in November, when railroad freight cars became available), some 41,951 Jews, including at least 6,053 children under age sixteen, had been sent to Auschwitz. This number included some 6,500 arrested August 26–28 in the Unoccupied Zone, of which Nîmes was a part, who were forwarded to Drancy for the final one-way voyage in cattle cars. In this instance Vichy handed over Jews from an area not

---

20   On July 16, 1995, Jacques Chirac made a remarkable speech in which, for the first time, a French president recognized the responsibility of France in the roundup of the Jews on that day fifty-three years earlier. He said. "France on that day committed an irreparable act. …It is undeniable that this was a collective fault." Seventeen years later, on July 22, 2012, the newly elected French president, François Holland made a discourse on the site where the *Vél' d'Hiv* formerly had stood, wherein he praised President Chirac for his "courage and clearness." He was unequivocally clear about the role of the French and a certain state organization in leading the way in these *rafles*: "The truth is that the French police, based on lists that they themselves had established, took charge of this operation …the French gendarmerie escorted them [the Jews] to the internment camps. The truth is that not a single German soldier, not one, was mobilized in support of this operation." He headlined his speech as "A crime committed in France by France." *Le Figaro*, July 23, 2012, page 3.

occupied by German troops. This is astonishing and is the only instance like it in Western Europe during the war. For a time these roundup (*rafles*) operations caused outcries in France, especially by the people who actually saw the heart-wrenching scenes of families being led off. This was one reason that Laval pleaded for a hiatus in September. We know the German liaison showed no regret over the events, but we can also state that the two most directly involved Vichy leaders in that collaborative effort with the Germans, Laval and Bousquet, exhibited no remorse over their active involvement either. The numbers quoted above could never have been reached without the cooperative participation of the French police organizations.[21]

Five (out of thirty-five in the Unoccupied Zone) Catholic bishops or archbishops spoke out against these Jewish arrests, starting in August when the archbishop of Toulouse, Cardinal Saliège, condemned these arrests from his pulpit. However, the Protestant Pastor Boegner was the most consistent protestor to the Vichy government concerning Vichy's crucial role in these scurrilous affairs. On August 20, he described what he had gleaned about the Jewish deportation process in a letter to Marshal Pétain: "The 'handing over' of these unfortunate foreigners happens in many places under inhumane conditions which have aroused the most hardened consciences and brought tears to the eyes of witnesses. Crammed into freight cars without any concern for hygiene, the foreigners designated for departure were treated like cattle." When he saw Laval in person on September 9, he was fed a propaganda line that the Jews had been sent to Poland to farm. Boegner said something after the war that could have been a reflection on the conscience of the soon-to-be-executed Laval: "I talked to him about murder; he answered me with gardening."[22]

The military developments in the World War through the summer of 1942 were, on the surface, very favorable to Germany, so one could see some basis for Pierre Laval's point of view. Most all the news from the Pacific was negative for the Anglo-American Allies. Singapore fell to the Japanese in mid-January, along with more than one hundred thousand Anglo-Indian prisoners of war, followed by the conquest of the Dutch East Indian colonies by early March. The fall of the island of Corregi-

---

21   Ibid., 217–219; *Vichy France and the Jews*. Ibid., 243, 250–252.
22   *Vichy France and the Jews*. Ibid., 355.

dor in May signaled the end of the American presence in the Philippines, and Japan's thrust along New Guinea to the South Pacific threatened Australia, which was relieved a bit by the Battle of the Coral Sea, a strategic victory for the American navy. It was followed early in June by the disastrous set back to the Japanese carrier forces at the Battle of Midway. In Russia, however, a renewed German offensive in the south resulted in the conquest of Sevastopol in the Crimea in May. That war was a costly one in casualties, but the Bolsheviks seemed to be bleeding more heavily than the Germans. Rommel had launched an offensive in Libya in January, and the Desert Fox bagged thirty-five thousand more Brits when the tough nut of Tobruk in Libya fell in June. Things looked uncertain for the English, who now faced an Africa Corps advance on Egypt.

An abortive Canadian-British amphibious raid on the port of Dieppe on the northwest coast of France suffered 60 percent casualties in a major setback for Churchill in August 1942. All this while the critical Battle of the Atlantic was intensifying and the German U-boats were slowly putting a stranglehold on the British Isles, with the growing level of Allied merchant tonnage losses on an unsustainable course.[23] Whatever the level of knowledge the average French person had of these events, it could not contribute to the reduction of their general uneasiness about France's near-term future under increasing German occupational repression. As the fourth winter of the war approached, France felt the added discomfort of more English bombing raids on its population centers.

September started off ominously for French workers of both sexes, because only approximately forty thousand workers had volunteered to work in Germany since June under the existing Réleve program. Laval, threatened by Sauckel, enacted a law that forced employers to formulate lists of all male employees, ages eighteen to fifty, and all unmarried female employees, ages twenty-one to thirty-five, from which the Vichy government could select workers who had to go where the government chose to send them (i.e., only Germany, at this time). By December, Sauckel had his 250,000 workers, whose French families were none too happy. This collaboration endeavor that forced French labor to work for the Nazi war effort in Germany was the genesis of what would become, in 1943,

---

23 *Vichy France.* Ibid., 304.

the largest source of youthful new members for the resistance. Laval continued to be the preferred Vichy official with whom the Germans wished to bargain, and their support kept him in power in spite of efforts by the French fascists Doriot and Déat to supplant him.[24]

When a German army started on October 4 to invest a faraway Russian city, Stalingrad, located on the Volga River, it most likely did not gain much notice in France. What certainly did draw their attention was the battle of El Alamein, which raged from October 23 through November 5 in North Africa's ongoing Western Desert campaign. Rommel's German-Italian forces were routed by Montgomery and retreated posthaste into Libya, where some trucks and fuel supplied by Vichy awaited them. Vichy was nervous about their North African colonies' fate, in light of increasing rumors of an Allied invasion, along with fears of stepped-up German demands for use of their Tunisian ports and airfields as resupply centers for Rommel. One of Laval's last two bargaining chips for seeking concessions from Germany and maintaining neutrality vis-à-vis the United States was about to be raked in by the croupier of war.

Operation Torch, the American-led invasion of Algeria and Morocco, took place on November 8, 1942. By early morning, Laval had secured Pétain's written approval on an order for the French army in North Africa to resist the American invaders, which they made a good faith effort to do. In turn, Laval was forced by the Germans to make Tunisian airports available immediately for reinforcements to arrive for Rommel. Hitler summoned Laval to Munich, and Laval hoped that strong French resistance in Algeria might persuade Hitler to make a miracle concession of military supplies sufficient to protect what was left of France's empire. While Laval was en route, Admiral Darlan, who by coincidence was in Algiers visiting his son, realized that continued resistance was futile. He took control of the situation and convinced General Juin to impose a cease-fire in the city of Algiers. By November 10, all French resistance stopped in Algeria due to this confusion in command, and Hitler heard of this just before Laval met him. The meeting was over before it began, and Laval shuffled out with burning ears, empty-handed and uninformed that Operation Anton would take place the next day. The German forces moved south of the demarcation line and occupied

---

24 *France: The Dark Years*. Ibid., 220.

all of the Free Zone with no resistance from the Armistice Army, which had been ordered to stay in their barracks.

All of France was now occupied (but the demarcation line remained well into 1943), and on November 27, in Operation Lila, the Germans forced the French Armistice Army to disband and moved near Toulon, where the main French fleet sat at anchor. The French naval officers did not trust German assurances that they would not attempt to take over the fleet, so the crews were ordered to open the scuttle cocks and the fleet came to rest on the harbor's bottom. So it was that Vichy's two significant aces in the hole, its fleet and its Mediterranean empire, were trumped without one shot fired in anger at the Germans. Darlan went on to play a confused Faustian role in the drama in Algiers, more appreciated by President Roosevelt and General Mark Clark than by Winston Churchill or General Eisenhower or certainly by Marshal Pétain. This confusion in command ended abruptly when Darlan was assassinated by a young royalist on December 24, 1942, in Algiers. On November 17, Pierre Laval had managed to cover his flanks within Vichy's shrinking power base with the new Constitutional Act 12, which empowered him alone to enact laws with his own signature. Marshal Pétain, still widely admired by the vast majority of the French public, was left in his position but his days of power were over. Shunted aside, he had begun in this catastrophic period for Vichy to show characteristics of his advancing age: passivity, indecision, and exhaustion.[25]

Laval's return to power and what he did at first had given impetus to mostly private, *attentiste* thoughts. However, on July 14, 1942, a demonstration of at least ten thousand people took place in Toulouse, where for two hours people celebrated their France of de Gaulle, the republic, and liberty, all while singing "La Marseillaise." It was not a unique demonstration that day in the Free Zone, and it represented feelings and aspirations more for the unknown future than for the known present. The Réleve was on their minds, certainly, and the Jewish roundups were about to shock them with their impact. The committed and aggressive Vichy fascist Benoist-Méchin wrote, "The Anglo-Soviet propaganda, the difficulties in food supply, the forced levies on French labor and the general presence of the German occupation, has pitted 90 percent of the people against Germany. This hostility directly reflects on all those who

---

25   Ibid., 222–227.

want to cooperate with Germany."[26] And that hostility was certainly most focused on Pierre Laval.

Pierre Laborie summed up this feeling succinctly in his usage of an internal intelligence memo issued upon the occasion of the reorganization by Pétain of his cabinet, which put Laval back in power: "Opinion has the regrettable tendency to consider him [Laval] once and for all the agent of the Third Reich in France."[27] This appraisal was made in April, and it only intensified as the year passed and came to its unhappy ending for France. As Jean Guéhenno forcefully put it in his journal the day after the Americans invaded French North Africa, "No, Mr. Laval is not a saint, nor is Pétain. They are only two imbeciles who believed that Germany would win the war and committed themselves along with us to that country."[28]

Unfortunately, the syntheses and interceptions for 1942 that were available in the Gard archives were limited to the months of January, May, November, and December. The January synthesis reported continued sympathy for the marshal and deplored that his orders were poorly implemented. "Father Pétain treats us well, but his commissioners don't obey him. It is always the same thing." People expressed satisfaction that France was not directly involved in the world conflict and lauded Pétain for his safe guidance. "Thanks to Pétain, France is in the process of reemerging from its decline." Numerous criticisms were recorded about life's difficulties, especially recriminations concerning poor food supplies. The report called the people "wise" who did not complain and gave the "imperfect organizations" credit for not making the situation worse. It appeared to be an editorialized effort at a back-handed compliment, which went on to say life would be misery for all but the rich if these administrative operations did not exist. There would have been much outcry if this statement had become general knowledge. Finally, the marshal's predictable Christmas statement about the continued plight of the French prisoners of war in Germany was noted.

The German retreat from Moscow reanimated Anglophile hopes in the Gard: "The Russian front is freezing; for the first time Adolph [sic] has made a grave mistake; my friend Frits, spoke candidly in French

---

26 *L'Opinion Française sous Vichy*. 269, n2.
27 Ibid., 265, n3.
28 *Journal des Années Noires*. Ibid., 299, entry dated November 9, 1942.

that 'I've had enough.'" Impartial people were even happy to see the Axis victory streak snapped. However, many did recognize what they considered the downside of a Russian victory: "a Bolshevik sway over Europe would be something worse than a German victory." An equal amount of opinions expressed that a stalemate in Russia would benefit France: "Let both of them suffer the worst; that's how we can reap profit from a role as arbitrator." The Nippon-American war elicited many comments, most of which were pessimistic. There were sympathetic expressions for the Allies over the heavy American and British naval losses. "The English are again tested [referring to the devastating loss of two battleships, HMS *Prince of Wales* and *Hood*, to Japanese land-based aircraft off Singapore on December 10, 1941], but they will not give up hope." Other Gardois demonstrated *schadenfreude*: "The English lose their most magnificent ships; Mers el-Kébir is avenged." Citizens who only thought about France feared that the entrance of Japan into the fray would only prolong the war and worried about the fate of French citizens in Indochina.

The report stated that the local bourgeoisie was more patient in coping with daily living conditions than was the working class, who were exasperated with the black market that the more financially secure people, including the bourgeoisie, could afford to utilize. "We need to double salary levels. We are being exploited. Only those with cash have the right to live. Let's hope the screw turns on them." The working classes considered the administrative strictures as restrictions aimed at making them, the poor, suffer. The outlook was for troubling reactions to come from the poor. Workers were pleased to hear that they would be paid for the Christmas holiday shutdown, but the proprietors groaned and groused about having to comply with the order. The high cost of living was mentioned frequently by workers, owners of small rental properties, functionaries, and retirees, who blamed peasants and business owners for urban and rural cost inequities. They wrote, "Peasants speculate on other people's hunger," while the farmers responded with statements like "We are hindered and exploited by regulations that are imposed upon us." The city dwellers came back with accusations: "The peasants don't appreciate the numerous favors the government does for them and they even chortle about the urban suffering." The report maintained that recent energetic anti-Jewish, anti-Gaullist, and anti-Communist measures enacted by the state were generally approved. Protestant enclaves were accused of being divided over the Vichy government goals: "Saint-Hippolyte du Fort is very Gaullist and anti-National Revolution." On the other hand, personal denunciations were liable to be a pretext for sanctions imposed by various municipalities and their functionaries. The local press was compared to the Swiss newspapers, which were mentioned as being very popular in the Gard. The National Revolution's goal proposing the creation of large families was highly unpopular: "Now is not the time to have children, as so many basic necessities are lacking."

The meeting at Saint Florentin-Vergigny between Pétain and Goering was mentioned for raising hopes that some prisoners of war would be coming home, as well as for anticipating the development of a peace agreement between France and Germany. But some people took anti-collaboration stances: "I cannot imagine how the Darlan-Laval gang can join with these German parasites who feast on humanity." Some credit for arranging the Saint Florentin meeting was given to the earlier get-together of Darlan and Count Ciano, Mussolini's son-in-law, which led to the release of some French POWs held by the Italians. The report maintained that the morale of prisoners held in Germany was high, and the men were united in their approval of collaboration, along with being anti-English. It stated that the prisoners objected to any letter from home that took anti-Vichy positions. These statements might be editorializing for the closed readership of the report. General Weygand's retirement was looked upon as something forced by the Germans. An extract indicated approval of the Workers Charter of October 1941 by the local syndicate leaders but no rank-and-file reactions were mentioned. This was not surprising as the Charter of Labor was meant to neutralize trade unions in France under the Vichy regime.[29]

Surveys were attached from the two groups of the *Chantiers de la jeunesse*, Youth Work Groups, located near Le Vigan. This Vichy organization was set up by General de la Porte du Theil to get young urban men of military age off the streets and put them in supervised work camps in the forests for eight months of hard work and some moral classroom instruction.[30] One group (No. 18) mentioned long early-morning marches in the cold to cut down trees and said they needed

---

29 *Vichy France.* Ibid., 217.
30 Ibid., 164.

extra bread rations. Of 150 youths inoculated against diphtheria, 100 became ill because they had eaten beforehand. One youth said he ate better in the camp than back home. The camp discipline was mentioned as being "strict." Another said that orders given could be stupid: "We are like cogs in a machine. This morning the order to dress, undress, and redress was given five times and the chief said it was an order, so no questions." Another wrote, "We work like Negroes with hardly anything to eat. I want to go home." The other group (No. 45) apparently had a different experience, with complaints registered over insufficient food and wine, which caused the work output to be reduced. "We have no wine; the meat supplied is less than 25 grams per day and the bread only 350 grams and some days only 200 grams." The cadres at this camp were indicted for being poor leaders and inadequate to the task at hand. Only 20 percent were deemed worthy according to the report. The medical shots caused the same fainting spells that occurred in the first camp. Of the 1,755 letters that were intercepted and read that month, 16 percent reported good morale, and 80 percent were indifferent. The balance of comments was judged as indicating low morale.[31]

The next summary report was four months later in May, and the key item forming public opinion was identified as "simply put, inadequate food supplies." The allocating authorities continued to be severely criticized, in spite of the first appearance on the market of fresh spring vegetables in the countryside. City dwellers said, "It is only getting worse and worse." Rural folk complained, "A three-hour-long wait in the ration lines, even with tickets for cutlets and cabbage, yet when my turn came they ran out of the vegetables and the pieces of meat were tiny. I could have cried." A teacher was bitter about the farmers: "The gutless peasants send you away without an egg after having walked ten kilometers to their farm. I hope they are different where you live." In Nîmes the food situation was no better assured, as one urban dweller asked a friend in the countryside: "The weather is beautiful, so don't we stand a better chance of obtaining food where you live? In Nîmes it is impossible, and there are only 250 grams of vegetables per person allowed in the stores. That's nothing, so one must tighten one's belt another notch. It cannot go on like this. I have five small ribs for dinner tonight, but what about tomorrow? Perhaps I'll find a salad or a bunch of radishes. Until today,

---

31   ADG. 1 W 42. Ibid. Periodic report marked No. 35 for January 1942.

there was no meat for fifteen days in Nîmes. I hear the officers' military families have meat three or four times a week and are favored by the supply department, so they don't wait in line like we do."

In Alès, it was the same situation: "Food supplies are becoming even worse, and are really hard for all households. There are no potatoes in the Gard, and we hear they are rotting in the nearby departments of the Ardèche and Lozère. All one can find are rotten spinach and mushy artichokes. Everyone is hungry except for the grocery merchants as the barter and black markets are very active. Even when we are authorized to buy vegetables in a given week, you can't find any. I swear I have not been able to purchase any vegetables the last three days." People were bitter when allocations were approved and then rescinded, which they only found out when their rations were turned down. No potato seeds were available for private gardens, so that would make the next winter even more difficult. Peasants groused over the high individual cost of fifty thousand francs for poor-quality horses and about chickens that couldn't produce enough eggs because adequate feed was lacking. For all these shortcomings, the blame was laid at the feet of the regulatory administrations. Local people heard of the level of inefficiency at the nearby *Camp de la jeunesse*: "Our chief made us plant five hundred kilos of peas in rocky soil which only merited fifty. If I had done that at home, you would have beaten me, and I would have deserved it." The black market was decried: "We struggle against the black market but to survive, one must make use of it or die of hunger. Our poor aged marshal sacrifices himself to save France yet is surrounded by men who only think of their own stomachs. Their wine cellars and mills are full. Their servants spread the word and the employees of stores who supply them are not deaf, dumb, or blind."

The Reformed Protestant churches were very active on behalf of the prisoners of war in Germany. The Catholic bishop of Nîmes, who was closely allied with the prefect, had his letter intercepted, the subject of which was his visit to a nearby parish: "I was graciously received by the mayor but was disturbed to see a word missing from the marshal's motto, so I added one: *God*, Work, Family, and Country."

The Alsace-Lorraine refugees were reported as being consistently against collaboration. The report writers were surprised how much these people deported from their homeland hated the "Boches." The Joan of Arc Commemoration was noted, but people spoke of their disappointment in the lack of food for the event compared to the prior year. Some 2,500 people were estimated to have assembled, but one person's description of the event ended with "but this May 10 event made me think of the shameful debacle that began two years ago." One person castigated the British for their bombing raids on Paris: "Let's not doubt that they will receive imminent justice for their murderous attacks." Another individual described Laval as "always calm and peaceful" and compared his performance to that of Louis XI after the Hundred Years War. Another, evidently a dedicated Collaborationist, said: "Laval's return to power can scarcely please the English who want us to reenter the war to protect their finances and especially their dastardly domination of the world. God protect us! The New Europe will know how to protect itself without the Great Anglo-Judeo-American lords of finance; with Laval we certainly have a New France within a New Europe; and in the future we will avoid all the wars where history has revealed the presence of a perfidious England, taking their shameful profits." [32]

Also in May, a survey was taken clandestinely on the 66th Company MOI (Military Organization of Indochina) stationed at Valleraugue in the Gard, at the request of their commander (1st Indochinese Legion) in Agde. All 106 of the letters written by the indigenous soldiers and posted for Indochina were read. The daily quantity of rice and soup, accompanied by one complete meal per day, was judged insufficient. Work had been increased, but complaints were negligible. There were no comments on their leadership, but it was noted that one officer in the 67th Company had been attacked and wounded over the pretext that the men had been given too little to eat. Evidently the men had gone through a period when letters home had been forbidden, as the comment was made in thirty-seven letters about this fact. Some twenty-one agitators had been detained over some political unrest, but its cause was attributed to friction between groups from different locales in Indochina. A group called the Society of United Hearts was accused of causing hatred and jealousy. Two letters described the wounding of M. Simon over the insufficient food complaint, which also noted that he was replaced. A certain Tung wrote "that as a result of the imprisonment of about twenty others, discipline was hardened and work augmented.

---

32   ADG. 1 W 31. Synthesis for May 5–19, 1942, dated May 20, 1942.

No one was told anything about the cause of this affair, which was very troubling to the men." The writer was very disgusted. Another writer, Nyugen, stated that although he had money in his pocket, he could not buy any additional food to ease his hunger and thirst. Hien wrote home: "I'll be unhappy here until our return to Indochina. I don't know whom I can cry with at night." It was most doubtful that any of these men would return to Cambodia, Laos, or Vietnam until 1946 at the earliest, and certainly not before being politically vetted by the French.[33]

The report for July 26 through August 25, 1942, highlighted ways to cope with scarcities: bartering wine for oats and clothing for food. More complaints were registered concerning illegal slaughtering of animals, the sale of vegetables over the taxed price, and in relation to the high pricing of grapes by the wine cooperative in Bellegard. Illicit arm sales were mentioned, but they were for hunting purposes. Because of adverse public reactions to the roundup of Jews in August in Nîmes, any remarks touching on Jews in the Gard were closely observed.[34] A telephone call was intercepted at the Protestant Reformed Church in Nîmes that stated that on a departed convoy, three out of five persons were "saved," while the other two were said to have left on a later train. The call was placed by someone at the French Officer School in Aix-en-Provence, and he talked about the Jewish transit camp near there, les Milles. Ominously, brackets were placed around the names mentioned in the conversation, which indicated that those individuals were to be placed under observation.[35] A woman at Uzès wrote about the French police roundup of Jewish people in the duchy on August 26. "I felt down in the dumps all day. They shipped all the Jews to concentration camps. The gendarmes woke the unfortunate ones up at 5 AM, and it was en route! They were brought to an assembly camp near Alès. We have nothing to envy the Occupied Zone for. I ask myself why we don't baptize ourselves German immediately so we could avoid having two separate police forces and spare ourselves all these duplicate efforts. There is certainly no reason to be proud to be French."

A Nîmoise mentioned the agitation in her neighborhood over the

---

33   ADG. 1 W 42. Sondage dated May 20, 1942, marked 54–56.
34   Ibid. Police Investigations dated August 25, 1942
35   ADG. 1 W 31. Telephone transcript dated August 25, 1942, marked No. 1415.

assemblage of the foreign Jews "to go work in Germany, men and women side by side, it's truly abusive, and it appears there were some heart-rending scenes. It is truly inhuman. There is even talk of some suicides. Since yesterday the uniformed Cub Scouts carried pots of jam, fruits, and packages of all sorts to the synagogue. However, there is not one word of all that in the newspapers, and it has been going on for days." A Jewish woman in Nîmes was understandably fearful and beseeched her military son to help her: "I learned some bad news and don't know what to do. This morning they sent 500 Jews from Nîmes. I am very fearful but one must have courage to face such suffering. Darling, can you find a place for me to hide, so I can save myself for my last days? I'm so distressed that I can't act, and only you can help me. The next time they will come to pick me up, and you won't see me ever again. I have only fifteen days left, and they will never take me alive. Do something for me." A Nîmois telexed Pastor Boegner to ask him "to intervene to delay the departure of Elisabeth Stenitz from the camp of les Milles so that she could enter legally into Switzerland. Her visa had been obtained; however, a general Protestant charity guarantee for Jews has been declared insufficient grounds for protection by a screening commission, and the first departure of Jews from les Milles is scheduled for tomorrow."[36]

On September 2, 1942, Avraum Ternatinsky, a Russian Jew living in the Gard, wrote F. Feigenbaum of Lyon-Villeurbanne that he should not stay around Lyon, as the next Jewish roundup was imminent, and he and his wife, Berthe, should flee at once to Provence with their son, François, who had a safe passage card and thereby escape "the executioner." He ended by writing "there are everywhere brave people ready to help us. There is hope that in spite of everything, happy days await us yet." On October 13, a police prison official in Lyon wrote his regional counterpart in Marseille that "the said Feigenbaum has been led to the concentration camp at Rivesaltes, and Ternatinsky, the uncle of Berthe, will eventually suffer the same fate." An elite mobile police unit, the *Groupe Mobile de Réserve* No. 5, was stationed at Nîmes to control certain organizations and aid in Jewish roundups. One member's letter was intercepted on September 23, for which he was judged indiscreet. He mentioned "his group had proceeded to arrest some Gaullists and

---

36 Ibid. Documents marked Nos. 1969–1971, dated August 27, 1942, and No. 1322 dated August 29, 1942.

Communists first and then some Israelites in the evening and that the windows of the German labor office had been broken." The night ended without the exchange of gunshots he had anticipated or hoped for. Three days later, Prefect Chiappe wrote the head of the GMR [*Groupe Mobile de Réserve*] "Comtat" in Uzès to investigate this loose-tongued Georges Clerget, and on September 28, 1942, he received his answer that Gardien Clerget had received a tongue-lashing in addition to a punishment. Administrative justice had been imposed.[37]

Then there was the investigation report concerning Mlle. Violette Mouchon, stemming from some of her letters that had been intercepted. This Parisian, aged forty-nine, had arrived in Nîmes in June 1940 from the exodus and had moved in with her father, a retired military general, who had occupied himself with the Franco-American Union, a local friendship group. Mlle. Mouchon, a Protestant, was a National Commissioner of the nondenominational French Boy Scout Federation, which was headquartered in the city of Vichy. The report observed that this explained her ongoing relationship with various Protestant pastors, in particular Pastor Boegner of Nîmes, who was the president of the French Protestant Federation. Mlle. Mouchon was also the president of the Protestant Inter-Movement Committee for Evacuees (CIMADE) and was very active with this organization, formed to aid refugees/evacuees of any nationality or faith. She thereby aided many "Jews," in whose company she was frequently observed. The report gave her compliments for "good conduct and morality, and the information received about her was most favorable. Although she was not politically active, it seemed she did not approve of the measures undertaken by the government regarding the Jews, for whom she has exhibited great solicitude. In rendering these facts, her case merited continued surveillance, and she would be the object of such by my organization."[38] Violette Mouchon survived the war and later coauthored a book published in 1968 on CIMADE's clandestine activities that outlined how they helped the Jews. Her associate within CIMADE, Madeleine Barot, had been mentioned in the telephone conversation intercepted on August 25, which

---

37 ADG. 1 W 35. Letter dated September 2, 1942 marked No. 201 and letter dated October 13, 1942 and marked No. 1221. Letters dated September 2, 26, and 28, 1942 and marked respectively Nos. 5265, 50, and 231C.
38 ADG. 1 W 35. Ibid. Letter dated September 29, 1942, marked No. 5862/5980T from the Special Police.

discussed the Collège Cévènol at Chambon-sur-Lignon, where many Lyon-area Jewish refugees were sheltered before fleeing elsewhere. Mlle. Barot was also "an observed" person by the Nîmes police for her suspected activities.[39]

The summary report for September 26 through October 25, 1942 was marked "Very Secret" and it concerned ongoing investigations in the Gard. The document related to seventeen investigations, most of which were again related to food-supply issues. The arrival of rotten spinach, onions, and milk was looked into, as well as the faulty administrative instructions, which reputedly delayed the distribution of fifty-four tons of potatoes. A black market in sheep, green beans, and onions also was investigated as were several barter markets of potatoes for cigarettes and/or wine. Illicit traffic in ration cards for bread and other foodstuffs also was listed, as were more ominous-sounding items like death threats, illegal sales by a gunsmith, and trafficking in safe-conduct passes.

The final report available for 1942 was for the month of December. It featured the assassination attempts made on December 8 and 25 against the German occupational troops recently arrived in the Gard. The summary noted that it was deplorable that public officials had failed to take actions to counter Gaullist and Communist propaganda efforts. Tensions were said to have lessened somewhat, as the emotions associated with the German order to disband the Armistice Army had calmed down and the relations between the Nîmois and the Germans had been correct, at least up to those assassination attempts. However, discontent over the vicissitudes of daily life was only increasing and the fear of heavy German requisitions of supplies added to that unease. The widespread divergence and disarray in public opinion was noted and deplored by the report writers.

The increasing difficulty in providing food for livestock was mentioned, as well as the fact that industry and commerce were in a sorry state due to the multitude of problems faced. The Gard's ability to distribute adequate food supplies to its citizens diminished every day, due to the fact that the food-producing departments did not deliver the allocations the government imposed upon them. German demands for quartering of their troops were becoming harsher. Individual acts of violence were on the rise.

---

39   *Vichy France and the Jews.* Ibid., 207. See footnote 93.

Anti-national behavior was a discussion topic. If anti-Vichy propaganda was more discreet since the arrival of the Germans, the militant acts of the Gaullists and Communists were more pronounced in numerous ways. Bombs were exploded in Nîmes on the eighth and twenty-fifth of this month, and several threatening letters from the resistance organization COMBAT were intercepted. Printed and radio propaganda appeared to be coordinated in a prudent but effective fashion. Oppositional groups were increasing in numbers and efficiency. Many Gardois listened to the Free French broadcasts from London or Algiers and spread the news they heard by word of mouth. Such pro-Allied propaganda was aided by the latest German seizures of local hostages. People didn't hide their feelings: "Our morale, confidence, and hope are excellent." Others regretted that officials did nothing to prevent this propaganda. Police inaction was decried against Communist intrigues, and the weak sentences handed out by the court tribunals were deplored. "Here, covert Communist action is being planned and no one responsible makes any effort to think that they must act to counter it."

The unease aroused by December's outbursts was seen as calming down, bit by bit. Correspondents began again to pay attention only to personal concerns. Thus, food worries and shortage sufferings caused malaise and discontent. This worry weighed heaviest on public morale in the Gard. Rumors added to the demoralization of the people, which was abetted by the poor quality of reporting in the French press and radio. One major rumor whirling around concerned the forced mobilization of young French men and women to work for the Germans.

There were very few comments on military events. However, the successes achieved by the Red Armies in Russia and the British in their bombing raids on Italy were noted and given tacit approval. Anti-German and anti-English comments were noted as being about equal. People fervently hoped for an improvement in living conditions in 1943. While some desired an Allied victory, others wanted improved French-German relations. They longed for an end to the demarcation line to come about from the Laval-Hitler meeting, and some saw in the Christmas and New Year message exchanges a reason to have confidence in France's future: "We ought to raise a toast towards having a recovery of France and its role in the New Europe."

Relative to internal matters, the beginning of the month saw many lively comments on the scuttling of the French fleet in Toulon. The irony of conflicted opinions was shown by the following comment: "For many a great hope is born. For others it is nothing but consternation and complexity." These extremes upset others who considered that the French were egoists, systematic in their criticism. "I've had it with France. Too much discord and the I-don't-give-a-damn attitude and incomprehension. I hope this test will destroy the country." The fact that France did not seem able to learn anything from its defeats was troubling to others. Optimists said one should not despair: "In spite of all that is happening, the marshal is there, there is still a government and a French administration, and all can be worked out."

The paucity of prisoner of war returns was blamed by some people on the recalcitrance of young workers to volunteer for the Relève. Partisans of collaboration were beginning to think that its time had passed, and others were only sarcastic about the chance for peaceful cooperation between the Germans and French people. Many questions were asked about the attitude of the Vichy government: "Here the vast majority is pro-American and inquire of themselves how to interpret the feeling of the marshal." More people were losing confidence in the marshal's government. "However, even if the actions of the dissidents [de Gaulle's forces] are generally severely judged, and the assassination of Admiral Darlan only provoked outrage, it is astonishing that many of yesterday's loyalists are passing over to the side of the dissidents. One member of the PPF even said that Laval should negotiate an agreement with the Americans."

As for the marshal, the personal respect and admiration for him had not seriously diminished but one encountered intercepts that reproached him for having too much faith in others: "The poor marshal—he trusts people and they betray him." The rebuke most frequently ascribed to the government was its lack of energy. "What a mess at Vichy! What a band of crabs around the marshal. The feebleness caused by his eighty-five years costs a lot because of the rogues who take advantage of him." They accused his government of taking no action against the Gaullists and Communists, of tolerating the black market, of keeping almost all the old functionaries, and of not changing the attitude in a new administration, which has resulted in turning the people against the new state. It was judged so inferior in its performance that many yearned for the Germans' efficiency: "The Germans ought to handle our food supply. Don't you agree? Even their enemies wished that it were so." It often was so handled, but the French food supplies were rather requisitioned by the Germans for feeding Germans in the Reich or in France.

Quite a few writers fixed the blame for France's current problems on the Jews, Communists, and Freemasons, and foresaw a civil war in France if the Russians defeated the Germans, allowing the Red Peril to march westward unopposed. Others blamed the Third Republic: "Putrid forfeiture by a General Assembly dirty with pride, ashamed of our race, such are the fruits of Republican democracy." In spite of the fact that the majority of opinions were carefully concealed, one could detect many traces of spirited opposition to the government of the National Revolution. The opposition was centered in the working classes, the Protestant bourgeoisie, the students, and the refugees and deportees. They wanted to return to the old way of doing things and were full of schemes against the German troops in the Gard who "take everything." They felt the end of the war was coming nearer. All difficulties were laid at the feet of the self-centered rich or the peasants. The fact that there was no French solidarity was a common complaint and the city dwellers said that only the rich could afford to eat. Winter famine was feared, as were unspecified troubles that loomed ahead.

To the complaints of a general penury of food, the high cost of living, the sins of a developed black market, and the general scarcity of all merchandise, workers were adding their recriminations against Laval's Rèleve. The forced departures to Germany were deplored, and many workers would not leave unless threatened with sanctions. Although voluntary participation remained the rule, police pressure on designated workers was such that they could not shy away from going. Some were just resigned to their fate and others openly expressed their anger.

One citizen wrote that the decree issued by the authorities to hand over personal weapons had drawn much criticism. He thought it was ineffective, as those who wanted to resist or murder Germans would never cooperate, while those honest citizens would deprive themselves of their arms, which would then become a stock of weapons ripe for pillaging by the Communists in case of a revolution. The dissolution of the Armistice Army and the circumstances surrounding it caused much emotion from its men as well as the local citizens, many of whom described how the French barracks had been surrounded by German tanks and machine guns. The confrontation ended peacefully, and the only incidents involved some of the demobilized soldiers systematically taking guns home. "The chiefs say take what you want. Some even took their horses." The officers were especially depressed by the disbanding of the army and accused the heads of government of treason. Their low morale was reflected in statements like this one: "What's the truth? What's our duty?"

Lowered morale moved on to increased material fears, and the fate encountered by the French army only heightened concerns over tomorrow's uncertainties. However, when the dismissed troops learned they would receive three months' severance pay and the promise of a job, their passions cooled, except for fears that those jobs could lead them to work in Germany. A small number seemed interested in joining a new Vichy military organization about which rumors had circulated, but most felt it would be under German control and were not interested. The army men were split between those who wanted to exact revenge on the German occupation forces for the actions of November 27 and those who were still loyal to Vichy and accepted the fact that the military must follow orders. The families with military sons or husbands in North Africa were confused: were they now dissidents, or were they being forced to fight for the Free French and Allies? They were also uneasy about who would receive the military pay allotments, if anyone.

It was noted that the German troops had been "correct" so far in their local relations with civilians, which did not awaken much appreciation from the public. Some unfavorable comments were heard, but several people felt that this represented not much of an evolution in the formation of public opinion. "Some find things worse as a result of the occupation, while others see advantages to be gained. In reality opinion seems to have scarcely altered and pro- or anti-German feelings have not been modified by the events of the last few weeks." Rather, people had quickly adapted to the German presence by acceptance of a *fait accompli* accompanied by neither hostility nor friendliness. The mood seemed to be one of ambiguity. Some accepted the Germans as the lesser evil: "If we didn't have these victors, we'd have Communists, and it would be worse." On the day after each attack in Nîmes on German soldiers, the mood definitely was uneasy, and these attacks drew general condemnation as the citizens feared German reprisals, particularly the taking of hostages.

In the political arena, the Legion—but especially Joseph Darnand's elitist offshoot the SOL (*Service d'ordre légionnaire*, formed in early 1942)—was noted as seeking an expanded role within Vichy. There had been talk that Darnand would become the Minister of the Interior. These feelings caused the sending of many telegrams to M. Raymond Lachal, president of the *Légion française des combattants*, on behalf of various Legion sections in the Gard. These machinations resulted in a general feeling of disbanding about the Legion. "They have had enough. They are disgusted. They only want one thing done: dissolve the Legion." Everywhere there was great disarray and astonishment that there was a rudderless, weak government. "The interior needs a strong man with balls ... a government without someone like that is a tumble, a great collapse." The same feeling even existed among the members of the PPF. The collaborationists wanted action and sought to integrate themselves in a close-knit fashion with the German troops. The Gard's Socialist party did nothing but translate circulars of their new president.

The local farmers had endless problems in raising their crops in the fields. It was impossible to acquire new equipment or repair old farm implements. There were no plows, which were needed now. No carburant substitutes were available either, and feed for cattle or horses did not exist. "Horses are dropping in the fields in a sad cadence." All transport was scarce, and Farm Services was incomprehensively slow and thus discouraged the peasants from planting. Any further attempts to furnish the peasants with military horses was ceased, as the Germans had confiscated all of them. Relative to wine production, the weather had been decent for caring of the vines. Vegetable availability was nil as the farmers were hoarding them. The olive oil crop was a disaster, with an average of only fourteen kilos output per each forty trees. The Gard's total output of potatoes for the season was only 1,684 tons. The demobilized local garrison was made available for forest work, and at least Farm Services was offering the Indochinese military companies for labor in the Nîmes region. There was an alarming situation in feed stocks, especially for horses, with no solution offered. The deliveries from the Supply Services for the last three months had been sadly deficient, partly due to a lack of transport, troop requisitions, and administrative slowness and paperwork obstacles. Such scarcity caused the slaughtering of milk cows as well as many horses. Use of cattle and oxen increased with the general lack of horses. Pigs were in short supply, so the prices were high and peasants were slaughtering for their own consumption. The purchase of ersatz substitutes had dropped off precipitously because of German homeland demands.

Industry registered weak activity due to the application of a decree furloughing workers in large industrial concerns from December 20 to January 3, 1943, because of road transport shortages and railroad restrictions. Other habitual deficiencies cited were the lack of primary or manufactured materials, decline in availability of specialized laborers due to the Relève, and German restrictions. "At this moment all the workers are working for the Germans." The mining activity at St-Laurent was reopened for German needs. The tube factory at Bessèges stopped production due to machinery problems. The steel industry lacked smelting material, and the chemical factories had no basic components. Shoes could not be produced, as rubber and glue were unavailable. Hosiery production was shut down, as there was no cotton, rayon, or bonded fiber in stock. The absence of credit-worthy customers and difficulties with spare parts suppliers also affected the production of steel, iron, wood, and smelt, as well as automobile repair shops. Additional reductions in electrical power adversely affected the Gard's critical mining industry, and shipments of coal were reduced because of a lack of rail freight cars. Therefore, some key companies on priority lists in both zones had received only partial allocations for December. The Relève and German requisitions had siphoned off all expert labor. Some decommissioned army personnel had been made available to work in the mines, but they lacked experience. Pechiney Chemicals in Alès and Froges and Camargue were at normal production levels, averaging seventy tons per day of calcinated aluminum. They were trying to create substitutes for other processes. Socipic in Beaucaire, which produced industrial chemicals for the wine industry, was hurt by a lack of primary ingredients. The factories with normal production for the Alès mining basin were Ciment Français of Beaucaire, Maison Progil of Le Vigan, les Carburants Français, and la Maison Rey, which made explosives.

Commercial activity was lackluster due to nonavailability of merchandise and lack of transportation means. Some local small-business activity was created by the German troops stationed in town. "We are selling all sorts of knickknacks and are even raffling goods off in the stores." Gun merchants' sales were strictly controlled. Wine sales in stores were slow, and the merchants were impatient for the new wine's delivery. Shippers could not fulfill their orders, so they allocated the quantities, but demand was low, except for wines with high degrees of alcohol, but they couldn't be found, as the market to Germany was favored with a twenty-five-franc export tax incentive per hectoliter. The domaine owners had difficulty in reserving their marc residue, and there were complaints that there was a complete lack of direction within the National Group of Import, Sharing, and Concentration of wine "must." Fruit and vegetable shipments were basically restricted to the Gard and very limited at that. Business with the Occupied Zone was limited to wine shipments to Paris and upper Burgundy's Cote D'Or. Source Perrier made its regular shipments to Paris. Commerce with the colonies was nil, as the invasion in North Africa had cut them off totally. There were daily wine shipments to Germany; Pechiney shipped thirty tons of arsenic to Spain this month; Maison Danzas shipped 3,800 hectoliters of wine and wine "must" to Switzerland. Heavy freight transportation methods were in crisis, due to the absence of locomotives and railway freight cars, commercial delays, and shutdowns. The SNCF was highly criticized. Merchandise was commonly stolen in transit. There was little road traffic freight, as things like tires, fuel, and repair parts were all in short supply. The presence of German troop vehicular needs had put even more pressure on private French transportation firms.

The crisis in food supplies was left for last and described as worse in December than November and deteriorating each day, with increasing complaints from both the people and food-distribution agencies. Local farm producers refused to bring their produce to town markets and preferred to sell directly to neighbors at more profitable untaxed prices. Administrative procedures that were labeled "stupidities" discouraged the farmers from selling away from their home bases. The wine-centric

Gard had to depend on other regions for vegetables, and there was a two-hundred-ton deficit in that key nutritional category during the last two weeks of December. The city dwellers, whose deliveries were the most affected, were the ones who suffered the most: "We line up all the time, and in the last twelve days my grocer hasn't had a single vegetable." Meat was doled out sparingly: "It has been decided to distribute ninety grams of meat only in the mining district and Nîmes." The result achieved for the exclusive use of these two areas of population concentration was actually short six tons of meat. There were complaints about the nearby Bouches-du-Rhône and Vaucluse departments getting better supplied. "Nothing here but in Arles they got 225 grams and in Avignon 140." The distribution authorities were powerless to requisition items that had to be obtained from nearby departments, which produced scarce things like butter, eggs, milk, and meat. For example, milk deliveries were short every day between ten thousand and twelve thousand liters from all sources of supply, and the children suffered: "There is a definite progression in the mortality rate of young infants." The mining region was favored with additional food supplies, as coal had to continue to be extracted for shipment, and the work was grueling. They got extra rations of potatoes, salted fish, and chestnuts.

The Germans had placed many requisition orders, and they applied pressure on suppliers to get results. They had gotten olive oil through such measures, and farmers who feared such demands killed their hogs and chickens early and hid them for consumption during the rest of the winter. The people blamed the Germans for buying up everything, no matter what price, even contingency supplies. The Protestants in Nîmes were very upset over the Germans taking over their nursing home and forcing out its sick inhabitants so troops could be quartered there. Schools were treated in similar fashion and "after ten minutes discussion, the German officers bang their fists on the table and threaten to take over the school by force, and citizens view this attitude as very peculiar." Other acts of force by the Germans included shooting at fishermen who ventured out on their boats to fish without permission, as well as destructive acts of random vandalism by their troops. The presence of the German occupation troops in the Gard did not turn the Gardois overnight into resistants; to the contrary the vast majority of citizens remained firm *attentistes.*[40]

---

40   *Nimes at War.* Ibid., 197–199.

Although German garrisons were stationed in Nîmes, Alès, Le Vigan, and later in St-Jean-du-Gard, most German military attention was given to the coastal zone. But the wait-and-see population certainly had their eyes and ears focused on these uniformed intruders as 1942 came to a not very happy ending.[41]

---

41   ADG. 1 W 42. Monthly Report No. 12, 1942, marked Nos. 89–99.

Opinion in 1943

Shifting Gears into the Passing Lane—Adieu L'Attentisme

"Stalingrad is liberated, Rostov is threatened, and Tripoli is taken. Roosevelt and Churchill have met in Casablanca and have decided their terms for ending the war with Germany, Italy, and Japan: Unconditional Surrender." —Jean Guéhenno, January 21, 1943[1]

"For the last eight days all young men, ages twenty to thirty, are in lines at the town halls signing up [for forced labor in Germany] like galley slaves. If there had been an atmosphere of resistance, if all the functionaries had been complicit to sabotage the orders, the Germans would have been forced to have armies of police to assemble these convoys." —Jean Guéhenno, February 22, 1943[2]

"The marshal has spoken to the young men taken off to work in Germany; what nobility of heart and spirit 'demonstrate in your gestures, your words, by the quality of your work, by your spirit of creative initiative, the genius of our race … My thoughts will not leave you on your way or in your new surroundings (*dépaysement*), let me be proud of what you do.' What an arrogant view; the old imbecile relates it all back to himself. New scenery (*dépaysement*), what a stroke of inspiration!" —Jean Guéhenno, April 5, 1943[3]

---

1   *Journal des Années Noires.* Ibid., 313.
2   Ibid., 320.
3   Ibid., 332.

"All the young people in the classes of 1940 through 1942 must leave for Germany July 1. Some will flee to Spain. Others will hide in the mountains, the Massif Central." —Jean Guéhenno, June 12, 1943[4]

"There were twenty-three prisoners of war from this village. Three came back as a result of the *Relève*. But ten young men have now gone back to Germany due to the obligatory work service (STO), and there are now thirty prisoners. Long live the marshal! ... Italy has capitulated." —Jean Guéhenno, Montolieu, Aude, September 8, 1943[5]

The Resistance organizations in France had developed slowly after 1940 and needed to take extreme precautions in order to have a chance to survive, especially in the Occupied Zones. They were called networks, limited in numbers, and were often formed into cells, as security measures like independence and secrecy were key to their existence. Their primary tasks were intelligence gathering, sabotage, and maintaining escape routes and, by necessity, they had to liaise by and large through the British, even when they dealt with the Free French in London. After the war was over, some 266 accredited networks were recognized, which comprised approximately 150,000 agents.[6] These networks or *réseaux* were not organized for encouraging the French population at large to oppose the Germans or Vichy. That purpose was reserved for the other resistance entity, the movements, and they also grew in 1943 in numbers, maturity, and coordination. For the movements to succeed in their social and political purposes, they needed to gain members through publicity, so their organization names were used on newsletters they started to publish and distribute clandestinely. These publications, whose print runs grew significantly in 1942, became an integral factor for achieving those ends.

The networks and movements had sprung up in both zones in haphazard fashion, and some morphed from a network into a movement along the evolutionary pathway of French resistance, or were destroyed

---

4   Ibid., 344.
5   Ibid., 352.
6   *De Munich a la Libération*. Ibid., 244.

like Boris Vildé's *Musée de l'homme* group, while others were absorbed by another existing movement. By 1942, various competing resistance movements had grown up on either side of the demarcation line, and Jean Moulin, a courageous ex-prefect, had, at de Gaulle's personal orders, been parachuted back into the Unoccupied Zone on January 1, 1942. His assignment was to gain for de Gaulle the fealty of the major southern resistance movements so that their men would be ready to coordinate their military movements under Free French leadership, when the appropriate time came. This took great patience, perseverance, and persuasive powers by Moulin, as the leaders of the three major movements in the Vichy area—Henri Frenay of Combat, Emmanuel d'Astier de la Vigerie of Libération-Sud, and Jean-Pierre Lévy of Franc-Tireur—were protective of their respective organizations' independence. However, some successful anti-German/anti-Vichy demonstrations in major southern cities on May 1 and July 14, 1942, resulted in the three movements' rank-and-file militants putting pressure on their leaders to cooperate. A huge step was taken on January 26, 1943, when Frenay, Lévy, d'Astier, and Moulin agreed to form a single organization, the United Movements of the Resistance (MUR), while continuing to publish their separate newspapers for widest achievable impact.[7]

On that same day, the Casablanca conference between Roosevelt and Churchill ended, but not before de Gaulle and General Giraud had been summoned to appear before them, concerning the next steps the Free French armed forces were to undertake under Anglo-American command. Rommel had to be cleared from his redoubt in Tunisia, and there were plans to invade Italy soon after that would have been accomplished. It was no secret that Roosevelt had a strong dislike for de Gaulle and that Churchill tolerated him, but they both wanted more French troops made available for fighting the Germans. Roosevelt wanted General Giraud pushed as a substitute for de Gaulle, but Churchill knew that would not necessarily happen easily. So nothing of consequence came out of the meeting about France's immediate future, except that the two Frenchmen were to cooperate in raising more Free French forces. However, de Gaulle had measured his rival and recognized his Achilles' heel. Giraud was a one-dimensional warrior, whose purpose was to make war but who was horrified by politics. De Gaulle wrote in his autobiog-

---

7   Ibid. 263. *France: The Dark Years.* Ibid., 434–436.

raphy about meeting privately with his challenger: "(Giraud) You speak about politics to me. (de Gaulle) Yes, I answered. For we are at war. For war is political. He heard me but he wasn't listening." The struggle would be unequal and finished in six months with Gaullism taking firm root as the basis for France's future.[8]

On January 13, 1943, Hitler had declared to his people that Germany was threatened by total war. Twenty-one days later, on February 3, the meaning of this was truly driven home to the German nation when a special announcement was made over the radio that the battle of Stalingrad had been lost, along with the remnants of Paulus's Sixth Army, which had surrendered the day before. This was a watershed for the German army, which from that moment on would be defending Fortress Europe from attack, all along a gradually shrinking periphery and no longer launching grandiose offensives to expand it. The people of Germany were not alone in feeling the effects of this total war, and in France the demands from Germany for supplies and labor would significantly increase in support of defense of their homeland.

The campaign to free Tunisia commenced in late November/ early December before Rommel had fully withdrawn into his Tunisian redoubt. Hitler ordered it to be defended, and that turned out to be another colossal strategic blunder. Between mid-November and end of January 1943, more than 240,000 fresh German and Italian reinforcements, along with tons of supplies, were shipped or flown into Tunisia. These new troops inflicted six thousand casualties on the untested Americans in February 1943 at the battle of Kasserine Pass, as they and the British and some Free French allies attempted to enclose the German and Italian forces in a Tunisian pocket. After the British and American forces were reorganized under a unified command headed by Sir Harold Alexander, the final battle for Tunisia began on April 17, with the Americans advancing on Bizerta from the west and the British pressing north and then east on Tunis. The campaign concluded on May 17 in a second unmitigated disaster for Germany, which approached that of Stalingrad in significance. Some 250,000 Axis troops surrendered, and all of North Africa fell into British, American, and Free French hands. The eyes of these combatants and their civilian popula-

---

8 *De Munich a la Libération.* Ibid., 280–281, n1.

tions were now focused on the vulnerable Mediterranean underbelly of Europe—Italy.[9]

On February 16, 1943, Laval, pressured relentlessly by Sauckel for more able-bodied workers to go to Germany, announced that the three post-World War One male baby-boom classes of 1920, 1921, and 1922 were being called up to meet new German labor requisition numbers, with no prisoners of war to be released. This forced labor demand, the Compulsory Labor Service (*Service du Travail Obligatoire* or STO), turned out to be a seppuku short sword stroke for Pierre Laval and his Vichy government, as well as, to some extent, the German occupying forces in France. It provided for no exceptions or excluded groups, and Sauckel boasted that "only France had filled its first two quota contributions 100 percent, thanks to the good attention of Vichy." It is ironic that the approximately 650,000 workers that STO provided to Germany were called "deportees," and that fact contributed to the general decline in attention the French paid to the Jews, who continued to be shipped off to Auschwitz. The STO sword was as sharp as a Japanese hara-kiri blade, as its first thrust cut deep into the support for Vichy, even among core adherents, and then its lateral cut spilled out many gutsy and hungry young men to augment the ranks of the resistance.

These were the young men who fled cities, towns, and villages to join the Maquis bands in remote areas in the Alps, Massif Central, Pyrénées, and Cévennes. Very few could be armed, even if the groups they joined were actively involved in sabotage efforts or actually implementing limited attacks on the German occupation troops or suspected collaborators. The reason was that the weapons were in very short supply, as their primary source was British air drops, which were dangerous, often inaccurate, and carefully controlled by the English. These young men who evaded STO were known as *réfractaires*, and they contributed more significantly to the drop in support of Vichy and it programs by the general populace than they did to the active resistance, who could not use the majority of them. Their parents obviously were concerned about them and feared German and Vichy operations designed to round them up. Additionally, many other citizens thought the whole STO program not only smelled of collaboration but also was patently unfair. These

---

9   Rick Atkinson. *An Army at Dawn* (New York, Henry Holt and Company, 2005), 5, 537.

same citizens were willing to aid the evaders, further eroding Vichy's support. Some people, especially those who lived near remote areas where the *réfractaires* concentrated, lost faith in Vichy's ability to prevent civil disorder as the hungry young men often raided henhouses and vegetable gardens at will in search of food. Some citizens or even banks were robbed at gunpoint by young men turned into fugitive gangs. I will note many examples of the use of the term "terrorist" employed by people who lived near areas where these types of incidents occurred. STO vitiated public enthusiasm for Vichy on multiple levels, and its opponents were lost forever by Vichy.

On January 30, 1943, Vichy formed an armed paramilitary volunteer group, the Milice, to take action against Vichy's perceived internal enemies, be they active resistance groups or *réfractaires*. In carrying out this role, these enforcers of collaboration acted in concert with the German authorities and troops and earned deep-seated hatred for themselves and the Vichy regime by their vicious actions. Laval supported this organization, which was led by Joseph Darnand. It evolved from a core of militants Darnand had formed in 1941, the *Service d'ordre légionnaire* (SOL), whose purpose was to protect Legion demonstrations. Julian Jackson estimates the Milice's numbers at 25,000–30,000 maximum, and its policing role for the maintenance of internal order increased during this year as the formal police organizations became disenchanted with actions supporting unpopular Vichy policies.

The Milice drew its members from Communist-hating activists, Catholic zealots, fanatical Pétain loyalists, and young naïve drifters like the one killed at the end of the Louis Malle film *Lacombe Lucien*. The first real Milice member was assassinated by the resistance on April 24, 1943.[10] Laval never really controlled the Milice, as it was Darnand, the committed fascist, who actually swore a personal oath of loyalty to Hitler and had become an SS officer who pulled the strings. Pétain himself actually lost luster due to his support of the Milice and Darnand, which the marshal disavowed only in August 1944. It had become the official enforcement agency of the Vichy state and prior to the liberation was the most hated organization of that state.[11]

Sauckel's obtuse toughness with Laval over providing more French

---

10 *France: The Dark Years.* Ibid., 230-231; *De Munich a la Libération.* Ibid., 388.
11 Ibid., 232–234.

workers for Germany succeeded initially, and 250,000 young workers departed France in March 1943 alone. But the negative reactions to STO caused the second demand to fall to only 37,000 by the end of May. The exodus to the isolated mountainous areas of France was in full flood. Hitler's new "golden boy" of the German war economy, Albert Speer, took objective notice of this failure and decided to do something about it, as he recognized that France was directly and indirectly a major contributor to the Reich's wartime economy. Speer found a like-minded technocrat in the person of Jean Bichelonne, the French Minister of Industrial Production, who saw advantages in cooperating with the Germans. Bichelonne could keep French workers employed in France, although their employment would be mostly in German military projects. He negotiated agreements with Speer in September that relieved Laval of Sauckel's pressures and ended the drafting of French labor for work in the Reich.

This so-called Speer-Betriebe industry classification not only guaranteed work for one million French workers and kept them in France but also assured decent delivery of scarce primary materials and allowed for an 80/20 split in production allocation: 80 percent for Germany and 20 percent for French needs. The total number of Frenchmen who in 1944 were working in France or Germany to support the German war effort is impressive, and it wasn't much lower, if at all, in 1943.[12] Jean-Pierre Azéma estimates there were 3,600,000 total laborers working directly for Germany in this regard, split between 2,000,000 in France and 1,600,000 in Germany. Using German sources some years later, Philippe Burrin put the gross number at just over 4,000,000, split between 2,660,000 in France and 1,314,000 in Germany, which included prisoners of war and workers commandeered from France to work in German factories. The grand total represented 37 percent of all French workers between the ages of sixteen and sixty, an impressive figure to say the least.[13]

We will see—ad nauseam, perhaps—many additional comments during 1943 in Gard SCT reports and citizens intercepts about the con-

---

12   Ibid., 208–209.
13   *La France a l'Heure Allemande*. Ibid., 470, n3. Burrin mentions the fact that there was other indirect help upstream in the French economy (examples like wine, Perrier water, requisitioned foodstuffs, etc.), which supplemented the German wartime economy. Altogether, as he states, these were massive contributions.

tinuing challenges faced in daily life, including but not limited to food and heating/cooking needs. A brief comparative review of the tonnages of foodstuffs and other products that Germany directly requisitioned or "exploited" for its own use during this fourth year of the war, will allow us to assess the severe challenge the great majority of average French families faced in feeding themselves.[14]

	1941–1942 Crop (in tons)	1942–1943 Crop Increase %	
Cereals	485,000	714,000	+47%
Forage	458,000	686,000	+50%
Meat	140,000	227,000	+62%
Vegetables	98,000	107,000	+ 9%
Fruits	59,000	118,000	+100%

The foodstuff quantities shipped to Germany made it significantly harder on the French market to satisfy its own demand, and in one way or another, prices rose concomitantly due to supply/demand factors. Additionally, agricultural production indices compared to a baseline of 1938 were 17 percent below that level in April 1943, which gives an indication of deeper pressures in the marketplace. An example of the increasing level of hardship experienced is the fact that the weekly ration of meat had to be cut about this time to 120 grams.[15] France was the market basket for Germany in any measure of overall foodstuffs provided, even greater than Poland.[16] There was another element that helped drive up prices, which involved the huge occupation subsidy that the Vichy government had to pay every ten days into a special German account in the Bank of France. A very favorable exchange rate of twenty francs to one mark had been set by the Germans, and a significant amount of that favorably rate-adjusted money provided by France was paid back to the German occupation forces in France, which they used to buy whatever they liked and thereby drive up prices further on the black market. This effect spread throughout France after it was fully occupied in late 1942.

The efforts Jean Moulin undertook to unify the resistance movements,

---

14 *De Munich a la Libération*. Ibid., 211, n1, 209.
15 Ibid., 215, n1; *L'Opinion Française sous Vichy*. Ibid., 375.
16 *Vichy France*. Ibid., 360.

after they joined MUR in January, continued unabated as its various leaders made trips to London to meet with de Gaulle or his delegates, in hopes of gaining advantages for their specific organization. Moulin's mission had expanded beyond the old Free Zone, and his role became more complicated as he interacted with the different movements based in Paris. Various French resistance groups were champing at the bit to take action, as STO had swelled their numbers, leaving them with many more idle hands. But the British were against wholesale arming of any French resistance groups, north or south, as they felt any early outbreaks would be counterproductive and could result in disastrous setbacks. Moulin's life was made even more complicated by the presence in Paris of another de Gaulle agent, Pierre Brossolette, who had differing ideas about movement consolidation efforts in the north. By May, however, Moulin, who enjoyed de Gaulle's explicit support, took advantage of that as well as his considerable powers of persuasion to achieve his primary objective: obtaining agreement among the movements to support a joint resistance council.

On May 27, the National Council of the Resistance (CNR) met in Paris. Its sixteen representatives incorporated the major movements, political parties, and trade unions, and although suspicious looks traversed the room, Moulin prevailed and had de Gaulle declared head of any provisional government destined for France.[17] This happening certainly bolstered de Gaulle in his attempt to shunt aside Giraud's effort to gain legitimization as the sole leader of the Free French in the eyes of the Allies. De Gaulle would never gain the respect of Roosevelt, but he won the support of FDR's commanding generals, who recognized the many shortcomings of Giraud, the man who detested politics. As Harold Macmillan wrote late in 1943 about Giraud, "I would suppose that never in the whole history of politics has any man frittered away so large a capital in so short a time."[18] By November, Giraud was formally relegated to a strictly military role—and a diminishing one at that. Moulin had done his difficult job well within France to pave the way for de Gaulle, who would never see him again.

On June 21, a resistance meeting took place in a northern suburb of Lyon, Caluire, where Moulin and several other resistance leaders were arrested by the Gestapo. To this day there still is debate over whether the

---

17   *France: The Dark Years.* Ibid., 452–456.
18   Ibid., 460, n50.

arrest was a case of betrayal. One member at the meeting was arrested by Klaus Barbie, the Gestapo chief in Lyon, on June 7, but was released. Common sense would dictate that this individual never should have been permitted to attend this meeting, but it happened. As a result of his capture and subsequent torture, Moulin died on July 8, without revealing anything. The ashes of this brave hero of the French Resistance were moved to the Panthéon in 1964 by a grateful French Republic, which his brave efforts had helped reestablish.[19]

Two days later, on July 10, 1943, the Allies commenced Operation Husky, the campaign to take Sicily, when the Anglo-American armies of Montgomery and Patton disembarked on that island's southeast coast. On July 19, in a hastily arranged meeting near Venice, a distraught Mussolini begged Hitler to pull back from Russia so as not to sacrifice Italy in a delaying action. While Hitler harangued him about turning Sicily into an Allied Stalingrad, aides continually updated Mussolini on the first massive American bombing of Rome, which killed many Romans. Mussolini scurried off from the inconclusive meeting with the Führer and one week later was placed under arrest by King Victor Emmanuel III, who replaced him with Marshal Pietro Badoglio. The general assured Hitler that the Pact of Steel would go on, but the writing "Fugi" was clearly on the wall. As one Roman woman wrote in her personal journal, "Italy has had enough heroes."[20]

The Sicilian invasion was a prelude to the effort to peel off Italy from Hitler's Axis, which was viewed especially by Churchill as the easier and more logical next step to undertake against fortress Europe. The memories of the Dieppe fiasco lingered and the British were realistic about how much time would be necessary for the American build-up in England for a cross-channel operation. Thirty-eight days later, on August 17, the hard-fought island campaign against the German and Italian defenders was over. Five thousand Allied soldiers died, and double that number, equally split between Germans and Italians, died in the defense of Sicily. Another 140,000 prisoners, mostly Italian, were taken. The Allies made a costly blunder, however, by allowing forty thousand

---

19   Ibid., 461. De Gaulle also had the support of the US ambassador to Britain, John Winant.
20   Rick Atkinson, *The Day of Battle* (New York: Henry Holt and Company, 2007), 142.

Germans and seventy thousand Italians to escape across the Messina Straits and reach the Italian mainland, where they could fight on.

The Allies invaded Italy at Salerno on September 9, some twelve hours after General Eisenhower announced on Radio Algiers the unconditional surrender of Italy, which Marshal Badoglio confirmed on Radio Rome one hour later. Italian forces were disarmed by the Germans, who turned the defense of Italy into a lengthy war of attrition. Stiff German resistance slowly yielded tough defensive ground, especially around Cassino. Churchill did not achieve the quick victory he had hoped for in this hard underbelly of Europe, and Rome would only fall on June 5, 1944, when there still would be all of northern Italy to conquer. The remaining German forces ultimately surrendered to the Allies on May 2, 1945. During all this time, troops on both sides were tied down in a very costly campaign. In the meantime, the Russians had launched a massive counteroffensive at the end of July 1943 along the entire Eastern Front against the German armies and their disheartened allies. The Germans had to cede vast expanses of Russian territory while retreating inexorably westward past Smolensk and then Kiev in the Ukraine, which fell to the Russians on November 5, 1943.

On September 8, 1943, German troops moved in to occupy the areas of southeastern France that Italy had occupied since November 1942, stretching from the French Alps opposite Geneva down to west of Nice. The thirty thousand Jews who had taken refuge around Nice, as well as the Jews in Italy, were now directly threatened by the Final Solution. On September 13, Free French troops invaded Corsica at its southern end near Ajaccio, while some thirty thousand Germans escaped from Bastia at the northern point of the island to Italy, where they helped stiffen the Nazi resistance. By October 5, Corsica became the first French department liberated, and de Gaulle was warmly acclaimed in Ajaccio three days later. He had double reason to be pleased by this greeting, as on October 2 he further reduced Giraud's stature to little more than a cipher. The normally aloof general had maneuvered to get the French Committee of National Liberation (CFLN) to make him annually reelectable as its unique president, while Giraud became military commander in chief of the Free French forces, giving up his copresidency and becoming subject to dismissal by decree.[21]

---

21   Ibid., 244 ; *De Munich a la Libération*. Ibid., 290, n3, 391.

The military developments of 1943 were such that the majority of the French realized this was the beginning of the end for Hitler and his German military machine. Even Pierre Laval might have had his doubts about the inevitability of a German victory. Publicly, he continued to speak of Germany as the barrier that stood between France and Bolshevism, which appealed to some right-wing bourgeois class elements who continued to support Vichy's collaboration policy. He still tried to convince Hitler to agree to an independent French partnership in the Reich's shrinking Europe, but Hitler ignored him. The intense dislike of Laval by the French for his personification of collaboration reinforced their hatred of the Germans. The Milice was the Vichy organization most detested by the French for its active collaboration with the Germans. The resistance movements and networks were becoming stronger in both organization and activity during 1943, but most of the forty million French men and women were nowhere close to budging from their seats, devoted to scratching out a miserable living. Additionally, they were ambivalent about the war for several reasons.

First, acts of resistance brought about harsh German reprisals, which people feared could touch them or their families. Second, liberation meant increasing air bombardment and subsequent invasion with its creation of battlegrounds on French soil. Third, many people believed that a class civil war would break out in France, should a victorious Red Army threaten to arrive from the east. *Attentisme* was a political mind-set consistent with waiting for events to take shape before making a decision. It was characterized by temporization, immobility, opportunism, and some degree of resignation. When Laval introduced STO, he enraged many French people, as it now was obvious to all what the true relationship was with the occupier. First, Pétain's promise that he would be a protective shield to keep the French in France was broken with the principal rural class, the peasants. Not only were their men in German prisoner-of-war stalags, but now these farmers could be called up indiscriminately to join their war prisoner relatives in Germany as forced laborers. Second, the refusal by the *réfractaires* to go to Germany represented a fundamental break with *attentisme*, a dynamic that caused many people to reflect on that stance. The vast majority of these draft dodgers never fought in the resistance, but their clandestine presence and the privations they faced among the rural people were mirror-like criticisms of a wait-and-see policy.[22]

In actuality, Marshal Pétain became even more of a mythical symbol in the year that had passed since the exhausting crises he endured in November 1942 and later in November–December 1943. As we have seen, Laval held the reins of power, which continually frustrated the old man, and in September he and some loyalists tried to work a trick on Laval to support a more democratic constitutional change, through which they could hopefully appeal to the Americans, as they thought Badoglio had done from Rome. Laval would be the Mussolini character, taken to prison, and Pétain would seek an armistice for France with the Allies. Pétain wanted to announce this on the radio but the Germans got wind of the court intrigue and saved Laval by forbidding Pétain his radio time on November 13, 1943. In a fit of pique, Pétain rebelled by ceasing to do any duties, a situation that caused Hitler to take a firm stand with the old man. In December, Abetz brought a letter instructing Pétain to form a new government loyal to Germany or quit, and by December 18 he capitulated and accepted all of Hitler's terms. Pétain was powerless, and Laval had to form a new cabinet of committed Collaborationist ministers some of whom he did not necessarily see eye to eye. Rumors of Pétain's helplessness reached some of the public, which provoked expressions of sympathy toward him.[23]

The French public, not being privy to all these Vichy court machinations, continued to show reverence to the father-figure the marshal represented, as he was something they could loyally hang on to, even as his power diminished. An unambiguous dislocation had existed between the Collaborationist wait-and-see policies of his Vichy government and his image of a patriot who had stood up to the Germans. This had given the people the opportunity to cling fast to Pétain the man while at the same time ignoring the actual collaboration of the Vichy regime, which had become more and more obvious. That dislocation had become more difficult to sustain since STO was implemented and the uninterrupted Allied victories on the battlefields had become apparent. In December, Vichy propaganda was placed under Philippe Henriot, a categorical Collaborationist, and he continued to work hard to stoke societal

---

22　*L'Opinion Française sous Vichy*. Ibid., 286–287.
23　Ibid. 289, n2; *France: The Dark Years*. Ibid., 232.

fears about civil war and foreigners. The November arrest in Paris of the Manouchian group, whose members spectacularly gunned down Sauckel's deputy Julius Ritter, became part of this effort.

The *Affiche rouge* was a vibrant red propaganda poster that announced the execution of twenty-three Communist foreigners with unpronounceable Slavic and Jewish names, who formed the Manouchian group. Hunted down over a period of time by a specially committed French police task force of more than one hundred agents, the provocateurs were stigmatized for their foreign origins. But the fact remained that these men and women had made a choice to resist the hated STO by shooting one of its top German agents in public. These men and one woman all died with courage for their conscious act of resistance. The debate within France over the number of resisters has been fierce over the years and generations. There is no doubt that the numbers of active participants in the resistance movements grew during 1943, but it is likely that that number, like that of committed Vichy Collaborationists, was relatively low compared to the overall French population. For example, by 1994 the number of holders of the card issued by France to recognize Voluntary Resistance Fighters (CVR) was 260,000. This might be too restrictive a number, as Julian Jackson points out, but it is indicative that the number should be in the hundreds of thousands, not the millions, and with it being most likely considerably less for the diehard Collaborationists.[24]

Pierre Laborie espouses an interesting hypothesis about what was going on in most people's minds in this period, which he labels "the logics of the imaginary Pétain." He argues that this feeling allowed many millions to maintain a state of loyal paralysis through their imagined image of the marshal, which toward the end of 1943 helped the majority of French people justify a state of anomie, wherein they chose to do nothing except grind through daily life. They took refuge in inaction, which they interpreted as the best way to support what they construed to be the double game of Pétain, to play the Axis off against the Allies for the fantasy resurrection of France. An *attentiste* posture allowed one to be for England or against the German occupier through the demonstration of one's blind faith in the marshal and by demonstrating this through not openly contesting his collaborationist policies. Fidelity to Pétain was

---

24 Ibid., 477.

best signified by such inaction and was an expression of patriotism. This attitude was normal for collective imaginations confused by uncertainty and conflict, where inertia was a safe harbor in support of the marshal's *beaux gestes*. The ambivalent attitude of the French people is exemplified by their loyal feelings in favor of the marshal and their subsequent disassociation from his regime, to which, in truth, he was the indispensable contributor. Subconsciously, however, most French people shared responsibility with the marshal by tolerating his *redressement* policies, which often had contradictory beliefs, through their unquestioning deference to his person. We will see evidence that the people in the Gard thought less and less of and about the marshal, but we also will witness brief periods of remission in the decline of adherence to *maréchalisme*.[25]

The first SCT synthesis available for 1943 was for the month of March, and it commenced with summaries of antinational activities. The agents ascribed demonstrations that took place at the departure of STO deportees from Nîmes to Communist attempts to use "seditious propaganda" to stir up the populace. "The Communists assembled at the railroad station singing the 'Internationale' and screaming against Laval and Pétain; in a Gardois village young people about to depart for work in Germany attacked some members of the veterans' Legion." It was stated that a Nîmes police inspector was gravely wounded by a "terrorist," who was arrested, but some people attempted to free him and these assailants were jailed and sentenced to death or lifetime forced labor. New acts of sabotage were reported against the two main railway lines from Nîmes that went west to Montpellier and north to Alès. The BBC broadcasts were described as being always "feverishly" listened to by the people. The SCT writer gratuitously commented that the increase in anti-Vichy manifestations was upsetting to the citizenry: "These bad elements are getting bolder." The public reacted strongly and negatively to Sauckel's second STO labor quota requisition that left for Germany in March, calling for "an end to it all," while the rumors that certain coastal localities in the Gard might be evacuated had made many people nervous and agitated. The difficulties associated with daily living were described generally as having entered a second stage. There were very few comments on events in Russia, and the rumors about an Allied invasion of France this year had abated.

---

25   *L'Opinion Française sous Vichy.* Ibid., 296–297.

On internal matters, the censors mentioned that the opposition to the Vichy government had grown very intense, and people disregarded its directives and paid no attention to its promises. The vast majority was absorbed with coping with daily exigencies and accused the occupant of causing such hard times and desired "an end to all that as soon as possible." The whole situation was one big mess, made worse by the inordinate German troop requisitions of supplies, and the result was ill will everywhere. "The current climate is less and less favorable to collaboration and no one except for some Nazi adherents speaks of Franco-German rapprochement." However, the Allies didn't seem to gain from those sentiments, and if a few interpreted Allied bombing in France as a prelude to invasion, most feared its spread. The people preferred that the bombs all fall on Germany. American inactivity in Tunisia was commented upon. Additionally, their bombing runs over Brittany and Normandy were mentioned as undercutting the initial sympathy the French felt toward them. The Communists were credited with being the most energetic resistance group, both in recruitment and activity. Their partisan support came primarily from the working class, and they were very prudent in expressing themselves in private communications. On the other hand, fear of Bolshevism was frequently mentioned in correspondence. Disappointment in Allied progress, however, or a fall-off in enthusiasm for them due to bombing campaigns did not translate into any reinvigoration of support for the Vichy government or its policies. To the contrary, the level of criticism was very lively in expressions about the divisiveness that abounded as well as complaints about the ineffectiveness of Vichy's administrative organizations. Comments ran the gamut: "We face terrible tests due to our internal divisions and above all the government lacks energy. We need a Bonaparte, a dictator with a cudgel. Our weak government would lead us to civil war with the Communists if the Germans weren't in place. The railroad guard is useless due to its poor organization."

The people realized that the inauguration of STO would cause an unrelenting demand for the massive sending of local labor to Germany. The report called attention to the extreme anger and disorder provoked by the first departures in January and February but maintained that the situation remained under control. The groups singled out for being most agitated over the STO requisitions were the parents of the young men forced to leave for Germany and those who listened to the BBC broadcasts. The actual deportees manifested their dissatisfaction by uttering chants and displaying protest placards upon assembly for departure. The report stated that sanctions had kept any disobedience with regard to departure orders to a minimum, and that letters from workers already in Germany helped calm things a bit. It went on to say that sympathy existed for the youth who were forced to go, but it reputedly was tempered by the fact that earlier classes had to fight in the war and that many of them still were prisoners of war in Germany. The biggest reason for complaint was over exemptions issued, and those cited were for agricultural workers and students. "These categories we know from the law as written were not exempted so unless they are for instances of some few individuals who were favored by parents exerting influence with local Vichy officials, this is a straw man comment."

Some people expressed the fear that the STO law would also be extended to young women, as the *Relève* had been. A valid comment could have been the fact that people were still complaining that so few prisoners actually had been exchanged under the promises made by Laval relative to that *Relève* program. In fact the number of prisoners returned to France under the misleading "one prisoner for every three skilled workers sent" deal between Laval and Sauckel was approximately fifty thousand, while four hundred thousand actually went to Germany under the *Relève*.[26] Furthermore, rumors had been spread by the Resistance press that when STO workers actually reached Germany, they were dispatched to the Russian front to participate in Chancellor Hitler's announced European mobilization in his crusade against Bolshevism.

Other false rumors were said to have been concocted about the Germans rounding up all Frenchmen aged eighteen to fifty-five in anticipation of an Allied invasion, as well as misleading news about purported evacuation plans for certain areas in the Gard. This latter matter had upset public opinion greatly and seemed to have had its origin in efforts to quarter the German troops of occupation, as well as knowledge of the existence of official Vichy contingency plans for a potential invasion in the south. Some misguided mayors were blamed for causing these concerns, partly based on the fear that the Allied bombing campaign would extend into the Midi. Most people were skeptical about the

---

26 *Vichy France*. Ibid., 368.

Milice's campaign to increase its membership locally, but a few correspondents put their faith in the belief that it could be a counterweight
to fears about a civil war. The Legion was considered moribund, and its
prestige was sinking, with the Milice being the sole pro-Vichy organization that was proactive.

The report referred to letters coming from the original Occupied
Zones in the north showing that public opinion had been influenced by
similar circumstances but was more aggravated in tone due to the longer
period of occupation. The STO was primary followed by fear of Allied
bombings, not only in France but also in urban centers of Germany,
where French workers were concentrated. In spite of the fact that the
bombings harmed the image of the Allies, all over France the people
wanted the Germans out of their country. The heavy weight of paying
directly or indirectly for the German occupation was decried by some
as far worse than the actual presence of the German troops. Comments
were made about the apparent absence of the French authorities. Other
correspondents grumbled about the actions of the Resistance: "Of course
one should continue the struggle against Germany but not by playing
dirty politics against Pétain and his Government."

Reasonable temperatures were favoring spring planting efforts, but
extremely dry conditions had hurt potatoes, nut-producing fruits, wheat,
cereals, and rice, which could compromise future crop-reaping levels.
Horses and oxen for plowing were practically nonexistent, their prices
were prohibitive, and no feed could be found for them. Milk production
was very low, which had caused extreme shortages of related supplies
in the cities. People complained that the government agency in charge
of animal feed stocks seemingly was helpless to correct the situation.
There also existed a general shortage in labor supply to work the land.
The distribution of food was always criticized and the availability of
vegetables was worse this month than February, but that lack had been
somewhat offset by extra supplies of dry beans and pasta. Meat deliveries were poor from sources both inside and outside the Gard, although
salted beef made up for some of the deficiencies in Nîmes. Fats and milk
were unavailable, but the workers in the mining basin had received extra
quantities of potatoes.

Industrial factories had shut down production as primary materials
were not being delivered, and the general shortage in supervisors and

experienced miners forced work weeks of sixty hours in order to achieve the necessary quotas. Production of other products was hampered by shortages in electricity, transportation, and mechanical parts. Coal was in great demand, and the pressure was increased because the February quota had not been achieved. Workers were pressuring their bosses for higher salaries, which put them in a delicate position with the government. March's average production was 8,700 tons of coal and 170 tons of lignite. The Soulier mines achieved 2,500 tons of pyrite but projected only 2,000 tons in April. The steel tube factory of Bessèges was back in production after repairs were finished on their rolling mills. The Pechiney chemical plant reported normal production of copper sulfate for the wine growers in the surrounding departments. The Beaucaire cement factory's output was normal at 1,300 tons and anticipated being able to produce a supplementary 6,000 tons by April for the special needs of the German authorities. The Rey explosive works increased daily production to five hundred kilos in order to deliver the requirements of the German Todt organization, which could use double that quantity if the Saint Chame factory could supply additional components for use in manufacturing explosives.

Commercial activity continued to be slow, as there was a general lack of merchandise for sale. The wine business had been temporarily suspended due to changes in regulations. Simplified regulations that taxed only wine that was actually produced, which had "a simple appellation and fifty francs prime tax per hectoliter," were popular and allowed old orders to be honored. The Perrier works volume with the German army was unchanged, as were the shipments of wine and alcohol bound for Germany in February and March at one hundred freight cars shipped direct and three hundred more cars via indirect shipment. Railroad traffic was heavily encumbered by the Germans, so deliveries were reduced for local consumption. This resulted in a lack of rolling stock as well as engines. Covered rolling stock was much sought after for security reasons. Road transport was practically at a standstill due to the absence of fuel and spare parts, so having a travel permit was worthless. All river transport had been commandeered. The stock market was very slow, although a PTT loan was rapidly bought up. Business properties were very sought after by people of means.

The weight of the occupier's hand was heavier than it was in the beginning of the year. Individual Germans were more agreeable than they were collectively, and their lodging requisitions were especially onerous, which had led to instances of violence. Acts of violent resistance, arrests, and executions were commented upon. Many intercepts from western France noted the Allied bombings in Lorient, St-Nazaire, Rennes, Morlaix, Rouen, and Amiens, and the targets that included civilian casualties were severely criticized. "The crimes of St-Nazaire and Lorient have opened our eyes a lot," wrote one citizen about civilian casualties caused by Allied bombings of areas near the German submarine pens located in Brittany. Letters from French workers in Germany indicated a feeling of resignation and acceptance of life's conditions as they existed. Work was hard, but the food was sufficient. The slow delivery of mail from home in France was a frequent cause for complaint. Those workers who went to Germany with special skills under the terms of the *Relève* often protested that they were employed as common laborers.

The spirit of those demobilized from the Armistice Army was unchanged, as most only could hope for the formation of a new force and that feeling was generated by the desire for revenge against the occupier. The ex-soldiers were very negative about Vichy's promises for redeployment or work placement. However, in spite of their defiance they were anxious to find any local work to avoid being sent to Germany, which they said they would escape at all costs. Some officers exhibited their loyalty and patriotism but objected to how they were closely controlled by the authorities: "We are treated like illegal aliens."[27]

The summary for April highlighted the appearance in the Gard of heavy Gaullist propaganda, the purpose of which was interpreted as an effort to counterbalance negative impressions that the heavy bombings of the Renault works in Paris's Boulogne-Billancourt suburb had created after April 4. Civilian casualties among the Parisians had been very high, and most prior bombing raids had been limited to the coastal areas. Gaullist radio stressed the presence of the DCA, anti-aircraft guns manned by the French, on the grounds of the Longchamp race track as the reason for civilian casualties having occurred there during the pari-mutuel horse races. Jean Guéhenno expressed a different opinion in his journal, when he wrote with cutting irony that nothing must prevent

---

27   ADG 1 W 42, Control Technique of Nimes Report for March 1943, marked 103–112.

the betting on horse races from taking place, not even Allied bombing runs.[28]

Locally, some anti-Vichy leaflets were seized that had been dropped from the air. Additionally, an "open letter to the marshal from university students" had been confiscated from the mail. Dissident materials had been found in the Nîmes Railway Station and among the Third Company of PTT workers. Such materials increased and included advice on how to escape to England via Spain or by airplane or boat. There was a very systematic effort by the Gaullist propaganda to explain the reasons for the Allied bombing attacks, as well as to incite French youth against the *Relève* and STO labor commandeering programs. Communist propaganda was more discreet but also very active. However, overt attacks were fewer this month in the Gard, although some aggressive actions had been taken against police personnel, as well as sabotage endeavors against the rail lines and the central electric power plant.

On February 20, 1943, three members of the *Franc-Tireurs et partisans* (FTP) blew up a French brothel in Nîmes that catered only to German military and civilian clientele, in what became known as the Maison Caro affair. The explosion succeeded in killing five Germans and two French prostitutes. Fifty Nîmois hostages were rounded up and held for a month until two of the perpetrators were captured, and subsequently tried and sentenced to death. Eight hostages were sent off to work for the Todt organization and the two bombers, Jean-Robert Faita and Vincent Faita, were publicly guillotined in front of the state courthouse next to the Roman Arena in Nîmes on April 22, 1943.[29] Plaques commemorate the execution spot, one placed soon after the war and a new one added March 29, 2010, which honored Charles Bedos, the president of the local bar association, who was deported to Mauthausen sixty-seven years earlier for defending the Faitas. The April report mentioned that a plea for clemency to Marshal Pétain by the Faitas or their representatives had been rejected, and the court that had convicted and sentenced them was one of the special tribunals that

---

28 *Journal des Années Noires.* Ibid., 333.

29 *Nîmes at War.* Ibid., 235, n180. The original plaque reads "To the memory of Jean Robert and Vincent Faita. Heroes of the French Franc-Tireurs and Partisans. Guillotined on April 22, 1943, on this site, which was the prison, by order of a French government in the service of the Nazi Occupant. They were twenty years old ..."

Vichy had empowered to handle such cases of violent resistance. These "Special Sections" were detested by the French public. The report went on to comment upon the "great courage shown" by the two men at their execution. The existence of an organization whose object was to combat the Occupier was announced by a local correspondent who wrote, "I belong to a secret association based in Paris which has branches all throughout France."

In the opinion section, the statement was made that the people thought the present tranquility was only the calm before the storm and that grave events were to occur soon. The level of general concern was heightened by what were interpreted in certain locales as preparatory measures for evacuation of areas of some southern cities in light of the nightly alerts that had been instituted. This was consistent with measures taken in the Parisian metropole to protect the citizens against the heavy bombing attacks that had stirred up anger against the Allies. This renewal of anger at bombing raids that caused civilian casualties had not resulted in any Franco-German reconciliation and furthermore, approval of the Vichy government was very rarely expressed, and one pessimist expected it to dissolve.

There were fewer utterances of confidence in the marshal than before and little comment on his speech to the STO deportees of April 5, which was called a deception, as it did not reveal what he hoped to see accomplished. The public was confused and sought clarity but such official statements made for even more disenchantment, as too often illusory promises had been offered and never kept. Some Pétain supporters questioned the loyalty of certain high functionaries, such as ministers who were viewed as putting their feet on the brakes to hold back the National Revolution from achieving its purposes. There also were comments on the lack of energy by the government and expressions of fears about what the future held for the nation. "Apart from the marshal, there is no strong-fisted man in France," remarked one loyalist. Other Vichy supporters blamed the Third Republic's leaders for France's going to war and took pleasure in the French state's handing over Blum, Daladier, Reynaud, Mandel, and Gamelin to German authorities on April 5 for imprisonment in Germany. One stated, "It is a shame they were not hung from a post or shot tied to a stake."

Laval's government was rarely mentioned, except to associate it with the departures for Germany as a result of the *Relève* or STO policies, for which Pierre Laval was attacked in a vituperative fashion. Because the labor requisition numbers were met in March, there were rumors that there would be no more immediate calls for more workers, and that had calmed the situation somewhat. Some believed that the workers' conditions in Germany were not so bad, but relatives in the Gard had not succeeded in having their food packages pass the demarcation line, and they had been upset to hear that relatives north of the line could ship such packages to their kin working in Germany. Another false rumor was that people thought the Germans had requisitioned the young people only to get them out of France. Some relatives or acquaintances were approving of the young men who had fled the STO call-up, while others pitied the plight of those who had nowhere to go. Certain families complained about the inequity inherent in who got called for STO duty, and even the POW families harped about the arbitrary process for determining who might get repatriated. There were allusions, but they were reticent ones, to the fact that some 250,000 prisoners of war in Germany were reputed to have been put on leave to work on German farms, while they were still technically captives.[30]

The attitude of the uncommitted populace toward the belligerent parties, which touched upon the Allies' chance to end the war, had been affected by the Parisian bombings' casualties. Vichy propaganda had attempted to portray the effects of the Allied bombings as only contributing to death and ruination. They stressed that an invasion for liberating the country would only lead to greater suffering and destruction. This resulted in the spreading of fear among the population, as the effects of war were witnessed up close, which was in vivid contrast with what had been clamored for before the bombs rained down. The steadfast Anglophiles dismissed such wishy-washy opinionating and answered back that "they complain about anything the Allies do, when they do nothing and when they do something." Some others had shown loss of faith in the "United Nations," as they interpreted what little activity that seemed to be occurring in Russia since the conclusion of the successful Soviet winter campaign as being

---

30   *De Munich a la Libération.* Ibid., 209. The number of French prisoners of war furloughed to work on German farms by the beginning of 1944 in the "free workers" program was 900,000, according to J-P Azéma.

disappointing. More important, many Anglo-American sympathizers were opposed to a Soviet victory due to the general European fear of Bolshevism.

The Tunisian campaign, wherein the Free French forces had joined with the Allies in combat against the Germans, was creating great hope, but its pace seemed to be going slowly. Any successful termination of the North African campaign ironically had led to the fear that the next battleground would be on the French mainland. Therefore, the people wrote that they would like to see any new Allied invasion take place on Italian soil or in the Balkans. The attitude toward the Germans remained systematically hostile and irrational, wanting their forces out of France as speedily as possible. However, interpersonal relations between the Gardois and the Germans were good, as the citizens were now used to their presence and only groused about their food requisitions or some incidents. The masses showed no interest in collaboration, and the ordering of a New Europe interested only the most unswerving support-ers of Vichy. This hostility, joined with disappointment in the Allied efforts, made opinion live like the people—day to day, devoid of ideals, and indifferent to anything that did not touch them directly, such as material wants and personal cares. It seemed there were only very few citizens who were discerning enough to be uneasy about France's situ-ation, among them the adherents of *La Seule France*, who felt the fate of France was in their hands and not outside the country. But the vast majority of the public wanted peace at any price and obtained in such a way that it would be handed on a platter to them without any personal sacrifice.

Indications of an opposition in the making, based on revenge against the oppressors, were numerous. But that manifestation excited another segment of opinion, which feared it would create a civil war, and these counterbalancing elements of society thought that the presence of the German troops would preserve order. However, one militant trade unionist who was firmly among the opposition put it this way: "When you want to improve the lot of the people do you have to ask them first what will make them happy." The report's writer voiced disappointment that the government's efforts to effect improvements for workers was uncommented upon. Perhaps this was the case because the Worker's Charter implemented by Vichy in 1941 was designed to control union actions by denying them the right to strike.[31] The black market received lots of angry comments accusing the governmental agencies of victimizing the working class by tolerating its presence in the marketplace. The functionaries in the economic control sections, on the other hand, bemoaned their fate by claiming to have insufficient resources. The peasants were equally up in arms over what they saw as the imposition of excessive requisitions that they generally blamed on the Germans as having added to all the difficulties they faced. They felt enough discontent as it was and only saw these additional demands on their limited resources as backbreaking. The young people were equally agitated, particularly the students and the Vichy youth movement, *Compagnons de France,* a Boy Scout equivalent.

The Legion's activity was practically nonexistent, except for some in the social milieu, about which a Milice member was scornful: "It is always the same with the Legion, too many stay-at-homes, many of whom swallow what Radio London says." On the other hand, the Milice was very active and was intensifying its propaganda efforts. Their spirits were very high and they showed no discouragement in the least over the hostility they had encountered. "We are very badly viewed but I don't care. I only have one purpose, which is to serve the marshal whatever will come." Their leaders complained of the difficulties they faced in organizational shortcomings. The assassination of the adjunct leader of the Milice in Marseille was the subject of high emotion in their ranks.

The paucity of comments on political parties indicated that there was little going on. The arrest in Clermont-Ferrand of Colonel de la Rocque in March, along with other members of his PSF (*Progrès Social Français*) was noted as having put the brakes on their activity. He was deported to Germany and incarcerated in the same prison as Daladier, Gamelin, and Weygand. The result seemed to be that there were numerous defections and one militant complained about the result of the leadership's decapitation: "events separate the indecisive and the timid ones. Laval knows how to limit our resources." The organization of ex-members of the LVF into a group had encountered some difficulties, as some active volunteers who returned on leave from the Russian front had not shown up for duty and had been called deserters by one of their leaders.

---

31   *Vichy France.* Ibid., 217–218. It is not surprising that, relatively speaking, there was a heavy presence of trade union members in the resistance.

The radio and press came in for criticism, as they were considered more as propaganda organs than news services. Following the news of the April 4 bombings around Paris, the people with relatives in the metropole were critical about the fact that the reports were not specific as to which areas had been bombed. The public had to listen to English and Swiss radio to ascertain that the bombings had affected the Renault works and the surrounding localities of Boulogne-Billancourt. Correspondents accused French radio of being incompetent. The newsreel presentations in the cinema were booed when President Laval was shown announcing the easing of the demarcation-line restrictions. This newsreel, coming just after the largest STO deportations happened, was treated with derision and led to several demonstrations. The shift in opinion in the Occupied Zone was more pronounced than in the Gard, as the actual bombings occurred there in Paris. But opposition remained quite active in many outlying regions, especially in Brittany where the Anglo-Americans had always had strong partisans, whose actions were now reinforced by the STO departures. The Vichy government received short shrift, as were its organizations like the Legion and the Milice, about which little was commented.

The general agricultural situation was distressing. The growing season advanced, but the overall dryness continued, and the fears were for a poor harvest, even though the recent rain had brought a temporary improvement. The delays in seed delivery caused by the lack of transportation also held back meeting demand levels, especially in potatoes, sunflower seeds, and dry legumes. Plowing had been hindered by the German requisitions of horses and labor; also contributing to the possible poor harvest season were poor availabilities of farm supplies like manure and chemical-based fertilizers, and implements like iron farm tools or even nails for repairing fences or barns. Animal husbandry was rendered difficult by the lack of forage, which inhibited weight growth as well as causing poor milk output. One peasant wrote, "In order to save their animals, people must participate in the black market." The wine season appeared encouraging, but the poor availability of copper sulfate raised concerns, and some producers complained that some domains had been favored in its distribution at the expense of others. Cereal production would be poor in barley and wheat, due to the low level of precipitation, but oil-producing plants would exceed their quotas. The fruit trees were flowering well, which probably would mean a good picking season, and early seasonal fruits and vegetables would have a good result. All farmers were looking for horses, pigs, and oxen, but supply was low. Tax collections for produce grown for personal use were highly resisted.

The heavy complaints continued over food resupply, which was critical in certain rural communities. Vegetable and market garden quantities were behind last month's output. The variety was nil, and the poor gathering result caused a slump in weekly outdoor market sales through the lack of produce. The supply of meat was precarious in spite of efforts by people high up in the resupply department to make more meat available. The late deliveries of fats did not make up for the amounts that had been promised. The milk supply was augmented by deliveries secured from areas outside the Gard so the overall quota was met for the month. Overall, however, the situation looked bleak.

Shortages for industry were everywhere and in everything: primary and secondary materials, coal and electricity, transport, packaging, and spare parts, all of which contributed to holding back manufacturing output. If the primary materials were available, valid orders could have been filled for metallurgy products, shoes, and textiles. The chemical industry lacked lead and copper for use in producing agricultural products. The Gard Gas Works and the coal industry were short of industrial lubricants and the mines lacked sand workers and explosives for mine excavations. Auto repair shops were shuttered due to the non-availability of automotive repair parts. The lack of coal and electricity supplies for both commercial and private consumption in all zones was the root cause for many complaints against governmental organizations, and those reductions in energy supplies had been getting worse. Labor requisitions also affected negatively some factories' output. Other factories feared industry consolidation.

The most important departmental industry, the coal mines in the Alès basin, which was controlled by the Committee of Bituminous Coal, had a small increase in coal production, but a decrease in lignite during the month of March. Actual output figures were about 9,000 tons of coal and 1,250 tons of lignite per week. Most of the coal supplies were requisitioned for military-equipment-producing industries in France or Germany.[32] The Pechiney factory continued to produce about sixty

---

32   *Vichy France.* Ibid., 237, 355 n37. Robert O. Paxton estimated France was

tons of aluminum oxide daily, and secondary chemical production of arsalumine, arsenic, sulfate, and acids remained unchanged. Some copper sulfate deliveries were expedited to the wine producers in various departments. Initially, the French Cement Societies of Beaucaire had delivery problems, as the availability of rolling stock was unpredictable and limited, but then production of cement had to be totally ceased, as many of their laborers were requisitioned, and there also were no packing materials. Small business was at a standstill and the scarcity of general merchandise had driven prices upward. The too-numerous and confusing administrative regulations that were in effect hurt these small businesses so much that they were driven to resort to bartering for transactions.[33]

The May report began with recent military news from North Africa and the comment that the renewal of labor requisitions for the STO had affected public opinion negatively toward the Vichy government. People interpreted these new demands for young workers to go to Germany as direct consequences of the recent agreements concluded between President Laval and Chancellor Hitler. "It is a bad sign when Laval goes there [to a meeting in Germany with Hitler on April 29, 1943] ... all men will have to go." Favorable expressions of confidence in the marshal were as rare as critical ones. There was only one comment on his recent speech that showed appreciation for his hopes for living to witness a world without war. The recent exhibit in Nîmes consecrated to him was not mentioned at all.

The most commented-upon subject in the May report affecting public opinion was military events, and specifically, the focus was excited comment about the Allied conquest of Tunisia. The relatively rapid destruction and complete surrender of the Axis forces had surprised the people and had elicited commentary on what was perceived to be the low morale that existed even among the German troops, in comparison to 1941–1942. There was hardly any mention of the Eastern Front, and all future speculation after the fall of Bizerte and Tunis was about where the next invasion by the Anglo-Americans would take place. Many in the Midi exhibited a real uneasiness in their letters that their country

---

limited to about 35 percent of their prewar coal supplies during the war years. Coal production in France stayed close to 1938 levels, but because of German requisitions, French coal consumption fell below the levels of 1890.

33　ADG 1 W 42 Contrôle Technique of Nimes Report for April, 1943, marked 122–128.

would be next on the Allied list. A real fear existed among the Gardois that southern France would be transformed into an active battleground, with dire consequences for Vichy, as the view was that many Frenchmen would come out in active support of the Allied invaders. Some saw a chance for a negotiated peace, thanks to the Tunisian victory, along with rumors that the Allies had met with Spain, and whatever they read into the marshal's May 2 speech. By month's end, these hopes were dashed, while those afraid that France was next for invasion had turned their eyes toward Italy or perhaps the Balkans as logical places for a second front to occur. The Anglophiles were a bit deceived—or at least disappointed—as they now foresaw a waiting period for France. Also, the air attacks against Bordeaux reawakened local fears that there could be a fresh breakout of Allied bombings on targeted cities in the south of France.

The new STO requisitions of young people for work in Germany were seen as a direct result of the visit of President Laval, Vichy's head of state, to meet with the Führer. All society was nervous, but if the emotions did not rise to the level of last March, it was because the numbers were greatly reduced, thanks to deferments and exemptions given to conscripts in some departments like the Gard (90 percent) and the Correze (100 percent). The reasons that the STO administrators could not raise high numbers were that agricultural and industrial workers, especially in the coal mines, along with students, bank and insurance company employees, and the Milice were all exempted. A comedian said, "There only remain the hairdressers." Now the people were afraid that it would be the Germans who would take over the composition of the lists for labor requisitions. Police were sent to search the homes of those requisitioned to cut down on defection, and the youth called by STO for departure for Germany from the Chantier camps were closely supervised. These brutal moves caused violent reactions from those in the public with family members involved. Authorizations to send deep miners to Germany were highly criticized by their communes.

Letters concerning POWs were numerous, and the content was very contrasting. Some indicated numerous returns of prisoners to France and talked about the conditions in the stalags and the morale of the prisoners who were still there. These letters also said the prisoners who had returned home were disappointed by the low morale of the people at home and commented that conditions were worse than in the prison camps. The POWs who remained were bitter and had very anti-German attitudes. In France, the nonliberation of young POWs with agricultural backgrounds caused consternation. In fact, the situation was worsened as the *Relève* and STO had taken peasants out of France to work in German factories. The announcement that 250,000 POWs had been furloughed to work on German farms and/or factories did not sit well with other prisoners or their French relatives. Some who did not have relatives as prisoners commented favorably about the POWs being "freed" to work outside the prison camps. The opposition was very discreet in its correspondence: "More than ever, one must keep to oneself what one truly thinks." The exception was the numerous positive comments on the Allied victories in Tunisia, often accompanied by the express desire for revenge on the German occupiers.[34]

The July report was pessimistic about what was perceived as a stalemate, perhaps referring to events on the Eastern Front. However, the Allied invasion of Sicily on July 10 had renewed hopes for an end to the war and the defeat of the Axis powers. The last days of July were mentioned for the increased optimism found by the SCT, occasioned by news reports concerning Mussolini's fall from power. The general feeling was that peace would be forthcoming between the Allies and Italy. There were very few references to Marshal Pétain and almost none to Vichy governmental undertakings, except for one writer who lauded President Laval's remarks to a prisoner-of-war assembly that was reported in the press: "I have very much admired Laval's speech. He will never be understood. We are spoiled by our total inability to comprehend his actions." The people's spirits were full of bitterness and weariness in spite of the recent hopes expressed about Allied advances in Italy, which in no way compensated for the sufferings they had endured from difficulties encountered in daily life.

The penury of food supplies forced mothers with families to rush off, seeking sources of nourishment with the utmost urgency, which often was met with frustrating disappointment and continuing hunger. The rise in the cost of living was dramatic for the average, nonspecial-

---

34   ADG 1 W 42 Contrôle Technique of Nimes Report for May, 1943, marked page 3–4.

ized workers, retirees, and small property owners who were forbidden to increase rents on their tenants. The hue and cry against the new tax increases was very loud, and the salary adjustments just announced were loudly deemed insufficient. All these oft-expressed difficulties augmented the complaints against governmental officials who were charged with absolute incompetence, which in turn nourished the opposition groups, pleasing some correspondents. "The people are disgusted and that reinforces their interior discontent. They cannot conceive how such a dire situation everywhere can persist for so long."

Again, rarely did the opposition express its true thoughts openly, but when it opened up, it was in the form of virulent anti-German feelings. Conversely, the relations with the local German troops remained good, and even those who disliked them didn't hesitate to work for them if the opportunity arose, either to escape deportation or earn higher salaries. "At least 80 percent of us French work for the Germans and even an Anglophile obeys and collects the higher salary the Germans pay them." On the other hand, Germanophobia was especially high among the working class and the Protestants, who gave aid and shelter to the *réfractaires* who had fled the STO. "The general population tolerates the presence of these labor delinquents because they act correctly, but more importantly, if they don't harbor them they will gain the enmity of the Protestants and their pastors." The people were unhappy in the Gard and that discontent was expressing itself more manifestly in a growing opposition, which had a fundamental antipathy to what they perceived to be the contrary attitude of the Vichy functionaries. "They seem to want to act in such a way that all goes badly. There is something wrong with people who want to have the system fail."

The STO administration was attacked by everyone, and the most common complaints rose against the methodology for selecting which laborers were to go to Germany. General disorder and ambiguity reigned due to the confusing and contradictory regulations put into place by the administrators. The student classes were both astonished and angry over the uncertainty it placed them in. The emotional anti-STO reactions were described as being reduced from June, which underplayed the angry reactions that still existed: "They only deport our men so that the English can't count on them. In spite of that the resistance movement is growing here organizationally and after the war there will be a settling of accounts." The report maintained that on the whole, the young people were resigned to departure (more so than their families, it said) and the number of *réfractaires* in the Midi was described as appearing to "being limited enough."

However, there were enough such refugees from STO acting as foresters in the Cévennes mountain area of the Gard that German paratroopers had been dispatched in a military operation to assault them in early July 1943. The lightly armed *réfractaires* were surprised, and an un-

One side of St-André-de-Valborgne's Monument to the Dead of the Great War 1914—1918. Note the seven Broussoux family members listed from this remote rural town of well under one thousand people.

equal gun battle ensued, wherein the German soldiers, at a minimal cost to themselves of a few wounded, captured, killed, and wounded most of these evaders at a deserted camp in Aire de Côte. This was a remote forest area of the Cévennes near Mt. Aigoual, the Gard's highest point, and which was accessed via St-Jean-du-Gard and St-André-de-Valborgne. The report continued that the French police were ineffective in following up their attempt to get more STO escapees to turn themselves in, but the local authorities and clergy had some success in that endeavor. The SCT stated that fear of reprisals against their families could have influenced the majority of young people to surrender, if the report was accurate. The writers of the report concluded that it was astonishing that no sanctions were invoked against either the young people who gave themselves up or their families. Robert Zaretsky describes this same action by the German column on July 1, 1943, of "sixty to eighty soldiers who fell upon the evaders who had settled in an abandoned youth camp." The disorganized resistance by what can be described as an inexperienced and poorly trained réfractaires/ Maquis group resulted in seven young Frenchmen killed; some fifteen wounded were captured along with about twenty unwounded youths, at the cost of seven German wounded. The commandant of the French police at St-Jean-du-Gard was arrested by the Germans for giving aid to the armed evaders. Jacques Poujol wrote that this debacle "gravely discredited the Resistance in the Cévennes," which could be true for the time, yet it was not an end but a beginning.[35]

The SCT staff construed letters from workers in Germany as being "practically all unanimously favorable" and went on to state that letters from French workers in Austria were similar in outlook. The *Relève* was not referred to and any mention of it was said to have disappeared from all mail. It was unclear if this meant the STO as well. On the other hand, the announcement about prisoners of war being furloughed to work outside the stalags in Germany—the so-called statute on free labor— had elicited numerous comments in correspondence between prisoners and their families. It appeared that prisoners in the camps were reluctant to join this program but as soon as they left the camps and were assigned to a farm or a factory, the majority of prisoners found the experience satisfying. It was estimated that around 60 percent, or about nine hundred thousand French POWs undertook this kind of work assignment at some time in their stay in Germany.[36]

Reactions to military events included the continued Allied success in the invasion of the Italian island of Sicily; their steady advance against

---

35 *Nimes at War.* Ibid., 235–236 , as well as notes 182 and 183 on page 236. Poujol also stated that of the young men captured at Aire de Côte (he used the figure of thirty-nine, not thirty-five) only twenty returned alive from the concentration camps to which they were sent by the Germans. This proved to be a costly price to pay by these untrained réfractaires and their families, no matter what the SCT report said. A French web source, http://www.lyceechaptal.fr/telechargement/ Concours_de_la_Resistance_2010/Pour_01-03-2010/Cederom_la_Resistance_ en_Lozere/_xml/fiches/21827.htm, confirms Poujol's figures. It also names the traitor, a former disgruntled camp member, who led the Germans to the campsite.
36 *The Unfree French.* Ibid., 200–201.This ties in closely with the figure used by J-P Azéma for 1944, referenced earlier.

Present day (2012) road leading to the location of the Aire de Côte engagement of 1943, about two kilometers west towards Mt. Aigoual. The road turns into a dirt track which becomes a hiking path to the mountain approximately eleven kilometers away.

the Italian and German defenders was followed with great interest in the Gard. The people were buoyed by this favorable news and were increasingly less reticent to comment upon the Allied progress, which they welcomed. One reason for this attitude was that the Anglophiles dominated the population, and another reason was their refusal to give in to the long war's effects when they could catch a valid glimmer of positive hope for it to end German domination: "We view with great joy invasion as the beginning of the end." The fact that "the struggle is localized [for the moment] to southern Italy gives us hope that we will be saved from harm," was the normal reaction.

Such examples of euphoria were far from being unanimous, and if it was a majority of writers who would welcome an end to the war and therefore their difficulties, many others feared what the future might bring. Many in this minority agonized over the national destiny when they envisaged the group and individual consequences of an Axis defeat. They realized that the Allies wished to destroy fascism but questioned what they would put in its place. Even many among the uncommitted worried in this regard and did not wish for the return to a government like the Third Republic. Great distress was displayed about anything that would result in disorder, revolution, or civil war, and those potential events were associated with the specter of Communism: "Will we see the Commune and the Black Flag over the City Hall?" was a frequent question posed.

An invasion of France was seen as a realistic event in the offing and only truly desired by the militant Anglophiles or those who foresaw such a military action as bettering their future situation, such as those young people who were liable to be sent to work in Germany under the STO. The spread of Allied bombing campaigns to the south was very much feared, as even was the widening bombing of Germany due to the vast number of French workers located there. This type of anxiety was on the rise since the air raids on France had spread to Le Creusot, Sochaux, and around Paris. There were two schools of thought developing around the bombing campaigns, which were juxtaposed to one another. First, there were the numerous writers who deplored that the Allies were bringing ruination to France by their indiscriminate bombing runs, and the numbers of people who felt hostility toward the aggressors was growing, according to the frequency of this type of comment in correspondence.

On the other side of the coin were those French who excused the raids in their letters as being necessary and responded by saying, "That's war," when they were asked about the innocent civilian victims.

Philippe Henriot appeared to have been warmly received at a conference he gave in the Duchy of Uzès. He had an intense voice which made him a mesmerizing speaker who swayed a lot of people when he was put in charge of Vichy propaganda in 1944. He aspired to be the French Goebbels. However, his published propaganda articles or his broadcasts on the radio continued to be the object of many lively criticisms.[37] "I no longer listen to Vichy Radio. They upset me with their discourse. Other [unnamed] sources inform us more frankly." The Legion's members had opinions that showed a noticeable degree of disillusion, which indicated they were losing ardor for the cause. "The only thing they do is in the realm of social events." The rank and file of the Miliciens, on the other hand, was very dedicated to the cause of the Laval government, even more so than their leaders, who were disappointing in that they failed to give their followers direction, as they seemed to have doubts about the future fate of the organization.[38]

August's report listed numerous activities described as "antinational" throughout the Gard, including numerous assassination attempts, railroad track sabotage efforts, crop burnings, resistance tract distributions, and protest demonstrations. The people saw a close connection between these terrorist acts and events on the battlefields outside France. One correspondent showed this tendency in writing: "They blow up transformers and locks and burn wheat. The end is approaching." The mining basin was a particular area of concentration for such anti-government actions, and the management leaders complained that the government was too supine in its efforts to suppress the widespread subversive

---

37 *De Munich a la Libération.* Ibid., 234–235, 296, 298. Henriot, a staunch Catholic and dedicated enemy of Bolshevism, joined the Collaborationists and became the Minister of Information and Propaganda in the Vichy government. He was a supporter of the Milice and used his frequent radio broadcast chats to exhort them and others who so wished to join in to hunt down "terrorists, stateless people [Jews], and criminal assassins." He also was a Laval copycat who broadcast on December 19, 1943, that "we will save the French in spite of themselves." *France: The Dark Years.* Ibid., 530–533.

38 ADG. 1 W 42. Contrôle Technique of Nimes Report for July, 1943, marked 159–162.

propaganda that abounded. The bosses maintained that all manner of pretexts were used to stir up the miners against the regime. "The miners won't go back to the mines unless someone provides them with bread." That would hardly qualify as a pretext. Letter writers frequently blamed the Communists as the originators of such violent actions: "Here we also have murders that are committed for unknown reasons which people attribute to the communists all along the line." Others tried hard to ascribe the crop fires to acts of individual revenge. Rumors abounded that the Communists detained in Nîmes's jail were actively planning for what was referred to as future actions. The rumor mongers probably feared efforts would be made to escape.

Public opinion reflected the desire for an Anglo-American victory, which was perceived as the road that would lead to an end to their suffering. Less and less attention was paid to whatever the Vichy government tried to do, as people felt its fate was tied to the fortunes of war: "Its collapse is inevitable and we will celebrate its fall as the end to a frightful tyranny and the coming of a new era of liberty." The head of the government, Pierre Laval, was very often harshly criticized. Those who did mention the marshal limited their remarks to deploring his powerlessness and lamenting how his efforts were checked. "The poor old guy is just content to give his speeches and get himself drunk on his words." Rumors floated around about important governmental changes in the offing.

On the Italian front, Mussolini's dismissal had brought forth great hopes for a separate peace being declared between Italy and the Allies, an event which could lead to the disintegration of the Axis pact and the ultimate defeat of Germany. This early reaction was offset by the new Italian government's announcement that it would continue the war, but people continued to question the true intentions of Italy and some feared that seditious elements there could pose risks to France. "We can't afford to let the Communists who groan in Italy's guts to come over the border into France." The victory of the Allies in Sicily (on August 17, the island was secured) offset these fears of Communism to some degree. But that impact was in turn dismissed by government loyalists as not being decisive, as they viewed Germany as still being very strong militarily, and they foresaw a long struggle ahead before any German defeat.

Yet the people who felt this way were the minority, and the plurality, the Anglophiles, were optimistic that the war could end in a matter of months or even weeks. The majority made no comment on these matters and simply let themselves be drawn along by the train of events and limited themselves to wanting peace to replace war as soon as possible. Fundamentally, although the vast majority of people lived for the present, it did not mean that they were not without concerns for the near future, which included the bombing campaigns and an invasion of French soil. The air attacks on the nearby French airfields at Istres and Salon-de-Provence had increased the level of anxiety. Now the war seemed more real, being much closer to the Midi than before, when it had appeared remote. Yet the southern people still exhibited apathy and fatalism about these bombing raids, which were approaching them, it seemed, inexorably.

The numerous, violent attacks that occurred all around the department, strangely enough, did not seem to bother the correspondents, who described what had happened without expressing any measure of disapproval. However, the fear of Communism was definitely on the rise, and many writers felt that France would not escape its consequences. The apparent alliance between Gaullism and Communism provoked reactions such as: "What I fear above all is a Russian victory, for then our poor France would be kaput, and the Communists wait for this moment with undisguised joy and the Gaullists are in intimate communion with them. That's tidy!" Yet some people did complain that terrorism was not suppressed enough: "The guilty are still free. The police are in concert with them." With the exception of some dedicated militants, the majority of the population who had once favored Franco-German collaboration was now very fearful of the turn taken by outside events that favored the Allies. They were anxious about potential reprisals and not without reason, for their adversaries did not conceal their desire to seek vengeance as soon as the circumstances would permit.

People were burdened with life's difficulties and they grew increasingly discontented with this ever-worsening situation; each segment of the population criticized one and the other, be they government administrators, peasants, workers, or small businesses owners and employees. Their objections were focused on the French spirit, which they stigmatized as being blind and ignorant to the grave predicament in which they found themselves. Any vacation time that summer did nothing to lessen this incomprehension and malaise.

Bitter recriminations were expressed endlessly by and against farmers and functionaries. The former focused their ire on requisitions of their labor supplies, as well as what they viewed as the myriad hindrances the administrators threw in their paths or to which hard circumstances contributed. The latter loudly protested their reduced time for holidays which they considered a form of governmental bullying, perpetrated by their bosses. Changes in their pension retirement plans gave vent to abusive attacks, which contributed to the opposition against the administrative leaders. Their verbal attacks made them look disloyal, and they were accused of sabotage, which only added to the accusations made by the common people against all the functionaries, from the bottom to the top. All this was made worse by the disgust over the high cost of living, with the level of salaries called totally out of harmony with the cost of everything. This was one point upon which both the bosses and the workers were in total agreement. People also harbored extreme resentment against the heavy tax increases, especially the owners of rental properties who were astonished to have been forbidden by law to raise their tenants' rents.

The violent anger over further STO departures had only grown in its intensity of opposition: "It is outrageous and untenable for us who are left behind to do all the work." The ones summoned by STO tried to avoid it by every means possible, as they were afraid of being sent to German factories in urban areas where Allied bombing raids were concentrated. The young designees and their families were provoked to take any action imaginable to avoid showing up for that duty. The numbers of evaders were growing enormously, and any workers or POWs who returned from Germany found it very hard to get their old jobs back. Many of the young fugitives thought that it would be a temporary situation for them to wait for the war's end to save them. Others joined together in bands in distant places in the attempt to form partisan groups: "we can safely await the uprising when it comes which will be the right moment to join it." Another wrote that "German troops are very active against these bands, and a dozen young men have been captured in the Cévennes and sent back to Nîmes." Others deplored the deaths of several young STO evaders in the tiny village of Thines in the Ardèche.

For those who obeyed and departed to work in Germany, conditions very much depended on the region and type of industry in which they went to work. Letters intercepted from them did not indicate high levels of complaints, except about the poor clothing available, which was the same experience of the furloughed prisoners of war who went to work in the same factories. Even the ex-POWs said they couldn't complain too much about their conditions, but some refused to go under the German free-worker program because of an active propaganda campaign in the prison camps against it by commando groups of French prisoners.

The celebrations marking the third anniversary of the Legion's formation unfolded without incident. Nevertheless, eleven persons were arrested, but the event was in marked contrast to the imposing parade that took place in Nîmes two years earlier in August of 1941. The number of the public who attended the 1943 ceremonies was very low, except for the spectacle held in the Roman Arena. Some people indicated their satisfaction with the attendance, but many others did not hide their disappointment. The false rumors that circulated about the disbandment of the Milice had succeeded in the organization's cutting back in its activities. Its leader in the Gard denied such rumors: "The marshal has ordered its continuance; you understand, it is he, Marshal Pétain, who has said that." The report went on to say that the organization seemed to have enjoyed some rejuvenation by this statement by exhibiting a more courageous attitude.

However, the activities of other movements, meaning the Resistance, had focused their propaganda efforts against the Milice. It was interesting that this section of the report failed to mention that the Milice headquarters on rue Emile Jamais in Nîmes had been attacked with a bomb prior to August 14. No one could doubt the fact that the Miliciens were in the crosshairs of the Resistance.[39] Political party activity continued to be very much in abatement, and the local Francist group in Nîmes was described as being in full disarray. A comment was made about a PPF parade in Paris on the Champs-Elysées exciting its adherents but not many Parisians. Some ex-Chantier groups from the Dauphiné and Auvergne were in Gard camps in transit for STO duty and were temporarily working under German troop supervision. The Auvergne contingent was assigned to the wine fields, but it was a bit early for

---

39 *Nimes at War*. Ibid., 205.

wine-picking time. The Dauphinois boys' morale was very bad and their leaders were blamed for their anti-German attitude. They were said to work slowly and only talk of desertion. The Auvergne boys were more content with their fate, although under certain adverse circumstances they showed some antagonism toward the German troops.[40]

The synthesis for the month of September emphasized in its overview that acts of "terrorism" were practiced all over France but particularly in the Burgundy region. In the Gard, the area most terrorized was the mining basin, where a great number of attacks had been committed against the railway lines, as well as through acts of industrial sabotage. To these campaigns of murder, explosions, fires, armed attacks, and threats, some worker strikes had been added, the first of which had been initiated by the grape-harvesters against the cooperative wineries. The next work action was taken by the coal miners over their hourly compensation, which had taken the form of a work slowdown concentrated in the major coal centers of the Alès basin. These movements were based on demands for increased salaries, but it was reported that the Communists had influenced the situation by advocating that workers undertake a general strike in printed tracts they had distributed. The Communists were also trying to infiltrate the ranks of the rightist party as well as the religious groups. Foreigners were also aiding the cause by distributing a pro-strike Communist tract in Spanish that suggested "the gathering of a national assembly with all the parties of the right and the Catholics." Some refugees from the Spanish Civil War were known to have taken up residence in the Gard.

"Dissident" radio broadcasts from abroad were always very closely followed. There was apparently no effort to control such broadcasts and people took no precautions to conceal the fact that they had their radios tuned in to those frequencies. "In Nîmes in broad daylight in the street you can hear Radio Algiers from a nearby open window and at night it's the same with Radio London." The STO *réfractaires* were joining resistance bands in increasing numbers, and it had been revealed that they had participated in some abductions as well as some armed engagements. It had been reported that air drops by the English were occurring

---

40   ADG. 1 W 42. Contrôle Technique of Nimes Report for August, 1943, marked 170–174.

up in the Puy-de-Dôme for the purpose of supplying various resistance groups.

Events in Russia and Italy had impacted the evolution of local sentiments in the month of September, along with the increase in terroristic acts and the continuation of Allied bombing raids. What was perceived as a state of disarray had led the people to have a tendency to reproach the marshal for this deteriorating situation. For some time prior, he had seemed to have been forgotten, but allusions to him now were more frequent than to the chief of the government (Laval). A fresh outburst of anti-Semitism had been noticeable in correspondence and some new roundups of Jews had occurred. These happenings had not stirred up an outcry in public opinion like before, and the report suggested that accusations of Jewish responsibility for triggering the prolonged war and their involvement in the black market were reasons for this attitude. Such anti-Israelite stances in correspondence were much more written about than in the previous months.

The people's apathy was firmly shaken in the beginning of the month by the announcement of Italy's unconditional surrender (September 8). Immediately, an optimistic hope appeared in correspondence, with the common prognostication made that the war could end in a few weeks. Overall, general satisfaction with the Allied victory was accompanied by sarcastic swipes about the Italian armed forces, which were meant to pay them back for the stab-in-the-back-invasion of France in June 1940. This reaction was fleeting due to the quick countermeasures by German forces in Italy, as well as their swift entry into the former Italian Occupation Zone in southeastern France. The rescue of Mussolini by the German commandos caused a great sensation among the populace.[41] When the effectiveness of the German counteractions was realized, the Gardois registered great disappointment. People questioned

---

41   *The Day of Battle.* Ibid., 244–245. On September 12, Captain Otto Skorzeny and his 108 men made a glider landing in broad daylight on Gran Sasso, an Apennines ski resort only accessible by a funicular lift, and freed Mussolini without much, if any, resistance from the 250 carabinieri assigned to guard him. The Germans flew Mussolini to meet with Hitler, who according to Goebbels "now realizes that Italy was never a power, is no power today, and won't be a power in the future." For all his shortcomings, Mussolini had kept the Jews safe from the Nazis both in Italy and in their French Occupied Zone. Shortly after their meeting, that was no longer to be the case in either area.

why the Allies did not combine their Italian operations with an invasion of France, especially in light of the fact that heavy bombings of airfields and railway lines had occurred at that time in northern and western areas of the country.

Any confidence in a swift ending of the war evaporated, and a new view of a longer war caused further disillusionment among those who were anxious for the Allies to arrive and thereby bring an end to their suffering. In any case, the apparent Russian advances on the Eastern Front had left people indifferent, dashed hopes among the Germanophobes, and fed the fears of people who foresaw the possibility of a revolution in France brought about by Communism. The nationalist element did not conceal the fact that they considered the German army to be a bulwark against Bolshevism's encroachment into Europe. There were only a few comments on the occupation of Corsica by the Allies. Some people, however, did take pride in the island's liberation by Free French forces. The approach of the Allies closer to the hexagon's Mediterranean coastline had revived apprehensions over an invasion of the Midi. The bombings of Paris had forced the English propagandists to seek excuses to counter the high emotions that had been raised over the widespread destruction of urban areas and the many civilian casualties.

Some apologists for the English cited the presence of German pursuit planes and the French DCA anti-aircraft weapons. Subsequent bombing attacks shut up these apologists, who now limited themselves to statements like "*C'est la guerre*" or "It is necessary to finish what we have started." Overall, the Parisians had reacted more sharply to the second attack than to the first one, which had appeared to be an isolated event or the consequence of a mistake. One cannot imagine how quickly the opinions of at least 50 percent of the people were altered. The English seem to have lost much of the esteem the French had felt for them and which had taken great victories to create. Hostility toward the Americans was even more widely expressed, and their daytime bombing blunders were violently criticized with an animosity far above that felt toward the English. There were many writers who dismissed out of hand the efforts of others who attempted to justify such aggressive acts.

The bombing of Nantes helped revive anti-Allied sentiment in the Gard. That opinion was found in many letters, because military targets had not been hit; the proof was that the city was in ruins and the civilian population alone had suffered immense loss of human life: "It is sad to say that the Nantais now understand that these slaughters of civilians do not advance the war aims; they have had enough of cheering on the bombings of Lorient and St. Nazaire." It was reported that the actual or anticipated forced evacuation of certain coastal areas had caused great uneasiness among those who were or could be affected, many of whom feared again to be unwilling participants in another exodus like that of May–June 1940.

The reaction to the first "terrorist" acts had mixed results with regard to moving public opinion. If certain segments saw Communist-led endeavors behind the violence, others tried hard to excuse them as actions by individuals. The rural fires on farms were particularly attributed to acts of vengeance against peasants who were accused of being active participants in the black market. But when these attacks were revealed to be well planned and coordinated, many people were disturbed by this revelation of perceived Communist influence, which added to the great uneasiness about what the future would bring. The reinvigoration of these fears underlined the high level of anxiety that the bourgeois and nationalist supporters of the Vichy regime were experiencing over concern for their future personal safety.

The most enthusiastic Collaborationists were highly worried by threats of murder or attacks, and thereby had a tendency to be proactive in defending themselves and their interests. Others who were slightly less aggressive in nature took different precautions, like moving closer to areas more sympathetic to the Vichy collaborative aims and their National Revolution, or where they could disappear into the general population. The firm conviction that France would not escape a revolution or civil war was confirmed by complaints over what was seen as the pusillanimous reaction by the authorities. "If we had a serious police force, this would not be happening again, but the way in which they conduct investigations, it is no wonder that they turn up no one." The police could not win, as they were also reproached for arresting militants who for a long time had no known personal involvement with politics or terrorists. These feelings gave new impetus to criticism of the government's inertia.

Such fears of revolution were reinforced by how difficult it was to cope with the exigencies of daily life. The managed economy was perceived as inefficient, which added to the general malaise and brought about an opposition that the government was powerless to offset. Citizens felt the government did not understand the problems caused by the lack of interagency communication and coordination. The result was the issuance of regulations that were in complete conflict with one another and led people to think the following: "Not content to do nothing, they sabotage their work and discredit the regime."

The large cities suffered deeply from insufficient supply, and citizens were angry to see a vibrant black market mock their distress levels.

"Everyone makes a fist in their pocket and bites their tongue. But fellows, the explosion will be terrible."

"A violent anger had welled up in the workers against the rich, the peasants, and the public officials who endlessly prattle on about their fight against the profiteers without ever taking any action whatsoever."

"The country is infested with gangsters who openly steal right in front of a complaisant police force and Gaullist city fathers who sabotage the Marshal's work," so said an angry loyalist.

The disproportionate increase between the cost of living and the salaries and wages paid, retirement, and pension amounts offered, etc., stirred up a general discontent. A local transportation association wrote a circular to its membership, which said, "There is no need to emphasize how much the politics of compensation works against social stability. Many of the increases in wages announced are yet to be applied or are so insignificant that they only evoke derision." Both large and small property owners considered themselves very bullied by tax increases, and the practical effect was to diminish their gross revenues, as they, by law, could not pass on these increases to their renters.

The increased level of discontent with government measures was especially revealed in the continuing opposition expressed to the STO labor requisitions. This unhappiness also existed in the syndicate ranks over the Work Charter's false promises. The dangerous attacks on railroad-line guards resulted in many of their duties being turned over to German troops. The families of POWs still in Germany became increasingly bitter, and the majority were against their family members participating in the free work program to which many prisoners had been furloughed. The stoppage of leaves was the subject of a great many negative comments.

The Vichy Information Services were very heavily criticized: "Radio is greatly faulted for its terseness in reporting on news that is important." The inaccurate communiqués on the bombings of French cities were widely deplored. As the press had concentrated their reporting recently on cities bombed other than Paris, the request for news about families and events concerning the capital city was much less. The reporters indicated that they were furious over certain instructions issued them to follow by local authorities.

The Legion's continued inactivity demonstrated the ineffectiveness of this supposed bulwark of Pétain's National Revolution. It lost membership, and in 1942, its activist members had joined the *Service d'ordre légionnaire* (SOL), which later became the Milice.[42] Yet some degree of uncertainty reigned even within that organization: "We are told nothing, and it is ridiculous to leave us uninformed. If it continues I am quitting." Part of this uneasiness was created by the assassination of some of its members, which caused some defections. Others were stalwart and only wrote of seeking revenge. "The blood of martyrs is the seeding of future harvests" wrote a student at the civil servants' (*cadres*) school at Uriage. A discreet propaganda was circulated within the Milice in favor of joining the Waffen SS. In politics, it was noted there were only 167 adherents in the PSF (*Parti social français*) of the Gard. The Monarchists took sides in the arguments between M. de la Rocque and M. Charlet, who were in the Comte de Paris's Secretariat. Some propaganda pamphlets were intercepted from the Socialist Legion.

The Chantiers were in a crisis state of disarray, as departures for its youth to Germany were on the horizon. The morale of the two groups in the Gard, one assigned to work for the farmers and the other working under German supervision, was very low. The young people had exhibited opposition to their rumored departure for work in Germany and had written of seeking revenge, which seemed to have been stirred up by their leaders. One youth assigned to the Todt Organization[43] wrote: "Our chiefs find that we are always doing too much. They are puffed up,

---

42 *France: The Dark Years.* Ibid., 230.
43 *The Unfree French.* Ibid., 116–117. The Todt organization was responsible for large-scale construction projects and employed French labor in France to achieve their aims. Many French workers, some 250,000 by 1944, worked on these projects. Much of the activity was related to building the "Atlantic Wall" defenses against the anticipated Allied invasion of France.

and we are waiting for them." The indications were that many desertions were anticipated and the youth didn't bother to conceal at all their intention to join the resistance.[44]

The audacity of "terrorist" attacks increased without cessation, and group actions were undertaken against the Camps de Jeunesse, which were located in fairly remote areas. These high levels of attacks were the predominant subject of October's intercepted correspondence. It was noted that police operations had managed to hold back terrorist activities in some regions of the Gard. Heightened levels of Gaullist and Communist propaganda were meant to convince public opinion that their sole object was to fight the Germans and the black market profiteers. This effort portrayed Resistance groups as advocates of righting grievous wrongdoing: "In the Haute-Vienne and the Corrèze, the Resistance is the law, and it sets the prices that peasants can charge and defends their requisitions of food for the people and themselves." The general strike effort around France seemed to have failed, and the only serious one took place in the Pas-de-Calais. In other areas, one noted only some lessening of output or sporadic work stoppages. The letters intercepted from political detainees indicated that they had maintained a brave front in order to keep their morale and spirits up. They were self-congratulatory over whatever concessions in their treatment in prison that they said had been granted and often attempted to influence their guards to gain their complicity in efforts to escape.

Shortages in fertilizer, adequate transport, and especially horses continued to contribute to poor food production. The payment of agricultural price supports for commodities that the government promised was very disappointing, and the farmers accused the agencies of being too parsimonious. Both large landowners and small farmers were fearful that the lack of forage for farm animals would have a disastrous effect, and what was available was too expensive and arrived way too late. On the farm labor front, the enforced return of the Italian field workers to Italy was greatly bemoaned. Their labor was very important to crop picking in the Midi and the farmers saw no way in which to find substitutes. It was envisaged that the Agricultural Corporation experiment with wine-for-potato exchanges would be expanded to other food cate-

---

44   ADG. 1 W 42. Contrôle Technique of Nimes Report for September, 1943, marked 182–187.

gories on a much larger scale, including categories such as grains, forage, and dry vegetables. Based on price parity, two kilos of potatoes would be exchanged for one liter of wine. The chestnut crop was reported to be excellent, but the producers criticized the tax for being insufficient. There had been demand for labor from the Chantiers to gather crops in the forest domains. Due to the shortage of animal fodder, substitutes like vine shoots were being sought and small mills were being created to grind them up. Tobacco plants were being cultivated on two hundred more hectares of land. Olive gathering for sweets had been authorized for ninety-five additional tons. The overall olive crop looked promising for producing a good-quality product.

Deliveries of fresh vegetables from sources both inside and outside the Gard were below the prior month. Complaints continued to increase about insufficient supplies and limited variety, although the last five days of the month had brought some improvement. The meat supply was very difficult, as deliveries were only partially met. The official tolerance for the black market only had made things worse. The General Supply Department threatened to cut off deliveries of wine to departments that had not kept food delivery promises to the Gard, due to their lack of controlling their black markets. Fat content rations were only honored in proportion to the grossly inadequate deliveries made. Anticipating a tax increase on potatoes, the produce departments held back deliveries by delaying shipments. Only one kilogram per family was distributed in the last days of October. The local collectives tried to improve food availabilities by working closely with producers, but results were dictated by supply, so prices continued to rise. The average daily milk supply was down, aggravating the already huge deficiency that added to the risk for children and sick people. Egg collections improved, thanks to the sanctions imposed on prior offenders.

Industrial activity continued to be paralyzed in all sectors by the never-ending difficulties in securing means of delivery transportation. Additional problems were caused by the lack of lubricants, raw materials that were indispensable for production, and labor. The poor availability of operating credit also handicapped industries. The complete lack of rubber tied the hands of tire production. A German-French commercial treaty was signed with the Ministry of Production, which reserved to France the entire production of furniture and hosiery, plus some other similar articles. This treaty was seen to benefit in the future the sizeable local hosiery manufacturing industry. The loss of Italian labor had a negative impact on the industrial sector. There was a definite drop in the output of coal from September in the Gard's key mining industry, even though lignite production improved a bit. Because of the lack of availability in the bituminous sector, some industrial plants shut down. In chemical plants, the extensive stocks of copper sulfate more than offset the weak production levels experienced during the month of October.

Small business commerce experienced a general slow-down in its activity, and the wine suppliers protested over the huge allocations awarded to the supply corps. The business was adversely affected in wines over the 10 percent alcohol level, because of the massive purchase requisitions for the German market and the distilleries. The wine business also was hurt severely by the lack of road transport, and railway cars needed to transport liquids. Finally, it was forecasted that this year's wine harvest would be below earlier estimates, and that the late heavy rains experienced would significantly lower the strength of the wine.

Fruit shipments destined for urban centers were down, as the needs of the German operational troops took precedence. The overall tonnage reserved for canning was raised. Aromatic and medicinal plants added important volume. The by-products for food grains also thrived. Significant shipments of wine and fruits went north out of the region to the German troops and the cities, while Source Perrier continued to enjoy good business. Every product destined for use in Germany was allocated to railcars, so shipments left unimpeded, as did Germany-bound supplies of the chemical product aluminum hydrate. The serious transportation problem had grave repercussions on the commercial exchanges. Additional limitations on rail transport were anticipated. Because of the lack of railcars and engines, expeditors held back their shipments. Robberies also happened frequently in railway yards. The shortages in road transport caused by the lack of solid or liquid fuels, tires, lubricants, and spare parts just added to the already aggravated situation.[45]

The November 1943 report stressed a wide variety of attacks around the department. The Armistice Day ceremony was an occasion that ignited various outbreaks of violence outside Nîmes, where the year

---

45   ADG. 1 W 42. Contrôle Technique of Nimes Report for October 1943, marked 189–190, 194, and 198.

before a large crowd in the evening had routed the police and SOL after singing *La Marseillaise* and shouting "Laval to the hangman's post."[46] The presence of German troops in Nîmes one year later certainly had something to do with crowd control. A bomb exploded in Nîmes at the Legion's headquarters, taking one member's life on November 15, 1943. The local resistance movement carried out this attack on the Legion, because they firmly believed that organization was guilty of supporting collaborationism.[47]

Elsewhere in the Gard, particularly in the mining basin, factories and railway lines suffered damages caused by sabotage. Vichy loyalist groups attempted to undertake counteractions against the terrorist bombings, but because the attacks were so uncoordinated, it was very difficult to uncover any organization responsible for such violent acts. The Communists or other resistance criminals were accused of the numerous armed attacks against individuals or small enterprises. But these same resistance groups printed warning tracts that indicated their uneasiness with the resultant disorder that resulted from such poorly planned, haphazard assaults. Some intelligence had been gleaned by the authorities about the recruitment methods of the clandestine armed resistance forces. They were successful in enticing recruits from the STO nominees and the DCA military units: "Our army grows more and more but we must wait a good month or more to train the new recruits for operations."[48]

Public opinion was focused, as usual, on how the lengthy war impacted the challenges everyone encountered with daily living, and the people paid scant attention to outside events (unless seen with their own eyes), which were not viewed as relevant as food supplies, winter home-heating requirements, or the high cost of living. Life's ongoing and increasing difficulties dashed hopes so much that a fatalistic viewpoint was ever more prevalent, and even the most sensational news couldn't make a dent in that outlook: "Morale fatigue grips the people from cares of all sorts as it is hard to find food and the war's prolongation tests the character of the most hearty souls."

Even the marshal seemed enveloped by this general indifference. The

---

46   *Nimes at War.* Ibid., 198.
47   Ibid., 203.
48   DCA (*Défense contre avions*) forces were anti-aircraft batteries manned by the French.

incidents that prevented him from speaking to the nation on November 13 revealed comments from a minority, which showed their complete indifference, even to a situation that had a direct impact on the nation. That statement was revelatory, in that word had reached the people that the Germans had forbidden Pétain to speak on that occasion. We will see in December 1943 and January 1944 that the numbers of Gardois who didn't "give a damn" were more significant than a "minority."[49] The report laid the blame for this prevailing attitude at the feet of foreign radio broadcasts' propaganda efforts, which garnered many more correspondents' "ears and comments" than those made about Marshal Pétain having been muzzled. Rumors about the dismissal of the marshal (we know it was he who had threatened to dismiss himself) were said to have provoked real emotion as anarchy and disorder were feared for France, which the report indicated was caused by the marshal's supposed withdrawal. There were some references to purported actions that extreme rightist groups would take if the marshal were really dropped. The text of the constitutional act that gave full power to Laval was known but rarely commented upon, yet the antagonism that existed between the marshal and Laval, the head of the government, was widely comprehended by the people.

Other acts by the Vichy government seemed to have passed unnoticed, including the dismissal of Mr. Hubert Lagardelle, a syndicalist intellectual whom Laval had picked to head up the Labor Ministry upon his return to power in 1942.[50] Vichy's laws were treated with contempt and the only attention paid to them was how to overturn or circumvent them. The harshest criticism here was reserved for the law on farming leases, land taxes, and the politics of government finances, which all were viewed as a means to bully honest folks and allow dishonest traffickers in the black market to enrich themselves considerably. There were also frequent attacks on the new regime placed in charge of the state schools. Finally, those who favored the Workers' Charter, and the Peasants Corporation complained about the indifference of the workers and the peasants, as well as the underhanded campaign by the heads of industry against the factory social committees prescribed by the charter. These committees did some good but the workers were mostly not interested

---

49   *De Munich a la Libération.* Ibid., 392; *France: The Dark Years.* Ibid., 232.
50   Ibid., 59; *De Munich a la Libération.* Ibid., 193n5.

in them.[51] The evident indifference of the general population was caused by the perception that the government caved in to hindrances of all kinds, acted as though it was business as usual, that times were normal, and lacked energy.

The increasing development of attacks, along with the impunity of terrorist actions and the seeming tolerance by the government of the resistance groups, gave credence to the opinion that one could only count on oneself. Additionally, the majority of writers didn't raise the least objection until those acts touched them personally. It was said that in Burgundy, Corrèze, and Savoie, the terrorists enjoyed an unchallenged authority and were warmly greeted by the people due to the actions they took against the black market profiteers: "It is Vichy who will no longer command in the Yonne [upper northeast Burgundian department], but it will be the Resistance which will reign supreme."

Among the Vichy militants, some conservative ones obeyed prudent counsel while the more activist ones were inclined to fight (with arms) fire with fire, but neither side was disposed to ask for the help of the authorities. Perhaps a reason for this was disclosed by interceptions from the police, which revealed that any aid from them would be illusory as they preferred to come to terms with the terrorists than to fight them. "We don't go out, or we would run into them" admitted one gendarme in a letter. In light of such inaction by the police, some writers hoped that orders to repress the resistance would be assigned to LVF members, who had been ordered back from Russia.

Approximately one-half of Doriot's anti-Bolshevik fighters were found unfit for combat by the Germans and sent home to France.[52] Speaking of the Eastern Front, not many people wrote glowingly or rejoiced in the Red Army's successes, as people generally limited their comments to uttering an opinion that a German defeat was unavoidable. The Allied foreign ministers meeting in Moscow in late November/early December was mentioned; great hopes were cited in that correspondence about it that was interpreted as proof of the high level of anti-German feelings in the Gard. However, the recent speeches of Churchill and Hitler were cited to confirm the opinion that the war would last

---

51 *France: The Dark Years.* Ibid., 297.
52 Ibid., 194.

longer, and that a goodly number of months would have to pass before reaching the end of German power.

The fears of an imposition of Communist rule in France were fueled as much by the growth in terrorism in France as by military events in Russia that seemed to point to a German defeat. Intercepted letters gave high credit to the role attributed to the Communists in North Africa and Corsica for the expulsion of the German forces. In reality, this was of doubtful credence. Some correspondents were appalled by what they considered as reckless naïveté by some people who denied that a Bolshevik peril existed and were still ready to take "the extended hand."[53] However, in light of the reality of this danger, an evolution was noted among several letter writers who indicated that they now considered Germany as a lesser evil than Russia. Many were those who persisted in adopting a wait-and-see attitude on subjects such as this one.

The references to the Anglo-Americans were less frequent in November, due to their slow advance in Italy against fierce German resistance. These were indeed ironic references as their opponents were no longer the Italians. On the other hand, as time elapsed after the heavy Allied bombings of Paris and Nantes, so did the level of angry feelings that had been attributed initially to the heavy civilian casualties caused by these air raids. Although an invasion of the Mediterranean coast was still dreaded, few people believed it was likely to occur. That was not the case for the English Channel area, where many intercepts by the SCT from the Seine area indicated very high levels of fear about an Allied landing. In any case, many people now did accept the fact that an invasion might just be a bad necessity for putting an end to the war. An air attack on Toulon, the ordering of some evacuations of coastal areas, and the announcement on the BBC of further bombing attacks planned on French cities by the Allies, increased the anxiety of the people by the end of the month.

Although the STO departures for Germany had been suspended, the Germans continued to demand French labor for defense projects within France. However, workers assigned to these projects in both the north and south zones complained of the fact that they had few tools

---

53   Robert O. Paxton informed me that this extended hand quotation was an "echo of a famous statement by Thorez in 1936, [which] offered cooperation with other anti-fascist patriots."

and were often just standing around idly doing nothing, while French projects or enterprises cried out for workers. Angry recriminations were recorded concerning the unequal treatment of French youth on standby call for STO duty, should the suspension be revoked. They felt helpless to sort out their future and considered that those who evaded STO were only threatened in a meaningless fashion. Under these circumstances, the youth who met their obligation could not even obtain leave in Germany. "What a perfect lacking of authority," one lamented, and those who had stayed behind in France did everything they could to remain. The difficulty in sending or receiving packages, the refusal to issue proper clothing, the incompetence of the Social Insurance Department, and the suppression of the half-salaries of certain free workers all contributed to the creation of more and more dissatisfaction among the recruits and their families.

Comments were generally unfavorable to French radio and press agencies, in contrast to foreign sources, whose broadcasts were frequently lauded, especially Swiss radio stations. The Legion was experiencing continuing defections. "All month long I see no one there [Alès]." The Gard's Legion chiefs had publicly announced that their organization shared nothing in common with the LVF or Milice. It would seem that its members were fully aware of this distancing. There were social (meaning "charitable") activities undertaken by the Legion still, but there was some friction in this regard, including hostility expressed by the Red Cross against the Legion's efforts. The latent antagonism between the Legion and the Milice had certainly come out into the open this month, and war was declared between the Milice and the Resistance. The situation was not favorable for the nationalist parties. "A wind of defeat blows over the country, and even the PPF seems to be in retreat, lying low with no visible activity." Apparently the JOC (*Jeunesse Ouvrière Catholique*) had been infiltrated by the Francists, who had close ties with the Milice. Oddly, the correspondence between members of the LVF at the Russian front exhibited high morale and maintained a great confidence in a victory by the German army.[54] In the following month of December, a change took place in the person charged with supervising the preparation of the Contrôle Postal Technique (SCT) reports. Now, Inspector

---

54 ADG.1 W 42. Contrôle Technique of Nimes Report for November 1943, marked 194–198.

Third Class Piquet had that responsibility. He changed the reporting design to a significant degree. As only two reports and a multitude of letters exist for the period from December into the first quarter of 1944, it makes sense to take them up in the next chapter.

Opinion in 1944

Apprehensions, Real and Imaginary, Preying on a Stressed-Out Public

"New message in the press from the old Tartuffe [Pétain]: 'Listen to a man who is only there for you and who loves you like a father … I beg you …' Two years ago he was ordering us to obey without thinking or making a whimper. What a fiasco from ordering to begging!" —Jean Guéhenno, December 25, 1943[1]

"We learn new horrors daily. Some young *réfractaires* have been hung in Nîmes and in different villages in the Midi [seventeen at Nîmes]." —Jean Guéhenno, March 24, 1944[2]

"Nothing is more frightening about the terrorists than their purity. What the cowards and the traitors fear in them is just that … The France which seeks refuge in that purity has found again its sense of grandeur." —Jean Guéhenno, March 25, 1944[3]

"On May 27 [1944], an aerial attack on Nîmes, whose rationale has never been explained, resulted in two hundred and sixty-five deaths and more than three hundred wounded."[4]

---

1   *Journal des Années Noires*. Ibid., 376.
2   Ibid., 397.
3   Ibid., 405.
4   *Nimes at War*. Ibid., 242.

"One thing is certain: France could not escape its misfortunes alone and we owe our liberty and rediscovered honor to these young Englishmen, Americans, and Canadians who fight and mix their blood with the young Frenchmen who would not be enslaved." —Jean Guéhenno, June 12, 1944[5]

As 1944 began, the population of wartime France was shaped like a baguette, with small crusty points at the two ends, encapsulating the large mass that represented well over 90 percent of an anxious populace who were "completely disoriented and ready to throw itself, like a lost child, into the arms of those who will bring peace."[6] The two small opposite ends of this familiar French shape represented the Vichy state adherents, like the Milice and the active members of the Resistance. If all the French people represented by this metaphor were willing to face the truth in a mirror, they could only conclude that Germany was losing the war and that loss would be accelerated during the new year by an Anglo-American invasion somewhere in France. This long-awaited event would create a dreaded double front for the German Wehrmacht to face, adding to the inexorable pressure being exerted on them along the wide Russian front. However, there was little doubt about the lassitude, ambiguity, and ambivalence that drove the large majority of Frenchmen as they sought a peace that would not cost them too much in bombardment from the air or from battles on the ground. And in a certain manner, the amorphous center was at the mercy of the two opposing tiny minorities' pressures on them from what became known through effective Vichy propaganda as the terrorist threat, in the form of Maquis groups or, on the Collaborationist side, the Milice.

As December 1943 ended, the Vichy older guard of Pétain and Laval were very strictly controlled by the German authorities, with the day-to-day running of the Vichy security apparatus passing in early 1944 into the hands of Joseph Darnand. He energetically took up the reins of internal security while acting in conjunction with the German police forces in France, with the express purpose of preserving order and preventing anarchy. He improved upon the special section courts started by Pierre Pucheu in 1941, so that "terrorists" could be executed more

5   *Journal des Années Noires.* Ibid., 415.
6   *France: The Dark Years.* Ibid., 535, n25.

summarily, and ordered the French police to work with the occupiers. Since the gendarmes were becoming more unreliable, he appointed dedicated Milice members to positions of importance in the police to give the force more backbone. Darnand's initiatives were supported by the efficacious propaganda efforts of Philippe Henriot, who was attentively listened to by the French in his twice-daily broadcasts from Paris, in which he effectively intoned fear-mongering, anti-Maquis, anti-Communist jeremiads. In March, these two were joined by Marcel Déat, whom Laval had been forced to name as Minister of Labor. By May, sixty-seven prefects or sub-prefects had been replaced with appointees loyal to the collaborators operating under Darnand's control. Angelo Chiappe, now in Orleans, was one of the Vichy loyalists promoted to a regional post.[7]

What the French populace so fearfully anticipated was commenced by the Allied air forces on April 10, a two-week bombing campaign that was concentrated around the major population center of metropolitan Paris, where on the twentieth alone, that raid killed or wounded more than eleven hundred civilians. Marshal Pétain's German minder, minister/plenipotentiary Cecil von Renthe-Fink, as well as Otto Abetz, approved of the marshal's carefully orchestrated visit to Notre Dame Cathedral on April 26 and the luncheon that followed at the Hotel de Ville, to demonstrate Pétain's solidarity with the Parisians who had suffered from the Allied air raids. An approved Parisian paper's headline shouted out: "The Marshal Acclaimed by the People of Paris." It went on to report: "At Notre Dame, the chief of state, President Laval, and members of the government joined in the ceremony dedicated to the memory of the French citizens massacred by the Anglo-Americans."[8]

Pétain made a brief speech to the crowd assembled on the place outside the Hotel de Ville, and perhaps the former myth surrounding his personality was resurrected for a short time, which certainly would have suited the purposes of his German handlers. However, there were contrasting memories from witnesses at the event, and one, from a friend of Claude Mauriac, remembered the impact that the French tricolor flag made on a young mother and her child, which caused them

---

7   Ibid., 530–531.
8   *L'Opinion Française sous Vichy*. Ibid., 298.

to shed tears, as it was the first time the flag had been allowed to fly there since the German occupation of Paris in June 1940. The greater numeric contrast was four months to the day later when de Gaulle, rapturously greeted by the whole of Paris on the Champs-Elysées, cried out: "Ah, it's the sea."[9] By April 28, the marshal was, without doubt, back in his straightjacket when he broadcast a speech on French radio, closely monitored by Minister of Propaganda and Information Henriot, wherein he strongly condemned the terrorism perpetrated by the Resistance.[10]

Even though the actual numbers of opposing forces of resistance groups and Miliciens, with their committed collaborator supporters, were numerically small, their internecine struggles had become increasingly violent. The hostility between the Milice and the Maquis was kept white-hot by the incendiary radio propaganda broadcasts of Henriot. Historian Jean-Louis Crémieux-Brilhac estimated that 30 percent of Henriot's broadcast editorials between February and April 1944 were devoted to offensive denunciations of the Maquis. Some of them were rebroadcast up to three times. The effectiveness of Henriot's anti-Maquis invective was incontestable, and newsreels still exist from that period that attest to his brilliance as an orator. The Resistance took revenge by assassinating him on June 28, 1944.

Henriot certainly had an influence in bringing about an early tragedy for a large Maquis group that jumped the gun in March 1944 on the plateau of Glières in the Haute-Savoie. Some five hundred Maquisards had gathered there to receive British air drops of arms and supplies and to resist probes by a force of Miliciens that Darnand had ordered there to prove to the Germans his seriousness of purpose vis-à-vis the Maquis. Both Henriot on Radio France and Robert Schumann on the BBC helped inflame things. Ultimately, the German command got fed up with inept Milice efforts and ordered more than six thousand of their troops into action on March 24, supported by a Milice force. The fight was unequal and some 150 brave but foolhardy Maquisards lost their lives, with an additional two hundred suspects hunted down and killed by the Milice in the following weeks. Perhaps some other Maquis groups learned a lesson about premature action, but it seems reasonable

---

9   Ibid., 299; *France: The Dark Years.* Ibid., 536.
10   *L'Opinion Française sous Vichy.* Ibid., 299

to conclude that the Glières resisters were victims trapped by the general Maquis desire to obtain arms from British air drops, their only source for significant weaponry.

The Glières incident begs the question: what did the vast majority of the French population feel about the Maquis bands or other fugitives who had increased their operations significantly during 1943. The image of the Maquis in peoples' minds certainly depended on the proximity of their covert activities, and its representation varied over time. The remote Cévennes was an area highly associated with such goings-on for the Gard and its adjoining departments. But the appearance of armed resistance bands there turned out to be highly disturbing to significant sections of the local populace, as its development was unforeseen, which caused the conflicting emotions of sympathy and fear. People's imaginations and opinions were liable to run wild under such unstable conditions, and the opposing forces, both French and German, could use propaganda based on the fear factor to manipulate a confused general public.

We have witnessed how the French press and radio, operating under the adept guidance of Philippe Henriot, used hackneyed and hostile images, especially during 1944, to influence public opinion against resistance bands. The Resistance wasn't very effective in countering this image in their appeal to a people who were currently more hungry and afraid than still worried about their 1940 humiliation. The heavy-handed German propaganda campaign exaggerated the numbers and importance of "terrorist" activities, in order to justify the unimaginable level of violence they employed in their reprisal actions. This armed resistance phase added new intimidations and perils to a public already beset by many difficult years full of fears. Natural empathy for the Resistance groups was strongly offset by wait-and-see reactions and fears that led to antagonism.

These enmities were derived from two sources: one was fed on by Vichy propaganda efforts to transform public opinion about the Resistance, while the other tagged on directly from Maquis activities that affected the local people. The first sought to undermine the Resistance by denigrating their motivations and members while appealing to well-known fears that moved the population. "Suppression of crime and terrorism" were the trite phrases that were repeated daily in the press to drive home Vichy's propaganda methodology, which employed pithy alternatives for variety's sake: "Terrorists, Communist terrorists, Jewish terrorists, foreign bands, criminals, assassins, murderers, Reds escaped from Spanish prisons, international brigades, Communists, anarchists, bearded gangs who prepare the way for the triumph of Bolshevism, criminals, looters, plunderers, thieves, scoundrels, arsonists, villainous bombers, starving pack of pillagers."[11] Playing on more common rural fears, Vichy linked the Maquis with being gallows birds, killing blindly, torturing, putting the countryside to the torch, raiding farms, burning haystacks, robbing banks and tax collectors and tobacco stores, demanding ransom, and robbing the shopkeepers. The bottom line, however, was that Maquis attacks often brought the wrath of the Germans down on innocent civilians, as the Maquisards disappeared into the countryside.

As noted earlier, the contempt heaped by Henriot on the Maquis during his broadcasts at the time of their defeat at Glières was largely based on these terse snapshots, which hardened public opinion against the Maquis. In areas like the remote mountains of the Cévennes, the second descriptive grouping was more effective in building up negative opinions about the Maquis or the faux-Maquis, when bands of STO evaders acted as though they were in the Resistance. We will see surveys and letters denoting how public opinion turned against the Maquis due to their robbery of banks and small merchants and their stealing of food and cars. Rural folk interpreted these acts as banditry by undisciplined STO refugees who needed to provide for their daily needs while being on the lam.

However, if the Germans undertook punitive actions based on reprisals, the surrounding population would often swing back to sympathize with local resistance bands as a result of their absolute rage against the bestialities that the Germans perpetrated. An early resister, Jean Cassou, reported to Emmanuel d'Astier de La Vigerie, the founder of the Libération-Sud resistance movement, "When one visited a village burnt out and pillaged by the Germans, not a single word of recrimination was uttered against the Maquis and the Resistance. You found yourself in the midst of a sort of fierce acceptance."[12] The bitterness against the "terrorist bandits" had some element of superficiality associated with it,

11   Ibid., 303.
12   Ibid., 305, n1.

as the neighboring folk, except for diehard collaborators or committed Miliciens, were, in the depths of their souls, at least tolerant of the Resistance. Ordinary citizens did comprehend that the organized Maquis was committed to ending the war by contributing to the defeat of the hated German occupier.

Pierre Laborie writes that wavering fear could not explain away the fact that the population was moving in the direction of implicit support of the Resistance through the showing of differing types of "solidarity" or intermeshing. Their proximate presence required networks and infrastructure for support to avoid destruction. This he called an objective solidarity that could be observed in how the agents within the PTT were often their willing eyes and ears, and how peasants showed their obdurate nature by refusing to answer questions put to them by the collaborative forces. A second solidarity was made manifest in the direct actions the Maquis undertook. Their varied forms of attack proved the hollowness of the regime, and the counteractions of the Milice and Germans further undermined this despised combination. Posters were hung on walls which described Miliciens who were candidates for assassination. Such acts turned fear to the advantage of the Maquis, especially when the executions were carried out. The fact that the Maquis refused to submit and often was successful in violent actions gave impetus to the public's gut rejection of the enemy.

Public demonstrations that the Resistance carried out in defiance of the Vichy authorities—however short-lived—had a strong influence on the local witnesses who watched them. These manifestations created binding ties with the public, which contrasted with the loss of regard for a disintegrating Vichy. Finally, there were deep mental solidarities that drew upon the traditions of the areas where the Maquis bands were strong. In the Cévennes, an area with a long history of Protestantism and opposition to encroachment, the spirit for resistance was readily at hand. This tradition of revolt against the authorities stemmed from the early days of the Cathar heretics to the Protestant Camisard revolts in the sixteenth and seventh centuries against the Catholic kings of France. From such local solidarities, the timing was becoming riper for the fabric of France in 1944 to be rewoven.[13]

Elsewhere in Europe, the Allied advances continued to squeeze

---

13   Ibid., 306–311.

Hitler's forces. The Red Army had entered Rumania early in April, and on May 17, the German lines finally gave way to the Anglo-American forces around Monte Cassino. A Free French Expeditionary Corps, led by General Alphonse Pierre Juin, fought bravely in this horrific battle.[14] Rome fell on June 4, just two days before D-Day/Jour J took place on the beaches of Normandy. It was not surprising that the level of violence on both sides within France was increasing. Prior to that time, in February and March the Germans conducted raids against active Maquis bands, which resulted in the burning of the village of Ardaillès near Mont Aigoual in the Gard, and the slaughter of sixteen civilians in the commune of Les Crottes in the Ardèche.[15] All this was preceded on March 2 by the reprehensible hangings that took place in Nîmes, where fifteen randomly selected young men from the St-Hippolyte du Fort area were taken back to Nîmes when the Bir Hakeim Maquis that the Germans were pursuing couldn't be located. The Nazis hanged them a few at a time from trees or a bridge to set an example, indicted by what was pinned to a couple of the bodies: "This is how French terrorists die." The hanging ropes were left in place by order of the commander until August 24, just five days before Nîmes was liberated.

But all these atrocities did nothing to stop the continuous beat of actions by the various Maquis bands operating out of the isolated Cévennes. In June and July, there were 216 attacks recorded by the police for the Alès district: 181 robberies; 11 acts of sabotage; 7 kidnappings; 10 assaults; and 7 murders. The vengeance imposed by the German SS Das Reich Division just after the invasion was infamous: 99 "resisters" hanged in the main square of Tulle in the Corrèze, and 642 civilians massacred in Oradour-sur-Glane in the Haut-Vienne.[16] In preparation for the invasion, on May 27, a wide Allied bombing campaign took place over twenty-five French cities. Nîmes, a target of limited strategic value, was among those bombed, where almost six hundred casualties, including 265 fatal ones, resulted. An official reported in June on the lassitude evident in Nîmes and how the populace was "deadened" and

---

14   *The Day of Battle.* Ibid., 472.
15   *France: The Dark Years.* Ibid., 533.
16   Ibid., 546.

wanted it all to end and "to be finished with a situation that had become untenable."[17]

Now let us examine the final two SCT reports available to see what they had determined. We will compare them to some research done along similar lines in Montpellier and Toulouse and then review numerous communication intercepts I found in the Gard's archives from the same period, many of which are cast in a very different color. The cover page for the December 1943 report summarized all the anti-Vichy intrigues for the month and included a letter from a resistance group member to a judicial magistrate and several threatening telephone calls from anonymous callers. Quite a few printed tracts were intercepted during the November/December time frame from groups attached to the French Liberation Committee. Included were:

- "Essor: The Future of Students," No. 1 of December 2, 1943.

- Socialist Party tracts: Liberation No. 153 of November 2 and No. 155 of November 15, 1943.

- Communist tracts: "The Promotion of France's Liberation" and "Against the Looting of French Livestock."

- This report reflected for the first time an attempt by the SCT to quantify public opinion, based on the subjects addressed in the letters intercepted, read, and analyzed during the month of December. This was accomplished at a time just prior to the departure of the extremely pro-Collaborationist prefect, Angelo Chiappe, for a regional prefectural post in Orleans in the Loiret, on February 6, 1944. The raw numbers for the individual letters clandestinely opened and read for the month were 44,205. The numbers that follow each subject indicate the number of references gathered during the month relating to that *italicized* topic listed. Items in **bold print** are the author's emphasis.

---

17 *Nimes at War.* Ibid., 238–242.

General Weariness: 1,278 (Out of 44,205; 2.9% of total)
Due to the war: 771

"The war does not settle anything, neither for people, nor for morale, nor for health [well-being]."

Difficulties of Life: 343

"The most absolute disarray reigns here. The masses become more and more passive."

The Absence of POWs and STO Deportees: 138

"Above all else, we miss Daniel [a POW engaged in the free worker campaign in Germany] who has stayed there for ages. We hoped for a leave for him when he started working free this summer but it never happened and for some time now he has told us not to count on it at all. We fear for him with all the bombing attacks in his area."

Uneasiness: 1352
Due to bombings: 548

"They get nearer as Toulon is only fifteen minutes flying time away. Next time it will be Montpellier."

Evacuations: 49

"Some areas are affected, but soon it will be everywhere. Everyone is shook; no one knows what to do; we are in a trance."

Fear of Invasion: 126

"What will come out of the Churchill-Stalin conference? We are frightened for the upheaval in France that will come from an invasion. When will this nightmare be over?"

Fear of Terrorism: 374

"Each night we fear noises. Fire and blood abound all around. Why not, as no one is punished."

Fear of Revolution: 88

"Bolshevism is coming, and it won't be a French variety. Let's hope we open our eyes before it is too late."

Fear of Denunciations: 13

"It's deplorable that we French sell our fellow citizens to the Germans. Several have been executed already because of this infamy."

Fear of a Long War: 291

"There is vague pessimism all over. A few months back people thought the war would be over soon. Now they think it will last long."

Complaints over the Increase in the Cost of Living: 193

"I am writing about the misery in the villages of retirees, minor functionaries, and people with low salaries. The answer was that my contention had merit and would be studied. Will it lead to an improvement?"

Complaints about Low Salaries and Pay Increases That Arrive Late: 95

"No one has the right to take something away belonging to somebody else. But some people are poor. What can one do to improve their salary? If I were to be the judge, I would willingly lessen their problems."

Uneasiness for the future: 78

"Even though the present is no fun, I fear there is no rest or peace for us even after the war, and I fear civil war will pit Frenchman against Frenchman."

Confidence in the Marshal: 11

"Opinion in Paris seems to turn back to the marshal, but can one bet on opinion, this illogical and changeable rogue of a horse?"[18]

---

18 By this stage of the war the people were making very few references to Marshal Pétain in their letters, and ones critical of him were appearing. Julian Jackson supports this trend with a similar example from the Var for the months of December 1943 and January 1944 during which some 90,000 letters were read

Approval of the Marshal's Attitude: 7

"[Following his being forbidden to broadcast by Hitler] we are fated to find again the Third Republic. Marshal Pétain's attitude is courageous enough. How are we to settle this most grave crisis we have had since May 1940?"

Allusion to his Christmas Message: 4

"I heard such a poignant, courageous, and full of hope message of the marshal's. When will we French understand that we must unite and think only of France?"

Opinion in Favor of the Government: 13

"Laval does the best he can in politics, but no one understands it."

Indifference and Regret to Government Actions and Lack of Energy: 18

"We have Girondins when the Mountain is necessary. The public has no interest in any organizations conceived by Vichy."

Oppositional Spirit: 22

"The miners' thoughts are upsetting to us. Eastern Front successes by the Russians puff up their Red hopes."

Terrorism: 131
Reproaches against it: 61

"[Attacks] they caused some damage but not enough to stop the train service which would have been bad [had the damage been substantial] for a good part of the workers would have been lost their jobs and we don't need that." "They are just bandits under the guise of patriotism." "The real guilty ones are those who train and pay them."

---

by the SCT, with the Marshal only mentioned in 151 letters, of which twenty-five percent were in critical terms, often of his advanced age. We will see the same trend continue in the Gard when we add together the December and January report totals for Marshal Pétain. People were fed up with hunger, lack of heat, and all sorts of frustrations from the four-year long war. *France: The Dark Years.* Ibid. 483.

Excuse it: 17

"Armed attacks increase, and thefts are common and the majorities of people accept, justify, and excuse this situation. How sad and what disarray." "Some deserve what is happening." "You attach an importance to things of little significance that you support. You speak of civil war and it distorts seeing things as they are."

Prudence: 29

"Don't partake of politics. Don't support anyone."

Regret over Reconciliation between Catholics and Protestants: 6

"Abbé Sorel spoke of himself as willing to be shot by his colleagues. That is a condemnation of the French clergy which should not be involved in politics and when it does, always appear foolish."

STO: 121
  Opposition and Criticism: 22

"The most gullible let themselves be taken in but the others slip through the mesh. Is it worth pampering those unfortunate infants to afford them such a future?"

New Fears about Departures for Germany: 24

"At school the kids are worried about a new census for call-up."

Concern over Leave Being Late: 21

"Look at the loyalty of men who call themselves French and who are not afraid to trample underfoot the promises they give to their comrades."

Initiatives or Wishes for Not Returning to Germany from Leave: 37

"There is no reason for wanting to return to Hanover. He would rather work for a German company in France. Why return there to get bombed, and then he isn't even sure that the factory will still be standing there."

Foreign Opinions: 258
　　Anti-English Opinions: 21

"Perfidious Albion follows another purpose which is to keep us down forever."

Complaints about the Bombing Raids: 53

"I cannot understand: why there still are Frenchmen who approve of these collective murders of civilians."

Faith in the Allies: 25

"Let them decide to finish it. Without being blindly confident in Albion, I think thanks to them we will get out of this fix with the least damage."

Critics of Allied Inaction: 81

"It's a pain in the neck that their promise to come is not realized, and they are dropping in my esteem for as strong as they are they could have come this year."

Unfavorable Opinions of all Foreigners: 14

"I have been misled and am totally dispirited, as we masses have all had enough, knowing that we've been toyed with by a clique which controls the world and is looking to tear us limb from limb." "Last year everybody was for the Allies. This year they are not for the Germans, but they say that the English aren't so dear to us either."

Hopes for a New Europe: 9

"We are at the point where the Germans and the French find themselves fused together as one."

Hopes for a German Victory: 6

"I hope Germany wins, which would be the best for our country."

Opinion That the Teheran Conference Will Speed Up the End of the War:
10

"Stalin is pressing for movement. Then who knows what awaits us?"
"Let's hope that the lethargic state is awoken so the war can be vigorously pursued."

Opinions on the Speech of Marshal Smuts of South Africa: 5

"Better to end the war first than to dispute over peace terms." "Smuts has told us some hard truths."[19]

Complaints about the Resistance/Dissidents and Unfavorable Comments on the Algiers Committee: 44

"Dissidence has finished its role, and Giraud and Georges are finished. As for de Gaulle, he is in with the Communists while waiting for them to throw him overboard." "One feels the troubled, hesitant opinion out there. There are military deceptions and the dissidence in the resistance ranks is unsettling."

Miscellaneous

Criticism of the Administration: 24

"Our leaders debate while the situation deteriorates endlessly in spite of the creation of a corps of functionaries who are totally incompetent."

Criticisms of Propaganda Services: 7
"Some real accurate information would be better than all the junk and propaganda on the radio."

Criticism of the Educational System: 35

---

19 Jan Smuts was a South African patriot, statesman, and general who fought against the British (and Winston Churchill) in the Boer War, and later served with Churchill in WWI. He was made a field marshal in the British army in 1941 and knew Churchill so well that Rick Atkinson quotes him speaking of Churchill on page 3 of *The Day of Battle:* "In great things he is very great, in small things not great." He was referring to Churchill's penchant for trivia or small details.

"The children are really behind and have too much inactivity. There appears to be politics behind that situation."

Hopes for the Future: 48

"If the French would begin to show self-respect again, that would represent a renewal of moral strength as the moment approaches to gather around the conference tables. We are searching for a commanding leader around whom to crystallize our hopes."

The Economy.

Olive Crop Satisfaction: 36

"The olive crop is very abundant and the people are ecstatic."

Planting Season under Bad Weather Conditions: 37

"The land is inundated and the poor crops are ruined."

Olive Oil Pressing with a Limited Number of Mills Functioning: 27

"This pressing season is idiotic. These polemics must cease. The mills are overworked and they don't want to accept any more olives. What an embarrassing situation."

Difficulties in Finding Farm Labor: 87

"One cannot find any more workers and the Italians are gone."

Critical Situation for Feeding Livestock and Lack of Horses: 99

"Things are in a pitiful state in the Midi for the animals. I have six horses and nothing for them to eat by the end of the month." "The supply center of Marseille refuses to give me any oats because my milk cows don't produce any milk allotment. If they cannot eat, how can they produce milk?"

Commerce.

Slump Due to No Merchandise Available: 43

"It is an infernal situation as there is nothing to sell. You have to wait, I tell you. If that lasts a few months, there will be a total paralysis."

Wine Business: Influence of Events on the Wine Business in Hard Times for the Domestic Market Versus the Export Market Boom [primarily to Germany]: 19

"Some people are so pressed to have income that they sell at prices below the tax if they can do it. It was to the contrary a year ago." "It is easier to export 50,000 hectoliters than to ship 2,000 within France." [A hectoliter equaled 100 liters.]

Industry

Multiple Hindrances to Industrial Production Including Shortages of Labor, Raw Materials, Electricity, and Coal: 158

"Look how we have been reduced here in labor, it is necessary to ask 'Peter or Paul' and the run around is annoying and difficult." "It is imperative to get the assurance of electricity supplies or close our factories Wednesdays and Thursdays every week. The running of the business is impossible; please indicate our supply levels in December." "Here the situation is getting harder and harder; we jump through rings to operate and there is little or no coal."

Consecutive Drop in Coal Mine Production Due to Lack of Freight Cars: 8

"Today it is even worse, and what is really annoying is that one day there are several cars, and the next none at all. It's horrible that it is so screwed up."

Demands for Coal from the Mines from Factories or Industrial Enterprises in Dire Straits: 92

"Urgently need my December coal allocation."

Factory Closings Due to No Electricity Supplies: [number unreadable]

"The factories will have to close this year." "We're furloughed two days a week as there is no power to drive the motors."

Transportation.

Package Theft: 108

"I don't know if I told you that in an Ardoise railroad station 4 out of 8 employees, including the boss, were jailed for stealing packages. It's a big subject for discussion in the region."

Complaints about the Lack of Transportation Rolling Stock and Concomitant Halting of Railway Line Traffic: 229

"There's no cars to ship anything. There's so few engines that the stations are all cluttered up. We have lots of orders but no means to ship them. All rail shipments are halted until we get new instructions."

Bad State of Road Transport Equipment: 17

"It's a disaster as there are no liquid container trucks because after three years of continual use they are at the end of their usefulness."

Fears of Reductions in Rail Travel: 44

"It is practically certain that soon one will not be able to ship anything, for the engines will be assigned other priority tasks by the people in charge and that will mean that the cities will be denied their food supplies."

Food Supplies

Unhappiness over Resupply of Food Necessities: 212

"We cannot get much and we even still have all our ration tickets!"

Comments Favorable to Resupply: 162

"We are getting enough to eat to get by. We no longer wake up with noisy stomachs."

Satisfaction in the Improvement in Food Resupply in the Gard: 195

"I find it improved for some time now."

Complaints on Late Delivery of Food Supply and the Absence of Products with Fat Content: 390

"We have not had one gram of fat content in November in our household!" "It is very rare to find fat products (*les matières grasses*)."

Complaints about Materials for Heating and Cooking: 80

"We have nothing to warm up our homes."[20]

Statistical Report of Information Gathered in the Postal, Telegraph, and Telephone Interceptions during the Month of January 1944.

This report was drawn up using:

- 15,164 opinions collected from 34,213 letters read

- 782 opinions collected from 47,367 telegrams read

- 1,263 opinions collected from 7,945 telephone communications listened to.

The numbers that accompany the titles of the different paragraphs represent the number of references relative to the subject treated. The opinions cited between parentheses were taken from literary extracts of the correspondences.

Addressees:
Inspector General, Head of the Contrôle Techniques Services, Hotel Thermal, Vichy. Copy No. 1.
Prefect of the Gard, Nîmes. Copy No. 2.
Principal Inspector 1st Class and Regional Inspector of SCT, Marseille. Copy No. 3.
Archives, Copy No. 4.

---

20   ADG. 1 W 42. Contrôle Technique of Nimes Report for December 1943, marked 205–215.

Nîmes, January 31, 1944.
Inspector 3rd Class Piquet
President of the Mixed Commission (PTT)
of the Contrôle Technique of Nîmes.

All anti-national intrigues:
>Tracts intercepted from all resistance groups:
>>"France d'Abord"
>>"Libération" No. 161–162
>>"Front National" No. 1–2
>>"La Marseillaise" No. 2
>>"La Scène Française" No. 1
>>"La Resistance Paysanne" No. 1

Fears of a long war: 417 (291)

"The United Nations and the Axis are both very puffed up and neither one is ready to surrender."

Invasion noises: 94

"The invasion will take place up north and in less than a month after that the Midi will be liberated."

Anglophobic sentiments: 313 (21)

"It's abominable. And to hear that there are people who like them!"

Because of the bombing: 168 (53)

"They have no excuse, and it does not benefit their cause; to the contrary many French people are changing their minds."

Because of Anglo-American inaction: 76 (81)

"They talk a lot but I think they just wait for others to win the war for them."

Those satisfied with Allied actions: 55 (25)

"The news announcements are more and more satisfactory. We follow their advances with great interest."

Germanophobia: 33

"I don't care for the Germans; it's a fact because I see what they are doing."

Sympathetic to the Occupants: 34

"They are very correct. You can't complain."

Unfavorable to all belligerents: 32 (14)

"Neither one is worth a damn."

Admiration for the war effort by the Russians: 17

"It's going well in Russia."

Public Opinion Information:

General weariness, sadness, anxiety over the future: 7,008

General weariness: 2899 (1278)

"Invasion hurry up so one either lives or dies." "It must be finished by all means necessary as the people cannot hold on any longer and that shakes us to our foundations."

Anxiety over the future: 1478 (1352)

"The future is not bright." "I'm waiting for many things to happen as one hopes and fears at the same time."

Fears of troubling times and acts of terrorism: 697 (374)

"These bandits are a prediction of civil war. Can't our leaders rein them in? It is only a matter of time before it happens."

Fear of bombing raids: 952 (548)

"Now it is our turn."

Invasion fears: 741 (126)

"I absolutely don't believe it will happen, but I act like everybody else and I am suspicious about it."

Fears about the renewal of STO call-ups: 201 (24)

"He told me that 400,000 youths are going to be gathered up and I had better anticipate the problem."

Criticisms of new requisitions of labor and steps to take to escape the STO: 264 (59)

"All we hear about are resistant camps, fake IDs, and ration cards, et cetera. What is certain is that the one subject of conversation is about fleeing."

The conflict:

Hope for a quick termination to the war: 549

"We are getting to the purpose: the end."

Terrorism: 476 (431)

"One must be calm and take precautions to hide during a time of terror."

Disapproval: 206 (61)

"All these bands are playing at doing harm, and they operate right under the eyes of the gendarmes without being checked at all, which is unbelievable."

Approval or excuses: 43 (17)

"Here all they await for is the order to march."

Requests for more vigorous repression: 16

"Let's hope that Darnand grabs some of these bandits."

The Chief of State (Marshal Pétain): 35

Approval: 29 (11)

"The humblest or the greatest can carry his grain of sand to our marshal who will drink the dregs of the bitter cup."

The Government: 61

Favorable comments: 8 (13)

"I have been hopeful for some time and feel that we are well led."

Opposition to the government: 39 (22)

"I hope this year the IIII [Fourth] Republic will change all that."

Administration criticism: 74 (24)

"We have enough difficulties without being bored by an idiotic administration."

Complaints about cost-of-living increases, salaries that are too low, and insufficient and tardy increases: 368 (288)

"If this life continues yet a bit we will have nothing. The only things people think about are retirement, salaries, and savings."

Fears about evacuation: 916

"Emotions have run high since this morning, as the newspapers published an official note prescribing the inhabitants in certain coastal areas to evacuate their homes. Although it is happening, everyone here is for not budging. The 1940 exodus was a test that no one wants to take again."

Hopes for invasion and liberation: 134

"We are ready!"

Fatalism: 101

"Our liberators kill us. All the terrorists and Communists are marching. Let's hope that Providence will look out for us."

Disapproval of the dissidents: 44 (44)

"They are all making Marx's bed. They are our Kerensky."

Critics of the propaganda services: 29 (7)

"The papers inform us of nothing. The little that one learns is by word of mouth and the radio."

Favorable comment about Philippe Henriot's radio chats: 15

"It is too bad that he did not reply sooner to the bombast of Radio London and Algiers."

Hopes for the future of France: 239 (48)

"France will rise up; she is synonymous with liberty and justice."

Food supply:

Favorable opinions: 727 (357)

"We see more fresh vegetables nevertheless in the markets than other years."

Unfavorable opinions: 826 (212)

"Our food supply, it is famine!"

Lack of milk, bad quality, and its high cost: 93

"There is not a bottle of milk in Nîmes! The doctor attributes this terrible outbreak to spoiled cans of condensed milk."

Lack of products with fat content and grievances over their non-availability: 736 (390)

"There are many cases of sick people due to lacking fat in their diet."

Criticisms of the black market: 203

"Our town has no food and the administrators have concealed the black market records."

Complaints about inadequate heating fuel supplies: 268 (80)

"For fuel we lack coal. We can scarcely heat the cooking top or stove."

Agriculture:

Difficulties in obtaining seeds, fertilizer, and the bad state in finding any agricultural materials: 44 (38)

"If we don't get seeds soon, it will be too late. We've done the sowing but what will be the result without the fertilizer? We can't find replacement tools or get the money to repair the broken ones."

Lack of labor: 64 (49)

"How can we succeed if they take away all the men?"

Lack of forage: 42 (99)

"Even with good credit, it is not to be found."

Complaints about requisitions, taxes, and regulations: 41

"Soon they will oblige us to give them more than we reap!"

Industry:

Difficulties in obtaining raw materials: 103 (82)

"We can't complete a project as the supply problems paralyze us."

Lack of coal and electricity: 71 (33)

"The factory is closed for lack of coal. The closure days due to being without any electricity put sticks in the wheels so that activity is very weak."

Lack of means of transportation: 33

"No transport means we are paralyzed."

Lack of personnel: 62 (43)

"We get complaints all the time from being handicapped in our lack of workers."

Commerce/Business:

Supply difficulties: 90 (43)

"For our business, we are in a terrible state with absolutely no materials to make the goods."

Concerning transportation means: 56

"Due to the real world inability to find railway cars, it is useless even to take orders."

Reaction to working only three days a week: 14

"We close two days a week, but I don't understand that measure as there is no improvement."

Complaints about little transportation and voyage difficulties: 460

"No more way to travel, and it looks like there will be no trains scheduled."

Slow traffic: 386 (229)

"There's no transport, as the rail lines are cut."

Stolen merchandise: 154 (108)

"Those we receive are always pillaged."

Irregular postal delivery: 88

"Lots of correspondence never arrives."

Shipping cost increases: 46

"Shipping is becoming unaffordable."

Financial news:

Devaluation of the franc and inflation: 26

"Better to spend it today while it is still worth something, as tomorrow it will be worth less or nothing."

Confidence: nothing to report

Military information: nothing to report

Information on foreign affairs or interior investigation: nothing to report.

Information on the Chantiers de Jeunesse:

Uneasiness over its dissolution: 12

"It is as much to say that the Chantiers equals the STO."[21]

Six months later, at the end of July 1944, the nearby SCT in Montpellier issued a report showing citizen opinions/concerns for the Hérault Department, which included material drawn from 93,721 letters, read surreptitiously. From these they had derived 86,759 opinions based on the format and method of tabulation they employed, which was most likely not exactly the same as Commissioner Piquet's.

---

21 ADG. 1 W 42. Contrôle Technique of Nimes Report for January 1944, marked 35–44.

Concern	Number of Opinions	Percentage
Fear of Bombing	25,175	29
Food Supply	24,661	28.5
War Weariness	15,145	17.5
Transport	7,019	8
The War	5,603	6.5
Invasion	4,999	6
Terrorism	2,001	2.3

In the larger city of Toulouse, which is in the Haute-Garonne Department some two hundred kilometers to the northwest, the results were very analogous to those listed above for the same time period, based on 123,440 letters analyzed and 91,633 concerned opinions formed.[22]

Concern	Number of Opinions	Percentage
Food Supply	24,281	26.5
Fear of Bombing	17,574	19.2
War Weariness	8,788	9.6
Invasion	5,796	6.3
Opinion of Belligerents	5,478	6
Terrorism	4,406	4.8
The War	3,608	3.9
Pessimism	2,900	3.2

Let us now compare the concerns that were uppermost in the minds of the Gardois in the periods for which we have quantitative reports, December 1943 and January 1944. The Hérault Department is just east and contiguous to the Gard, and its economy also was largely based on viticulture. The more densely inhabited Haute-Garonne was more urban-dominated, in that Toulouse's population represented nearly 50 percent of the entire department's inhabitants. Different criteria obviously were used for the compilation of the three area report summaries of key concerns.

---

22   *L'Opinion Française sous Vichy.* Ibid., 318–319.

December 1943		January 1944	
Concern	Number of Opinions	Concern	Number of Opinions
Uneasiness	1,352	Weariness	7,008
Weariness	1,278	Invasion	1,657
The War	771	Food Supply	1,553
Fear of Bombing	548	Pessimism	1,478
Terrorism	505	Terrorism	1,173
Food Supply	374	The War	966
Transport	229	Fear of Bombing	952
Invasion	165	Transport	460

The ranking of concerns varies slightly, but the overall worries in these three areas, all of which were departments in Vichy, are consistent. The length and fears directly associated with the war are four commonalities (weariness, fears of bombing and invasion, and war in general), and the vicissitudes of living under these conditions are two others (food supply and transport). Terrorism and pessimism have a relationship with future fears of what would happen to France in the aftermath of the war, as the Communist Party had been and still was a factor in these areas of France. In the Gard reports, another factor stands out like a sore thumb. Among the 78,418 letters read in these two months, along with the 47,367 telegrams and at least 7,945 intercepted telephone calls that were enumerated only for January, there are only forty-six total references to Marshal Pétain. This does not mean that all people detested him, but it does indicate that he no longer was the imagined force of solidarity that he or his image had been earlier in Vichy's four-year history. The Gard's concerns were predominantly associated with a list of anxieties caused by a war that was not yet over, the end of which was foreshadowed by a coming invasion that would be aided by a growing resistance movement. It is also telling to reflect that the total number of references to the Vichy government in these two months was only 113, of which 81 percent were unfavorable.

I have tried to present the SCT reports in an unaltered fashion, but it is highly probable that the SCT analysts in Nîmes wrote portions of their reports with it foremost in their minds that their prefect, Angelo Chiappe, was a committed Collaborationist. However, the true cares of the Gardois can certainly be recognized in these and earlier monthly reports. An editing, from time to time, also can be identified as something meant to appeal to Chiappe, which often appears obvious. For comparison's sake, I would like to finish this chapter by drawing on some 111 letters, telephone call transcriptions, and telegrams I uncovered from late 1943 up to and including the first months of 1944, which are unedited and revealing in the various apprehensions illuminated. Most but not all of these citizens were ignorant that Prefect Chiappe would be moving early in February 1944 to his new regional post based in Orleans, which he very much coveted. As we know, he would return to Nîmes under arrest following the liberation of France, to be placed on trial for collaboration during the period referred to as the *épuration* or purge.[23]

1. One telephone conversation described steps recommended for protecting significant wine stocks in the event of an actual **invasion** by Allied forces that might cause widespread destruction in the environs of Nîmes. An insurance agent suggested to the wine owner an indemnification policy that might cost up to five thousand francs every three months to insure the owner's wine against "risks of war," with a 1.25 percent incentive in the event of no claim. Business went on in spite of fears associated with the war, in this case a possible invasion.[24] Jan. 1944

2. A Nîmois replied to a friend in Montpellier that he thought both areas might be **evacuated** but in spite of keeping a valise packed, he had no idea where he could possibly go in the midst of winter. His letter ended by noting that an announcement had appeared, indicating that all males between the ages of eighteen and sixty might be called to report to the camp of Massillan to await events. He likened having to report there to being a prisoner and wondered what had happened to their beautiful France. Jan. 30, 1944

3. Another Nîmois recounted the poor level of provisioning avail-

---

23 *Nimes at War.* Ibid., 245

24 ADG 1 W 40. The vast majority of communications that appear in the following forty pages come from this file folder. Individual words in **bold** font tie into the major concerns mentioned by the departmental populations cited in the SCT summaries referenced on pages 210–211.

able and the high prices (380–420 francs per kilo) demanded for goose, declared "freely available" by the government, which only the rich could afford. The rumors of an imminent forced **evacuation** due to an Allied **invasion** in the south caused consternation among the citizens, as did the fear of **bombing attacks** because of a recent air raid over Montpellier. In consolation, he would eat his dried vegetables and potatoes before they spoiled. Jan. 1944

4. A writer despaired over her young daughter's school being occupied by the **Germans**, which caused the students to be spread out all over their village. The villagers, however, especially the children, were overjoyed by the celebrations attendant to the Tet festival by the Twentieth Indochinese Company that was located there. The playing of French military airs by the band during the three days of celebrations was uplifting to everyone's spirits. Jan./Feb. 1944

5. One Nîmois feared for his son, who planned to march in a parade in a nearby camp named Le Blanc, because the camp had previously been attacked by **"terrorists"** and the apprehension was that they would strike again. His daughter had met some German troops in town, and he sympathized with them and wished the other citizens would not treat them as pariahs. His fears indicated some concern for the fate awaiting collaborators. Jan./Feb. 1944

6. A deep feeling of gloomy **pessimism** for the future of France was revealed in a letter written to a friend on the coast near Spain. This Gardois feared **evacuation** orders and the placing of all men up to age sixty into a local concentration camp by the Germans. Phrases like "catastrophes, one more terrible than the other or blood and fire" abounded, along with the imploring of heaven to save them from these fates worse than death. **Terrorists** were also decried for their bombing attacks that broke storefront windows, which could kill innocent civilians if they coincidentally were walking in front of such a location. Jan./Feb. 1944

7.   In a telephone conversation between two people in Nîmes and Alès, the subject touched on **evacuations** ordered in areas where the Germans anticipated Allied **invasions**, and the point taken is that these evacuations had not improved the availability of agricultural labor. The conversers were dismayed that requisitions from the remaining agricultural labor pools were increasing to meet German demands for French labor to work on German defense projects within France. The conversation ended with one person stating he was going to Marseille to ask Vichy to intervene to help keep agricultural workers on the job, as he viewed the result would be a more disastrous situation for food supply if this trend was not reversed. The likelihood of this gentleman succeeding in his wish would have been very doubtful. Jan./Feb. 1944

8.   A correspondent in Alès was affected by the **fear of bombardments** but especially by **terroristic acts**. He wrote he had visited a family whose parents were murdered by some "Spanish terrorists" but "feared what will become of everybody under such dire circumstances, where the situation gets worse every day and life is very uncertain." Feb. 1, 1944

9.   Another correspondent wrote that the situation was calm where he lived except for some **terrorists**. However, his current visitor, M. Jean, the president of the Legion, and his brother-in-law had just returned from Paris and Vichy and told him that orders were about to be issued to **evacuate** all areas in the Gard within twenty-five kilometers of the coast. Should this agonizing event actually happen, the writer felt that he need not be displaced. Jan./Feb. 1944

10.   A resident of St-Jean-du-Gard wrote that an acquaintance's truck was stopped by a **terrorist** Maquis band between there and Alès. The band requisitioned all the meat they were delivering and all their tobacco rations, which they had paid for the month of February. They also demanded to look at the identification papers of all people in the delivery car to make sure there were no members of the Milice among the passengers. The writer humorously stated that he would go tomorrow to

St-Jean to ask the man who was robbed for some cigarettes.
Jan./Feb. 1944

11. M. Cabon of Nîmes penned a complaint about the organized
     bands of *réfractaires* on the loose that **terrorize** by pillaging,
     robbing, and murdering, so much that one does not need to
     have a curfew imposed in order to stay locked up at home for
     self-protection. He blamed their organization on Communist
     leaders who turned them into thieves and assassins who did
     their bidding, so that France succeeded in falling lower than it
     was during the abysmal time of defeat in the summer of 1940.
     He ended pessimistically by indicating that there was no one
     who could get the better of them. Jan. 30, 1944

12. A former supporter of Marshal Pétain and current admirer of
     Philippe Henriot's daily broadcasts lamented that the dissidence
     (resistance movements) had brought the country to its knees
     in these current unhappy times. The writer's lady acquaintance
     did not wish to leave Nîmes for the countryside in Chassagne
     for **fear of the Communists** who dominated the surrounding
     area in the Corrèze. Jan. 31, 1944

13. A grippe epidemic was mentioned that had been particu-
     larly deadly for some older people, and the writer saw in it a
     metaphor for the destruction that would happen when the
     United Nations arrived to save their area of France. He had
     received late delivery of a postcard sent from an East Prussian
     stalag, where a relative was a prisoner of war, that indicated
     how low the prisoners' spirits were and how poor the diet was
     on which they had to survive. The fear of what would happen
     to the prisoners in the midst of the approaching Russian offen-
     sives was very evident. Another dread apparent in the Gard was
     caused by the rumors concerning **evacuation**. The sabotage
     attacks were mentioned as happening off and on in the mining
     areas and were attributed to well-organized Communist efforts,
     but the concern was that they represented the calm before the
     storm. Jan. 1944

14.   The writer was asked his opinion of the English in light of their recent bombing raids. He labeled them "bastards," based upon his experience in the 1918 war, when he felt they were only out for themselves. He went on to say that France could only count on itself. He mentioned the forced **evacuation** of coastal areas from Béziers to Aigues-Mortes of women, children, and aged persons in anticipation of an Allied **invasion**, which he said would head up the Rhône Valley. He mentioned that food supply had improved a bit but coal or wood for fireplace burning, as well as cooking gas, was all but nonexistent or too expensive. Jan./Feb. 1944

15.   A Gardois wrote a friend in the Ardèche to ask if he could come there to stay with him if the **evacuation** orders that had recently been posted were invoked and enforced. He reported that the police had forced the residents of Grau-du-Roi to evacuate that Gard fishing port. He stated that he would not leave his home unless obliged to do so by the authorities, but had heard that the food rationing cards were taken from people who refused to leave. The evacuation announcement indicated that their destination would be around St-Hippolyte-du-Fort. He did not believe that any **invasion** would occur on the shores of the Gard, but admitted that everybody was in a great state of worry over such a possibility. Jan./Feb. 1944

16.   A youthful member of Lasalle's Maquis wrote friends how they went to block the route of a purported column of Milice that had come to punish the resistance groups based around that section of the Cévennes. The "cowardly" Milice never came, but that did not lessen the triumphant parading of armed and uniformed militants in the streets of Lasalle later that night, in a protest to honor some of their fallen friends at the recent Aire de Côte action. The missive ended with "Long live Free France, De Gaulle, and the Maquis." Feb. 2, 1944

17.   A second evader from the **STO** from the Bouches-du-Rhône had a far different attitude in contrast to the prior writer, as he wished only for a return to normalcy. He was not interested in resisting, only in avoiding the STO, perhaps by returning to

employment in the mines or by joining the police, if he could succeed in having strings pulled in his favor. In any case, he felt that by March, he would have to move again to avoid a worsening situation. He noted that youthful Maquis elements prowled all around, and the **Milice was afraid to come**, and that hostages might be taken. While observing there was new legislation relative to French labor employed by the Germans in France by the Todt organization, he did not find it very reassuring. Feb. 1944

18. A resident of Lasalle described the events that started at the monument to the First World War dead with a moment of silence, followed by a jubilant parade and wild celebration that lasted from 10:00 PM to 3:00 AM the next morning. The young **resistance militants** were enthusiastic about being armed, but the citizen felt they were as yet poorly trained, and he deemed them most happy to be able to move about freely. However, the remark was made that the crowd seemed as large as any prior July 14 national holiday festivity. Feb. 1944

19. A telegram addressed to the mayors of Aubais and Calvisson requested lodgment for two families with children from a M. Baille in Aigues-Mortes, who was trying to help out these **evacuees**. Feb. 4, 1944

20. A telex from Nîmes to Paris confirmed the arrival of plentiful shipments of fruits and vegetables there; while in Alès, only some fruits arrived but very few vegetables were received. Feb. 4, 1944

21. A member in Nîmes of Doriot's anti-Communist party, the PPF, wrote a higher official in Passey, Haute-Savoie, that he had been meeting with the canons of the Cathedral of Nîmes, as well as various priests in the diocese, to encourage them to support the Party. He reported that their bishop, Monsignor Girbeau, had recommended that they avoid politics, but the priests were for the marshal, and many supported the PPF, while there were some few elements who were anti-Collaborationists. The correspondent stressed that he had **pushed**

the Party's anti-Communist stance, as the clergy considered Bolshevism to be their most terrible adversary. A certain Jean Hérold-Paquis [a well-known Collaborationist journalist] was coming to give a conference, and the writer would distribute invitations to the priests who had shown interest in supporting the Party. Feb. 2, 1944

22.   A student in Nîmes, in what would have been the military call-up class of 1945, informed an acquaintance in the Haute-Garonne that he and his classmates were doing the minimum studying possible, spending time in the cinemas and/or playing billiards while **waiting to join the Maquis in order to avoid the STO.** He indicated that most of the class of 1944 already had taken this course, and his class would be next to "be among terrorists, Communists, thieves, pillagers, murderers, and God knows whom else," but all manner of good living based on a cornucopia of supplies, and even women, were there for the taking. Optimism reigned in his soul. Feb. 4, 1944

23.   A young man was dismissive of people whom he labeled idiots because their only concern was about their stomachs and well-being. He was pessimistic about peace coming in 1944, as progress was too slow. He noted that people in Montpellier were fleeing to the Cévennes for safety, and that Grau-du-Roi was also deserted due to the **evacuations.** He was aware that Chiappe was leaving to become the regional prefect in Orleans and wondered if that event caused some people to worry about their futures without him, as his replacement was not yet announced. However, he felt that Chiappe had no regrets about quitting Nîmes and suspected the feeling was reciprocal from the Nîmois. Feb. 1944

24.   A mother wrote her relative expressing her inquietude about her sons having **to cope with the new STO regulations,** which she thought would affect one million more men between the ages of eighteen and sixty. She fretted over being unable to advise them of what course to follow and regretted the uncertainty surrounding her sons being unable to take their baccalaureate examinations. Finally, she and her husband chose to be

in accord about the fact that their children should obey the law. She expressed regret concerning the announced departure of Prefect Chiappe, as she worried about the loss of his influence on the occupying authorities. She closed, noting that the family priest had offered a sermon addressed to the youth who might have to go work for the Germans, which she found very moving in how it touched upon their expected suffering. Feb. 1, 1944

25. A woman in the small Cévènol village of Sainte-Croix-de-Caderle wrote a friend about how dangerous the environs were between there and Lasalle due to the bands of **armed terrorists**, or as her friend preferred, *réfractaires*, that were out and about on the routes. She said that the gendarmes were so afraid after the recent Lasalle demonstrations that they would not even raise a little finger in resistance. She prayed for a return to stability in the country so that one could hope again for the future. Feb. 1944

26. A lady from Nîmes who lived near where the prison was situated was returning from the cinema on Friday night at 10:30, and noticed four suspicious-looking men hanging out on the corner, which gave her cause to be fearful. The next day she heard of **the escape of the twenty-six prisoners and the abduction of four police agents**. Things had become lively late that night, as both the French and German police circulated around the quarter frequently but could find nothing. The writer was concerned that this was just the beginning of difficult times. Some people were exultant over the escape, while others were made very uneasy about the future. Feb. 1944

27. Another correspondent related the details of the escape of the prisoners, who she said were aided in their breakout by an inside jail keeper. The four police agents were found naked, as their uniforms were stolen for subsequent use by the men who set the prisoners free. The writer predicted this would mean **civil war**! She also complained about the **bombings** of nearby Midi population centers and feared that Nîmes would soon join the list, which would cause citizens to flee the air raids. She lamented that German rail workers must come to get their French coun-

terparts to do their duty, and she was still an avid **supporter of the marshal**, whom she said the people had deserted and no longer listened to. He had saved so many lives by signing the armistice and ending the war, but now it would start up again for a long time and **France would become a terrible battlefield,** where no one was to be spared. She pitied the poor, unappreciated marshal who had been so patriotic and devoted to France. She knew how active the resistance movements had been in the Haute-Savoie and Savoie departments and categorized those areas as being under siege by the Germans, with no one entering or leaving, and hoped that the Maquis, which had been **terrorizing** the people, would be destroyed. Feb. 7, 1944

28.   The wife of a police inspector charged with outside investigations was fearful that her husband was in danger. She stated that he was being observed by those groups responsible for **terrorism** and pleaded with M. Maurice Therault in Vichy to have her husband reassigned to an office post for his safety. She maintained that events worsened with each passing day in Nîmes, and the date of this letter placed it just after the date of the large-scale evasion from the central prison. Feb. 9, 1944

29.   A letter from near Alès was full of uneasiness over the overt demonstrations and manifestations of what the writer called the Gaullists around there and the neighboring towns of Lasalle and St-Jean-du-Gard. In his town, the armed and uniformed young members of the Resistance marched in good order one night under their colonel, singing patriotic songs, before observing a moment of silence for their comrades who had fallen the year before in the Aire de Côte. They operated each night in the vicinity of Lasalle with impunity, and the fearful gendarmes were powerless in their presence. In St-Jean, the police station was barricaded even in daytime, and the police only went out with their revolvers drawn and always in groups, never alone. No one went outdoors at night, as the police could not protect them. **All those who were collaborators or Miliciens—in short, anyone who was not a Gaullist—received a small replica of a wooden coffin with a noose inside.** Those who

received them in St-Jean include Deleuze and Dordarier, the mayoral secretaries; Laval, whose truck had been stolen by the Maquis; old Larguier, the peasant from Fumades who sold eggs at twenty francs each; Captain Perrier, Commandant Malaval, and others he didn't recall. "I don't know what to make of it, but I am afraid it will end badly like in the Haute Savoie, for example. It would suffice to send shock troops to Lasalle but who knows what would transpire after they would leave. On all the routes leading in the Milice stop all the passers-by; in brief, we are like in a **state of revolution**." Feb. 8, 1944

30. A telephone conversation between two Nîmois covered actions purported to have been taken against the resistance in Nîmes by the Milice, which these two men applauded. They discussed how of seven men recently arrested, three had escaped from the central prison, and the remaining men were all foreigners, Polish or Russian, etc., but not Spaniards, to their surprise. The afternoon of their conversation there had been a **terrorist caught by the Milice** behind St. Paul Cathedral, and two grenades and a weapon had been confiscated. They wished that type of action would be taken against the resistance groups operating around Lasalle and Bagnols and talked resolutely of wanting to join authorized groups like the PPF, the PSF, or the Francists in any such punitive moves. One asked the other to volunteer, as he had no fear. Feb. 8, 1944

31. **A *réfractaire* wrote from Lasalle** that he considered himself almost accepted by the Maquis to join them in wide-ranging actions, after having witnessed a lot. He was disgusted by the peasants' actions in refusing to sell to them anything. He said their cows didn't give much milk, and they only had two small pigs that they would only sell at astronomical prices. He was happy to hear that one of his fellow *réfractaires* "requisitioned" one of these pigs. These peasants sold potatoes for twenty francs a kilo and eggs at fifteen francs each, and he estimated they had made "two or three millions since the war began." The evaders have "promised" to visit the peasants again soon. He was disappointed that these peasants didn't treat them better, as they

were only four refugee families, which was not too much to complain about from his point of view. Feb. 9, 1944

32.   A doctor's daughter wrote from Anduze on February 10 that the roads were unsafe due to all the **bandits operating with impunity**. She reported that on the prior Sunday, a truck and an auto both had been stolen from M. Laval of St-Jean, and yesterday, 1,600 liters of olive oil had been confiscated from the owner of the Trabuc Mill in Mialet. She accompanied her father on a house call in the countryside at 7:00 PM and was fearful all the time, but nothing transpired. Another doctor would go out at night only if it was a question of childbirth. The husband of Mme. Roumegous had forbidden her to ever leave the house at night. That seemed to be good advice, as M. Roumegous was the regional and departmental leader of the Milice, living in Nîmes, and whenever he visited Anduze, he always was accompanied with a good guard that he had set up. Feb, 10, 1944

33.   On February 12, two Nîmois, who approved wholeheartedly of the efforts undertaken by the Milice to counteract the Resistance, were in a conversation on the telephone, and the call initiator spoke guardedly about an "important personality" who would be announced soon and who **would continue the Milice's "formidable work."** They talked in admiration of their former prefect, Angelo Chiappe, and the man who knew the inside information, which he would only divulge in person, said that "Angelo will be happy" upon hearing it. The person called answered "that Chiappe had phoned that morning and invited him to visit him in Orleans." Feb. 12, 1944

34.   A Nîmois corresponded with an acquaintance in Vichy and wrote that they most certainly would be in agreement about the announced free distribution of the texts of speeches made by **Philippe Henriot, Vichy's Minister of State for Information**, which frequently were delivered via radio broadcasts. The writer felt that Henriot should have been appointed to his current position long ago, but he went on to indicate that he and more than one hundred Nîmois were disappointed that

day when they visited the Information Center, where they were told the notebooks containing those speeches were not available. He asked his **friend in Vichy to visit Henriot's office** to alert them about this distressing fact. Feb. 1944

35. A mother in Nîmes wrote her daughter in Paris what she had heard about the purported **evacuation** of Grau-du-Roi, which was that a train was dispatched by the French authorities, but it returned empty as the people refused to leave. The next rumor was that the angered authorities would order the residents to leave with only a maximum of thirty kilos of luggage, instead of with their furnishings that were said to have been allowed before their refusal to leave. She informed her child that her father listened faithfully to Vichy radio and **subjected the family to lectures concerning Henriot's perceived wisdom**. She ended her letter by informing her daughter, "that is, at least, a compensation for not being at home in Nîmes." Feb. 10, 1944

36. A resident of Bagnols-sur-Cèze replied to a friend who lived in Marseille that although there were empty rooms for rent, the owners refused to accept people who were being withdrawn from coastal areas unless they were forced to comply with an order to **evacuate**. "Since our department was not under such orders, one could not oblige these bad French people to welcome refugees into their lodgings. There were vegetables to be found here, but meat was hard to get, and fats were even rarer and we had none in December, and in January the weekly allowance was only 125 grams of olive oil. We can only anticipate more bad days to come and only idiots believe that the Allies will provide us with everything we need. **I say what Philippe Henriot says: 'Why are they awaiting to invade us if the Germans are so down the drain?'**" Feb. 16, 1944

37. A resident of Pont-St-Esprit wrote of sensational **terrorist** endeavors in her town. First, over Friday night, gasoline was robbed for the second time from "mother Gurs," right from under the noses of the gendarmes who were right next door, and "no one saw anything!" Second, at 6 AM the day before the terrorists stole 700,000 francs from the post bank, and

they took the motorcycle of Dr. Vleu as well. He was surprised to find it the next day where he had left it, with a note from the terrorists, which contained a 5,000-franc bill that he was instructed to keep in compensation for its use. The gas had also been topped off in the cycle's fuel reservoir. The writer expected that the doctor would not leave his motorcycle outside his door anymore, though. Feb. 1944

38.   A Nîmois indicated to a correspondent that new military orders had been issued, effective the next day, which would only add to their miseries. The coastal zone would be under German control like in the north of France, and the brief note ended with the observation that they all would be wise to lay in extra provisions in anticipation of bad things to happen, like **an invasion**. Feb. 14, 1944

39.   A young **member of the Milice in Nîmes** wrote to his girl-friend's father, a resident of Monaco, about his daily activities, which included patrolling in the countryside, arresting suspects, and guard duty. He had so much duty that he apologized for his brevity of communication. He went on to say that he and the daughter were taking instruction in oral presentation from the leader of the Milice and each participant must choose a subject. The one he had chosen was "Monaco, the shame of the National Revolution," and he requested that his correspondent gather some precise data for use in his argument, such as "**to know what incited the prince to make his country into a jumble full of spies, Jews, and English**." Feb. 1944

40.   The curé of Lasalle wrote a friend about the rounding up by the reinforced gendarmes of a band of *réfractaires* who had been led by a dangerous local **bandit,** whom other *réfractaires* had rejected as a pillager and robber of local farms for his own personal profit. This individual, Léopold Fougairolle of St-Bonnet, was captured along with his wife, two of his three sons, and some other stooges, without any effusion of blood, "Thank God!" Subsequently, some other members of the band were arrested and the search continued. This was the latest happening in Lasalle, which otherwise was peaceful and quiet. He

mentioned by name two men who resided in the Pas-de-Calais, who evidently were known to his correspondent, indicating that one had left and the other was ready to go at the first signal. This Protestant curé, a man of peace, said no more. Feb. 1944

41.   A young man wrote his sister from prison in Nîmes, reproaching her for hurting his self-respect by **accusing him of not being patriotic enough**, but in the sense that he did not support Vichy. He refuted her by asking if the people she cited had really done their military duty, as he had in 1940, when he had been awarded the Croix de Guerre with citation. He and his comrades had suffered low morale as a result of the debacle, but they were uplifted by knowing they had fought for ideals in which they believed, and their suffering strengthened their patriotism. He admitted he was imprisoned for fattening up some corrupt functionaries but blamed it on the rotten society in which they lived. Yet he regretted that he was imprisoned inside while comrades he knew on the outside struggled on, risking their lives. He ended by writing that he was anxious to fight again in the service of France. Feb. 15, 1944

42.   A report of activities of the LVF branch in Nîmes was cited for the period January 25 through February 10, 1944: The local population was very alarmed over the eventuality of **an invasion** as well as local **terrorist** attacks in Nîmes and around the Gard. "Our enemies are in the driver's seat, and we only wait each day for new attacks. In politics, there is even hostility, jealousy, and dissent among national parties of similar outlook like the PPF, Francists, and others. This is in contradiction to the union that is so wished for by the French." In social and work questions, there was growing discontent among the working class over the fact that nothing had been done to ease the high cost of living. Feb. 11, 1944

43.   On February 15, a Nîmois wrote a friend in Grenoble that the departmental vice president of the Legion, M. Silhol, who had kindly given them some wine last December, had been assassinated that morning in his mayor's office in St-Hippolyte-du-Fort. Everybody was upset upon learning this news, and his

father was very sorry as he considered him to be a classy person. Evidently, **some terrorists** came down to do it. "You cannot be sure about what tomorrow will bring." Feb. 15, 1944

44.   Two Nîmois conversed on the phone about the Gerard **Silhol assassination**, which took place about 10:00 that morning, calling it horrible and lamentable, and that although Silhol had received threats, he reputedly did not know his assassins. The call terminated with both parties calling it a disgusting and cowardly act. Feb. 15, 1944

45.   A correspondent in St-Hippolyte-du-Fort wrote moving details to a relative on the **killing of Mayor Silhol** at 10 AM in his mayoral office in the presence of four or five powerless secretaries. Two assassins shot him twice in the head, after which they mounted their bicycles and pedaled away. Silhol was a judge in Nîmes, and it seemed that he had condemned two men to death. It appeared that vengeance could not be made to wait. "The times in which we live are frightening." Feb. 16, 1944

46.   A lengthy letter from a resident of St-Hippolyte-du-Fort recapped recent events for the benefit of the French fascist **Marcel Déat** c/o general delivery in Alès. (Déat had recently joined the Vichy government as the Minister of Labor, in this final year for that government.)[25] The writer described the entry of three armed youths into the post office the day after the **murder of Mayor Silhol**, at 6:30 PM. They did not rob the bank but cut phone wires and removed fuses so that the employees, of whom the writer was one, could not communicate with the police. They succeeded in this endeavor and then locked up the employees and went to join their group, which had surrounded the gendarmerie, in **order to free two compatriots arrested that same morning**. They returned one hour later after liberating their friends and disarming the "*flics*." The youths set the postal workers free and then sped away in a car with their revolvers and submachine guns in hand. The postmaster was so frightened that he needed a drink, which

---

25   *France: The Dark Years.* Ibid., 530.

didn't help calm him down, as the writer took great delight in describing how his boss made repeated errors in balancing the day's receipts. Feb. 17, 1944

47. A man from Avèze in the Cévennes wrote a relative in Paris about the anxiety rampant in his area. He was upset with the young former students who had taken refuge in the area, because they were enthralled with the "patriotic" Maquis who robbed, murdered, pillaged, and set fire to places, encouraged by these spineless young assistants. The writer was a **great admirer of Gerard Silhol**, whom he called a true patriot, who had accepted the position offered by "our directors" [Legion or perhaps Milice] to lead the St-Hippolyte delegation, where the Communist elements were very restless. He had died on the field of honor, the **victim of a cowardly assassination**. The whole region of Lasalle and St-Jean were poisoned by the *réfractaires*, who joined the Maquis to obtain weapons in order to rob their food and exact their revenge. Feb. 17, 1944

48. Another resident of St-Hippolyte described the makeup of a local band that stole tobacco, olive oil, and rations cards and pretended to be *réfractaires*, which was not true at all. He named the son of a family who was in this group and intimated that individual was one of **the two youths who entered the Mayor Silhol's office and shot him dead**. He averred that many people saw these men because it was fish-market day. He related that these *réfractaires* wanted to free two members of their band who had been arrested. They were about thirty in number, armed and ready to shoot, when they surrounded the gendarmerie and the post office. They had cut all telephone wires, so no calls for help could be made, and by 7:30 PM the police had surrendered the two prisoners. "One of these days things will turn nasty at St-Hippolyte. But I pray that ceases as it is terrible to witness such discord between us French." Feb. 17, 1944

49. Another letter was intercepted that discussed the central prison escape by twenty-five youths, as well as the Silhol assassination. This Nîmoise stated that fifteen of the escapees had been

recaptured, but the rest could not be found. Evidently, her son Jean had aided the Milice for several nights in searching for the former prisoners, which made her fear for his safety. **His support of the Milice** has caused a political split in her family, as her husband, Robert, was furious with him, and he had a raging argument at the dinner table with his daughter, Renaude, who supported her brother. When Odette, the wife, mentioned **the murder of M. Silhol,** Robert replied, "Terrific—one less of them to worry about. He was very angry and if I could not calm him down, our hours of leisure would be full of constant bickering. Everybody is hyper and there is blood in the air." Feb. 19, 1944

50.   Another resident of Lasalle regretted the murder of Mayor **Silhol,** the cousin of a friend who had frequently hunted on the Silhol property nearby. She described the former mayor as an honest man with only the best intentions but not too diplomatic in his dealings with the Gaullist opposition, which evidently had been the cause for his murder. She was highly indignant about "this cowardly murder as well as against many imbeciles in Lasalle, who were willing to excuse this crime. There was much to despair about for our country." Feb. 18, 1944

51.   A letter from Bagnols-sur-Cèze indicated that the area where the correspondent lived had been surrounded for eight days by one hundred policemen. They had conducted many searches of numerous homes at dawn or in the middle of the night, but while nothing was found at one of their neighbors, many arrests were made. One neighbor was arrested at work and transferred to the Nîmes prison. But during this time period a robbery took place in the Regional Farmer's Bank by three **armed bandits,** who ran off with several hundred thousand francs after cutting the telephone wires. The bandits then raided a distillery, where they drank lots of alcohol and then entered a house and demanded food, as they were now hungry, putting their cash and weapons on the table while they ate. In the meantime, the distillery owner, M. Cotton, had phoned the police and many came from the surrounding towns of

Remoulins and Pont-St-Esprit to capture the robbers, who were sound asleep on the straw in the home where they had eaten. The robbers were two Russians and a young Polish student who spoke excellent French and had been in the region for six months. A friend, Claude Rochetin, had his small truck requisitioned by the gendarmes to help in the operation. The letter continued to describe **the robbery of 700,000 francs from the postal bank in Pont-St-Esprit**, in which the employees and the police were overpowered on the prior Saturday at 2:00 PM. It ended with a remark that **terrorism reigned** supreme in the region. Feb. 17, 1944

52. In a telephone conversation between Nîmes and Marseille, complaints were heard about an official in the prefecture who was involved with censorship. The two individuals said they knew the prefect and officials in Vichy, as well as a certain M. Vogt and M. Bonefoy, and admitted that they see the censor every fifteen days when he borrowed 200–300 francs from each person he visited. They accused the censor of being a nitpicker, but not in his choice of his collaborators. Someone named Bernard always backed up the censor. The two groused over finding a way to force the censor to stop his attacks on whatever it was, or at least quarantining him somehow. Nov. 29, 1943

53. One displeased Nîmois opened his letter by stating he had returned his medal for distinguished service in the military to the prefecture, because he was the object of a police report that accused him of selling tomatoes and onions at prices above the legal limit. "We are living under a police regime which does not please me. We live under such a flurry of regulations that [no] one can understand which end is up. For every person who works, there are two who distribute the orders and three who take charge of controlling them, not counting the judges and the jailors! That is why the black market is so successful: it is quick, direct to the end user, and without paperwork. I am convinced that if one created a Minister of the Black Market with commissions, committees, circulars, et cetera, the black market would not last more than one month and everyone

would return to a market properly regulated as soon as it would be possible." Dec. 1943

54. A Nîmois feared that commercial rail traffic would cease as it would be commandeered for military purposes by the Germans. The city was bound to suffer by not being able to receive adequate food resupply. However, he went on to recount that officials associated with the trains and railway station were accused of thefts of packages placed for shipment via rail. The accused included a railroad station supervisor and two police-men whose job was to watch out for theft in the station. The writer even received a package that had been rifled. He sug-gested that someone should be executed for such transgressions. "What a rotten society, devoid of authority or discipline." He cited further examples of malfeasance: directors and inspectors of food supply arrested; justices of the peace as well as police commissioners detained for illegal possession of food rationing cards. "The future of France will be sad, as it will rest in the hands of the **terrorists** who will have to cope with the prisoners of war, who will return physically and mentally diminished." Dec. 1943

55. **A letter was favorable to having armed Miliciens around,** as they were good protectors of the bourgeoisie and business owners. "In their town of Aimargues, a German captain arrived with a company of Russians who had been deserters and came from all sorts of rotten races, including Mongols, Tartars, Sibe-rians, and Ukrainians. When the German officers supervised them it was OK, but as soon as they left, the Russians ran out to bang on the doors, demanding wine. The experience gave a glimpse of what life would be under the Russian heel to our citizens, and the poor German captain had a miserable life trying to control them and said he would prefer to go back to fight on the Russian front. Finally these Russians were ordered to the coast at Aigues-Mortes, and the captain returned to see us and complained that the same things go on at the new post. Maybe not every one of them was so bad but 85 percent were." Dec. 1943

56. The writer in Nîmes called the year about to terminate, 1943, a very bad one, and he did not have many hopes that the new one would get anything but worse. "1943 saw France slide more and more into the depths of the abyss. Will 1944 see us pull together and have a surge of energy to get us out of this descent? In my opinion we cannot remain strangers to this conflict where our fate and that of Europe is hanging in the balance. **A new energetic government should align us alongside the Axis**. This would have grave consequences for us and undoubtedly we would expect a redoubling of the **bombing raids** by our dear liberators. But it is the only means for us to avoid Bolshevism and allow the reestablishment of our empire and our place in the world that we have momentarily lost." Dec. 1943

57. An expediter for La Grande-Combe Mines in Avignon's depot telephoned the mines about a needed shipment of twenty tons of anthracite and was told that it could not be shipped because the mines were not provided with enough ten-ton-capacity coal cars. Additionally, the mines were very backordered because of not having enough labor or material. The depot asked for favorable treatment but was told the outlook remained bleak. Dec. 29, 1943

58. A Nîmois wrote an acquaintance in the north of his opinion that 1943 had been a better food supply year than 1940–1942. "Prefect Chiappe had released much supplemental food for the December holidays, including meat, pate, jam, eggs, fowl, rabbit, and animal organs. Potatoes also were adequate in supply but there were a few complaints by consumers over ration cards not being honored. **Fat supplies were totally lacking,** but what can one do? The vegetable merchants don't have too much variety and it seems to be limited to carrots, turnips, and the edible part of the cardoon. If one wants cabbage, it is necessary to choose one of those three as a substitute." Dec. 1943

59. A Nîmois wrote a friend in Montpellier that an acquaintance had four hundred kilos of potatoes, which might come in handy if the Anglo-Saxons and their Free French allies invaded the south of France, as the **bombings and invasion**

would cut off all supplies. He also was of the opinion that any invasion would advance very slowly, comparing it to the Italian campaign. The writer was a committed supporter of Vichy and **loyal follower of Philippe Henriot's broadcasts,** including the one of New Year's Day, which he thought was sublime and better than any Sunday sermon. He had a deeply negative view of the local clergy, whom he considered devoted Anglophiles and Gaullists, except for Bishop Jean Girbeau of Nîmes, who still remained faithful to the marshal. He also was a devoted listener of a certain M. Jean Hérold-Paquis, who was an Anglophobe and always ended his discourses by saying **that "England, like Carthage, must be destroyed."** He contended that the Anglophiles were beginning to realize that they were no better than the Germans, and in spite of hoping that an invasion would change the situation, they again would be deceived in that hope. His reason for this was his belief that the French coastline was so well defended that havoc would be wreaked on any attempt to invade. He maintained only the French could succeed by being placed in the first rank of invaders, not the English or the Americans. "My God, what a muddle we are in!" Jan. 2 1944

60.   A young man who was the leader of the JEN (Young New Europeans) in Nîmes wrote one of his family that they were composed of twelve girls and eight boys, which was not very many, but in fact two-thirds of their adherents were in Germany in either the LVF or the SS, while some unfortunately had been in one of the Camps de Jeunesse. He ended by stating that obviously they (les JEAN) were very **National-Socialist (Nazi)** and firmly believed in a European victory. His family member, to whom this letter was written in Bordeaux, was also in the section JEAN, an acronym not spelled out but in which the A most likely stood for Germany (*Allemagne*, in French). Jan. 4, 1944

61.   A telegram was sent from the village of St-Victor-la-Coste in the Gard to the head of the National Young Legion in Vichy, expressing at this time of hope and fear **their devotion to the**

National Revolution and its leader, the marshal, and asking that this message of fidelity be passed on to that esteemed head of state by his group. Jan. 4, 1944

62. **The wife of the departmental head of the Milice**, a resident of Anduze, wrote her friend in Geneva, Switzerland, that France was currently at the same point in time that had preceded the outbreak of their Civil War in Spain. She blamed the English radio for exciting the French to kill their compatriots, join the *réfractaires* or the Maquis, and commit crimes—pillaging, raping, etc.—in order to feed and clothe themselves in the name of patriotism. These acts were eliminating the people who were trying to safeguard order in France by avoiding a revolution: the prosecutors, the judges, the royalists, the priests and the Miliciens. Often these acts were simply efforts at vengeance. France was ill-equipped to handle this situation, and there never had been so many crimes. She assured her friend that both their families shared the same political viewpoint and used as proof the fact that her husband was the leader of the Milice, which made her proud but also fearful of the future. "France must reorganize itself around interior order so it can regain its strength and energy, but there is little evidence of this yet, except for the Milice. There are bad days yet to come" is how she closed her letter. Jan. 1944

63. A resident in the coal mining center of Bessèges wrote his family that he feared that his relative, still a prisoner of war in Germany, would not come on leave as the feeling of solidarity among the prisoners made it unlikely that he could quit those comrades, who would have to stay behind in the stalag. "At home in the mining basin the workers' productivity is high. **Occasionally, he receives Communist tracts in his mailbox** but that does not worry me." Feb. 2, 1944

64. A Nîmois indicated in his letter that the holiday season, which was a sad one, had passed but people again were taking up the refrain of the previous September, that major events like **an invasion or bombardments** were about to descend on their countryside. He heard that the end was near and wondered if

Germany would capitulate and let all her land be pillaged by the Russians. Only the future would instruct them, and he saw only somber days ahead, even though for the moment there were no bomb-raid alerts. He recited the food supplies they enjoyed during the December holidays: pâté, one egg, 150 grams of olives per ration card, and 120 grams of beef per person, plus some potatoes and green beans. They received that winter sixty kilos of potatoes, which was a plentiful allotment and allowed them to eat hearty soup. "Certainly there was no fat for cooking, and meat was scarce from time to time. We were able to purchase some oats on the black market, but the high price will prevent us from buying any more." Feb. 1944

65.   A Parisian acquaintance wrote Mme. Clauzel, 10 rue de la Tresorerie,[26] Nîmes, that the recent bombing attacks around Paris had caused enormous mourning for the dead. They had to stay one hour in the bomb shelter, and the electricity had failed, making the stay even more lugubrious. He continued remarking that German reprisals were coming in a week or two against the English or the Resistance, and the suffering and crying that resulted would give them their just deserts. He was sure that Mme. Clauzel, the wife of a Vichy-appointed provisional administrator for Jewish confiscated properties, agreed with him. He wondered if she suffered much as a result of **terrorism** in Nîmes. He believed these acts were beginning to open people's eyes, but it was too late. He saw the hand of Moscow behind all the events unfolding in North Africa, Corsica, and foresaw Communism approaching the ports of France. "If I would not suffer too much, I assure you that I would not mind the arrival of Stalin's barbarous hordes in Paris for a few days. That would settle the hash of some idiotic Gaullists in a very just fashion. It appears that M. Bousquet and M. Bedes have

---

26   In a subsequent chapter concerning the treatment of Jews in the Gard, we will encounter the same family name and address. Mme. Clauzel's husband would be appointed a trustee, or "*administrateur provisoire*," to handle Jewish property that was confiscated under the provisions of the law of July 22, 1941, in a policy of Aryanization initiated by Xavier Vallat, the first commissioner of the CGQJ. See *Vichy France and the Jews.* Ibid., 152–153.

been arrested. I don't know the first one but I do the second! I heard him make some frightful statements at Odette Caron's so I don't pity him at all." Jan. 1944

66. A doctor in Nîmes wrote some Parisian friends in a New Year's greeting for 1944 that it was doubtful that it would be much better than the year just past, but he expressed the hope that they could find the peace they so desired in good health without adding to the silver in their bodies from the receipt of a bullet in the neck. Their destiny would be determined by events that took place on the Eastern Front. "**If the Russians prevail,** I do not expect to hold very dear your skin or mine. So without loving the Germans more than you do, I consider when they kill Russians, they are doing us French, as well as the English and the Americans, an incalculable service, as none of us **can counter a victorious Bolshevism conquering the world.** As any such effort deserves a salary, I estimate that it is cheaper to pay well for such services rendered than to turn the cash register totally over to the tax collector." Jan. 7, 1944

67. A woman from Lasalle wrote her friend in Annency that her young gardener's aide had been convoked for three months of **STO duty** in the Bouches-du-Rhône area. He was so worked up over it that he was threatening to join a rebellious band operating in the Cévennes to avoid that requisition. Her son, Robert, who as a forester was exempt from such duty, planned on going to Nîmes to seek an administrative exception to consider the young gardener as a forester, so he could stay in his current job and thus preclude his fleeing to the disruptive bandit group. "He is intoxicated by all the wild rumors he hears about the band, and he will not be appealed to by reason." The correspondent was very worried over two or three robberies that the **bandits** had committed in the environs, which included their having broken into the tobacco shop, pillaging its contents, and stealing all the food ration cards from the mayor's office. Jan. 6, 1944

68. A young student in Nîmes waited incessantly for news of **the invasion,** as he considered that would mean the destruction of the Third Reich and the end to the war in Europe. He expected

this memorable date to be in the beginning of March, and his expectation was great for it to come to fruition. The aunt of the person he had addressed his letter to in the Haute-Saône agreed with him, and she hoped to visit him shortly thereafter. He concluded by observing that things were positive for the moment, especially on the Polish front. Jan. 6, 1944

69.   Two truck drivers commiserated on the telephone about the unavailability of good engine oil, or even wood or coal to power their alternative-engine vehicles in the absence of gasoline. They could not make deliveries for these reasons or other ones, like the absence of automotive piece parts for repairing broken-down vehicles. One of the parties had broken three connecting rods in his engine that month. The only oil available was recycled, which was very bad for the engine. They termed it "water" and reminisced over how they changed oil before the war every two thousand kilometers. They wondered over the fact that there was any truck that functioned and only saw the chance for improvement **when the war would be over.** Jan. 1944

70.   A man in Alès telexed a friend in Montpellier over the fact that his wife or daughter had **diphtheria,** and there was no serum to be had in Alès. He wondered if his friend could urgently find some anti-diphtheria serum in that bigger city. Jan. 10, 1944

71.   A Gardois wrote that a local outbreak of grippe was being diagnosed by the doctors as the Spanish grippe, which was upsetting to the medical community as it was spreading at the same time as some cases of **diphtheria**. "The local diet has been very deficient as there has been no butter, only an egg or two, and rarely any canned goods. Some vegetables were to be found but hardly any meat, so the cooking result is exclusively soup-based. We are in the years of thin cows. Pray that 1944 sees the end of this war, but we face a long perspective of agonizing days before that happens." Jan. 19, 1944

72.   A resident of Vénéjan, which was served by the railroad line that ran between Bagnols-sur-Cèze and St-Victor, sent a telegram to

a friend in Grenoble that **a bomb** attack had knocked down pylon number 421 on that line, and therefore all rail service had been suspended. Jan. 10, 1944

73. A farmer/producer reported that because he had not planted any sunflowers, the authorities had cut off any ration tickets for supplies of fats or olive oil, and he was at wit's end over this situation. To buy any oil was just too terribly expensive. This Nîmois was pleased to have two of his **rooms requisitioned by the German army** for a month, as the captains he lodged gave him sufficient food so that his family did not suffer at all. In truth he regretted very much their departure. Jan. 6, 1944

74. A retired general from Nîmes wrote a friend in Pau about his pessimistic outlook for the future. He feared that some provinces in France would again turn into **battlefields that would result in ruination and evacuation**. He noted that the surrounding countryside was devoid of road transportation, which had continued to affect negatively the food-supply situation. He feared the hint of Bolshevism coming, from what rumors he heard from sources in the North African colonies. "Strong emotions are on the horizon, which does not bode well for the people of France." Jan. 9, 1944

75. A functionary assistant to the director general of Food Resupply in Nîmes wrote his friend in Castres that **his boss had been imprisoned by the Germans**. He had continued to do his job in the best way he could, but the public was very suspicious of anything functionaries did, and not all of his associates had his attitude. He admitted that his wife had constant household problems, not the least of which was that of adequate food supply. He ended by saying that in Nîmes the black market had dried up, which he took as a bad sign, due to the fact that edibles were just not readily available. Jan. 8, 1944

76. A member of the rightist Francist group in Nîmes telexed his associate in Quissac that he would arrive Thursday for a gathering of the group, for which he would bring propaganda pamphlets. He had sent some berets but would bring his own to

wear at the ceremonies. He expected to have a truck for use to get to Quissac, in which he would carry the "bonbons," by which he meant uniform shirts for the participants to use that had been sent from Paris. Jan. 10, 1944

77.   An official of the coal company of Bessèges wrote that their company installations were the target of frequent **sabotage attacks**, against which their defensive efforts were not always successful. He castigated the inertia of public officials, whom he called complicit by allowing the **criminal terrorists** to operate practically unopposed. He called their supporters imbeciles who would approve the destruction of the nation's capital in order to save it. He observed that such people were crazy to bind themselves to such a cause. He felt that a state of civil war already existed. His friend's son was working for the Germans in Austria, and he believed that his own son would follow orders should he be called up by the STO to the same hard fate. Jan. 1944

78.   A woman in Nîmes wrote about the fate of her brother, who had been interned along with several other men from the city in a harsh camp in Compiègne. They were taken as **hostages after a bombing attack** on October 20, 1943, which resulted in the deaths of three German soldiers and wounded twenty-seven more on the Place des Carmes in Nîmes.[27] Since then, they'd had limited correspondence with the brother, for whose health all their family feared. They could send one package per month to him, whose contents were a constant concern. Their mother was very ill with a heart ailment that was not improved by her stressful worry over whether her son would ever return. The man's wife and young child were also despondent while they awaited news of his fate. "I wonder how things will end for France after **the invasion** occurs. This question is constantly on every person's mind. I hope my brother returns before that time of coming agony, as his presence will allow us to support better such hard blows as we anticipate will come. His absence is truly cruel." Jan 9, 1944

---

27   *Nîmes at War.* Ibid., 235.

79.   A man from Uzès wrote a lady in the Aveyron that he desired peace, and he felt it was fast approaching. His sister-in-law had written him, anxiously questioning whether that peace would not be worse than the actual war they were in. "One can only resign oneself to accept the misfortunes one encounters as after all, I did not cause the war and only want the war's end **with the boches kicked out of France's door**, and only that." He commented that what his correspondent was doing intrigued him and wondered about her new activities. He would be very much interested to learn much more details of what she was engaged in, if it were possible. He ended by writing that she was decidedly not of a race that would let it be beaten. Jan. 8, 1944

80.   A Gardoise wrote that life was full of sadness where she lived, too, as all the men in her husband's class had been called up for **STO duty**, and she awaited hourly for the police to knock on their door. She was expecting a child, and she worried that her husband, Edmond, would be taken away before its birth, which would break her heart. She realized that many families experienced the same situation when the men were called up at the outbreak of the war, "but they were leaving to fight for their country, and now those who are so torn from their homes are forced to do it for foreigners in order to serve a foreign country. It seems that is a more tragic circumstance. It seems that better days are far distant and all this worries her parents as well." Jan. 7, 1944

81.   One Gardois wrote that all the surrounding farmsteads were transfixed with fear. "Everywhere in the region the *réfractaires,* **terrorists**, or petty thieves stamp their Gaullist activities on the backs of the peasants, often with forceful blows or pillaging, with revolvers or machine guns in hand. The methods employed are so rough it is impossible to get justice. The French have need for a referee: the money is taken from the peasants as well as all their lard and provisions. If these not very amusing attacks were stopped after a reasonable minimum, one could say that it would not be so bad, but let us hope that this wave does not

reach us. One can only see what happens day by day." Jan. 10, 1944

82.   M. Blanc of Vergèze wrote a friend in Nice that the Germans had not bothered them and had been very correct in their behavior. He felt "that since Joseph Darnand [28] has been nominated to head up the French police that **the terrorist attacks** will dry up. He is a man with a fist of steel who is much needed." Jan. 10, 1944

83.   A resident of Pont-St-Esprit wrote her friend in Les Vans, in the neighboring department of the Ardèche, that she feared the worst as she lived near the Valley of the Rhône, which would be the natural passageway for any northerly **invasion route**. In addition to the turmoil associated with war and obtaining the necessities of life, she lived "under the near-daily torments **of terrorism** caused by the 'refractory' bandits who had hidden in the Chartreuse woods near Pont, and who come each night using death threats to rob from the citizens. The last three nights they stole private cars and trucks and broke into a gasoline station, besides bombing two or three private buildings, not counting their attacks on railroad tracks or electricity pylons. Each night at dusk we all barricade ourselves in our homes until the next morning and wonder if it will be our turn that night. The doctors all refuse to make house calls at night. I hope things in Vans are not the same, and if you have trouble obtaining food, at least you have security. All this frightens the children, our Colette included, who as a result is experiencing very grave mental crises." Jan. 16, 1944

---

28   *France: The Dark Years*. Ibid., 530–531. By 1944, the Vichy government had largely lost control to the French fascist elements in Paris, who were collaborating even closer with the Germans than Pétain had or Laval could. Darnand was its most powerful figure, and he firmly held in hand the reins over all internal security matters. As the French police had at last generally turned away from carrying out willingly the dirty work of the Vichy regime on behalf of the Germans, Darnand began to appoint members of the Milice to key enforcement roles in the interior security forces. They carried out many acts of violent repression as players in the orchestra led by Darnand, who conducted a leitmotif of fear, which was accompanied by the narration of Philippe Henriot, the voice of the New Vichy.

84. **A Nîmois member of the New European Youth Nazi-supporter organization** wrote his confrere in Paris about their latest activities in support of French fascists and their German backers. A friend from Sète had attended a congress held by the group in Paris and stopped in Nîmes to tell him about what transpired there. He heard from Paris that two other friends had joined the Waffen SS, and he asked his correspondent, Daniel Thaquenne, when he planned to join its French regiment. He mentioned in closing that he attended the funeral of a certain Bonhomme, who evidently had been a member of the Milice's permanent guard. Jan. 14, 1944

85. A young woman wrote about the administrative paperwork frustrations she had experienced while trying to register in a trade at the prefecture. She heard rumors that there would be a change of prefect and wondered if the replacement would be better or worse than Chiappe. **More young men had left for work in Germany** and an acquaintance named Roger, currently in Essen, had heard that he might be reassigned to the north of France. In actuality, it turned out to be the north of Germany near the border with Denmark on the island of Syte, where he suffered greatly from the cold, damp climate. She commiserated with her friend Lucie that "this same fate of miseries, cares, and suffering applies to us too. Now the **invasion** will come and it will be only a question of where, but it will mean ruination and grieving for France. You are far from the coastline and considered yourself more safe in Toulouse, but one never knows what war will bring and to where." Jan. 1944

86. A businessman in the Gard, who had been allocated Indo-Chinese labor, had made his second trip to the seat of the Vichy government to request replacements, as they had been taken away from him. This Marcel wrote his wife that he had been successful in his endeavor but would have to wait a few days for the **new laborers** to arrive. They lived in the Gardois commune of Grand Cabane, which was on the road to Arles. Jan. 14, 1944

87. A correspondent described how one hundred men had been called up on a Monday in the Gard to dig trenches and that

it would increase to two hundred the following week. Those selected were picked by alphabetical order and were watched over by German guards. The writer was relieved that the requisition stopped at that number and that the workers, who only earned fifty-six francs a day, did not break their backs handling their picks for such meager wages, as their guards were often fast asleep in the afternoon, having drunk too much wine at lunch. Jan. 1944

88. A purported admirer **of Joseph Darnand** wrote friends in the Aude department that his region of the Gard was relatively calm from the point of view of bandit activity, and contrasted it to the Aude where he had read in the Little Provence newspaper that the level of terrorism was high. When he expressed a hope that Darnand's "justice" would be as expeditious as that rendered to Mussolini, while going on to comment if it might not be too late, one could be suspicious about a double meaning. He ended his letter expressing concern that the publication of a nearby factory newspaper had been suspended by Vichy. His letter was sent on after opening by the SCT, but politically or otherwise, it could be interpreted as being full of opaqueness. Jan. 14, 1944

89. A telephone conversation initiated by Mr. Mahmoudi, a North African Légionnaire delegate, to the Legion headquarters in Marseille, was transcribed in which the caller asked for a French translator to accompany him to all the Alès basin mines, where he was to address the Arab laborers working there, digging coal underground. His thesis would be **"The Work of the Marshal since 1940,"** which would concern the circumstances of the North African Arab workers who had been separated from their families all this time. He explained that the meeting would be very fractious, as being an Arab he knew their mentality, and they felt ignored and abandoned by "their French comrades." He had asked to speak with a Dr. Bouyala, who was not there when he called, so he insisted that the message taken stress the importance of his request. Jan. 15, 1944

90. A young man who worked in the Grande-Combe mines wrote a friend who was in the First French Regiment in Le Blanc, of

the Indres department, asking if he would not prefer **to join a permanent Milice company,** as he planned to do in Nîmes on January 20. He enjoined his friend to be attentive to the orders of his superiors while he remained in that regiment. He was very happy about the fact that he was going to quit working in the mines, where he seemed often to be occupied carrying loose coal out in a shoulder basket. He apparently did temporary duty with the thirty men assigned to the local Milice caserne, but "hope to take Alice to Nîmes with me when I leave this black hole in four days." The day after he wrote his letter, he had to go to Alès to get some labor conscripts. Jan. 16, 1944

91. The engineer in chief of the Bureau of Mines in Marseille conversed with M. Damian in Alès concerning steps to be taken with some **unruly labor working in the mines of that basin.** Someone had wanted to send these insubordinate workers 150 kilometers away in the Var, but the caller believed such action would be unwise, as the majority of the men were repatriated prisoners, and to send them away from their homes would cause lots of complaints. He felt the wiser course was to turn the case over to the state's attorney for legal action, so that no one could accuse them of victimizing the recalcitrant men in such a brutal fashion. His interlocutor agreed this was the better course of action to follow as the prosecutor could constrain these men legally. Jan. 1944

92. After quoting Pascal's and La Bruyère's aphorisms about thinking, an Uzès resident asked her correspondent if she didn't think that they lived in the company of cannibals. "Some people surely don't waste their time while waiting to think. At 4:00 PM today, **four men armed with revolvers entered the Caisse d'Epargne bank in our little city.** With a truly admirable mastery they took all the money there was, about 250,000 francs, and left as they had entered, in perfect order, without haste or precipitation. The four or five bank employees, including the head of service, about fifteen clients, as well as the concierge and his wife, were all left speechless. A banal story you would say, and you would be right! We have only now the need

to announce the very close recovery of immortal France by conjuring up the so legitimate hope of the memory of Vercingetorix, Jeanne d'Arc, of Bayard or the Chevalier d'Assas, so that everybody can rejoice as it suits them." Jan. 14, 1944

93. A miner complained in a letter that the blue uniform he just had bought cost 440 francs and that the quality was complete junk. "It was truly a shame to see how we are trod upon by the Company. Like my co-workers I bought a pair of high work boots for which I paid 198 francs. Other companies sell the same boots to their workers for 120 francs, so it is hard to understand. The Company is also selling us potatoes priced at ten francs a kilo for up to 100 kilos, upon presentation of the proper ration card. Just this day I bought potatoes on the open market for 3.2 francs per kilo, and I purchased fifty-six kilos. If I had only wanted twenty-five kilos, the price would have been 6.5 francs per kilo. But all we do is protest to the Company and get nowhere. There are plenty of **bombing alerts,** and I am on call for them in the passive defense force, which is no fun. I hope our region will be spared the **horrors of an invasion,** for we have an understanding of what ruin will result from such bombing attacks." Jan. 23, 1944

94. Telex "Alès to Lyon re production in coal mines on Jan. 10 of 7,168 tons of coal and 126 tons lignite and 99 tons put into storage. Got 709 empty cars and dispatched 395 with the coal shipments." Jan. 11, 1944

95. Telex "Alès to Lyon re production in coal mines on Feb. 2 of 7,634 tons of coal and 150 tons lignite. Got 308 empty cars and dispatched 403 with the coal shipments." Feb. 3, 1944

96. Telex "Alès to Lyon re production in coal mines on Feb. 3 of 7,670 tons of coal and 135 tons lignite and 84 tons put into storage. Got 420 empty cars and dispatched 400 with the coal shipments." Feb. 4, 1944

97. Telex "Alès to Lyon re production in coal mines on Feb. 4 of 6,954 tons of coal and 157 tons lignite and put 100 tons into

storage. Got 284 empty cars and dispatched 380 with the coal shipments."[29] Feb. 5, 1944

98.   A woman wrote that on the prior Saturday, four young **bandits** had held up the Caisse d'Epargne of Uzès at gunpoint and relieved it of the day's receipts, some 250,000 francs. They showed a sympathetic spirit as they refused to rob an additional 110,000 francs that were on hand for the support of the prisoners of war, calling out that "this money is sacred, and we don't want it." She ended by commenting that some people can act correctly, even under the conditions of war. Jan. 18, 1944

99.   An Anduze resident, whose son Charles was in the **Milice** and whose daughter Josette refused to go out at night, wrote her friend in Bordeaux her complaints against the armed bands who hid in the mountains and raided at night. "They are a disparate mix of *réfractaires* from STO, Communists and Gaullists, fanatics or bandits, all labeling themselves 'patriots' and living from theft and pillaging, and secret slaughtering (of animals), etc. When the **invasion** comes they will be on the move to join in the assault. We take precautions and bar the entry at night. Our great worry is about Charles and the risk he is running as a member of the Milice. One could say they are foolish patriots,

---

29   ADG. 1 W 38. It cannot be ascertained from the thirty-eight telexes outlining coal shipments that exist in the files from "Minalais" in Alès to the Midicentre, Lyon, where the coal shipments were destined, or if they actually reached their final destination in France or perhaps Germany uninterdicted by Allied bombing attacks or French railroad workers' (*cheminots*) or Maquis' sabotage efforts. What seems to be certain is that the coal was consistently extracted and shipped from Alès in this period toward the end of the war in France. It is probably a valid assumption that these coal shipments were not destined for heating homes in the Gard or elsewhere in France. A better guess is that they were shipped for powering factory production for German military equipment. Robert Paxton maintains that the French could only count on about 35 percent of their prewar supplies for their own use, but their total production stayed at 1938 levels while internal coal consumption fell to levels below 1890s. (*Vichy France.* Ibid., 237, 355, n37.) In the thirty-eight telexes referenced above, a total of 284,203 tons of bituminous coal left Alès in early 1944, ranging from a high of 13,095 tons, which could have been two days' production, to a low of 2,347 tons. Shipments appear to have been made six days a week and the thirty-eight-day average of 7,479 tons is very much in line with thirty-six out of the thirty-eight shipments.

fanatics even, for they are risking their lives. I don't know how it will all end." Jan. 19, 1944

100.   A writer described the difficulties she faced in the winter with no heating fuel and electricity turned off by ten o'clock at night; she was only warm in bed in the evening. She froze in her kitchen, but since she was near the **evacuated** cities of Agde and Sète, whose residents were all searching for places to live, she was easily tormented by the fact that she would also probably have to leave. Her correspondent, who was from Lyon, had told her that she had not received any fatty materials, but she responded with irony that she had kept her December allowances and there were unlimited beautiful fat geese available at neighbor Albo's, but they cost 375 francs a kilo! The smallest one was 2.4 kilos, which was too expensive, but if her friend were here, they could share one, but she certainly could find one in Lyon. What she really missed was coal, and it had been announced that twenty-five kilos would be available per household, but it was not worth the trouble for someone to come to deliver such a small quantity. She had sent her radio out for repair but used an old one to listen to Philippe Henriot, who was truly splendid. It gave her such a pleasure to listen to him. Another odious **sabotage bombing attack** had taken place at Tarbes, which resulted in a horrible derailment. "This gives one pause to think about traveling." She told her friend that she thought she would have fewer problems in food supply and would be less hungry if she came to visit her where they had vegetables. "It is oil, meat, and desserts which are missing." Jan. 20, 1944

101.   A Lasalloise wrote a friend in Finistère that she prayed that God would allow them to see a new blossoming of peace that would permit France to rise from its ruins through order, peace, and honor. She went on to say that finding food where she lived was still difficult, unlike other areas richer in agricultural production. However, she was thankful to God that the current situation was no longer one of complete food shortage, and thanks to a bumper crop of chestnuts and an improvement

in the availability of potatoes over the prior few years, things were looking better. She explained that Lasalle had been greatly shaken by recent events, and things had become so enflamed due to the fact that the local Protestants had turned out to be so Gaullist that their patriotism had been overtaken by partisan politics. They were surrounded by the Maquis, which agitated the local situation, often dramatically. She cited the example of the **murder** in the center of Lasalle of a couple in their home who had **been leaders of the Milice and in contact, evidently, with the Gestapo.** It was the main subject of conversation and none of the guilty ones had been found. "Our community has been graced with tobacco, goat, and ration-card robberies. On the other hand, we have not suffered up to now from the war, as there has been no occupation or air raids. But we all wonder what will happen next but for the grace of God. People talk about an **invasion** but no one is certain where it will take place." Jan. 19, 1944

102.   A correspondent wrote from the Château de Fourques that she and her mother could not come to visit on Saturday, as all the men in the village, ages eighteen to sixty, had been **obliged by the Germans to work** on various projects since the day before her letter. Half the men worked six hours in the morning and the other half the same amount of time in the afternoon, which was when her husband, Maurice, did his work. Since only 150 of 300 men in the available labor pool were working this week, she felt her husband would only be working every other week. The pay she felt was insufficient as it was only 6.45 francs an hour. The same situation existed at Arles just like in the Gard. The next thing she expected to see happen was women being assigned to cook for the workers. Apart from that there was nothing new to report, except for the fact that there were practically no men left to work in the fields. Jan. 20, 1944

103.   A schoolteacher wrote from Nîmes that since October, there had been only thirty hours of serious course instruction, which was very depressing for her and her colleagues. She mentioned that her friend, who was on a farm with egg-laying chickens,

told her that the tax that had been imposed on her production was counterproductive. In Nîmes, the monthly allocation per person for fats and oil was announced at 210 grams, not the requisite 310 grams, but only 100 were actually delivered in December, as the rations were canceled. This forced her to buy a fat, force-fed goose weighing six kilos at 363 francs per kilo, or 2,504 francs in total, including the tax. She admitted this was expensive but it was totally used to make up for the absence of oil, fat, and butter in the household. "Even if one makes some economies, it can't pay the expenses if one has to flee **an invasion**. Nevertheless, I have my thirty kilos packed in my valises and keep my bicycle well hidden." She suggested that Maurice keep his eye on his bicycle, too. Jan. 22, 1944

104. A Gardois noted that there seemed to be many women who were pregnant, perhaps because there were advantages families with numerous children received in order to grow the population, but locally, he wondered where they would be able to go if forced to **evacuate due to the rumored invasion**. He listed Montpellier, Sète, Agde, and Béziers as places destined for evacuation, with Nîmes designated as a place to receive refugees, but no one was aware of the precise location of an invasion, and the Anglo-Americans had delayed, he felt, in order to gain time and demoralize the population. He thought it was more likely that the invasion would take place in the north, as there were many more German troops stationed there—300,000 he believed—and the Channel area was better suited to supply the invaders and was closer to Berlin. Paris, on the other hand, he said was already mined with trenches dug in the streets and the Germans would defend it brutally. He had it from a reliable source, who had just returned from Paris, that any after-war financial markets would be full of peril for shareholders, and the fate of many industries postwar would be fraught with uncertainties, and many would not be able to recover. For the moment, he personally was profiting in Suez shares, which had risen, then fallen, and now were on the rise again. **He mentioned that he listened attentively to Philippe Henriot**, who had spoken against what the writer said de Gaulle had tried to

do to influence the currency via the Bank of Corsica. He also maintained that the Gaullists were losing popularity in Paris and that German propaganda was on the ascendance against the dissidents. Jan. 22, 1944

105. A mother in St-Gilles wrote her daughter in Cannes that her husband, Henri, believed the Allies would not land near the Gard coast as its near interior, the Camargue, was too marshy and not ideal at all for tank maneuvering. They had financial cares, as their wine crop had not sold due to the lack of transportation and still sat in storage in the local wine cooperative, and should it be blown up by an explosion, all would be lost. On this day Henri had to work for the Germans for five days at a rate of fifty francs per day. Rumor was that the men who did not show up for work would be deported to Poland. She had written her daughter to give her some advice about the **evacuation**, which she said her daughter would ignore. Should the daughter have to come stay in St-Gilles, they would try to cope as best they could, but should things go badly she should know that they would all move on to the interior in the Ardèche if it were possible. Jan. 24, 1944

106. A telephone conversation took place between the Peugeot Garage in Nîmes and a garage contact in Alès over the **possible requisition of fourteen cars** by the authorities. It started with one party detailing how two German officers accompanied by two civil officials had visited the automobile dealer, and taken the identification numbers of fourteen vehicles without placing any orders. In response to the dealer's question they answered that they would not pay money or give requisition orders. This astonished the other converser as he said he had always experienced very correct relations in such instances. The originator of the call expressed his fear that they would return soon and commandeer the autos, paying nothing. The other party couldn't believe such a thing would happen, but cautioned his friend that since there were lots of people around who were not who they said they were, he had better check around and prepare a bailiff's contract. The dealer said such a confiscation would

be his ruin. The party in Alès said he could obtain papers that would block such a type of forced sales, and the Germans ought to pay ten thousand francs per car. He suggested that the dealer visit the prefect or sub-prefect, who should be able to issue him forced-removal cards that would guarantee at least the return of his investment. He offered to take any unused cars off the dealer's hands at a fair price. Jan. 26, 1944

107.   Two Nîmois spoke on the phone about an incident that involved one of them by chance at a major traffic circle in the heart of Nîmes. The party involved was driving his car and noticed something amiss, so being "a man of action," he braked his car instantly and jumped out to ask a bystander what was transpiring. The response was that some *réfractaires* were inside the public building, trying to steal ration tickets, and there were three policemen also inside. The driver thought it was all over and the **robbers** would have been handcuffed by then. All of a sudden, the terrorists came out of the mayor's building with guns in hand and told him to stick up his hands. As the car's engine was turned off, and he was standing alongside it, he could only obey. In the midst of a crowd, he could do nothing alone, so his 40,000-franc car was driven away as the escape vehicle. It was an unforgettable moment, and he couldn't help feeling that the crowd was complicit with the young robbers. "This is the first time such a travesty had happened in Nîmes," and all he could say was that "a state of **civil war exists**." No one had moved an inch or uttered one word of protest when his car was stolen; this proved to him that there were some very troubling elements in those moments of silence. "It was like those American films that we have seen about the gangsters. It was a sad commentary that exposed a frightening mentality, especially when one considers that there were gendarmes in the mayor's office when all this happened." Jan. 26, 1944

108.   A Nîmoise wrote that she wondered if the people were still so enthusiastic in their support of America. "The menace their Russian ally represents must now trouble those who are so used to an easy life full of wealth and abundance. Everybody speaks of

two **possible invasion** points, on both coasts at the same time. All these fibbers don't know anything; they are evacuating the Mediterranean coastline but only as a precautionary measure. I am still hoping for a split in the 'Allied' alliance which would cause some things to happen; let's hope it transpires. Last week the anarchists derailed a train in Beaucaire's tunnel by removing the bolts. Let's hope that Darnand will crush some of these **terrorist bandits.** What a sad life!" Jan. 26, 1944

109. Another Nîmois wrote his reaction to **a Henriot broadcast** of the prior evening, which was very pessimistic concerning the dangers of death and ruin the imminent Allied **invasion** would bring to France. This had caused him to reflect upon such an event. He thought there would be landings in the Midi either in lieu of an invasion in the north or to support such a cross-channel invasion. So a major invasion would take place in the south or, at least, significant commando raids would occur and war would come to the Midi. "Now Churchill has indicated that this will occur before March 15, but we could hope for it to take place later, but for certain it will happen during 1944. I think it will be very dangerous not to have a fall-back plan in this case and one must be prudent to prepare some place to seek refuge. I note that here in Nîmes no one speaks of this and that people carry on their lives in tranquility. Won't their awakening be a very rude shock?" Jan. 26, 1944

110. A policeman in Nîmes mentioned that beginning the next day, the shifts would be increased from eight hours to twelve, from seven in the morning to seven at night, or the reverse for a night shift. "Twelve hours is very long, especially at night when even well dressed against the cold, my feet and back get frozen. In Alès, a city about 100 kilometers from here, the **terrorists** stripped the clothes off all the guarders of the peace but did them no further harm. They even let one policeman who was wearing civilian shoes, keep them. Not too far from Nîmes other terrorists have driven off several police trucks filled with gas and oil supplies, but they did not hurt the drivers. You see that there is no danger as they know how to arrange their affairs. For the

moment the most annoying thing is to have to work twelve straight hours. Truly I have it up to here with the thought of working twelve-hour shifts, and I have found a scheme where I could make more money than a policeman as an insurance agent, and when we return to the normal eight hours I will be able to do it. Finally, in twenty-four days I can take some leave but that depends on whether the English will arrive by that time, because I think the invasion is approaching." Jan. 1944

111.   A second Nîmes policeman expressed concern over grave events he felt would soon transpire. He advised his correspondent to warn Henri to stay on his guard, although he did not feel he would be grabbed for work. He wished he could visit, as he knew there was repair work to do on the pipes, but he could not come as now he must work twelve-hour shifts. He feared that he would have to cope with the *réfractaires* and did not relish that fact and wished he could avoid getting involved. However, "it was simply not just a question of youths hiding out to avoid work, as they are under the control of pillaging and massacring **bandits.**" He went on to describe an incident where two armed *réfractaires* almost ambushed a police patrol in which his brigadier comrade was involved. They faced off against each other for a moment, and then the youths withdrew without causing any deadly confrontation. "People call these *réfractaires* patriots but what will be their attitude at the next meeting?" The policeman told his friend that he did not wish that any next meeting would result "in the need for crosses to be erected." The writer thus made a distinction between dead "bandits" and "live" patriots.[30] Jan. 1944

These letters certainly recite the litany of fears that were reflected in the SCT analyses from Nîmes, Montpellier, and Toulouse. Fears about what problems would be posed for people ordered to evacuate or those who would have to accept evacuees as lodgers were very commonly expressed. Worries over invasion were equally widespread, as were fears of Allied air raids, as they both conjured up death and mayhem and

---

30   ADG. 1 W 40. End point of this file folder, which commenced on page 212.

the ruination that occurred under battlefield conditions. The trepidation associated in civilians' minds with "terrorism" caused by "bandit" groups was very widespread. Fear of bodily harm might be exaggerated, but with food being short, families were rightly averse to having supplies requisitioned by the numerous young men hiding out in remote areas to avoid the STO. Then again, organized bands of armed "terrorists" were frowned upon by large numbers of civilians who feared hostage-taking by the German troops and the retaliation it brought.

We also have witnessed some examples of worries about commerce as well as complaints over the lack of labor available to support agriculture or the coal-mining industry. The strictures associated with heating and food supply challenges were mentioned frequently, but people were perhaps tired by now with repeating that category which had been a drumbeat for four straight years. The frequent mentioning of the Milice, Philippe Henriot, and the murder of Mayor Silhol were interesting for the fact that they most likely were meant for the right-wing portion of the audience for whom the reports were prepared in Nîmes. Prefect Angelo Chiappe himself is mentioned a few times, both before and after he left for his new posting. But the vast majority of subjects mentioned in these communications were the common fears associated with what I call the rumors and risks attendant to the approaching resolution of four dark years of war and occupation. The concerns enumerated in the unscientific surveys that are found beginning some forty-odd pages back also existed in the mind's eye of the Gardois who wrote, telexed, or telephoned their thoughts during the dissolution phase of the Vichy experiment. We have read correspondence wherein people voice suspicions that their mail is being read. In this grouping, nearly four years after the defeat, it would seem that pro-Allies people had learned to write or phone only with extreme caution. Perhaps that is the reason we don't see many comments about de Gaulle being the strongman savior in the wings.

Camps and Communes

Les Chantiers de la Jeunesse: *Monitoring Opinion in the Youth Camps and Towns outside Nîmes in the Gard*

"From dawn to dusk, whether in your healthy quarters or your well-organized work sites, you will vie with each other enthusiastically in your firm determination to grow stronger through the pursuit of moral and physical purity. You will also compete with cheerfulness, and your songs and games will demonstrate to the country that the joy of undertaking activity is stronger in your hearts than the bitterness of any ordeal." —Mission Statement of the *Chantiers*, by General Joseph de La Porte du Theil[1]

Letter dated March 19, 1942, from the Alès Chamber of Commerce to Angelo Chiappe, Prefect of the Gard:

"In answer to your letter of March 4, 1942, we have the honor or answering your request to furnish you with a preliminary list of the names of all Jewish businesses in the subdivision of Alès. Attached is a list of all the Jewish businesses on the Place d' Alès."

The names and particulars of eighteen Jewish businesses were appended, nine owned by French Jews, and nine more owned by foreign Jews, mostly from Poland. Eight days later, a second letter was sent to the prefect from the Alès Chamber of Commerce, reporting that "the mayors of the following communes have indicated that there are no Jewish businesses

---

1   Pierre Giolitto, *Histoire de la Jeunesse sous Vichy* (Paris: Perrin, 1991), 548. The date when this statement of purpose would have been issued would most likely have been in summer/fall of 1940.

located in the jurisdictions of Saint-Jean-Du-Gard, La Grande-Combe, Bessèges, Genolhac, and Saint-Ambroix."[2]

As the Vichy regime took over the reins of power after the signing of the armistice in 1940, one of the issues they faced was how to treat the residue of male youth of France in the Unoccupied Zone. According to Jean-Pierre Azéma, there were approximately one hundred thousand young men of military draft age who had not been assigned to basic training units, and the question was what to do with them. Marshal Pétain viewed this as an opportunity to imbue the moral tenets of his evolving National Revolution into these young men's characters, especially those who lived in the cities, by returning them to the soil through hard physical work—in most cases, forestry. The Germans, who had suspicions about the implicit military quality of this program, begrudgingly went along with a program headed by retired Artillery General Joseph de La Porte du Theil in the late summer/early fall of 1940.[3] With any military draft now forbidden, the *Chantiers de la Jeunesse*, the name assigned to the organization, established camps in remote forests or mountainous areas, and these venues served as locales for a compulsory, eight-month national service for all twenty-year-old males.

There, far from the corrupting cities, the first class was drawn from the pool of youth mentioned above, to experience rigorous outdoor activity under their camp leaders (*chefs*). Hard forestry labor was accompanied during daylight by some technical training and/or French history lessons, finished off by organized games and campfire singing to imbue comradeship. Its purpose was to create an idealized youth community, whose foundation was to be based on a high level of moral education. Trips to rural communities were meant to instill love of the peasantry in the youth. In actuality, the youth were at odds with the harsh military-like discipline they endured through cutting down trees to make charcoal, while suffering hunger, harsh weather, boredom, and insipid brainwashing. Although the Germans feared that the *Chantiers* were being trained as a covert military force, they were really there for indoctrination with Vichy dogma, based upon scouting and Catholic social

---

2   ADG. 1 W 137, marked 243–246.
3   *De Munich a la Libération*. Ibid., 94.

order, while serving under traditional military discipline. The letters that were sent to and from the camps in the Gard were closely monitored by the SCT, and we will detect easily the level of ennui and discouragement that was reflected in what the youth wrote.[4]

The camp leaders generally stayed loyal to their campers, the regime, and especially to Marshal Pétain. No one was more loyal to the marshal—or his campers, for that matter—than their supreme leader, La Porte du Theil. In November 1942, while inspecting *Chantier* camps in French North Africa, he coincidentally witnessed the chaos attendant to the American invasion and occupation. He returned voluntarily to France to continue his work with the French youth in his camps, and what he observed in North Africa caused him to fear what would happen if an invasion should occur in the French hexagon. He warned his camp leaders that "the only way to maintain internal peace" would be to adhere to "the most absolute loyalty toward the marshal, the sole responsible figure ... and sole guarantor of national unity. ... He has received a mandate to lead us, and the enlightenment for that will never fail him."[5]

An irony was instantly made apparent to the young *Chantiers* themselves after February 16, 1943, the date when Laval was forced to impose the *Service du Travail Obligatoire*, or STO program. The camps became traps in the form of easy roundup points for the campers themselves to be sent to work for the Germans. La Porte du Theil tried in vain to get Laval to exempt his campers from the work program.[6] Before the beginning of large-scale avoidance of the STO by *réfractaires* fleeing to remote areas containing Maquis groups in the fall of 1943, the general most likely was chagrined to report the following to the marshal about the month of July: "Eight thousand of the sixty-three thousand called to the *Chantiers* in July 1943 did not show up." In the same month he received a report based on a troubling letter intercepted from a *Chantier*

---

4   *France: The Dark Years.* Ibid., 338–341; *Vichy France.* Ibid., 163–164.

5   Ibid., 287–288, including quotation from Robert O. Paxton, based on his note 6. He mentions that General de la Porte du Theil was transported to Germany by the Nazis in May 1944. This forced deportation worked to the general's benefit as he was acquitted by the High Court of Justice of any collaborative involvement during the French trials after the war. Paxton remarks in the note, "It was typical of German inability to distinguish between Vichy nationalists and the Resistance."

6   *De Munich a la Libération.* Ibid., 193.

who had deserted a camp: "You have only to see the ease with which I move around the region. The police, the gendarmes, the civil authorities, everyone is for us. They pretend to act to obey government orders."

By November, a report on *Chantier* desertion was even more distressing: "There is not a mayor who is not complicit."[7] However, according to Philippe Burrin, in the final quarter of 1943, only 12,953 French workers went to work in Germany under STO requirements, and it was doubtful there were many *Chantier* youth included.[8] A final irony is that neither the French government nor La Porte du Theil lost their enthusiasm for saving French youth through state-sponsored endeavors. Robert Paxton points this out by noting that both the general and his "brother" in moral reeducation of French youth in Vichy, Jean Borotra, the Basque tennis star, were made members of the *Haut Comité des Sports* by the French government in the 1960s.[9] Now let us turn to the intercepted letters written from the *Chantier* camps in the Gard, mostly from 1943, which served as the basis for the survey summary pages prepared by the *Commission Mixte des PTT*, of the *Contrôle Technique de Nîmes* (SCT). These reports do not indicate to whom they were copied, but they certainly were available to Prefect Chiappe, if not also to any interested parties in the *Chantiers de la Jeunesse* organization headquartered near Clermont-Ferrand.

In December 1942, the watchful eyes of the SCT secretly monitored the correspondence written by youths assigned to several *Chantier de la Jeunesse* camps in the Gard. The camps were located near Laudun, sixty kilometers northeast of Nîmes on the Cèze River; Le Vigan, situated in the Cévennes national forest approximately eighty kilometers northwest of the departmental seat; and Anduze, a gateway city on the Gardon River to the Cévennes communities of St-Jean-du-Gard and Lasalle, about fifty kilometers northwest of Nîmes.

Of the 1,512 letters written, 1,462 (96.7 percent) were read clandestinely for opinion content and then resealed and sent onward to their addressees. The major subjects that the SCT censors highlighted for analysis by their superiors were campers' comments on food, clothing, and shelter; morale; work; furloughs; and discipline. Categories of

---

7   *The Unfree French*. Ibid., 260, n48. 267, n78. 268, n85.
8   *La France a L'Heure Allemande*. Ibid., 194, n37.
9   *Vichy France*. Ibid., 344.

lesser interest to the young campers were sports and physical education, country and the National Revolution, hygiene, and intellectual development. The five major subjects were most consistently emphasized in the letters written home. The opinions registered were logged in on charts by the SCT tabulators as good *(bon)* or bad *(mauvais)*. Bad marks generally ran two to one over any good ones. Food was the number one topic of concern, a subject extremely important to twenty-year-olds away from home, which comes as no surprise, considering their work was very physical. More revealing, perhaps, was the low level of interest demonstrated in subjects so esteemed by Vichy and La Porte du Theil: the National Revolution, country, discipline, leaders, sports, and intellectual development.

Food was a highly commented upon subject in all the camps, although its quality and quantity did vary from camp to camp. If quality was good, quantity was insufficient, and vice versa. However, the quality of food was judged to be very irregular and the important bread ration deemed insufficient. Campers realized that the cause behind the failure to maintain a good replenishment of food supply was associated with the problems Vichy had in general distribution of important commodities like foodstuffs. The camps were in remote areas and as delivery trucks were commonly unavailable due to breakdowns or lack of fuel, camp chiefs had to resort to employing mules, if they were obtainable, to transport supplies. The campers had some eye contact with the recently arrived German troops and understood their presence placed extra demands on nearby peasants, who occasionally had supplemented the campers' rations.

The bad weather conditions caused by incessant rains not only negatively affected camp morale but also the health of the young campers. They worked outdoors under wet conditions and lived in barracks that were leaky. Surroundings such as these rendered their straw mattresses damp, contributing to poor health and inadequate sleep. Rudimentary illumination in the huts made nighttime trips to the latrines difficult, which caused further camper frustrations with their living conditions. A lack of clean drinking water had occurred in some camps, which led to cases of dysentery.

None of these conditions boosted morale within the camp; in fact, campers' morale was very low and apathy was common in their manual work. The leaders appeared not to react properly to the campers' ennui. The suppression of furloughs and rigorous control over their right to receive packages from home led many to leave a bad taste in their hungry mouths. The more seasoned campers were anxious to go on leave. *Chantiers* who worked off-site, such as the charcoal makers, or groups who occasionally got to eat lunch at farmers' homes, sought to retain such assignments. Morale was negatively affected by the friction between the city boys and the campers drawn from the rural areas. Jealousies broke out between these groups over differing work assignments, as well as diets apportioned differently for manual labor versus artisan endeavors, "which resulted in egotistical and contemptuous actions," or so wrote one of the "intellectual" city boys. The organization of the Christmas and New Year's holiday festivities temporarily improved morale by keeping people busy inside, especially in preparing for the entertainment shows. However, this indoor respite from the rain caused work output to suffer greatly in tree-cutting and brush-clearing endeavors, which were critical camp measurements. The strict discipline employed in these isolated camps caused hostile complaints about those leaders who were particularly harsh. Collective punishments for petty theft and kicking up rumpuses were frequently handed out and were badly accepted by the youthful recipients. The relevant points of concern were best expressed in the actual words of the campers, as extracted by the SCT analysts from their surreptitiously intercepted correspondence.

Young Rancoule wrote his mother that although he was disgusted by his life in the camp and the work did not interest him at all, what he found bizarre was that instead of being horrified by physical labor, he got a sort of perverse moral thrill by doing "civil" work, especially with the pick and the axe. While the idea of developing the *Chantiers* was something positive for French youth, its application in the camp was far from successful in his eyes, as the supreme spirit among his fellow campers was fixated, first and foremost, on food. "It was our sole preoccupation: to eat! We only think about that or being in our quarters [housing quality ranked in importance just after eating] or by taking leave or playing skittles. We only do what we are ordered to do or is necessary; the rest do as little as one can get by with."

A camp mate from the Pyrénées-Orientales department wrote his former teacher that he had heard a rumor about the beaches in that area, the *Côte Vermeille*, having been transformed into a forbidden zone by the Germans. He found this distressing news, which caused frightful thoughts. But after a bit, his hopes rose again, for the campers always retained confidence in the massive liberation of the *Chantiers* (or did he mean escaping over the frontier into nearby Catalonian Spain?). Another camper tersely reflected on the resentments felt in camp caused by the invasion of the Unoccupied Zone by the Germans in November. He wondered if it meant that their role as *Chantiers* would be more demanding and arduous. Another youth wrote his father that after returning from the cinema, campers from the adjoining barrack caused a commotion by entering their quarters and turning all the beds upside down. After kicking them out, they slept with closed fists, only to be awakened at midnight and ordered to go on a two-hour march. He accepted this harsh treatment, reflecting that "one must take the good with the bad, as it was not worth grumbling since everybody was in the same soup."

Young Gaston informed his girlfriend from Castelnaudary in the Aude that there were moments the campers were totally discouraged and made to feel like idiots. He gave the example of that morning, when they were given orders to dress and undress and repeat the process five times. "It is painful to hear the leaders simply respond that an order is an order, and it must be executed without speaking up or questioning it." Another camper wrote that they were going to a farm for a good meal, and that "every camper especially cared about eating and the rest, nobody gives a damn about." But he ended by saying that the campers were really not unhappy. The leader of the workshop wrote that what they were really lacking was a good cook. The rations they had were plentiful—even fats, chocolate, sugar, and dry vegetables—and they truly ate too much. The quantity of food left over from meals would make any civilian jealous.

Another camper expressed his dissatisfaction with life in "this castle of grief," where they worked like "Negroes and are given hardly anything to eat." He wanted to go home to see his buddies and eat well. Another youth was doing better by being a team leader and didn't find the work or food too bad. He was happy that he had only two months more before his discharge. He did complain about being ordered to march twenty kilometers the prior night at midnight, but took it a bit philosophically, as he was one of a group of sixty campers suffering the same fate. Young Jean Serre described "a grand game" assignment given to his camp group, which was to march to a designated village of 263 inhabitants, Lirac, and make a full investigation about what the people were doing. His specific task was to learn about local customs and youth activities. Another youth penned that as of January 5, they would go to the rural commune of Rossignac to work in agriculture, which he hoped would be more interesting than cutting down trees as a forester.

Another young man wrote that he had not received his tobacco allowance and that an hour of gymnastics was a bit too tough a routine to do. They were told to dig a trench to direct water away from the barracks but only worked when the chiefs were around. He described how the food they received was inadequate. He mentioned that they bought a newspaper daily but he thought the reports about the *Chantiers* were all fibs. Another camper mentioned the dissolution he had experienced about life as a *Chantier*: no inspiration in individual or team spirit, only incomprehension, constraint, crudeness, and dishonesty. It was the life of an integral, mindless state. Another camper wrote his friend in the Canet beach area that his sole purpose was to perform his work admirably in the eyes of his chiefs, but the work assignments were not much to write home about.[10]

Young Vidal wrote a letter, in which he stated how pleased he was to be a charcoal burner, as there were only three of them and they worked "unsupervised and independent of all the campers and the leaders, have a cozy barracks, which is well heated, and prepare our own meals with double rations. Each night we play cards until 2300 and can sleep until 0800 the next morning. The normal campers are up at 0600 and work all day under close supervision, while no one orders us around at all. If I could, I would stay in this job for my whole eight months obligation." Young Dejean remarked how "arduous things had been, rising at 0630 and not quitting until 2000 hours with not a single minute to ourselves. Our activities included conferences, sports or gymnastics, and an hour of workshop. In the afternoon, it was cutting trees or clearing woods for use in the manufacture of charcoal. The work is worse than being in prison but it will end on December 23, as we will go to St. André de Buèges for Christmas and New Year's. The second work stage will be from January 4 to 15, and I hope I will fail it so that I could be eliminated from the second work session."

---

10 ADG. 1 W 42. Marked 64–66.

Young Hournet said "the chiefs, who know nothing, only want to hear 'yes, that's right, chief.' Thirty-one of us were working with trowels, and we have plenty of cement and quicklime but the result was a complete fiasco. One real accomplished mason would make a fortune with all the material at hand, including lumber and windows. The army is no match for a civilian worker." Young Pelisson was enthusiastic about the mission of the *Chantiers* for regenerating France under the motto of Dumas's famous protagonist, D'Artagnan, "One for All, All for One." Another *Chantier* enthusiast gushed over the benefits he saw in how the camp program would prepare him better to participate in society later in life, while another youth said his team treated him royally. A third camper said he ate quite well and doubted that the same quantity of food would be available in civilian life. The next youth mentioned all sorts of food they were fed, but lamented at the end of the list that they were in total ignorance of news of outside events. A far different attitude was expressed by another camper who decried how poorly they were clothed, in a way that made them look like a bunch of beggars or straw men not even fit for the crows. A final camper commented that the activity was so poorly organized that for a chief to be awarded a star or a braid of command would be a travesty and an insult to his comrades.[11]

Young Marcel wrote home that the *Chantier* life was "worse than the army, where at least one learned how to use a gun. All I do is work in the kitchen as a cook in the morning and afternoon with a break for one hour of gymnastics. We are only taught to sing like stupid idiots while saluting the flag, and that is how our days are spent in raising up France." Another youth inscribed that "he had been thrust in the role of a leader for his boss, who was absent." He was enthusiastic about playing the boss but felt his group members were "all idiots, completely twisted, deficient in physical and moral strength, as all were the sons of alcoholics." Another camper, one of the "intellectuals," was reading a book on the poet Verlaine when his leader entered and frustrated him by stating that the only education in the camp was "work." He ended by saying that "the food is so abominable that it was wearing everybody down, which will lead to the cessation of any work."

Another camper complained that the food was "worse than that given to the poorest people in Montpellier. We are working at cutting

---

11   Ibid. Marked 59–60.

down trees, but we cannot understand for what greater purpose." He theorized that the purpose of the *Chantiers* was to give youth a national education, but he questioned if the result was really worth the money being dispensed. He believed that their military-like training had aspects of a camouflaged army associated with it, and that the Germans were fully cognizant of this fact. A mate wrote that group morale was "excessively low. The only lucky ones are those assigned to work for the farmers, as they get fed kilos of lard, sausages, and cheese, plus are issued supplementary bread ration cards so they can lessen their hunger in this fashion," while he could only get by because of what his parents managed to send to him. He was going to the infirmary and not just for fifteen days but until reforms were made. He could not fathom why the chiefs couldn't realize how bad things were and act to take steps to correct the terrible situation.

Another camper informed his brother that although the food was not badly prepared, they just were not fed enough quantity to subsist. The living conditions were unbearable, as it was freezing in the barracks, where the roofs also were leaking from the continual rain. He frequently had to sleep on the floor and water was difficult to find for washing oneself or even drinking. If only he could be given some interesting work, then he could avoid the feeling of languish with which he was beset. He noted that the Germans apparently have some control over the allocation of their food supply. Another youth wrote his parents that he hoped "the food allowance would improve now that Chief Mattler has returned after fifteen days in the infirmary. The food supplies we receive were brought from the railway station at Thoirez by mule train, since the trucks were continually broken down and in repair shops awaiting nonexistent parts. Now the menus must be placed on the doors of the dining halls, clearly indicating the quantity allowed per camper."

Young Mouchet wrote that food delivery was not consistent, and because of this, nourishment was "the only concern and subject of conversation." He was unhappy with the fact that after Christmas, his group would have to leave for a mountainous camp area in the Cévennes, in order to make room for a group of naval *Chantiers*. Another young man, given to exaggeration, reported that everybody was "dying from hunger" and that food was "not copious enough to support the hard physical labor we must do. If I was in the army, at least I could say that I am serving my country, but here I am just starving without accomplishing a damn thing." He was surprised that the Germans had not dissolved the *Chantiers*, as if they believed that the chiefs and the youth there were neutral, they were sadly mistaken. Young Jean wrote that he could hardly wait for the diversions of Christmas.

Another camper bemoaned the fact that chopping wood was hard work, made worse by his boss who did not tolerate anyone who stopped wielding his axe, nor did he allow any conversation. If the daily quota was not achieved, supplemental hours must be worked until the prescribed quota was reached. His stomach was always empty, and he needed more food sent from home. He ate four times less than back home but worked four times as hard. It was true that everyone was famished, but he felt ashamed to write home over such petty things. A young athlete wrote that he had chosen to play rugby over football (soccer), as they had more road trips for matches. He mentioned they had just played the prior Sunday at Millau and had a competition planned for Decazeville. They had also played against Capdenac [sic], Villefranche, Rodez, Perpignan, and Montpellier. Such frequent road trips probably had a compensatory nature of being fed better meals. Finally, young Paisardier wrote home that his group was praised by their chief for a work detail well performed, but others received blame and had to work supplemental hours due to their poor results. On Sunday he could not leave camp, as he was to receive his second inoculation.[12]

Now we turn to secret surveillance undertaken by teams from the SCT of certain cities and their suburbs (the French word *l'agglomération*) within the Gard that were located outside Nîmes. It was likely that most of these eight communes were singled out for special monitoring due to the political makeup of their working classes, which were often associated with the French Communist Party.[13] The majority of the towns were concentrated in the important mining basin around Alès. The towns surveyed included La Grande-Combe, Bessèges, Salindres, St-Gilles, Le Vigan, Beaucaire, Aigues-Mortes, and Alès. Three of them, Alès, La Grande-Combe, and St-Gilles, were selected for multiple correspondence interceptions in the summer and fall of 1943. A total of 6,058 private letters (88 percent) were clandestinely opened, inspected

---

12   Ibid. Marked 62–63.
13   *Nîmes at War*. Ibid., 38.

for opinions or investigative follow-up, and then sent on to their final destinations, out of 6,888 mailed.

La Grande-Combe was a mining community, approximately sixty kilometers northwest of Nîmes, somewhat beyond Alès. Private correspondence was secretly surveyed three times (*le sondage*, in French) between June and November 1943. The first one was taken on June 11. Categories of opinion that were focused upon included food supply (including cost of living, rationing, and housing conditions), work (together with salaries, unemployment, work conditions, and foreign workers), community health, and levels of confidence in governmental leadership.

Local public opinion was strongest about the general inadequacy in food supply. The community was extremely dissatisfied with food distribution and its associated difficulties, and the written protests were very vociferous. However, in reality, the mine workers and their families did not have much of a problem, as they already received extra rations from the mining companies themselves. The rest of the people griped vigorously and begged that they be sent supplemental packages of food by relatives outside the area. Other common issues that people lamented about were the need for policemen, the high cost of living, and insufficient salary levels. The National Assistance Bureau had been dispensing many free meals, but the announced suspension of this program at the end of the month was widely deplored. Health concerns existed—cases of typhoid and diphtheria were discovered—as well as the poor physical condition of children. Parents were very upset about the lack of remedies for improving their children's health. New, inexperienced miners felt they were well treated by their bosses, who seemed to show themselves understanding of their situation. With regard to perceptions about communal mayors, there was only one very general allusion to the fact that some local authorities had attended the recent Legion Congress.

Food, meat, and fat materials were singled out as being insufficient in quantity and irregular in delivery. The poor availability of fresh vegetables in the markets caused people to seek supplies from far away, in the Lozère or the fields surrounding Alès. Deprived of reserves for the winter, the families sought to find dried vegetables or potatoes, but they had been rebuffed by the farmers most of the time, or the prices were so high that their salary levels could not afford them. The black market's pernicious effect was very much felt. Some people had put their hopes in going out to gather up chestnuts. As for the miners, thanks to the supplemental distributions of commodities they received, they definitely suffered less. Staple agricultural supply was further hindered by the lack of certain chemicals for combating effectively the potato beetles that had infested the potato crop. Late in the year an important distribution of potatoes from outside the Gard had been made and additional food-stuffs provided by the mining company greatly relieved some household anxieties. Those who had no direct connection to mining employment continued to complain about insufficient fatty materials, the shortage of meat, and the poor milk supplies. Protests continued about the high cost of living and shortages in clothing destined for the POWs in Germany.

Many people commented on the host of young people of all back-grounds who had arrived seeking work in the depths of the mines, in order to escape being deported to Germany under the STO obligation. In spite of their doubtful ability to perform this difficult work accept-ably, employers make no objection to engaging them systematically on the spot. The bosses desired to keep up full production of coal output, so they instructed the experienced workers to treat these unqualified young men well and give them instructive help. Nevertheless, coal produc-tion had fallen markedly due to some technical reasons: poor supplies of mining materials, gas, and specialized labor. The mine bosses were frustrated by this shortage of skilled labor, which resulted in poor output levels. Additionally, the inexperienced, young laborers soon tired of this tough work and sought to get excused from it, while looking for differ-ent employment outside the mines. These trends would be unfavorable to the Grande-Combe mines, as its geological configuration required a large labor component. Additionally, frequent sabotage, particularly against the electrical supply, had caused lots of work stoppages. The extension of work to include Sundays did not make up for the down hours in the least, and serious precautionary measures were required to counter these acts of sabotage. Late in the year, concerted acts of sabotage closed off several wells, but the water supply was restored in just twenty-four hours, thanks to the quick response by German engineers and troops. [14] However, the lack of open railway freight cars to transport

---

14   Ibid. No. 9168 marked 83 contains a letter written November 15–17, 1943: "At this time the attacks are increasing and one saluted November 11th at 7PM the

coal was frequently mentioned as the largest impediment to shipping the coal that was extracted. Because of this fact, the retired miners who had been recalled to work had been laid off again. An increase in accidental injuries in the coal mines was a further obstacle to full production. The cause was attributed to a deficiency in caloric intake for the mine workers, whose labor required high physical exertion and the diet to support it. Something was amiss here, considering all the comments made in letters about the issuance of extra rations to mining families.

Very few workers were content with salary levels, as most all families in La Grande-Combe were very concerned over the increased cost of living vis-à-vis their earnings. The Miners Union spoke out on behalf of their retired workers, who complained that adjustments should have been made to their pensions to offset the increases experienced in the daily living expenses.

Few correspondents commented on the head of state (Pétain) or the head of government (Laval) as well as the general political situation. Laval was criticized for his lack of control over the black market, which caused further aggravation of the already inadequate food supply. Talk about the need to increase salaries was widespread, but it was counterbalanced by concerns that working hours would be increased. The morale of the people was one of calm resignation in the summer. The citizens were indifferent to most events, except for STO deportees and

---

evening before with three explosions over near Ricard that caused quite a bit of structural damage. The Germans did not take this laying down and at 2AM they called M. Ducastin in Alès whose response was not pleasing so they told him to get the repairs done in 24 hours or else. The engineers had to work all night and the specialists were on call as well. The cars were in motion all night like it was daytime and it goes without saying that André was hard at work. They came to get him at 10PM and he was at Ricard until 9AM. But the saboteurs will not stop at that and they tried to put the electrical depot out of order but failed in the attempt. Times are certainly not tranquil. The Germans made terrible round ups in Alès; Dr Conrozier was taken in handcuffs along with others to Marseille. Everyone is fearful but no one was taken from La Grande-Combe, however, the denunciations are plentiful." Another correspondent reported more serious consequences for personnel in La Grande-Combe or Alès: "There was sabotage in the Mine and the Germans arrested the Director, the Gendarme Captain, and the Sub-Prefect. The two first men were released and the Captain has been made responsible in place of the Sub-Prefect to see this type of incident does not happen again in the future. It is useless to tell you that sparks will fly. It is very annoying but one cannot do anything about it."

German troop departures. Only material things agitated them, like the cost of living and food availability. Tomorrow's uncertainties caused pessimism, and even Anglophiles failed to hide the lassitude they felt over the endless war.[15] The Legion's Congress did not evoke much curiosity, but traditional religious processions gained interest as people sought solace in church customs.[16]

Late in 1943, as the winter was felt, no one mentioned the government or even the marshal in their letters. Although there were some discussions of hopes for liberation, should an invasion occur, the subject was nuanced or offset by fears of increasing troubles that would occur as a result, like increased sabotage attacks. The arrest of guilty "provocateurs" was generally greeted favorably.[17] There was general apprehension about the future. Significant numbers of people wrote that they did not approve of all the sabotage efforts for fear of German reprisals, denunciations, and especially unemployment. All these factors weighed heavily on morale. The effect of war-weariness continued to have its negative consequence on the general situation, in spite of positive comments that mine engineers made about the majority of miners being courageous in their work ethic. However, material cares, concerns over winter's approach, and attacks that irritated people for their hindering communications or causing stoppage in working overtime profoundly affected the population. The miners were content to be exempt from rail-line guard duty, but this put extra stress on others, who did not conceal their anger. Hostage-taking disgusted everyone. Morale in La Grande-Combe seemed to be at an all-time low.[18]

Bessèges was another mining town, slightly to the northeast of La

---

15   ADG. 1 W 42. Ibid. No. 5094 marked 53. A worker brought to Alès from Vannes in the Morbihan (Brittany) wrote his friend at home in the northeast that after some administrative procedures that had taken a few days, they would commence work the next day. He hoped it would be for short duration as it would be painful, indicating that it might be work in the mines. He went on to indicate: "The people here are interesting enough and very open. The cost of living is much less than at Vannes for what one needs to get by. I feel the people are favorably disposed to the new political order that awaits them from across the English Channel, but that they do not really know the rigors of a real occupation like the one the Vannois have experienced."

16   Ibid. Marked 10.

17   Ibid. No. 2437 marked 26.

18   Ibid. Marked 82.

Grande-Combe. Protests about the poor availability of food dominated the mail that was opened. Delivery was very irregular and what did arrive was judged insufficient in quantity. Additionally, inordinately dry weather conditions were mentioned as hindering any chance to augment the diet with local fruit and vegetable production. The survey was taken in June, when German troops were active in the region. Their presence and the food requisitions they made locally caused considerable grumbling. All the people moaned about the black market and how it had driven up prices. Some mining families recognized the fact that the mining company tried to come to their aid through the issuance of a few supplemental rations. The rest of the population searched for food up on the mountain. On the plus side, a small number of people remarked that an extra ration of potatoes was made, as well as that the supply of butter was increased to some degree.

Workers were unhappy with management with regard to their salaries not being adequately increased. Since salaries were not sufficient to support a family, many women were forced to seek jobs outside their households to supplement family incomes. Although the mining company sought many ways to augment production of coal, those initiatives had failed, as the sub-par diet would not allow the employees to increase their working hours or output. Secondly, new workers were limited to young men fleeing STO, and they were very unqualified for the type of physical work associated with underground mining. People wrote in complimentary terms that the mines' directors were sympathetic toward these green young recruits and that the skilled miners treated them kindly. The impression they made was positive, as they seemed to accept with equanimity the good and the bad that they found in their new work. The Miner's Union chose not to make their demands known before they returned from attending their Congress's annual conference to be held in St–Etienne, July 2–3. In the local tube factory, production had been reduced due to the lack of raw materials and an insufficient labor supply.

Prefect Chiappe was criticized for trying to force the class of '42's young workers, who had been hired to work in the mines, to leave for work in Germany. There was not one single reference to the marshal, the government, or politics. The overall opinion was that morale was very low and headed lower, due to the privations being suffered. Everybody was fatigued with this situation and wanted an end to the war without taking any further part in that belligerency, in spite of there being a decided Anglophile tendency in the community.[19]

Salindres was another town dominated by the mining industry about fifty kilometers north of Nîmes. It was subjected to a clandestine opinion survey conducted by the SCT in July. Food was again the number one subject on people's minds, and all comments were negative and fairly similar to those noted in Bessèges. The grievances written on this hot button issue were frequent and intense. Home gardening in the countryside was hurt by the lack of rain. Everybody mentioned the total unavailability of fresh fruits and vegetables, and many attributed this lack to the presence of German occupation troops, who bought up anything available, no matter what the price. The high cost of living was causing more and more alarming reactions from the public. Health concerns were expressed, as cholera had been diagnosed in children.

Heavy production at the chemical products factory had resulted in the hiring of additional laborers, but the quality of these new workers was mentioned as being unsatisfactory. Experienced workers were hopeful that the chemical factory bosses would be able to offer some extra provisions for their employee families.

Some citizens wrote that the end of the war was approaching. Morale was affected negatively by the general problems associated with food supply, the dry conditions, and the elevated cost of living; all this affected the general outlook for the future. Current events left people indifferent most of the time, except for those who feared they might be displaced once military operations commenced in the south of France.[20]

The industrial and wine-producing town of St-Gilles was about twenty-five kilometers south of Nîmes, nearby the Little Rhône River and the Camargue wildlife area. Vichy officials suspected the Communist Party of having major influence in the area, which was reason enough for the SCT to conduct secret surveys in July and November. Not surprisingly, dissatisfaction with food supply was the major complaint, for it knew no political allegiance. Food distribution was abysmal in the St-Gilles central market, where endless lines formed and people seemingly had to wait forever with little result. Many writers commented

---

19   Ibid. No. 5326 marked 49.
20   Ibid. No. 5635 marked 47.

how important it was to have a small home garden and expressed pity for those who didn't have the necessary land or the means to get to Arles to seek supplemental provisions. The dry weather conditions meant cereal production would suffer that growing season. With winter's approach, people commented that fresh vegetables were hard to find, and their scarcity added to the steadily rising cost of living. The black market was harshly criticized, as were the Germans, for bidding up prices everywhere.

The dry weather also was blamed for causing the oidium blight to infect the vines of the nearby important Costières wine-producing area. This created a pessimistic outlook for the fall grape harvest. The small wine producers were continuously visited by individuals seeking to purchase wine, but most merchants had empty cellars by July. Additionally, wine barrel production had suffered from a lack of necessary raw materials. Bartering in wine had increased, which along with the black market, were indicated as areas of concern requiring strong counteraction. Comments in correspondence noted that shipments of wine and alcoholic products to Germany had slowed down. Observations were made that the commandeering of formerly available Italian laborers and the departure of French youth to Germany had severely reduced the labor supply, which was especially hard on agricultural labor needs. The wine producers, however, were reluctant to seek labor from outside the region, as this would put extra pressure on the food supply.[21] One wine cooperative, Distillery Antoine and Brunel, was credited with taking a unique step to improve the food rations of their laborers by exchanging wine for potatoes. Overall, salaries seemed to be sufficient, but industrial and commercial activities were seriously handicapped by the general lack of transportation.

---

21   Ibid. No. 8996 *"Annexe au sondage de Saint-Gilles*; letter of November 9–10, 1943 from Fernand X to M/Mme. Henri Fabre, *Proprietaire a L'Amerade*, Pierrefeu, Var, explained the local labor situation: "We cannot find anyone to come work either at Cernac or Saint-Gilles. That causes us great concern. You can only find people if you furnish them with food and we are badly located for that as there is nothing here. I have ordered potatoes using ration cards but it is not certain we will receive them. If I get them all, that is to say 500 kilos, we will make a sacrifice and take on one man for boarding, but that is tiresome as practically all the Italians and young Frenchmen have been sent to Germany, and the few available have gone to the farmers' fields where they can be fed. Lastly, we are going to gather the fodder we have cut, but there won't be enough to carry us through the winter season."

Concerning Vichy, many wrote that they had witnessed an increased spirit of opposition, thanks to the local demonstration on July 14.[22] Gaullist and Republican sentiments were widely disseminated via English and Dissident radio stations, notably Radio Algiers, and they were greeted with great smugness. Hope for improved conditions and an end to the war always were subordinated to the wish for an Anglo-Saxon victory in this community. Food supply and the general lack of agricultural and manufactured products had been the center of current preoccupations, but in spite of this, morale had been good and the population calm. The public joined in a peaceful religious march praying for rain, and the July 14 parade was not violent, even though it was pro-English.[23]

Another general preoccupation mentioned was the lack of fuel and materials for home heating. In health matters, it was noted that some children had become ill from drinking contaminated condensed milk. The locals were very weary and fed up with the overall situation. The people heartily disapproved of the presence of the unruly Russian POWs who were serving in the German army. On the other hand, the impression of the *Chantiers*, who had been detached to work in St-Gilles, was first rate because of the good morale they exhibited. These young campers wrote how satisfied they were with their job assignment, as the work had not been too difficult. The *Chantiers* youth had been exempted provisionally from STO, and they impressed the local population when they had to work for the German troops, by doing as little as possible.[24]

In August, a covert survey was taken in Le Vigan, the sub-prefectural, gateway city to the Cévennes. Food supply, that endless drumbeat, was the subject that evinced the most comment. At this moment, food provisions appeared satisfactory. Complaints were minor and most people recognized that early crops of local fruits and vegetables had been abundant. However, correspondence indicated that due to the current dry weather conditions, new market-garden production would

---

22   Ibid. No. 5866 marked 46. Mme. Bertrand-Dourieu wrote her husband on July16: "What a sad July 14, not a flag, not a bell rung, even when the people aren't at work. This morning Marcel Berrel said to me, 'We had the Republic, but no Republicans.'" This letter is in contrast to one of the same day from Pierette "X" of Saint-Gilles that ended by remarking about their July 14: "a big crowd in the streets and everybody, including me, was wearing their cockade."
23   Ibid. Marked 45.
24   Ibid. No. 8996 marked 84.

be less than the prior year. Plums were plentiful, and the chestnut crop looked promising. The production of animal manure for fertilizer was mentioned as being well below normal. The sub-prefect's decision to retain all the forage produced in the region for exclusive use of the local animals was lauded in some letters. Winter potatoes were mentioned as having benefited from a heavy rainstorm, although the initial crop was deficient in quantity. However, that same violent storm was called out for damaging many fruit trees and market gardens. On the positive side, delivery of plums increased, but the farmers were anxious to receive back their shipping cartons. Some fruit farmers wrote that russet apple shipments would begin in about a week, and the prices were expected to be quite high: forty to fifty francs per kilo.

Complaints continued relative to the high cost of living. Under economic activity, writers indicated that there was a general slowdown, with the exception that the hotel business had been prosperous due to the summer holidays. However, several writers regretted that the sub-prefect had classified Le Vigan and its suburbs as an urban center. That decree upset vacation-home owners and other villagers on the peripheries of the town, who worried their rental incomes would be hurt. The health of children in nearby vacation camps was closely followed in local correspondence. Some intestinal infections had been blamed on bad-quality bread. People also noted that pharmacies in town were very poorly stocked with medicines.

Some residents in Le Vigan mentioned their wish to give proof of their loyalty to the head of state and his government. However, they were not complimentary about the services of the press and radio. The second company of PTT workers were noted for making repairs to communication lines in a rocky path area for nine consecutive hours. They were expected to finish up by the fifteenth of the current month and then move on to Randan in the Puy-de-Dôme. No reason was given for why they were doing such substantial renovations in that remote area.[25]

Alès, the second largest city in the Gard, center of its important coal-mining district, and garrison to 1,560 German soldiers,[26] had its citizens' correspondence secretly scrutinized by the SCT in early August and mid-October 1943. Food was again the topic that dominated the

---

25 Ibid. No. 6388 marked 69.
26 *Nimes at War.* Ibid., 200, note 13.

letters written by the Alésiens. Supplemental supplies had been adversely affected by the poor yields experienced in family gardens caused by the dry weather conditions. Then a thunderstorm of exceptional violence on August 3 had ruined unpicked fruits and vegetables, further contributing to the local distress. The majority of the population sought their food source not in town but on "the prairie" or went seeking it in neighboring departments. Chestnuts were in demand but could it have been an unstated indication of desperation, as that item was no longer normally consumed as a staple (except in the far reaches of the Cévennes)? The complete absence of fatty materials and insufficient meat supplies were the objects of bitter criticism, and people exhibited a growing animosity against the black market. Individual families, fed up over the excessive prices that market gardeners demanded, turned to barter more frequently in order to cope with the high prices demanded. Some unanticipated deliveries of canned seafood and potatoes gave temporary relief to the citizens. Miners were beneficiaries of extra rations and had just received some additional provisions of cheese and sauerkraut. Some city dwellers hoped food supplies would improve if the German assault troops left on a rumored expedition into the Cévennes. The closure of bakeries had made people suffer and had caused the women to become very angry. Agricultural labor was difficult to find, and deliveries of foodstuffs, if available from other departments, were hampered by the lack of road transportation and even the lack of shipping cartons. On the other hand, thanks to the dry, hot weather, the vineyards were primed for an excellent grape harvest.

Health concerns included the cases of diphtheria and cholera, and the poor physical well-being due to under-nourishment and the reduced quality and quantity of foodstuffs. Worries such as these dragged down morale, which was reflected in the general tone of sourness and disillusionment evident in most letters. The Alésiens feared that the arrival of winter would again aggravate the difficulties in providing the basic necessities of life. Hopes were ascendant that the end of the war was near, due to news from the Italian front and the anticipated departure of German troops.[27] Whenever food supplies improved, the morale

---

27   ADG. 1 W 42. Ibid. No. 6358 marked 68. On August 3, M. André Gay wrote his wife concerning some suspicious events that took place that day in Alès: "Today the Germans distributed to us their bread reserves; there was a crazy crowd

of the people rose. This currently was aided by the vague optimism that existed about the war's early end. However, some citizens were worried about the Communists in the area, and those concerns were augmented the closer they lived to the coal mines. Other people with family members in Germany as prisoners or workers were anxious for two reasons: the intensified Allied air raids on Germany and the Red Army's potential treatment of their relatives when they reached the stalags.[28]

Concerning commerce and industry, it was reported that the shortage of railway freight cars, road transport difficulties, and weight limitations imposed by the SNCF on packages had all combined to cause grave damage to business. The activities of numerous industries would not be sustainable if this situation should be prolonged. The mines without adequate transport could only continue by stockpiling excavated coal on the spot. Many protests continued over salary levels that were judged insufficient to cover the cost of living. The miners were treated with kid gloves and an advantageous resolution of salary levels was in the offing, for both them and the metallurgists. A fire in the Tamaris factory had stopped production.

Railway guards came in for a lot of condemnation, which was reflected in disagreeable comments made about the municipality. Concerning rail transportation, the high probability of train cancellations was a subject of grave concern. Public confidence had been hurt by the many recent arrests made by the German police. Denunciations were dreaded and mistrust was widespread. The fear of violent terrorist attacks provoked great uneasiness. On the other hand, the drop-off in acts of sabotage that had been frequent in the prior months, hopes for salary improvement, and the assertion that the class of 1943 would not go to Germany produced a bit of reassurance. People wrote few appreciative remarks about Marshal Pétain, the head of state. When they did refer to him, their statements were solely sentimental in nature and nonpoliti-

---

and profiting from the melee the Germans threw into the air some powder whose intent was to burn the eyes. Everybody pulled out their handkerchiefs to wipe their eyes and the Germans used the occasion to film for a German newsreel from the steps in front of their caserne a contrasting scene of French people crying for bread. It really made one think about it all."

28   Ibid. Marked 67.

cal. Any allusions to the Vichy government were very rare and totally negative.[29]

In the mid-fifteenth century, Charles VII of France declared Beaucaire, twenty-five kilometers east of Nîmes on the Rhône River, the site of the Foire de la Madeleine, an important commercial fair for France. In September 1943 it became the site for a clandestine opinion survey conducted by the SCT. Again, the general category most mentioned was food supply. Complaints were plentiful over the fact that fresh vegetables were hard to find, no meat had been delivered for fifteen days, fatty materials were still hard to come by, and dry grocery supplies had suffered delays in delivery. However, people commented that fresh fruits were abundantly available and a distribution of tuna and eggs the prior week in the market had improved the supply situation. One read widely about habitual objections to the high cost of living and the black market.

Wine production was a key economic driver around Beaucaire, and with the wine harvest in full swing, correspondents judged that the current crop would be profuse and of good quality. The domaine owners were complimented for how they treated their wine-pickers. This temporary labor force was accepting of the food inadequacies, as their salaries had been raised. People did complain that foreign labor made up a significant portion of the work force, but this was because many of the local men were working elsewhere for the Germans. Small farmers made mention of their unease over the high price of forage. Shipments were very poor, as the railway station was often blocked, and river traffic had been momentarily suspended due to inundation problems along the Rhône. In industry, one noted that the nonspecialized labor in the chemical factory had complained over the toxicity of products they had to handle in their work. No health concerns were remarked upon except for normal childhood colds. People wanted a quick end to the war, and some expressed hopes that the country's youth would help pick it back up off the floor. There were hardly any written references to exterior events, such as the war or the future.[30]

Aigues-Mortes, a Mediterranean port rebuilt by Saint Louis in the thirteenth century as the embarkation point for the Seventh (CE1248)

---

29   Ibid. No. 8236 marked 79.
30   Ibid. No. 7236 marked 73.

and Eighth (CE1270) Crusades, was some forty kilometers southwest of Nîmes. Its opinion pulse was taken surreptitiously by the SCT in October 1943. There were bitter and loud protests over poor food supply: no meat or vegetables delivered for three weeks, very little fish, and the fatty-material allowance for September had not even been distributed. What little milk there was had been doled out sparingly between infants and ill people. There had been poor results in secondary crops like sunflower seeds, corn, and potatoes. The citizens beat the countryside in search of food. Everybody looked for food packages from relatives and sought to swap wine for potatoes. People regretted that they had bartered their salt allowance early, as it was now in short supply. Heavy rumors abounded concerning the secret slaughtering of animals. There were endless grievances expressed about the high cost of living and the black market.

Some wine domaine owners commented that it was difficult to provide enough food for the agricultural workers and therefore, the wine crop would suffer. Those same wine producers, however, seemed to be content with the pricing level and were hurriedly trying to empty their cellars via sales, as they feared what could happen if there was an invasion. At Salins, the gathering of sea salt had been finished (estimated at 160,000 tons). The shipping activity was lower than expected, due to the lack of fifty-kilo sacks, as well as transportation, so some workers were dismissed early. There was a slump in small business and crafts, as there were very few raw materials available or truck transport on hand to deliver the finished product. Fishermen complained about poor catches for filleting.

In health matters, the diphtheria epidemic appeared to have been checked but only after four deaths. There were many cases of tonsillitis, and prudent people were getting vaccinated. Two young children died from intestinal infections. There was no mention of the government or politics. The threat of terrorism, real or imagined, was feared; denunciation and death threats were anticipated. The general population was pessimistic and agonized over the following reasons: the approach of winter under deplorable food-supply conditions; and the construction of defense structures on the coastline that caused concerns about imminent invasion. If people were anxiously awaiting "deliverance," however, as it was rumored, none had the courage to mention it. The presence of the

Italians and the Gestapo preoccupied the people, and only the youth had retained their habitual carefree attitude.[31]

As we look at the surveys compiled for the *Chantiers* camps and the towns in the Gard, we can easily determine, no matter what SCT filtering existed, the main topics of concern for both campers and citizens—the lack of sufficient food to sustain life, and work. The definitions for these two categories were more simplistic for the camps of twenty-year-olds, and more evaluative for the townspeople. The campers' letters were secretly "polled" about the quantity and quality of food and in connection with what they thought of the work they had to perform. In the three surveys cited from December 1942, the food area was commented upon most, garnering nearly 50 percent of the observations amassed, and 65 percent of those young men were dissatisfied with what they were given to eat. The work they had to perform was very hard labor, and many city boys were not accustomed to tasks as physically strenuous as cutting down trees and clearing forest areas of brush. Work was mentioned 31 percent of the time, but it was not considered in a negative sense. Perhaps misery loved company, and of course, some sense of camaraderie in the midst of nature might have been felt, even if conditions were far different from urban upbringings. At any rate, these ratings were not very sophisticated.

The town summaries were perhaps a bit more refined, with food supply, rationing, and the high cost of living, all intertwined. Work was judged on salary, employment levels, type of occupation, and competition from foreign labor. All the marketing areas reported upon were surrounded by locales that consisted of concentrations of peasant farming activity. Between these two most-discussed topics, the food supply subject was touched upon in over 78 percent of the correspondence, versus labor at 22 percent. But the levels of discontent in both areas were closely aligned, at 88 percent for the food topic and 73 percent for work-related conditions. In the individual letters, there had been noted comments by workers concerning their cultivation of home gardens as well as townspeople, mainly the women, searching for food in the countryside from peasant sources. On the former point, Julian Jackson noted that "it was difficult to find food to buy, and many workers started to grow their own. Workers' gardens in the Loire increased tenfold in the

---

31   Ibid. No. 8056 marked 77–78.

period. If workers shunned politics it was often literally to cultivate their gardens."[32] These same comments applied undoubtedly to the Gard.

We have witnessed practically a total absence of political discussion in the various reports. The peasants, however, were not very welcoming to mine-worker housewives, unless they had ready cash in hand to pay for what they wanted to carry home. The acute commentator Léon Werth took close notice of peasant smugness in the Jura during the war years. He remarked, "Whatever occurs they at least will never go hungry … They are suspicious of everything, of Germany and England, of Communism and the government." But they shared one thing in common, which was the hatred of workers: "They envy us, but they do not envy our work. If there was a revolution they would come and take their revenge on us … they would pillage us."[33] Outright peasant greed or their self-protective measures against Vichy economic controls caused frustrations among the local functionaries, and one felt that only the presence of a gendarme on every farm could cause the peasants to obey the law. The peasants, who were such a critical component of the National Revolution, turned on it and even its leader, Marshal Pétain. In the nearby Hérault in 1943 it was reported that "the peasantry has lost all confidence in the government and in some cases, people go as far as to accuse the marshal of duping the agricultural population."[34]

---

32 *France: The Dark Years.* Ibid., 296, and notes 134 and 135.
33 Ibid., 290, note 100.
34 Ibid., 291, note 107.

Jews in the Gard

1940–1944

Academic Inspector for the Gard, Nîmes, 17 December 1940, to the Prefect of the Gard [Angelo Chiappe]:

"In reply to your letter of December 16, I have the honor to inform you that M. Cohen, teacher trainee of the Nîmes Lycée, M. May, teacher of the Alès Lycée, Mlle. Vergnes, head disciplinarian of the Young Girls School of Nîmes, and M. Chourik, intermediate school instructor, all fall under the scope of Article 1 of the Jewish Statute. In accordance with ministerial instructions, the [four] people concerned have been informed that they must step down from their positions by December 19." [1]

Police Chief, Saint-Gilles, January 31, 1944, to the Prefect of the Gard [Angelo Chiappe]:

Subject: Change of residence by Jews.

"However, the French Jew, Emmanuel MEYER, born 26 August 1870 at Marmontiers (Bas-Rhin), and residing in the commune since July 1940, had been arrested by agents of the Gestapo on 22 January 1944, and was taken away to an unknown destination." [2]

"Why Servan? The people will ask this, knowing that the maternal grandfather's name is Fernand Crémieux, and not being unaware that grandfather Schreiber was called Julius-Joseph, not Servan. To next-of-kin in on the know, Servan was the World

---

1 ADG. Enquêtes Juives, marked numbers 92 and 504.
2 ADG. W 140-143. marked number 626.

War I name Emile assumed while serving in the French army (Schreiber was too Germanic sounding) … For Robert, George, and Emile, the brothers Schreiber, it was the first step from that moment on toward Gallicizing their last name … To be a Jew in a Catholic land was not trivial; to be German in a French country was no less a problem; finally to be both of Jewish and German origin in Paris was worst of all." Re: April 1918 birth certificate of Jean-Claude Fernand Robert Servan-Schreiber.[3]

I n the prologue of this book, we witnessed how an investigation of Jews in the Gard was launched, thanks to "normal well-informed sources" in April 1941. Of course, as we have covered in subsequent chapters, this was at the time in Vichy's history when the First Jewish Statute and other associated anti-Semitic laws were operative. Prefect Chiappe ordered his inspector to report back his findings with urgency on "potential (read: black market) schemes by Israelites who reside in the Remoulins area" to monopolize the cloth business. Thus, most likely an informer was able to bring about the thorough examination of the two German-Jewish refugee families from the Saar, the Rothschilds and Levys, who lived in Remoulins. That they were innocent of any such plot probably paled in comparison to the inspector's feeling he needed to indicate to his superiors that he would continue to observe them. After all, they were Jews, and foreign ones at that. One family, the Rothschilds, had formerly been incarcerated in the concentration camp in Gurs, while the other family was headed by a stateless person.

The many concrete actions Vichy took against the Jews (as well as the Masonic lodges) were homegrown and intrinsic parts of the National Revolution. Marrus and Paxton have enumerated three fundamental, native goals of that agenda which were implemented starting in July 1940. The first objective was the stopping of any further immigration of refugees, especially Jewish ones. We have noted the irony of Germany injecting several thousand Jews from the Saar into the Unoccupied Zone and the howls of useless protest that emanated from Vichy. The second goal was an attempt to promote the reemigration of refugees already within Vichy's borders. Under wartime conditions as well as German

---

3　Alain Rustenholz and Sandrine Treiner, *La Saga Servan-Schreiber: Une famille dans le siècle* (Paris: Seuil, 1993), 182–183.

resistance, this effort was signally ineffective. The final and more successful goal was to eliminate the influence of that "other," the Jew, foreign
or French-born, from the spheres of public, cultural, or economic influence within French society. After the *Journal officiel* published the *Statut
des juifs* of October 3, 1940, Jews were singled out in a press release
because their influence "made itself felt in an intrusive and even disuni-
fying manner." [4]

Freemasonry was an early target of the conservative Catholic
elements in Pétain's Vichy government. Very different from American
Masonic lodges, the French variants had a history of anticlericalism and
support of the pro-Dreyfus movement in the early twentieth century.
Justice Minister Raphaël Alibert hit their lodges immediately when he
imposed a law on August 13 that abolished all secret societies. Examples
of how the bureaucrats in the Gard implemented this order still exist in
its archives. All public organizations had to demand that their employees submit a handwritten declaration attesting "on my honor never to
have belonged to one of the societies listed in Article 1 of the Law of
13 August 1940, having been banned as a secret organization. Furthermore, on my honor I promise never to rejoin this organization, should
it be reconstituted." The examples found in the archives were from a
M. Roger Nouet and M. Figuier, employees in Nîmes' Public Utility
for Gas, Water, and Lighting. Although it would seem these were two
non-Jewish Frenchmen, Jews would not escape the scrutiny of French
bureaucrats doing their duties under the plethora of Vichy's Jewish
statutes, laws, and decrees. [5]

Various public agencies and municipalities began to report back
with frequency to Prefect Chiappe about how they were complying with
the various Jewish laws that Vichy had implemented. On December 17,
the secretary general of Nîmes' Department of Veterans, Victims of the
War, and Orphans answered a dispatch of November 26 that he had no
Jewish employees in his departmental office. Similarly, on December
10, the Labor Department responded that there were no Jews among its
twenty-three local employees. On December 19, M. Michel, the agricul-

---

4   *Vichy France and the Jews.* Ibid., 13, 14, and note 52 (*Le Temps,* October 18,
1940); *Vichy France.* Ibid., 172–173.
5   ADG. Enquêtes juives. Both unnumbered but archived, dated October 2, 1940
(*Ste. Lyonnaise des Eaux et de l'Eclairage, Usine a Gaz de Nîmes*).

tural professor in charge of farm services in the Gard, listed himself and his nine employees for having made their individual declarations establishing their non-Jewish status. The quotation on this chapter's first page revealed that any teachers who qualified under the statute as Jews had to be dismissed. Such was the ordained fate of Messieurs Cohen, May, Chourik, and Ms. Vergnes, as of December 19. Jewish judges were not exempt either. On December 20, 1940, the public prosecutor of Nîmes informed Prefect Chiappe that only two of his personnel were affected by the law's proscriptions: M. David Cahen, a counselor to the court of appeals of Nîmes, and M. Léon Messian, a judge for preliminary investigation. The public prosecutor indicated that he had informed Vichy's attorney general *(Le Garde des Sceaux)* that the two individuals in question were Jewish. The responsible party would discharge them.[6]

The word declaration referred to the Vichy functionary form that each individual employee had to fill out, regardless of whether he/she was Jewish. The declarer filled in his full name, date, and place of birth, and his present address at the top. Next came individual questions: were the paternal grandparents—male and female—of the Jewish race? Were the maternal grandparents—male and female—of the Jewish race? The next question asked, if there was a wife, was she Jewish? Next came categories whereby a French Jew might gain an exemption from the law's employment prohibitions. They were four that included having served as a combat veteran of 1914–1918; having earned a military citation in that war; or having earned a military citation in the 1939–1940 campaign; finally, had the declarer received a military Legion of Honor or military medal. Forms for two individuals, Jules Faisse of Nîmes and Maurice Léon Jallaguier of St-Theodorit in the Gard, were filed in December 1940 and both indicated "no" to all questions about being of the Jewish race.[7]

On February 13, 1941, an official letter from the Minister of Public Education in Paris was sent to all prefects in France. It was signed by H. Luc, the general secretary for vocational education, and its opening paragraph read as follows: "The law of 3 October 1940 in Article 3 stipulates that access to and the exercise of all public functions other than those enumerated under Article 2 are only open to Jews if they qualify under

---

6   ADG. Ibid. Marked numbers 416, 395, 372, 504, and 513.
7   ADG. Ibid. Marked numbers 546 and 144.

one of the following conditions." The conditions cited were the same ones on the forms filled out by Faisse and Jallaguier in the prior paragraph. The letter continued:

"According to the established legislative definition [of a Jew], any individual with three Jewish grandparents, or two grandparents of the same race and a Jewish spouse, must be considered a Jew.

"It is incumbent upon you to conform to these regulations by undertaking an immediate investigation into the ancestry of all Regional and Departmental Inspectors for Vocational Education. Each Inspector must sign the attached form after having written in the names of his father and mother, and both his paternal and maternal grandparents. If he is married, the same information must be furnished for his spouse. Under Article 7 of the aforesaid law, [if qualified as Jewish] the Regional and Departmental Inspectors [concerned] must immediately cease performing their duties. Replacements will be appointed as quickly as possible. It is imperative that I receive your response to this instruction by the end of the current month."

Prefect Chiappe added some marginal, handwritten notes to the memo, urging a staff member to comply with M. Luc's request.[8]

One year later, Prefect Chiappe was still hard at work keeping the screws tight on any Jews working in his department. He issued a new directive, marked "Urgent," to all mayors and sub-prefects in the Gard on February 28, 1942, reminding them that "no Israelite could be employed in a public capacity" unless the aforementioned exceptions expressly provided for by the [Jewish] law applied to them. The memorandum continued: "Consequently you must issue a decree terminating the jobs of all such agents, contract employees, or temporary workers, who cannot take advantage of the legal exclusions.

"I look forward to receiving *by return courier* the list of names of those [Jews] retained in your service, specifying for each the reason justifying the exemption from which they have benefited." The small commune of St-Andre-de-Valborgne answered the memo tersely on March 9: "Israelites employed at the mayor's office—None."[9]

The case of the Gardois Jew, Edmond Danan, is illustrative of how the various administrative offices maintained their attention and adher-

---

8   ADG. Ibid. Marked 206.
9   ADG. 1 W 137. Marked 3, 2.

ence to the Jewish statutes and all their ramifications. On February 11, 1943, the CGQJ in Vichy wrote Prefect Chiappe inquiring why the Jew Edmond Danan was still employed as an accountant in the departmental Office of Potatoes at a salary of 2,700 francs per month. The letter also indicated that Danan had not filed a form indicating his status as a Jew, and that his boss, M. Legal, was unaware of the fact that he was Jewish. It makes one wonder how the CGQJ in Vichy gained all this intimate knowledge. The letter concluded: "Finally, may I draw to your attention that this Jew has not been included in the census, and his pretext is that he only was released from [POW] captivity three months ago and that he was not aware of the different measures that his coreligion members were obliged to follow."

On February 17, Prefect Chiappe followed up with a letter to the director in charge of all food supply for the Gard, to which was attached a copy of the correspondence from the CGQJ. In the body of his detailed letter, it is clear that Chiappe had already made inquiries about Danan's prior military service. He wrote: "However, I believe I must inform you about what concerns me, which is that M. Danan is not working in a prohibited job." Chiappe was very precise in noting that M. Danan qualified for exemption from the Jewish public employment laws due to an individual declaration Chiappe had obtained. Danan had proven that he had been a combatant in World War I, had also fought in the 1939–1940 campaign, and was a recipient of either the Legion of Honor or a military medal. However, the final paragraph as originally typed was crossed out. It had stated: "Under these conditions, contrary to the conclusions of the Head of Mission to the CGQJ, I judge that he [Danan] would be able to continue his functions, after being so advised by the CGQJ."

The last puzzle piece, at least for the Gard's bureaucracies, was put in place on February 20, when the head of food supply responded to the prefect. His letter stated: "As a result of information furnished me by the office of the departmental head of the Potato Bureau, M. Danan is the beneficiary of the following clauses a), b), and c), which according to the terms of the law of 2 June 1941, contained in the Jewish Statute, constitute an exemption in his favor." So Edmond Danan kept his job for the time being in early 1943. I found no record concerning his inclusion in any roundup of Gardois Jews sent for deportation east, such as probably was the fate of Emmanuel Meyer, taken by the Gestapo from Saint-Gilles in 1944.[10]

On June 14, the *Journal officiel* published an extract of the law of June 2, 1941, signed by Marshal Pétain, which ordered the registration of all Jews. Its Article 1 decreed that all people classified as Jews under the *Statut de juifs* had one month from its publication to go to the local prefecture to register. It went on to indicate that the individual must "make a declaration establishing their civil estate [residence], their family situation [single or married with children], their profession, and the state of their property holdings. The declaration will be made by the husband for the wife and minor children." Article 2 listed the penalties for failure to comply with this census of Jews, which included monetary fines, imprisonment, or both. The prefect, "without prejudice, had the right to order the internment in a special camp, *even if the person concerned is French* [author's italics]."

Prefect Chiappe refined this cataloguing of all Jews in the Gard on June 24 when he instructed all sub-prefects, mayors, presidents of special delegations, central commissioners, and police heads urgently to compile concurrently certain sub-categories for Jews. He wanted this information back by June 30, so he allowed some approximations for "French and foreign Jews, including Jewish refugees, and the separating out for both French citizens and foreigners, of 1) noncommercial Jews [N.C.], 2) Jews in commerce [C], 3) Jewish businesses, with both French or foreign ownership [SC], and 4) Jewish family heads [JCF]." Chiappe finished his written communiqué with the following: "This census is independent of the declaration ordered by the decree 2 June 1941 (*JO* of 14 June) and will be regularly published in the press." Something more than just listing the whereabouts and civil state of all Gardois Jews was afoot, and one could read between the lines that it would involve Jewish wealth and economic activity.[11]

The responses to Chiappe's instruction started coming in. The handwritten one from the mayor of Montfrin listed one non-commercial Jew, Ronis Beutioy, born April 17, 1906, in Rumania, as a refugee from Belgium. The letter stated that there were no Jews involved in commerce or any Jewish businesses in Montfrin and no Jewish family

---

10   ADG. 1 W 137. Marked 476–478.
11   ADG. 1 W 138–139. Marked 634 and 635.

heads. This report could be described as worrisome, as we will later devote much emphasis to the prominent Jewish Schreiber family who owned the Montfrin Chateau in the town and filed family declarations at this same time. However, the prefect's administration did maintain a Gardois commune ledger in Nîmes, which tracked these responses. It indicated one foreign Jew as noncommercial (evidently M. Beutioy), and five French citizens, who probably were the Schreiber family members who were French citizens. For Nîmes, the register showed 100 foreign and 150 French "NC"; 30 foreign and 50 French "C"; 4 foreign "SC"; and 110 foreign and 160 French "JCF." [12]

Between the tallies made from individual declarations and the one demanded subsequently by Prefect Chiappe on June 24, a consolidated report for all Jews in the Gard, by foreign nationality or French citizenship, was completed by the end of July 1941. The two-page report issued by the prefect for Vichy's use listed the foreign Jews in residence by nationality. There were twenty nationalities enumerated, plus Moroccans (protected French) and stateless people (*Apatride*), of whom there were fifty-one. Of the 738 foreign Jews listed, the largest numbers were from Poland (249); Austria (*ex-Autrichiens*) (102); and Germany and Turkey (84 each). There were even four people listed as North Americans. There were additionally 961 French Jews. The human inventory record was sub-divided for gender and children under the age of fifteen. There were, in total, between French and foreign Jews in the Gard, 970 men, 583 women, and 146 children.[13]

The CGQJ was invested with significant powers to limit or restrict Jews' access to their bank accounts. Later on in this chapter, I will explain how this affected the very wealthy Robert Schreiber. Postal bank accounts were very popular in France, and this type of banking establishment, a state entity, was a logical place for the functionaries to be directed to start under the applicable Jewish banking laws. The secretary general in Nîmes of the PTT, a division of Vichy's communications sector, wrote Prefect Chiappe the following letter on September 20, 1941:

"To permit my division to proceed with the Bureau of Checking accounts in Paris in its operation to block the postal bank accounts held by Jews, I must ask that the attached form be completed, after consulta-

---

12   ADG. Ibid. Marked 91 and 541.
13   ADG. Ibid. Marked 637 and 640.

tion of the existing file in the Prefecture, *with a yes or no*, as to whether the people indicated are Jewish or not.

"I would be most appreciative if you would urge your collaborators in your instructions to complete filling out the information on these statements with the shortest delay possible."

Chiappe immediately handwrote his instructions to his head administrators right on the director's letter. The attachment was completed for the fifteen persons specified, all of whom were listed as either Catholic or Protestant (no Jews). Among those recorded were a marquis and his sister, a countess, and a pastor and the son of a pastor. A letter to Prefect Chiappe of November 19 attests to the thoroughness of the lines of communications in this endeavor. It came from his chief of police, who had received a similar inquiry from his counterparts in Dijon and Orleans inquiring whether the five account holders who lived in Nîmes were Jewish. All the answers were in the negative under the heading "Jewish Race or Not." One of the individuals listed was a Mr. Moise Morin, Villa Dalila, route d'Uzes, Nîmes.[14]

Examples such as the last two quoted give pause to consider how thorough the investigations were sometimes in determining Jewishness. Morally, perhaps, this is understandable. However, accuracy in reporting Jewishness is very difficult to quantify, let along qualify at this early stage of Vichy's anti-Jewish campaign, well before the massive spring and summer roundups of 1942. Nevertheless, it is probably not coincidental that Xavier Vallat, the Commissioner General of Jewish Questions (CGQJ), issued the following bulletin to all prefects on December 15, 1941:

> Given the risks of fraud to which our services are more and more exposed, I have decided that in future I will only accept baptismal certificates under the following conditions:
>
> 1) That they antecede their production date by at least one year, and
>
> 2) That the signature of the ecclesiastical authority be duly notarized.
>
> I expect you to follow these instructions and inform interested parties as need be."[15]

---

14   ADG. 1 W 137. Marked 332/614, 336/618, 373.
15   ADG. Enquêtes juives. Ibid. Marked 507/617.

In complying with the declaration provision for the newest Jewish law, it was natural that certain Gardois Jews would stress the length and service of their family's French ancestry. Jean-Armand Hirsch of Nîmes was one such individual. On July 12, he wrote Prefect Chiappe the following typewritten and well-composed letter:

In adhering to the requirements of the law of 2 June 1941, it is my honor to inform you that I consider myself a Jew under the laws provisions. It is the same for my wife and my children.

Listed below please find the information required for me and my family members:

1. HIRSCH Jean-Armand, born at Luneville (M&M), 8 April 1900, married in Luneville 15 April 1928 to:

2. NORDEMANN Yvonne, born at Luneville, 15 January 1903. Born from this marriage:

3. HIRSCH Pierre, born at Asnières (Seine) 29 October 1929

4. HIRSCH Janine, born at Asnières (Seine) 28 May 1933.

Nationality: My wife and I are French of old stock (*de vieille souche*).

Concerning my paternal family, they are listed in the census taken in Alsace in 1784 by order of King Louis XVI. My great grandfather was born in Alsace in 1790. He served in Napoleon's Army and participated in the Russian campaign. My grandfather was a teacher for the French State, born at Haguenau (Bas-Rhin) 6 October 1821. My father was born at Thann (Bas-Rhin) 5 May 1859.

Profession: Commercial enterprise, established in Nîmes at 8 General Perier [sic] Street.

Assets: a) business revenue b) my personal dwelling.

I would appreciate receiving acknowledgement of the receipt of my declaration.

Be assured, Mr. Prefect, of the receipt of my most respectful sentiments.

Jean Hirsch

Pro forma, this letter was entered in the record and filed away with all the other declarations, probably not ever reviewed by the prefect. I have seen examples where having Jewish ancestors who had served in Napoleon's army did not preclude one being deported to Poland, if one were unfortunate enough to be swept up in one of the Jewish round-ups.[16]

As the Jews in the Gard complied with the law by filing their declarations, it is important to note the requirement to list their business affiliation and sources of wealth and assets. In earlier chapters, we touched upon Vichy's policy of Ayranization as embodied in the law of July 22, 1941, just one of the twenty-six laws and twenty-four decrees Vichy issued relative to Jews between October 1940 and October 1941.[17] That law, as published in the *Journal officiel* of August 26, 1941, proposed specifically to "eliminate all Jewish influence from the national economy." Fortunately this aim was unreachable, but the 1,343 trustees (*administrateurs provisoires*) Vichy did appoint in its zone worked assiduously at appropriating Jewish businesses and residences as allowed by the law.[18] CGQJ Commissioner Vallat wrote Prefect Chiappe a memo, the purpose of which was to tighten up controls on this process. It stated: "By virtue of the powers conferred on me by the laws of 29 March 1941 creating the Commissariat-General of Jewish Affairs [CGQJ] and of 19 May 1941 setting my powers, by decree I am designating Captain (*le Capitaine de Corvette*) Lecussan, as charged with the mission of Director for the economic Ayranization for the Montpellier region.

"I expect that you will fully cooperation in aiding and facilitating Captain Lecussan in his efforts to accomplish his mission. Vichy, 25 June 1941,

"Xavier Vallat, Commissioner-General for Jewish Affairs."[19]

Captain Lecussan's adjunct director, in performance of his function, wrote Prefect Chiappe on October 3, 1941. "I have attached a list of

---

16   ADG. 1 W 138-139. Ibid. Marked 837.

17   *France: The Dark Years*. Ibid., 363, 355. Julian Jackson notes that a total of 287,962 Jews registered under both the earlier German requirements in the Occupied Zone and the subsequent Vichy requirements for a Jewish census in mid-1941 in the Unoccupied Zone. In Vichy's area a total of 108,000 Jews made their declarations within two months. The overall number of Jewish registrations for both zones was about the same: 90 percent.

18   *Vichy France and the Jews*. Ibid., 152–153, and notes 116 and 117.

19   ADG. Enquêtes juives. Ibid. Marked 1836/164.

Jews presumed to be residents in your department. Have your services please verify that they have subscribed to requirements of the census of 1 August. Please accept, Mr. Prefect, the expression of my most respectful sentiments."

The attachment contained the names of ten Jews, mostly from Nîmes. Chiappe's "services" efficiently finished their research. Six individuals had complied, while four persons had not made their declaration. No one should be allowed to fall through the cracks.[20]

This brings us to the case of the Berr family of Mas Devèze, Chemin de Campagne, in Nîmes, who experienced the process of expropriation through the application of the Ayranization procedure. This Jewish family tried to challenge what happened to them under the Jewish laws. On August 18, 1941, the director general of the CGQJ's office in Paris, handling the appointment of trustees for Jewish-owned properties, wrote Prefect Chiappe. He requested that the prefect forward his letter to Messieurs Marcel and Georges Beer (sic) of Mas Devèze, which was a reply to a letter the Berr's had sent him on July 28, concerning the appointment of a trustee for certain of their assets. In essence, this CGQJ official said he could not answer their request, which was undoubtedly for an exception, until the "German authorities" to whom he had submitted their request had made a ruling. It takes little imagination to figure out the negative answer they could expect.

The eight members of the extended Berr family had been residents of Nîmes since the summer of 1940. This fact is established by the presence in the Gard archives of an identity card stamped Jew (*JUIF*) for each of them, as required by the law of June 2, 1941, for all Jews. The Vichy government originated the identity card system in France and found it efficacious to add this Jewish "refinement." All the Berrs were French citizens by birth. Marcel Paul, born in 1911 in Nancy, was married to Suzanne, born Scheyen in Troyes in 1918. Their children, Michel André and Claude Simone, were born in 1938 in Nancy, and 1940 in Nîmes, respectively. Marcel's three siblings also lived with him: Georges born in 1913 in Nancy; René in 1916 in Valence; and Paulette in 1922 in Nancy. Their mother, Jeanne Berr, born Kock in 1889 in Villefranche, rounded out the Mas Devèze household. The Parisian CGQJ office and their "German authorities" contacts probably became involved with

---

20 ADG. 1W 137. Marked 642–643.

the Berrs because they came from Nancy, which formerly had been the capital of Lorraine.[21]

The Berr family possession of Mas Devèze, a wine-producing domaine, was swept up in the tightening web of Vichy's Ayranization policy. Proof of this fact was announced in the *Journal officiel* on November 7, 1942, when the new Commissioner General of Jewish Affairs, Darquier de Pellepoix, appointed M. Paul Clauzel, 10 rue de la Tresorerie, Nîmes, as the trustee to control the Berr property and enterprise. The announcement applied to all "businesses, wealth, and tangible assets belonging to Jews", in this case, specifically, "the property known as Mas Devèze, situated at Nîmes, Chemin de Campagne, belonging to Berr, Marcel-Paul and to Scheyen, Eve [sic], his wife, living in Nîmes, and Berr, Georges, of the same address."[22]

Now we must fast-forward to three days after the Normandy invasion, when on June 9, 1944, the regional director of the CGQJ in Marseille answered Chiappe's replacement prefect concerning the Berr case. The Berrs had petitioned their case to the appeals court in Nîmes, which issued an order on May 22 to grant the Berrs a reprieve on the sale of the assets belonging to these Jews, the Berrs. The letter went on:

> Given that the order to sell came from the head of the CGQJ, and that the Judicial Tribunal has indicated its willingness to adjudicate the process in spite of your challenging their competence, I request that you take up this conflict.
>
> A firm decision is necessary for this conflict to be resolved.
>
> M. Clauzel, the trustee for the Berr assets has been instructed to contact you and to give you and the necessary information of which you would have need.

The prefect made some marginal notes on this letter, dated June 28, that, although not entirely legible, do indicate that the process was going forward toward some sort of resolution.[23]

M. André Carcassonne, the uncle of Marcel Berr, wrote Prefect

---

21 Ibid. Case 23121, marked 121. ADG. 1 W 139. All cards stamped in conformance with the Jewish law of June 2, 1941.
22 ADG. 1 W 136. Marked 255/496 and dated at Vichy, October 22, 1942.
23 ADG. Ibid. Marked 432/400.

Paganelle on August 31, 1944, to inform him that Marcel, his mother, his wife, his children, and his grandmother, all Jews, had been arrested by the Germans in their apartment at 18 boulevard Victor Hugo in Nîmes or at Mas Devèze on May 28, 1943. He pointed out that Mas Devèze had been appropriated by the CGQJ and that M. Pierre [in fact, Paul] Clauzel, a name that will surface again in our final "Jews in the Gard" story, had been appointed as its provisional administrator. M. Carcassonne informed the prefect that Marcel Berr had escaped the Germans in Nîmes and was somewhere in France unknown to him, and that he wished to be able protect his interests, especially as it was time for the grape harvest at Mas Devèze. So he requested a temporary appointment from the prefect to represent Marcel's well-being until he returned in person to Nîmes. On September 15, the prefect replied in the affirmative and gave permission to M. Carcassonne to go to Mas Devèze and act on behalf of his nephew so that the grapes could be harvested for wine production.

Mas Devèze still exists today, at least as a street near Caissargues, a commune two kilometers southeast of Nîmes. What my research did not enlighten me on was how many other of the Berr family members survived the war.[24]

A foreign Jew, Elie Afnaim, born in Constantinople, Turkey on August 31, 1895, had made his obligatory declaration at the Prefecture after the law became effective in mid-1941. His name is found on a tally sheet amongst the foreign "A's" as a shopkeeper, resident at 14 General Perrier Street, Nîmes. His wife, Regina, born Cohen, also in Turkey, and a child born in France, appeared on another declaration list of June 26/27, 1941. If the Afnaims had moved their residence after July 1, 1942 (which they did not), one of them would have had to return to the Prefecture to make that fact known within thirty days of moving. Undoubtedly, the Afnaim family was inventoried among the eighty-four Turkish males and females listed with other foreign and French Jews on the tally mentioned some pages back. Their child, having been born in France, seems to have been recorded with typical Vichy functionary attention to detail along with French Jewish children. M. Afnaim, like the Berrs, sought to protest the takeover of his business by the CGQJ and the trustee they had appointed on May 16, 1942. The enterprise,

---

24   ADG. Ibid. Marked 475/77 and 465/67.

Superfina, was a retail silk goods business "exploited by the Jew Afnaim." The letter from the regional director of the CGQJ in Marseille to Prefect Chiappe stated: "The sale [of Superina] had been set for 21 June 1943 and Afnaim had opposed it, forcing the trustee, M. Georges Royer to appear before the President of Nîmes' Civil Tribunal, who extended the date for the sale in order to consider the case, which liquidation was based on 'Rationed Material' [meaning the sale of silk]. The appeal has been submitted to the Court. The principle of separation of powers which allows the court to intervene makes it troublesome for our administration to carry out its duties. I ask you to employ your powers to instruct the Prosecutor General to seek a dismissal in the Appeals Court of this case based on the incompetency of the President of Civil Tribunal to rule on this matter."

There is no further archival record to prove whether or not M. Afnaim had a positive outcome similar to the one Marcel Berr subsequently obtained.[25]

On March 24, 1943, Prefect Chiappe handwrote a two-page letter to the Minister of the Interior in Vichy, in response to several of his recent telegrams requesting information as to whether there were any Bulgarian, Spanish, Hungarian, Italian, Portuguese, Rumanian, Swiss, or Turkish "Israelites" in his department who were interned or who wished to be repatriated. Chiappe answered that after researching all the residents of these nationalities in the Gard, "not one of these nationalities is interned, as I possess no internment camp in my territory. I have made an inquiry to ascertain whether there are any volunteers among these named foreign nationalities who wish to be repatriated, in effect conforming to the policy announced in your circular dated 22 January 1943 Pol. 12 forbidding requests for visas or passports coming from Israelites; again none of these foreign Jews has requested repatriation. Only the Spanish Jew, Bessudo, Jose, born 28 September 1894 in Constantinople, is a volunteer for his repatriation. I will keep you informed of any new requests for repatriation which might ensue."

Another list was to be maintained. However, all these potentially lucky "Israelites" were from either neutral countries or ones with which Germany was allied. Of course, the Axis allies, except for Italy, all had

---

25   ADG. Ibid. Marked 430. 1 W 140-143. Unmarked roster "A". 1 W 138-139.
op. cit. marked 637 and 640.

ongoing efforts supervised by the Germans to eradicate their Jewish populations.[26]

On April 5, 1943, Louis Darquier de Pellepoix's office administrator in Paris, M. Antignac, wrote all prefects, including Chiappe, ordering the census-taking of all Jewish school children. Its purpose was to study the feasibility of creating a primary school exclusively for Jewish children. Antignac requested the following information:

1. A summary of all primary education school enrollments in the department for boys and girls, with the specific number of Jewish students indicated as well.

2. This is to be summarized for course work student composition as well.

3. A similar summary for superior schools and courses as well.

4. List, with names and addresses, all Jewish teachers, male and female, who have been put on leave by the application of the law of 2 June 1941, and who would be acceptable for an exemption from the general order forbidding them to teach under Article 8 of that same law, if they would be willing to teach in a school reserved for Jews.

On May 18, 1943, Chiappe received back the summary he requested from his school academy inspector. It opened by reiterating how the report was formulated and went on to state: "There are no teachers or professors affected by Article 8 of the law of 2 June 1941 who are interested in teaching in a school establishment reserved for Jews." Nineteen schools spread out over the department had a total enrollment of thirty-three Jewish students. It is easy to imagine what the future might bring.[27]

On June 21, 1943, a more urgent matter for Vichy and their German occupiers was addressed in a telegram sent to "All Prefects in France." It came from the Obligatory Work Service (STO) chief in Paris and requested the following information in two days time:

1. the total number of Jewish males in your department;

---

26 ADG. 1 W 140-143. Marked 272–272.
27 ADG. Enquêtes juives. Marked 344/200 and 339/196.

2.   the number of your Jewish people born between October 1, 1919 and December 31, 1922;

3.   the number of Jewish male internees defined accordingly with No.1 and No. 2.

Chiappe replied the next day in his telegram to STO's Paris HQ. "This is in response to your telegram number 294 and offers you the following information: 1) total Israelite male population in my department—1156, of whom 512 are foreigners; 2) number of young Israelites born between 1 October 1919 and 31 December 1922—60, of whom 18 are foreigners; 3) there are no Israelites interned in my department."

The number of Jews must have been reduced somewhat by the raids to arrest Jews made by Gestapo elements in the Midi during April–May 1943. Nîmes was one of the targeted cities on April 19, and those raids speak volumes to the cross-purposes of different German organizations.[28]

Earlier evidence abounds that indicates the tightening of the screws on foreign and French Jews when the Germans moved into the Midi as a result of the invasion of French North Africa. On December 26, 1942, the regional prefect in Marseille wrote the prefects under his control in the Bouches-du-Rhône, the Gard, and the Var, a letter of instructions that furthered police restrictions on Jews. A new Jewish law had been imposed on December 11, 1942, that "prescribed the fixing of the word Jew not only on all identity cards but also on all Israelite food rationing cards." Appended to the letter was the press release announcing this edict. The second purpose of the letter was to "apply the instructions contained in letter number 18.743 of 6 December 1942 from the 14th Bureau of Territorial Police, relative to the removal of all foreign Jews who had arrived after 1 January 1938 in all localities situated 30 kilometers from the coast. Since this zone comprises almost the totality of the BDR, I intend to apply it to the entire department. I beg the Prefects of the Gard and Var vigorously to apply these instructions to remove all foreign Jews, by conforming to the stipulations of letter number 18.743 of 6 December, on which they were copied."

The prefects of the Vaucluse and Hautes-Alpes were also copied.

---

28   ADG. 1 W 137. Marked as 50 and 49. *Vichy France and the Jews.* Ibid., 308–309.

On March 1, 1943, SS Oberscharfuhrer von Stellvertr of the Sicherheitspolizei SD [better known as the "Gestapo"] in Marseille wrote Prefect Chiappe the following letter in German. Duly translated, it referred to an earlier letter of his dated February 16, 1943, whose subject was the registration of foreigners. It went on to say:

> As a result of the agreement between the head of the SD and the French government, the prefectures are required to maintain a register of all foreigners residing in their department.
>
> This register must be current as of 20 February 1943.
>
> The prefects must retain an updated copy for use of their services as well as for use by the SD.
>
> The regional prefect in Marseille will maintain a consolidated document for all the foreigners resident in the departments under his supervision, which will be put at the disposition of the SD Command in Marseille.
>
> I request that you inform me by 3 March 1943 of the total number of foreigners by nationality resident in the department of the Gard, accounted for as of the end of February.

Clearly, all foreign Jews were included in these registers for use by the SD.[29] Early in 1944, the SCT intercepted some Jewish communications in the Gard. A couple of letters were from Mme. Levi who lived on Grand Convent Street in central Nîmes, not far from the Maison Carrée. She wrote her son that a Mme. Berger had denounced their family, accusing them as well as M. Vidal of keeping pistols concealed in their homes. The German police had searched their residence but found nothing and then returned to ask for their papers and to inquire concerning the whereabouts of their children. A friend had been imprisoned for making a false accusation but was later released, as there was no evidence. A second SCT intercept from the Levi house concerned the rescue of twenty-six prisoners by a group of *"réfractaires"* from the central prison of Nîmes on the Friday prior to February 6. It described how the "terrorists" also had abducted four police agents who were listed by name and were still missing. The letter went on to indicate that on the fifth,

---

29   ADG. Enquêtes juives. Marked 270 and 334.

the German police came and arrested M. Vidal, which had upset Mme. Claude, a resident of the household. M. André, the tramway controller, had been shot in the leg by two Miliciens who caught him putting anti-Vichy propaganda into mailboxes. He was taken to the hospital where the Milice had him under guard. Nîmes was described as being subject to constant roundups, day and night. Police Chief Framagen was being driven to distraction but it seemed that some police reinforcements had been approved by Vichy.

Another Nîmois Jew, M. Weill, had his phone call intercepted by the SCT. He told a friend who lived in the mining basin that he was frustrated by the poor information available in the prefecture concerning which young men would be called to STO duty. First the answer was yes, and then no, which proved to the caller that the administrators knew nothing. The party called apparently worked for a mining company and said he had been getting call-ups for the class of 1943 already. He replied that in such cases, the young men named were already working in the mines and were therefore exempt from STO duty. This comment did not seem to dispel the anxiety of the call originator, probably because he or the young person he was concerned about did not work in a mine.

A foreign Jew who resided in Anduze was the subject of another letter intercepted by the SCT. He wrote a friend that his book had sold more than two hundred copies in the two local bookstores, and they seemed to be widely read, resulting in general consternation, due to the subject matter. He had received several anonymous hate letters, as well as some printed pamphlets, which labeled him as an international vagabond chased out by five countries before arriving in France. He related that scatological songs were circulated about him, along with many other invented stories. On the street, two or three people had screamed at him but his indifference was off-putting to them. Although his letter was not specific about the subject matter of his book, it was grist for virulent anti-Semitic outbursts.[30]

In May 1944, some other Jews were more vigorously involved in resistance activities against the Germans and their Vichy surrogates. Their stories were taken down on the telephone by Mlle. Remusat, who worked in the Gard's gendarmerie. One concerned the Polish Jew Kyjak.

---

30   ADG. 1 W 40. Ibid. Unmarked letters of January 31 and February 6, 1944; marked 41/83 of January 1944; marked 93/56 of January 31, 1944.

On May 1, at 11:00 PM, two high-tension electrical pylons belonging to the Society Grande Combienne of Lighting and Electrical Energy had been sabotaged by an explosive charge on the rail line between Alès and Salindres. One bomb had been found that had failed to detonate, which was brought back to the gendarmerie. The message ended by stating that "a Polish worker, Margan Kyjak, found carrying 15 detonators, was arrested by a GMR [French special mobile police unit] patrol towards 2300 hours. He has been taken to the Alès Central Police station. The German authorities there have been notified; they have alerted the Feld-gendarmerie of Nîmes."

The Alès sub-prefecture telephoned to give Mlle. Remusat the following message on May 10: "On 9 May at 2115 hours the Alès police were informed that Paul Reynaud, 43 years old, attached to the German Gestapo service, had opened fire with an automatic weapon on two individuals, who according to his testimony, had attacked him. The two persons in question were killed. They were Adam Kaczmarck, 40, a cook, resident of Hauteville (Ain), and René Nique, 25, residence unknown.

"Additionally, Mme. Marie Brès, 58, of 1 Market Place, Alès, and Jean Garcia, 6, of Sabaterie Street, Alès, received multiple bullet wounds. They were taken to the Alès hospital.

"A German officer reached the site of the incident and assumed control of the affair."

Mlle. Remusat received news of a serious incident at 2:00 PM on May 30 from the Nîmes gendarmerie. Her transcription read: "A murder took place in Nîmes on 29 May between 1230 and 1300 hours near the Mas of M. de Courcy, mayor of Bouillargues. The Israelite Kremmer was killed with a pistol shot. The victim was found ten meters from the road. She died a few minutes later. No identification was found on her except for a slip of paper indicating that she had been the object of a prior arrest by the German authorities. The gendarmerie was notified by M. de Courcy and arrived on the scene. The judiciary of Nîmes has been alerted about the incident. The body has been taken to the morgue." A handwritten remark was added to the report that confirmed it had been "seen by the Prefect."[31]

On March 23, 1944, Pierre Laval, as head of government, issued a

---

31   ADG. Enquêtes juives. Ibid. Marked 451, 2 May 1944; marked 249, 10 May 1944; unmarked 30 May 1944.

law at Vichy that made changes to how destitute Jews were to be supported under the Vichy social system (*fonds de solidarité*). Article 1 of law 172 effectively doubled an allocation (from 10 percent to 20 percent) derived from liquidated Jewish enterprises, for this purpose. Article 2 and 3 created a new 10 percent allocation, retroactive to July 1941, taken from all Jewish bank deposits under the control of the CGQJ, for the same purpose. Hence, the wealthier Jews, dead or alive, would increase the amount of money in the CGQJ's pot, which might or might not ever get into the hands of poor Jews in France. The final article announced that "the present decree will be published in the *Journal officiel* and be executed as a law of the state."[32] In five months time, both Laval and Pétain would be forcibly abducted and incarcerated in Sigmaringen, Germany, while administrative procedures in the Gard would be transitioning to Free French control.[33]

  Evidence of this evolutional change came in the format and form of a letter Prefect Paganelle issued on September 14, 1944, on stationery on which *Etat Français* was crossed out and *République Française* was

---

32 ADG. Enquêtes juives. Ibid. Marked 294. The following is a personal communication of April 15, 2012, from Robert O. Paxton to the author on this subject. "The *"fonds de solidarité"* came from the money generated by the confiscation and sale of Jewish property under the terms of the Law of 22 July 1941. Ninety percent of that money was deposited in the *Caisse des Dépôts et Consignations* and 10 percent formed a *fonds de solidarité* used to aid indigent Jews. I believe that some of the money raised by the billion franc fine levied on the Jews of France in December 1941 also went to the *fonds de solidarité*.

So I understand the 1944 law you cite as increasing the amount of money available for aid to the indigent, as of course the number of Jews who could not earn a living kept increasing. I don't think this is an increase in a tax, but an increase in proportion of the money from confiscated Jewish property used for aid to the indigent.

When the UGIF (*Union générale des israélites de France*) was set up in November 1941, it was assigned the task of distributing the *fonds de solidarité* to indigent Jews. It seems very bizarre that indigent Jews were receiving relief at the same moment that they were likely to be arrested for deportation, but those two contradictory behaviors do seem to have coexisted in the world of the Shoah.

Sometimes the two things intersected—on several occasions indigent Jews came to UGIF offices to get their welfare money, and found Gestapo agents waiting to arrest them. Near the end the UGIF offices warned welfare recipients not to come to the offices, but to receive their aid by mail. At the end, the UGIF staffs themselves were taken away."

33 *Vichy France.* Ibid., 329; *France: The Dark Years.* Ibid., 567–568.

typed in. Its object was dual fold: "Abolition of house arrest for British and American (USA) nationals and elimination of the word 'Jew' affixed to foreign Israelite identity cards." The Brits and Americans in the Gard could now move about without staying just in their commune of residence. As to the Jews, the word Jew was to be removed, as "no racial distinction" was permitted any longer. The concerned parties could retain their old identity cards in corrected form, or pay the corresponding fee and receive a "new" one in exchange.[34]

The prefect issued a press release two weeks later which announced a major policy change vis-à-vis any Jews in the Gard who had been dispossessed of their property. It stated: "In an order dated 27 September 1944, the Commissioner of the Republic for the Region of Languedoc-Roussillon, stipulates that all parties having acquired or taken possession after 26 June 1940 of property belonging to people qualified as Jews in the sense of German ordinances or of texts of a racial character coming from the Vichy government, must make said declaration within two weeks after publication of this decree, at the Prefecture or Sub-Prefecture."

The people so involved were to come to make their declarations at the 4th Division in the Secretariat for Jewish Interests at the prefecture, before October 12. This was one of the initial steps for restitution of Jewish possessions expropriated under Vichy.[35]

A Jewish official, Vidal Escojido, secretary of the Jewish Entr'aide (sic—meaning Mutual Aid) Committee, did not wait long to take the initiative. On September 22, 1944, Prefect Paganelle gave M. Escojido permission to access all Jewish affairs files held at the Commerce Tribunal or the Chamber of Notaries. This Nîmois, who would be acting "in the public interest," so wrote the prefect, was a Chevalier of the Legion of Honor and holder of the Croix de Guerre. Subsequently, on October 7, the prefect sent a written instruction to the civil and military authorities to allow M. Escojido, in his official capacity and accompanied by M. Picard, the head of Paganelle's office, to pass frequently on their mission between Nîmes and Marseille. The march for justice was on.[36]

On November 3, 1944, the commissioner for Languedoc-Roussil-

---

34 ADG. Enquêtes juives. Ibid. Marked 66.
35 1 W 136. Marked 104/9.
36 Ibid. Marked 26 and 27.

lon in Montpellier wrote all prefects in his region concerning important changes in procedural relations affecting the PTT. The memo stated:

> The committee instituted on October 8 for the purpose of reviewing certain restrictions existing within the PTT has published some redrafted instructions. Effective 25 October sealed postal correspondence has been resumed and as of 30 October interurban telephone service will be reestablished. This applies to all of Languedoc-Roussillon. However, relative to postal services, the following instructions will apply. Sending regular, express, or registered mail for private correspondence is allowed in all the territory of France, except for the following Departments: Meuse, Meurthe & Moselle, Vosges, Haute-Savoie, Doubs, Territoire de Belfort, Moselle, Bas Rhin, Haut Rhin, Loire Inférieure (St-Nazaire and Paimboeuf), Morbihan (Lorient, Port-Scorff, Port-Louis, Hennebont, Bolz, Pluvigher), Auray, Quiberon, Musillac, Roche Bernard.

These departments were either still occupied by the Germans or being fought over. The small step relative to "sealed mail" did not mean, however, that the SCT had been yet totally defanged.[37]

During this period of the liberation of France, we have witnessed steps taken to remedy the wrongs done to French Jews in the Gard under the Vichy regime and its CGQJ organization. The French language is known for the preciseness of word definition. What was carried out under the Ayranization policy was called, in French, *spoliation*, which means, in this sense, despoilment or the stripping of rights or possessions. The companies or individuals who were so despoiled were not limited to the Berrs or the Afnaims. Some internationally famous French firms, owned or controlled by French Jews, were taken over by trustees appointed by the CGQJ. As an example, in the *Journal Officiel De L'Etat Français* of May 16, 1942, the Minister of the Interior placed an announcement on behalf of the CGQJ. It proclaimed that companies such as Pernod and Cinzano, Chanel, Saint Gobain, Galeries Lafayette, and Banque de France, controlled by prominent people like the Rothschilds, Werthheimers, and Veil-Picards, had been placed under provi-

---

37   ADG. Enquêtes juives. Ibid. marked 1.

sional administration. No Gardois company or resident was illustrious enough to be included on this list, but obviously many suffered a similar fate that required rectification.[38]

Nearly three years later, on April 22, 1945, the *Journal Officiel De la République Française* proclaimed that in "Ordinance number 45-770 of 21 April 1945 its focus on the ordinance of 12 November 1943 and nullified the acts of despoilment carried out *by the enemy or under his control* [author's italics] and decreed that restitution be made to the victims of these acts and the return of any property of which they have been dispossessed (p. 2283)."[39] Several days later, a handwritten list containing twenty-six names was prepared by Gard prefectural functionaries, for the following purpose: "Under application of Article 28 of Ordinance 45-770 of 21 April 1945, this list (*Bordereau*) of declarations has been made at the Prefecture of the Gard by holders (*débenteurs*) of Israelite properties."

The vast majority of individuals resided in Nîmes, while only two were located in Alès. This probably was an initial compilation of trustees, as certain known *administrateurs provisoires* do not appear on this particular directory. However, it did include a certain M. Royer of 10 rue Colbert, Nîmes, of whom we will hear more shortly.[40]

On August 8, 1945, Prefect Paganelle received a letter from the Minister of Finance of the Provisional Government of the French Republic located in Paris. It stated:

Under the Vichy regime, the ex-Commissariat General of Jewish Affairs pursued inquiries under the policy of what was called Ayranization, concerning the owners of all types of property, of any presumed Israelites."

What happened frequently with this organization was that before these properties were assigned to a trustee or even sold or liquidated, their owners were asked to furnish original documents establishing proof of their ownership. These documents have been retained in the archives of the CGQJ.

Many of these papers could remain of great interest to those

---

38   ADG. Ibid. marked 149/229.
39   ADG. 1 W 136. Ibid. marked 12.
40   ADG. Ibid. Marked 7.

who were asked to provide them and have not been given them back. My Restitution Service would be very pleased to return them quickly to their original owners.

Consequently, in order to allow my service to proceed in the restitution of such material, I request that you announce its availability throughout your department in the press and on the radio, as indicted below:

Restitution of Israelite Ownership Documents

The Restitution Service possesses a number of important documents held in the files of the CGQJ belonging to individuals from whom this organization took over property administration.

The interested parties can actually claim repossession of these documents, by submitting the necessary precise information to the Restitution Service, 1 rue de la Banque, Paris 2e.[41]

The notice was published throughout the Gard on August 9.

On October 1, 1945, the same restitution finance minister wrote Prefect Paganelle on a sticky administrative matter. It was his third request (after May 29 and July 25) to the prefect for a specific CGQJ trustee's missing individual declaration. Apparently, the missing statement concerned M. Royer, resident of Nîmes, 10 rue Colbert, whose name had been on the list of April 21, but whose declaration had slipped between the prefectural cracks. Seven decades later, the implied admonishment remained in the Gard's archives.[42]

On December 6, 1946, Minister of the Interior Edouard Depreux wrote all prefects on what would seem to be a very delicate subject matter.

Objective: Destruction of documents based on distinctions of racial order among the French.

Under the Authority of the Government of the so-called French State, a text entitled "law of 3 October 1940, known as the Jewish Statute," had claimed to create between the French distinctions based on racial order.

---

41   ADG. Ibid. Marked 229.
42   ADG. Ibid. Marked 98/3.

The regulations it brought into effect forced persons considered as Jews to sign various declarations.

I recall that the law of 9 August 1944 which reestablished the republican legality in metropolitan France notes in Article 3 the nullity of all acts that establish or apply any discrimination whatsoever founded on a Jewish qualification.

Now it has been pointed out that in various administrative entities (Prefectures, Mayor Offices, Police Departments, etc.) some index card and paper files established for these purposes still exist.

In conformance with the spirit of the law of 9 August 1944 cited above, no more traces of the legislation of such [racial] exception under the occupation must remain [in the files] and *all documents based on definition of Jewishness must be destroyed* [author's italics].

Please address clear instructions on this matter to the mayors and <u>to all concerned functionaries</u> and report back on the implementation of these instructions.

Proof is in the pudding, at least for the archival and prefectural files in the Gard, where these items still exist.[43]

The Schreiber-Crémieux Family Alliance and Vichy

On January 31, 1916, Robert Schreiber and Suzanne Crémieux signed a marriage contract in the presence of the family notary, and the alliance was solemnized when they were married civilly on February 17. Both were French Jews: he was a self-made, successful newspaper publisher from Paris, and she was the progeny of an illustrious Radical Party political family who resided in Remoulins, the Gard. Robert, age thirty-seven, had been a military staff officer in the French army, who was training to be an aviator, and Suzanne, twenty years old, was participating in Belgian children's relief work.

Robert was the eldest of three brothers born to Joseph Schreiber and his wife, the former Clara Feilchenfeld, both of whom had immigrated to France from Prussia a few years after the Franco-Prussian war. Joseph and Clara became naturalized French citizens in 1894, while their sons

---

43   ADG. Enquêtes juives. Ibid. Marked 3/516.

were French by birth. Robert's parents were German Jews in France, whose financial state had been a modest one; it was for their sons to achieve significant levels of success. Joseph died in 1902, but Clara lived much longer and died in mid-1941 during the German occupation of Paris.

Suzanne was the youngest child of Fernand Crémieux, born in Pont-Saint-Esprit, the Gard, and the former Soltana Aghion, who had been born in the Jewish community of Alexandria, Egypt. Fernand Crémieux served over thirty years as a senator under the Third Republic. His more famous uncle, Adolph Crémieux, was born in Nîmes in 1796. He was a renowned jurist and served from 1834 until his death in 1880 as vice president of the Central Consistory of the Jews of France. He became the justice minister in the French Government of National Defense in Tours in 1870, which treated with Bismarck after France's defeat in the Franco-Prussian War. Ironically, it was Adolph Crémieux whose name was attached to the *Décret Crémieux*, the law of October 24, 1870, enacted by him, Gambetta, Glais-Bizoin, and Fourichon, which declared the 37,000-odd Jews residing in Algeria to be French citizens from that day forward.[44] Fernand Crémieux had a natural distrust and dislike of Germans, exacerbated by his service during the Great War. He demonstrated his suspicions about an alliance between Robert and his family by undertaking some inquiries into Robert's commercial interests. These included *The Echoes of Exportation: an Information Newspaper for Business and Industry*, which Robert had founded in 1908. That enterprise had prospered by being the first to introduce commercial advertising for its customers. The hefty sum that Robert added to his daughter's dowry helped him pass muster, and so the marriage took place as noted.

The wedding gained some unfortunate publicity, which understandably was upsetting to the young bride. She sent a February 28, 1916, clipping to Robert, who was back in the army. It was the lead article in the rabidly anti-Semitic journal founded in 1892 by Edouard Drumont, *La Libre Parole*.[45] Its headline blared: "Viviani has committed an act of indignity against our parliamentarian regime," because he

---

44   *Vichy France and the Jews.* Ibid. 4.
45   Ibid., 30–31. Paxton and Marrus explain that this paper and *La Croix*, published by an Assumptionist Catholic order, played very effectively to the fears of various social groups who felt threatened by the Jews.

had been a witness at the Schreiber-Crémieux civil wedding ceremony, which involved "a German yid." The commentary went on to state "that Senator Crémieux gives away his daughter to a Schreiber has no importance: a Jewess marries a Jew, that's all. It happens that the Jewess is born in France, and that the Jew is born in Germany, but both are neither German nor French: they are from Jerusalem." Robert and Suzanne Schreiber had three children from their union: Jean-Claude born in 1918, Marie-Claire born in 1921, and Marie-Geneviève born in 1930.[46]

With the war over, Robert returned to his newspaper, where he was director and editor in chief, and his younger brother, Emile, became coeditor. They shortened the masthead to *Les Echos* and relaunched it in May 1919. It became very successful and evolved over the years into the French equivalent of the *Wall Street Journal*. Emile became a married man when he took Denise Brésard, a Catholic, as his wife on May 4, 1923. Their first child Jean-Jacques Servan-Schreiber was born in early 1924.[47] He would become internationally famous as the founder of *L'Express*. The third brother, Georges, a medical doctor, married an assimilated Jewish woman, as Robert had, in 1920.

Robert began to accumulate a substantial fortune, which suited his strikingly beautiful wife Suzanne very well. From youth, politics had impassioned Suzanne, and she also avidly followed the feminist movement in France, where women were denied the vote until 1944. Robert encouraged her to attend the 1924 Radical Party Convention, where she joined other prominent women from the French League for the Rights of Women. From that year forward, she hardly missed attending that annual event. Suzanne had numerous personal advantages to ease her advancement in her political involvement: her family name and her father's contacts; her striking beauty and her social ease in the society of men; her desire to succeed; and the agreement of her successful husband to dispense his money freely so she could entertain lavishly in the Schreiber avenue de Montaigne apartment the likes of Herriot, Daladier, de Monzie, etc.[48]

In September 1925, Suzanne took her two children to spend three

---

46 *La Saga Servan-Schreiber*. Ibid., 135–136.
47 Ibid., 226, 232–234, 245–247, 249, 254.
48 Ibid., 269–270.

weeks at her parents' country home, La Cigale, in Remoulins outside Nîmes in the Gard. One day she was driving in the countryside and by chance passed through the village of Montfrin, where she noticed a château on a promontory above town. Robert visited it soon thereafter and fell in love with the place and the idea of becoming a châtelain, the owner of a countryside chateau. He purchased it and its immediately surrounding 3.5 hectares for only 110,000 francs, closing the purchase contract on November 14, 1925. He completely modernized its 3,500-square-meter interior with bathrooms equipped with running water, as well as twenty-eight telephones placed throughout the chateau. After Suzanne participated in an international conference for women's suffrage at the Sorbonne in mid-May 1926, she arrived to supervise the set-up of Montfrin Château, where she could entertain her political friends and Gardois acquaintances as mistress of an impressive manor.[49]

As the turbulent 1930s unsettled French society, so did diverging interests agitate the relationship between the two Schreibers. The different worlds of business and politics drew them apart and caused growing friction, as Robert felt that Suzanne did not pay enough attention to their children. He also maintained suspicions about her faithfulness to him, although he was no saint in this regard himself. In 1934, this led to a split when Suzanne announced she would accompany a political delegation which included her reputed lover, Pierre Cot, on a trip to Russia. Soon thereafter, Robert wrote his eldest daughter, Marie-Claire: "Your mother has gone to Russia, and I have decided that we will lead separate lives from now on. She will keep you girls, and I will keep my son." The Schreiber-Crémieux alliance had turned into a misalliance, although they still got together under family circumstances in Paris or Montfrin in the years leading up to World War II.[50]

Fast-forwarding five years, at 5:00 PM on September 3, 1939, six hours later than the British, France declared war on Germany. The Phony War (*Drôle de guerre* in French) was about to get underway in all its weirdness. Jean-Claude went to learn how to mount his modern horse, a tank, at the Saumur cavalry school in mid-September and trained there until March 1940. Two months later, on May 10, the French debacle com-

---

49   Ibid., 277–282.
50   Ibid., 363–366.

Montfrin Château today (2010).

The rough-hewn stone that marks the gravesite of Robert Schreiber, at a spot overlooking Montfrin Château.

menced as a result of failure in their military command and not from a lack of their soldiers' resolve. It was over in six days. By the end of May, Jean-Claude was among the more than 100,000 French soldiers who had escaped from Dunkirk to England.[51] He did not rest long on English soil, as he and most other French soldiers shipped out as soon as possible for Le Havre, where the civilians cheered them, not realizing that the battle for France already had been lost. He managed to join a part of his brigade near Evreux, south of the Seine, midway between Rouen and Paris. While there, he was awarded a morale-boosting military cross as a result of his two citations, and even managed to have Suzanne and Marie-Claire, both in ambulance corps uniforms, there to witness the award ceremony.

On June 11, Jean-Claude was back in action against the Germans, while retreating near Pacy-sur-Eure west of Paris, when he was shot in the thigh. Luckily, he was evacuated via train to Bordeaux, just after the Germans entered Paris on June 14. His wound healed so well that he was given two weeks' leave to recuperate. He decided to travel for that purpose to Montfrin, where he found his whole family among some one hundred Belgian refugees that Robert had put up on the grounds. While France's military fate was being determined, Suzanne received a phone call from René-Victor Manaut, a deputy and friend associated with Reynaud's government, who informed her that some ships had been ordered to Bordeaux to transport elements of the government to North Africa to help preserve the republic. He suggested that she consider leaving with her family on one of those ships, as the known examples of how Hitler treated certain societal elements in Czechoslovakia and Poland, especially Jewish ones, were not encouraging. Suzanne convinced Robert that it would be best to leave the hexagon. The Schreibers drove two family cars to Biarritz, from where Suzanne left for Bordeaux to pave the way for their passage from France to one of its North African colonies.[52]

On the night of June 16–17, Bordeaux was the scene where a crestfallen Paul Reynaud resigned his premiership and suggested to President Lebrun that he choose Marshal Pétain as his successor. Lebrun agreed and Pétain, who was committed to feel out the Germans about peace terms, formed the last Third Republic government. The composition of

---

51   Ibid., 412–414, 418–422; *France: The Dark Years*, 118–119.
52   *La Saga Servan-Schreiber*. Ibid., 421, 423–425; *France: The Dark Years*. Ibid., 120.

its members covered the French political gamut from conservatives to socialists, but excluded anyone from heading a ministry who was dead set against an armistice. The atmosphere was frantic, and uncertainty and confusion reigned, since the members of the new government feared the arrival of German troops before negotiations could commence. General Weygand, the current French army commander, was being strongly lobbied by his North African military delegate, General Noguès, to influence the new government to transfer to the colonies to continue the fight against the Germans. For one brief moment on the day of June 19, the cabinet approved that some government administrators and all assembly delegates should depart for Morocco to avoid being bagged by the Germans. Swiftly, Pétain's firm armistice adherents reacted and shifted the mood so that those who might actually leave would be cast in a light reflective of the nobles who fled Paris for Brussels at the start of the French Revolution, the *émigrés*.[53]

Suzanne Crémieux arrived in Bordeaux the next day, in the midst of that chaotic disarray. Under such stressful and fluid circumstances, no French officials understood what was really happening, as the new government suffered from poor military intelligence and was largely dependent on rumor. Suzanne met an acquaintance, Charles Pomaret, whom Pétain had appointed Minister of the Interior on June 16 (he would be replaced eleven days later). He informed her inaccurately that President Lebrun and almost all the ministers had already departed for Algiers. He counseled her to seek passage on the *Massilia*, a ship that was to leave that day carrying many parliamentarians from the port at the Gironde's mouth, Le Verdon. She telephoned Robert that she had been given the requisite papers to allow all the family to embark on the *Massilia*, and that he must leave at once with the children in order to arrive before the ship's departure. The car carrying the family arrived at 11:00 PM, having covered the three hundred kilometers from Biarritz and joined about fifty other cars parked in the fields by the estuary.

Robert met Jammy Schmidt, a deputy from the Oise whom he knew; Schmidt told him any further boarding would take place in the morning of the twenty-first. The family spent the night nestled among their valises in the field and the next morning, they watched German planes attempting to bomb shore batteries. Then, around 11 AM, Robert,

---

53 *Vichy France.* Ibid., 7–8.

Suzanne, and the two girls bade farewell to Jean-Claude, as they boarded the ferry bound for the *Massilia*. Jean-Claude, walking with the aid of a cane, turned to wave good-bye to his family and then went off to rejoin his unit at Limoges. Robert and Suzanne soon realized that there were only twenty-seven parliamentarians aboard, the vast majority from the Radical Party, and ominously not a single member was present from the new Pétain government. When Robert walked in to lunch, he saw at the head table Edouard Daladier, Georges Mandel, Jean Zay, Pierre Mendès France, César Campinchi, and Yvon Delbos. He joked, "There are enough here to form a ministry. If you are lacking someone for commerce, I'm your man." Apparently, this attempt at a joke was taken down by someone within hearing, for later Robert maintained that it was put in his dossier as a charge against him.[54]

The next day, the tone was decidedly more serious, as it appeared that rumor or confirmation had been received by the *Massilia's* radio operator that Pétain's armistice terms had been accepted on June 22 by the German military representatives at Rethondes near Compiègne. The deputies debated what to do; some wanted to return to Bordeaux and others were for heading to England to join de Gaulle. According to Robert, Georges Mandel had been a proponent of this latter course of action, and Robert maintained that he had discussed with Mandel his fears that they had fallen into a trap by departing Bordeaux without the government aboard. Reputedly, Mandel agreed with his assessment, but the ship's captain, Ferbos, refused to alter his orders to proceed to Morocco. According to Julian Jackson, the absence of the *Massilia* twenty-seven benefited the proponents of an armistice, as they were the strongest opponents of giving up the fight in metropolitan France.

Raphaël Alibert, Vichy's future Minister of Justice, who would play a central role in drafting Pétain's constitutional powers and the first anti-Jewish laws, passed on false information to Pétain about the German army not having yet broached the Loire River defenses. Due to this bogus intelligence, Pétain's new government chose to remain in Bordeaux, and for that reason alone, none joined the twenty-seven deputies aboard the *Massilia*.[55] Robert stayed in his cabin next to the one occupied by

---

54 *La Saga Servan-Schreiber*. Ibid., 429–431.
55 Robert Servan-Schreiber. *Journal* (Paris: Editions Leo Scheer, 2009), 448–449; *France: The Dark Years*. Ibid., 127, 152. 554.

Suzanne and her two daughters, wondering what fate would await them upon their arrival in North Africa. The ship entered the port of Casablanca at 7:45 in the morning of June 24. When the director of public security boarded the ship, accompanied by some policemen, he looked over the passenger manifest but offered no information, and simply told all the passengers that they had to stay on board to await the arrival of a higher official. A couple of hours later, Secretary General Morizé arrived in the company of General Lebrun, the military commander of Casablanca, and Morizé agreed to send a telegram to Herriot on behalf of four deputies, who asked for some instructions of what to do.

The next day, the answer was received: "I am doing what is necessary for the government." Some restricted movement within Casablanca's city limits was allowed on June 25, but the deputies were distinctly feeling a cold-shoulder treatment from elements of French officialdom. Jean Zay had experienced a scuffle with a French aviator on the dock for an old, perceived insult toward the French flag in a poem. That same day, the *Massilia* moved with all passengers aboard to an anchorage a kilometer offshore, and the passengers realized that they were interned for the moment. The voyage had certainly turned out to be a trap, as local French newspapers were already portraying the twenty-seven parliamentarians, who had left Bordeaux aboard the *Massilia*, as deserters. When they were finally permitted to leave the ship on June 27, the crowd hurled insults, calling them sell-outs, cowards, and deserters, and Georges Mandel was taken off by the police. The fact that Edouard Herriot only had his luggage aboard the *Massilia* would not save him from persecution, as he would be among those exiled to German-annexed Lorraine in 1942 for opposing Vichy.

Life under Vichy

The Schreiber family managed to disembark, find taxis, and head to Algiers in hope of returning to France as soon as possible. Robert and Suzanne, as well as any deputies not under arrest, had fully comprehended by now that the French authorities in North Africa had chosen not to continue the war against the Germans from their bases there but had elected to follow the orders of the Pétain government. It also had become clear that the deputies who had been aboard the *Massilia* were *persona non grata* in Vichy, where the National Assembly was to convene on July 10 to hold at Pétain's behest a constitutional convention. The Schreiber party of four continued to wait in Algiers and finally was able to book passage on a ship bound for Marseille, which arrived there on July 12, from where they set off for Montfrin about one hundred kilometers away. Robert, Suzanne, Marie-Claire, and Marie-Geneviève arrived at the Château to find 150 Belgian and French refugee children still there, in addition to a regiment of Senegalese *tirailleurs* who were now encamped on the château's commons. Upon visiting his mayoral office, Robert learned that Pétain's new interior minister, Adrien Marquet, had dismissed him from that position.[56]

Robert's return to Montfrin was duly noted, and the authorities in Nîmes were apprised of this fact, along with his arrival in Marseille from North Africa in the company of Suzanne and his two daughters. Therefore, the SCT commenced almost immediately to listen in to telephone conversations and intercept mail to and from the château. At any rate, Robert did not easily give up, relative to his removal from the mayor's office. He traveled early in the fall to Vichy to register his protest with Marquet's successor, Marcel Peyrouton, armed with a thick dossier. Peyrouton refused to give him an audience, but he did succeed in meeting with his chief office assistant, who was impressed with Robert's justifications for his voyage on the *Massilia*. However, he advised Robert to calm down: "What would you have us do? We have just dismissed over three thousand mayors, and it could well be that by acting so swiftly, several of them were let go in error. I suggest you give us some time and don't pursue immediate reinstatement. We will see what we can do." The

---

56 Ibid., 121, 127. Interior Minister Marquet was the mayor of Bordeaux when Reynaud and his fleeing French government arrived there in mid-June. Marquet was an ex-pacifist who believed France had been defeated by the Germans and did everything in his power actively to support Pétain's armistice cause and oppose those who wanted to fight on. As mayor, he made that very difficult for the latter and offered city facilities to make things easy for the former. He assisted Alibert in influencing Pétain to desist from sending representatives to North Africa to carry on the war. His reward, the interior ministry, only lasted from June 27 through September 6, 1940. Of the deputies and former cabinet ministers arrested for fleeing to North Africa, two, Georges Mandel and Jean Zay, both Jewish, were slain by French Miliciens in mid-1944. A third Jew, Pierre Mendès France, survived, having been able to join de Gaulle's Free French group in London. We will see later how he became aligned with the Robert and Suzanne Schreiber family. *La Saga Servan-Schreiber.* Ibid., 432–437.

The front side of the imposing Monument to the Dead in the spa city of Vichy.

De 1940 à 1944
sous l'autorité de fait
de Philippe Pétain
ont été arrêtées et déportées
par mesure de répression
ou de persécution
plus de 390 personnes,
hommes, femmes et enfants
nés ou résidant ou travaillant
à Vichy.
Plus de 240 d'entre elles
sont mortes dans les camps nazis.

Qu'il nous en souvienne !

The only place in Vichy where Marshal Petain's name is still mentioned. It commemorates the 390 men, women, and children of the city who were arrested and deported under Petain's regime, of whom 240 perished in Nazi camps like Auschwitz.

answer proved valueless, because soon after this interview, on October 3, 1940, the first anti-Jewish statute was promulgated by the Vichy government, which excluded Jews from elective office. Insult was added to injury when, four days later, Vichy wiped the 1870 Crémieux decree off the books, thereby stripping French citizenship from all Algerian Jews.[57]

Suzanne, although we will see that she would not become a total stranger to Montfrin Château, rented an apartment for herself and the two girls in Marseille during these troubling times for Jews in France, even the wealthy and French ones. Jean-Claude was still technically in the army but visited his mother in Marseille while on leave that summer. He had worries similar to his father's over the fact that their family, having Jewish, Masonic, Radical, and Republican roots, was now living at considerable personal risk under a Vichy state that was virulently inimical to those values. Robert had discussed these issues in July with his brother Emile, who had already decided to seek safety in converting to the faith of his wife and children, Catholicism, which was the preferable religion under the Vichy regime. Emile was baptized on July 30 in Sainte-Baudile Cathedral in Nîmes, and married Dénise again immediately thereafter in a religious ceremony. Robert and Suzanne quickly followed suit, when on August 13 Father Amat converted them to Catholicism.

Robert wrote years later that he strongly believed that he and his heirs should be people who subscribed to the desire to assimilate themselves fully to the ways of France. But at the time, he knew that this conversion would not allow them to avoid the inconveniences of the Jewish Statutes because their conversion took place after June 1940. His priest also informed him that baptismal day that he "would not be a good Catholic, but I know that you have always been a good Christian." About the same time, Jean-Claude made a similar decision and was baptized in a church at Ribérac in the Dordogne, but, unlike his father, he held firm religious convictions. As his father later said, "Of our three children, two are fervent and convinced Catholics: my son Jean-Claude and my younger daughter, Marie-Geneviève." At the August 13 private ceremony, however, Robert and Suzanne did not follow up, like Emile, with a Catholic marriage, as they had already been living separately for six years.[58] Robert received Vichy's official notice of his separation from

---

57   Ibid., 438; *Journal.* Ibid., 456; *Vichy France and the Jews.* Ibid., 4.
58   *La Saga Servan-Schreiber.* Ibid., 440–441; *Journal.* Ibid., 463–464.

his former mayor's post on August 17. Jean-Claude's Masonic allegiance probably helped move along his demobilization, which would officially take place later in the fall of 1940, when France's small Armistice Army was established with German consent.

As Jean-Claude awaited his separation paperwork while guarding the demarcation line, his sister Marie-Claire visited Montfrin with her usual friends, Jean Daladier, her pal on the *Massilia*, and Lana Marconi. She and Lana left in her car and arrived on October 15 to make a surprise visit on Jean-Claude in Taponnat near Angoulême. His army unit was posted there on the demarcation line separating the Occupied Zone from the Unoccupied Zone, splitting the Charente. Lana, who was quite strikingly beautiful, was born in Bucharest, Romania, in 1917, which made her about four years older than Marie-Claire, who was then nineteen. Marie-Claire announced to her brother that she was driving Lana to Châteauroux in the Vichy Zone, where Lana had been called to rejoin the ambulance corps. After doing that, Marie-Claire intended to travel on to Paris, which her brother recognized as a dangerous place for a young Jewish girl to visit. Jean-Claude soon ascertained that the relationship between Suzanne and Marie-Claire was rocky, due to their strong-willed mother's efforts to constrain the activities of her equally determined and stubborn eldest daughter. She was just going anywhere to escape her mother.

Jean-Claude called the ambulance corps in Châteauroux and found out his mother had arranged for Lana to be called there for service, which made it obvious to him that it was a ruse to separate Marie-Claire from Lana, which only resulted in pushing them closer together. He tried to persuade Marie-Claire that she could lead an independent life in Marseille and that he would enlist the help of their father in getting Suzanne

---

Robert Zaretsky in *Nimes at War* (103 and note 54) gives a somewhat different interpretation of these events. My feeling is that Robert Schreiber was not particularly religious, whether Catholic or Jew. He did desire to be considered an assimilated Frenchman and a French citizen. Additionally, he may have hoped that he could avoid some problems associated with being a Jew in France under the new laws in some fashion. However, in both the books cited, he mentions reasons why he objected to certain tenets of Judaism, and that he could not avoid the Jewish Statute's application to him. He was converted by Abbé Amat. Mr. Zaretsky noted that Bishop Girbeau refused to permit that conversion, but that did not prevent it, in my view, from taking place and the archival research documentation I found reflects that conversion.

to allow more freedom for their daughter. Jean-Claude wrote Robert that one thing certain was that Marie-Claire could not live with her mother. Suzanne had committed many foolish acts toward her daughter, and as soon as Marie-Claire made a friend, Suzanne became jealous and tried to separate them, just as she did in the case of Lana Marconi. He also went on to tell his father that Suzanne's trips to Vichy were being talked about and that she ought to be more discreet and circumspect in her actions. However, he could not dissuade Marie-Claire from continuing on to Paris, where she stayed with her mother's sister, Esther Alphandery, in her apartment near the Trocadero, and enrolled in a school to earn a Red Cross nursing degree. On November 3, she wrote Jean-Claude that her mother had written a disparaging letter to her, which she was ignoring. She was content with doing something purposeful on her own, and she would never disassociate herself from her family, "as mother believes."[59]

Being Watched

On September 12, 1940, a letter addressed to Suzanne Schreiber-Crémieux at Château Montfrin was intercepted by the SCT in Nîmes. It was from a political acquaintance who most likely was a fellow Radical Party member, M. Georges Bruguière. He had just written her sister Esther in Paris a long and painful letter after seeing her in a very ago-

---

59 *La Saga Servan-Schreiber*. Ibid., 444–447. Lana (Ecaterina) Marconi was born September 8, 1917, in Bucharest, Romania, and migrated to France probably sometime in the 1930s. In 1945, she became the mistress of the prolific actor, playwright, and filmmaker Sasha Guitry and starred as an actress only in films or plays that he wrote or directed. Married four times, he famously characterized her as, "the others were my wives; you will be my widow." His prediction turned out to be true as she remained married to him from 1949 until he died on July 24, 1957. (http://fr.wikipedia.org/wiki/Lana_Marconi, January 29, 2011.) Guitry, although he never collaborated in making films for the Continental Studios that Joseph Goebbels backed for the French film industry during the Occupation, continued to work in Paris during that time and led a life in high society, which often was frequented by collaborators and Germans. When the liberation took place, he was arrested along with entertainers like Arletty, Pierre Fresnay, and Maurice Chevalier. Guitry was soon released but operated under a cloud until August 1947, when the Paris Court of Justice decided that there was no case to make against him. As Julian Jackson points out, a poll taken in 1944 indicated a 56 percent approval for his arrest. His *joie de vivre* was exhibited openly in 1940–1944, and as he appeared not to have suffered like other Parisians, for this reason he was punished. *France: The Dark Years.* Ibid., 589.

nizing state, which he was sure Esther had communicated to her sister. He went on to inform Suzanne that "they were living in perilous times, but the trembling earth would not turn heads so solidly affixed to the shoulders as yours."

He felt that the advice Suzanne had received from Jean Montigny [a reputed lover of hers in the past] was good. He knew that Montigny "had become a close collaborator of Pierre Laval and was therefore well placed to share with you his concerns. But there was one thing that it was impossible for him to guarantee for you: for you to be useful in such a difficult position. I do not doubt his brotherly affection for you, although I do contest his actual influence. Be on your guard to not forget where he was personally parked and that he will steer clear of danger as much as he can. He will not be the only one from among your acquaintances who will find it his duty to inform on you if you commit some imprudence.

"The imprudence would be to return to Paris while the negotiations of which I have spoken to Esther were being pursued. My feelings in this regard are very definite. There are some lusty guys in the wings with very sharp teeth and clearly resolved to do away with the old personnel. Won't they be on the scene from tomorrow? I prefer very much that you remain out of range of their paws. It seems to me that the month of September will be decisive. You will let it pass, if you believe me, without demonstrating that you exist.

"It appears that a Jewish Statute is on the way to being developed. It is a very easy thing to do but I doubt that it will be considered adequate and after that the real difficulties will begin that will be hard to evade. All the more reason to arm yourself with patience while resigning yourself to do nothing to complicate your life."[60]

On September 12, at 8:45 in the evening, Suzanne telephoned a friend, Madame "Lola" in Vichy, telephone number 23.21, which conversation was transcribed by the Nîmes SCT. Suzanne's voice was picked up after the conversation had started, saying, "Yes, dear, I know that my apartment in Paris has already been searched three times. I will ask the maid to give me an explanation; however, they have always carried out the same routine. Tell Louise that I am pining to see her. I want to have some details about my office on the rue de Berry and especially what's

---

60   ADG. 1 W 40. Marked 14/432.

been happening there. If you have some fear about departing for Paris, come here and we will be happy to receive you."

Vichy: Don't be worried. I leave next week and will inform you about everything.

Montfrin: I'm going to Marseille to study the question you know about ... there is much to do. We can create a movement favorable to our purposes. You say that M. Rousselier has returned? That's good.

Vichy: The offices are open in Paris but my dear, there are only difficulties. I am going first to Châteauroux to look for some news and arrange my departure. It is quite difficult to arrange for a car ... I'm afraid there will be no gas to be had. I'll write you.

Montfrin: My dear, I would have wished that you would have been able to come with me.

Vichy: Impossible! Good-bye, dear Suzanne, I give you a big hug.

Montfrin: I do the same for you, my dear Lola, and good courage.

Notation by the SCT of Nîmes: "the number 23.21 at Vichy is a phone in the name of Chapard at Pont-Bentiron, Vichy."[61]

On September 14, Suzanne received a call in Montfrin from an unspecified caller located near Châteauroux (perhaps Madame Lola again?) which was again transcribed in the course of the conversation.

Caller: Did you receive the telegram in question?

Called party, Madame X: No, but I had the possibility to get the gist of its meaning thanks to the kindness of its recipient who verbally told me its contents. It came from Madrid and said, "I am returning to France," signed Nicoll with two L's.

Caller: I am very busy.

Madame X: Be very prudent, but I do believe you will not experience many difficulties. For my part, I do not know anybody there. M. Roger is at St-Lo. Myself, I don't think I will return there, as there are many impediments, among others the prefecture.

The following day another call was recorded. The caller was Lana Marconi, who placed the call from a number in Montélimar, and it was answered by Madame Schreiber in Montfrin.

Lana: I will arrive tomorrow at noon.

Mme. Schreiber: Did the general arrive?

---

61 Ibid. Marked 312.

Lana: We don't know. If a telegram arrives for me, open it and telephone Miss Schwab at Châteauroux to read it to her."

End of conversation. September 15, 1940.

On September 16, the Princess de Broglie called and was given the following message by whoever answered the telephone in Château Montfrin:

"Following the receipt of his telegram, Edna Nicoll wrote from the French embassy in Madrid to announce her return. This letter was addressed to Lana Marconi, who ought to arrive in Montfrin this afternoon. The general should arrive tomorrow. It was indicated additionally that Marie-Louise de Tocqueville was at Montélimar. Madame Schreiber will return from Marseille on Wednesday."[62]

On September 19, at 5:45 in the afternoon, Lana Marconi phoned from Montfrin Château to Miss Schwab at No. 3, Etrechet (Indre) near Châteauroux, to ask her to call Madame de Tocqueville in Paris and request that she go to Miss Marconi's apartment there to see what was going on. She also asked her to try immediately to get some gas-rationing cards sent to Montfrin. She was to convey the message that the travelers had arrived at their destination, which was stressed as being very important.[63]

Suzanne Schreiber sent two telegrams on October 23, 1940, both of which were intercepted and sent on to their final destinations. The first one, at 9:35 in the morning, went to Colonel du Vignaud c/o La Cavalerie in the Aveyron and read: "Emile [Robert's brother] is at his chalet, 'Nanouk' in Mégève, telephone No. 30. My best wishes, Suzanne Schreiber."

The second telex was sent at 5:50 in the afternoon to the Countess de Tocqueville, c/o the Hotel Ambassadors in Vichy: "Just received this moment the following telegram: [in English] Nicoll asks us to say very unhappy, cable often **stop** innocent of even a bad thought **stop** Geneva must give guarantee to british [sic] red cross who refuse to help **stop** take care apartment **stop** heart and soul bleeding despair Churchill clapham clericorum **stop** tenderly, await your call. Suzanne Schreiber."[64]

A month later on November 22, 1940, a phone conversation at 9:45

62　Ibid. Marked Nos. 310/F, 311/F, and 312/F.
63　Ibid. Marked No. 323/F-419.
64　Ibid. Marked 531.

in the morning between Countess de Tocqueville and Suzanne was over-
heard and summarized as follows: "Suzanne announces her departure for
Marseille on Tuesday. While speaking of her son, Jean-Claude, she says
that he is leaving for Limoges tomorrow but he hopes to be transferred
to Lyon soon. Suzanne asks Madame de Tocqueville kindly to telephone
René for him to confirm their meeting in Toulouse on the tenth of
December that she had arranged with him. Suzanne asks Madame de
Tocqueville if her trip to Geneva had been a good one. She answers yes.
Suzanne asks if there is something for Emma [not Edna?]. She answers
that there is nothing for her. Suzanne says that is dreadful, abominable.
Madame de Tocqueville shares her opinion."

Later that same day, Jean-Claude received a brief telegram from a
Denis Baschet, evidently an acquaintance in Lyon, inquiring of him:
"When are you leaving Montfrin? Are you passing by Lyon when you
return?"[65]

Marie-Claire had returned safely from Paris by December 2, 1940,
as a call she placed from Marseille that evening (Dragon 36.99) to her
father at Montfrin (13) was transcribed by the SCT.

Banalities were reciprocated and then Robert said: "I am thinking of
going to Mégève for about twelve days."

Marie-Claire: You're right. Since the government has decided to
move to Versailles, he [she talks of an unnamed person who probably is
in the cinema business] will begin to shoot his film in January. You know
our letters take four days to arrive and are all opened by the censors.

Robert: I don't give a damn.

Marie-Claire: Me also. I don't care either if that interests them. In
Marseille they have rushed to prepare things for the marshal's arrival;
all is completed including the decorations. There will be a new Praeto-
rian Guard! Come spend a few days with me, and we'll see some good
films. L'Estragouze has bought a property in Narbonne and he wishes to
become a wine grower … later he'll continue his film making."[66]

Marie-Claire returned to Paris early in 1941 and decided to visit
her parents' apartments, first discreetly visiting the concierge of her
mother's place, who told her the Germans had moved in. She did not
trust that concierge, so she left, saying she was just passing through,

65   Ibid. Marked 760.
66   Ibid. Marked 845.

but consulted some old neighbors she trusted, who confirmed what had happened. She next visited her father's apartment and was able to enter it and see that it was undisturbed, and that the valuable paintings her father had collected were still hanging on the walls. A few days later she was dumbfounded to see an article in the *Au pilori* titled "The Gangsters" that condemned her father, mother, and Emile Schreiber as vultures who used influence to obtain the honors that had been conferred on them and accused them of being Jewish Masons. The days of the confiscation of Jewish enterprises and wealth were fast coming, and the Schreiber clan would not escape the clutches of Xavier Vallat's SCAP provisional administrators.[67]

But the audacious Marie-Claire was not going to stand still for that to happen in Paris in regard to the paintings that belonged to her father and her mother. Her father's apartment was easy to enter, and she removed the most valuable paintings with the help of a friend and transported them to her aunt's place in a car. Her mother's abode represented a bigger challenge, as midlevel German functionaries slept there. She and the same trusted friend arrived at 8:00 PM, avoided the suspect concierge, and both entered the apartment at 6 rue du Bocador with their hearts beating with trepidation. The Germans were all still out, so they quickly carried the artwork down to the service entrance shared with number 8, whose concierge, M. Jaeger, was a Communist she knew and trusted. Marie-Claire entrusted the paintings for storage in his cave for safekeeping. With great luck, the two girls slipped out the normal entrance and returned to Esther's apartment on rue Magdebourg before the curfew. It was an audacious but impulsive endeavor, which turned out to be successful. It would not be Marie-Claire's last such dangerous undertaking.[68]

On January 20, Jean-Claude wrote his colonel in Limoges, where he was stationed, that he desired to reenlist in the Armistice Army in spite of the anti-Jewish statutes. He pointed out that he was a Catholic but of "Israelite origin," as he put it. "I want to be given the chance, as a young

---

67   *Vichy France and the* Jews. Ibid., 8. SCAP stands for *Service de Contrôle des Administrateurs Provisoires*, an organization that Vichy set up initially in December 1940 to counter German efforts in taking over French businesses, mainly Jewish-owned ones, in the Occupied Zone. Later the SCAP organization operated in the Unoccupied Zone as well.

68   *La Saga Servan-Schreiber*. Ibid., 450–452.

cavalry candidate of nearly twenty-three years of age, to be permitted to prove that he has reason to be proud of being French." A short time later, his request was refused as defective on the grounds that he was Jewish. His father's enterprises also came under assault from a centralized office for Jewish Affairs that had been formed by Admiral Darlan in March 1941. It was placed under the Commissioner General for Jewish Questions, Xavier Vallat, whose mission was to reestablish French control of the administration of Jewish affairs in the Occupied Zone. *Les Echos* in Paris was soon placed under the control of a M. Oudart as provisional administrator, and Robert asked Suzanne if she knew anything about him. She did not know him, but advised Robert to go to Vichy as soon as possible to try to protect his possessions in the Unoccupied Zone, such as Montfrin Château and its farming operations. According to what she knew at the time, however, she indicated that the Jewish Statute did not apply to one's habitat, so she felt Montfrin would be safe. Time, and not much of it, would tell as laws under Vichy were malleable, especially anti-Jewish ones.[69]

Meanwhile, Marie-Claire continued her risky project to move her family's valuable artwork collection from Paris under the German occupation. Through friends of her mother, she obtained a pass to exit Paris so that she could drive to a home in the suburbs, which belonged to a former housecleaner whom she could trust to safeguard the paintings. She borrowed a small truck with a tarpaulin cover, and on a Saturday morning, she managed to talk her way past an admiring German sentinel. He was reputedly more interested in arranging to meet her later for a walk than inspecting under the conveyance's cover the Vlamincks or Roussels that she was transporting to safety. She completed her mission and simply returned to Paris through a different city entrance. On April 3, she celebrated her twentieth birthday in the company of Lana Marconi, but soon thereafter, she willingly departed Paris for the Midi and the advantages of the Unoccupied Zone. Before returning south, she realized that the fact she was Jewish made some former friends avoid her. However, she did take pride in the knowledge that she was a trained nurse who had witnessed many interesting operations by dint of knowing Dr. Henri Mondor, a close family friend. She set off south, accompanied by her new friend, the intrepid Madeleine, the daughter of

---

69   Ibid., 449, 452–453.

her aunt's concierge, who had helped her remove the paintings from her mother's apartment.[70]

The two girls had just passed on foot the village of Bléré, which was to the east of Tours and on the route for the not-so-distant demarcation line, when they were stopped by two German military policemen who demanded their papers. The men took them in hand in order to check out their excuse for hiking in the area and locked them in a room of a nearby château. Soon they returned with news that they could not verify the girls' story, so they searched them more thoroughly and discovered a necklace with a torah-like charm on Marie-Claire's neck. She, "the Jew," was handed the mop and broom to clean up the room and later taken to a prison in Tours, where she was kept locked up for several weeks in the company of a group of local prostitutes. One morning, she was set free by the authorities without any explanation and even given back the Dunhill lighter that Lana Marconi had given her for her birthday. She returned to Paris, where she immediately met an ambulance driver she knew, who offered to drive her to an area in the Cher where it was safe to cross the line into Unoccupied France. She returned to her mother's apartment on rue Dragon in Marseille toward the end of May and found, to her surprise, Jean-Claude, who had just arrived after his demobilization in Limoges. The reason they had not gone to Montfrin first was that their father had been bluntly instructed to make himself scarce in the Gard.[71]

A second major Jewish Statute was promulgated by the Pétain government on June 2, 1941, the intention of which was to restrict further the job categories prohibited to Jews by the First Jewish Statute of October 3, 1940. Forbidden work categories were expanded for Jews, going beyond the original fields of education, high civil service, and cultural affairs to include advertising, finance, and real estate. The original law had promised a quota system and new restrictive, employment limiting allocations, or what became known as *numerus clausus*, were established at 2 percent over subsequent months for lawyers (July 16), medical professionals (August 11), architects (September 24), and dentists (June 5, 1942). Jewish students were only allowed to constitute 3 percent of the secondary or university population on June 21, 1941. Important for the Schreiber brothers, on July 22, 1941, the law attacked

---

70   Ibid., 454.
71   Ibid., 455–456.

Jews with business interests in order to vitiate their economic influence. This law allowed Commissioner Vallat or his successor to name provisional administrators for any Jewish businesses or pieces of property, assigning these officials the authority to sell or liquidate the entities as they deemed fit throughout France, including the Unoccupied Zone. The power vested in these individuals resulted in many predatory transactions that had a devious nature attached to them.[72]

In April, the month before Marie-Claire and Jean-Claude returned to the Midi, Robert Schreiber had received a telephone call from a special commissioner in the Gard's prefecture, requesting that he come to Nîmes for a personal interview. Robert hastily arranged to drive to the prefecture and get together with his caller, who met him and immediately said, "I have been given the task to ask you to leave your property and reside anywhere else but in the department of the Gard." The commissioner refused to give Robert any reason for this peremptory request and, with things at an impasse, asked Robert if he would rather meet with Prefect Angelo Chiappe, who might be able to enlighten him further. Robert and Suzanne both had been acquainted in Paris with Jean Chiappe, Angelo's brother, who had disappeared over the Mediterranean in November 1940, presumably shot down by the Italians, so Robert anxiously agreed to the meeting.

In a few minutes, he was ushered into the prefect's office, where Chiappe greeted him in a courteous fashion and offered him a seat. The prefect maintained that he also was ignorant of the specifics behind the request but did say, "In general, however, I can tell you that you telephone too much, correspond too much, and you see too many people." Robert objected to these generalities, and then the prefect made an offhand remark, suggesting that Robert was known to have called France a dirty country. Robert was incensed by this accusation, and explained that it was said in the context of comparing the cleanliness of French peasant homes to those of the Swiss and the Dutch. Robert's angry tone raised Chiappe's hackles and he replied, "You forget undoubtedly that you are no longer in the presence of a functionary of the Third Republic but before a prefect of the marshal and that my powers are without limit."

Robert would not back down and demanded a trial before a judge, with his attorney beside him. The angry prefect rose and was about to

---

72 *Vichy France.* Ibid., 178–179.

tell an official to take Robert away under administrative arrest, when he reflected a moment, calmed down, and sought a more reasonable solution. He mentioned Robert's friendship with his late brother and repeated in composed fashion his unfamiliarity with why Vichy had issued this edict, but said it was his duty as a Vichy official to carry out the expulsion order. However, he did not want Robert to oblige him to take more drastic measures and said, "You are free to go where you wish, except in the Gard. I know that your brother possesses a charming villa in Mégève; go there for two or three months. And when you will come back, you will thank me for having avoided imposing more severe measures." Robert admitted that there was nothing more to discuss, so he took his leave and prepared his departure for *Nanouk*.[73]

While his father was in Mégève, Jean-Claude installed himself in his mother's apartment in Marseille temporarily. The authors of *The Saga*, Rustenholz and Treiner, broach the subject of Marie-Claire's alleged lesbianism via comments attributed to Jean-Claude and Suzanne. Jean-Claude reputedly witnessed in his mother's apartment some altercations, verbal or otherwise, between Marie-Louise de Tocqueville, Edna Nicoll, and the Princess de Broglie over which of the trio "would succeed in putting Lana Marconi in her bed." He concluded that "the allegations of his mother were not without foundation: Marie-Claire would be homosexual!" By June 11, Jean-Claude and Marie-Claire had learned from their father that his mother—their beloved grandmother, Clara—was apparently on her deathbed at her apartment in Paris. Emile was refused a pass to cross the demarcation line at Moulins near Vichy, and so it happened that on June 16, 1941, Clara Schreiber died at age eighty-five with none of her sons at her bedside. This sad event was overshadowed six days later by the announcement heard on the BBC that the Germans had invaded the Soviet Union. This was an exponential expansion of Hitler's war in pursuit of his policy of *Lebensraum*, or living space, in his Thousand-Year Reich's quest for territorial expansion.

Jean-Claude left to supervise the management of Montfrin, as its

---

73 *Journal.* Ibid., 466–469. It is interesting to parse the words that Chiappe reputedly said to Robert, taken from Robert's diary written at some undetermined date. It clearly seems to indicate that the telephone calls and mail from and to Montfrin Chateau were being closely observed, and one could say this was an indiscretion by Prefect Chiappe, who was privy to SCT reports that were all stamped as very secret and not to be divulged to ordinary citizens.

farm lands provided for all his dispersed family's needs and it could not be neglected. Suzanne wanted to sell the property, and Robert wished to make a cash settlement with his wife, so that he could split the bulk of the estate among his children. Jean-Claude was charged by Robert to make legal enquiries, which he did in July–August, but the legal alternatives were blurred with the shadows cast by the recent Jewish Statute's regulations and what SCAP was implementing, even in the Unoccupied Zone.[74] In Mégève, as the skiing season neared, Emile wrote in his diary on October 25 concerning the hostage executions in Nantes and Bordeaux and how the French people were split over the subject of actions taken against the occupant's forces. He accepted Robert's too-optimistic bet that Hitler would be defeated in Russia by the end of 1942 and countered with his own that it would not take place before March 1943. Just around Christmas, their doctor brother, Georges, surprised them by showing up at the chalet, having fled Paris and the Occupied Zone, where he feared Jewish persecution and roundups. Georges mentioned that a cousin had been arrested in Paris during December, among some six thousand Jews rounded up, he said, in reaction to the killing of German troops. Georges's number was inflated, as the true figure was around one thousand prominent Jews, accompanied by a German demand for a billion-franc fine payment by the Jewish inhabitants of the Occupied Zone.[75] Jews were natural targets for hostage-taking, as a result of the small wave of assassinations that started with the killing of naval cadet Moser in a Parisian metro stop on August 21, 1941. *Le Matin* newspaper later put it succinctly in a headline for French consumption: "Jews, Communists, and foreign agitators constitute a national danger."[76] Jean-Claude joined his cousin Jean-Jacques visiting Mégève at Christmas for a short stay. Jean-Jacques was studying in Grenoble in the Unoccupied Zone in the competition to enter the prestigious Polytechnique or Science Po program. Jean-Claude was floating between work at Montfrin and Monte Carlo, where he had a girlfriend, Sabine Wormser,

---

74   *La Saga Servan-Schreiber.* Ibid., 456–457, 459.

75   Ibid., 460-461,; *Vichy France.* Ibid., 181.

76   *Vichy France and the Jews.* Ibid., 224–226. According to Marrus and Paxton, 743 French-Jewish professionals, including many decorated war veterans, were joined by about 250 foreign Jews in the arrests made in Paris on December 12, 1941. On December 15, ninety-five hostages were shot at Mont-Valérien prison, of whom fifty-three were Jewish.

the daughter of a wealthy banker. By this date, it had become apparent to even the upper-class Jews south of the demarcation line that they too lived under very precarious circumstances. [77]

Robert Schreiber would have been very concerned for his property and family to know about steps Xavier Vallat was taking in mid-1941 against Jewish property ownership, baptismal acceptance for conversion to Catholicism by Jews, and Jewish postal bank accounts. We read documentation on these edicts announced by Vallat under his CGQJ powers earlier in this chapter. It is worth repeating that on September 22, 1941, Prefect Chiappe received a letter from the PTT section head in the Gard who supervised postal bank-checking accounts, requesting "your permission for my administration to proceed with its operations to freeze the postal checking accounts as instructed by the Paris check account section concerning accounts held by Jews. Per the list attached, please indicate yes or no after consulting the census files at the departmental prefecture, as to whether the persons listed are Jewish or not. I would appreciate very much your instructions to that effect with the forwarding of the attached list to your colleagues so that they may complete their responses for returning the information requested with as little delay as possible."

Robert Schreiber's name was not on the attached list, but in due course a postal bank-checking account he held in Limoges was frozen. Chiappe handwrote on the letter in question, instructions to a secretary to forward copies to the sub-prefects in Alès, Le Vigan, along with two other involved officials in Nîmes.[78]

On October 4, 1941, the prefect received an inquiry from the regional office in Montpellier charged with supervising the "elimination of all Jewish influence from the national economy." In due course this meant that as soon as the proper ordinances had been put into place, the ownership of the Jewish entities placed under the provisional administrators should be transferred to non-Jewish owners. This letter was a preliminary step in that direction. It stated: "Attached is a list of presumed Jews whom we have been notified reside in your department. I would appreciate it if you would verify through your offices that these people have registered under the provisions called for by the census of August 1st, 1941. Respectfully yours, the adjunct-director." Ten names were

---

77   *La Saga Servan-Schreiber.* Ibid., 462.
78   Ibid. Marked 1744T.

attached, four of which had not registered. This list did not enumerate Robert Schreiber, but he would not avoid registering as required.[79]

Xavier Vallat was a deeply committed Catholic, whose virulent anti-Semitism outweighed his religious beliefs when it came to defining for his agencies' regulations of what constituted a Jew. He did not really subscribe to the fact that Jews were able to assimilate according to France's cultural heritage, but he was somewhat uncomfortable with the German ideas on racism as they applied to the Jews. A military veteran and ex-head of the Legion of Ancient Combatants, he wanted laws and orders obeyed, and he also wanted the presence of Jews in France to be reduced, so he ran his organization with his unique form of flexibility in defining a Jew, in doing what he saw to be his duty. If it took one part religion and one part racism to get the job done of reducing the Jews in France, he was for it in the performance of his daily job. In Alibert's original Jewish Statute of October 1940, a person was a Jew if he or she had at least three Jewish grandparents, no matter what their declared religion. Vallat was eager to make this definition agree with the terms of the Second Jewish Statute of June 2, 1941, as the Modus Vivendi for his CGQJ organization. He gave an interview to the government press agency (AFIP) on February 3, 1942, that confirmed his credo: "A baptized person or the son of a baptized person is Jewish if three grandparents were Jewish." And when a person had converted who had only two or fewer Jewish grandparents, the baptismal certificate only mattered if it were dated prior to June 25, 1940, a procedure more stringent than Alibert's original anti-Jewish first statute.[80]

On July 1, 1941, Robert Schreiber sent the following registered letter from Montfrin to Prefect Chiappe, the subject of which was "the application of the law of June 2, 1941 on the Jewish census." The letter stated:

"Although being a Catholic and having never belonged to the Jewish religion, and not being certain of the membership of my two grandparents in this religion, I declare myself a Jew under the application of the law, this declaration being valid for me, my wife, and my children. M. Prefect, sincerely yours, Robert Schreiber. Montfrin (Gard)."

---

79 Ibid. Marked 642–643. *Vichy France and the Jews.* Ibid., 152–153, and note 116. Marrus and Paxton also found a quotation from a speech given by Vallat ("Greed has been unleashed"), which certainly applied to many instances in this whole sordid affair. Note 115.

80 *Vichy France and the Jews.* Ibid., 88–92, note 45.

The declaration form read as follows:

Robert Schreiber, French nationality, born in Paris 22 March 1880, married with three children.

Profession: grower in Montfrin.

Possessions: home and agricultural property in Montfrin.

Military situation: Honorary Captain of Aviation, having participated in the campaigns of 1914–1918 as a Staff Officer and aviation pilot. Decorated with the Legion of Honor for military service, Croix de Guerre with four foreign citations won in action. Legion of Honor with the rank of *Officier.*"

Suzanne Schreiber, born Crémieux, French nationality, born in Paris 29 June 1895, no profession.

Possessions: dowry document, all from the French State, held in the office of M. Jacob, exchange agent in Paris. Chevalier of the Legion of Honor with exceptional deeds; Red Medal for work in Epidemics, War of 1914–1918; Commander with the Order of Public Health; in a position to prove being part of a seventh generation born in France, but probably much more.

Jean-Claude Servan Schreiber, born in Paris 15 April 1918, candidate for the Reserve Cavalry, 2 citations and 1 wound, campaign of 1940.

Profession: agriculturalist in Montfrin."

Marie-Claire Servan Schreiber, born in Paris 3 April 1921, student of Social Assistance.

Marie-Geneviève Servan Schreiber, born in Paris 13 December 1930.

Robert Schreiber had followed the letter of the law, which was his habit. However, he stressed the various awards and honors for himself, his wife, and his son, thereby indicating their loyal service to France, in addition to their conversion to Catholicism and the Servan name adoption by his three children. It was a vain hope as part of the pro forma declaration that the Vichy state required.[81]

A few days after Robert submitted his familial declaration, a certain

---

81   ADG. 1 W 138 marked 91. The letter is stamped received by the French State, June 28, 1941.

Jean-Baptiste Schweig wrote a letter to an official in Nîmes concerning his presence in Montfrin on the Schreiber estate. The letter read:

> I have Belgian nationality and wish to solicit your help in extending to me the authorization to stay in France. I hope you will study my case particularly as I escaped from a prisoner of war camp for Belgian soldiers in February 1941, and crossed the demarcation line on June 10, having been furnished with a pass by the German authorities, which is attached to this letter. I am lodging at this moment at M. Schreiber's, in the Château of Montfrin. Six days ago I was arrested by the French police and brought to Nîmes to have my case heard but I was released under cognizance that I would contact your Labor Department for consideration.

It appears that Robert Schreiber, who may have already returned to Mégève, occasionally came to Montfrin to attend to official Vichy paperwork and was still influential in the community.[82]

On June 14, 1941, an extract appeared on page 1476 of the Official Journal listed as No. 1333—the Law of June 2, 1941, prescribing the census of Jews. It was from "We, the Marshal of France and the Head of State, including the Council of Ministers," and decreed:

> Article 1: All persons who are Jewish as defined in the law of June 2, 1941, known as the Jewish Statute, must within a month of its publication, submit to the Departmental Prefecture or Sub-Prefecture in which they are domiciled or where their residence is situated, a written declaration indicating that they are considered Jewish under the law, and mentioning their civil state, their family situation, their profession, and the state of their possessions. The declaration is to be made by the husband for the wife, and by the legal representative for any minors.
>
> Article 2: Any infraction of the regulations required by Article 1 are punished by imprisonment set between one month up to one year and a fine set from 100 francs to 10,000 francs,

---

82   Ibid. Marked 634, 168, 91/541, and N, C, SC, JCF on Names of Cantons and Communes list.

MINISTÈRE DE L'INTÉRIEUR

Direction Générale de la Police Nationale

Direction de la Police du Territoire
et des Etrangers. — 4ᵉ Bureau

DÉCLARATION

DES

CHANGEMENTS
de résidence des Juifs

Les Juifs Français et Etrangers qui changent
de résidence doivent en faire la déclaration au
Commissaire de Police (ou à défaut de commissaire de police au Maire) de la commune de leur
domicile si la durée du déplacement prévu dé-
passe 30 jours.

Les intéressés sont tenus d'effectuer la même
formalité au cours des 48 heures qui suivent leur
arrivée dans la commune du lieu de destination.

Tous renseignements complémentaires peu-
vent être recueillis auprès des autorités de Police
ou administratives compétentes.

Les présentes instructions sont applicables à
partir du **1er Juillet 1942.**

Imp. Coop. L'OUVRIÈRE, 4, rue Guizot — NIMES

*The public notice informing foreign and French Jews of the legal necessity
to notify police authorities when they change residence.*

ÉTAT FRANÇAIS

Saint-Gilles, le 3I Janvier I944   194

LE COMMISSAIRE DE POLICE de Saint-Gilles,

à Monsieur   le Préfet du Gard

Changement de residence
des Juifs

Nîmes

En exécution de vos instructions en date du 4 Décembre I942, relatives aux changements de residence des israélites français et étrangers,

J'ai l'honneur de vous rendre compte qu'il n'y a eu au cours du mois de Janvier I943, aucun israelite français ou israélite étranger nouvellement établi à Saint-Gilles ou ayant quitté définitivement cette commune.

Cependant, le Juif Français MEYER Emmanuel, né le 26 Aout I870, à Marmontiers (Bas Rhin) qui residait dans la commune depuis Juillet I940 a été arrêté par des fonctionnaire de la Gestapo, le 22 Janvier I944 et dirigé sur une destination inconnue./.

A January 31, 1944 formal response by the Mayor of St-Gilles to the Prefect of the Gard, that includes the fact that a French Jew, Emmanuel Meyer, had been arrested by the Gestapo and taken off to an "undisclosed destination."

or only one of the two mentioned penalties, without prejudicing the rights of the Prefect to pronounce a sentence of internment in a special camp [read: concentration camp], even if the person involved is a French citizen.

Article 3: Some special rules will define the conditions to which the present law will apply in Algeria, the colonies, in protectorates, Syria, and Lebanon.

Article 4: The present decree will be published in the Official Journal and will be executed as a Law of the State.

Promulgated at Vichy, June 2, 1941. Ph. Pétain[83]

This general Jewish census instruction, the one to which Robert Schreiber had answered for his family on July 1, 1940, was followed up in a detailed letter four pages long from Admiral Darlan on July 12, 1940, sent to all prefects:

It is my honor to send you the instructions I announced to you in my telegrams of June 13 and 23 concerning the census ordered for all Jewish persons under the Law of June 2, 1941.

I particularly call to your attention the importance attached to this census, which is a public order measure, and that you carefully control its implementation and use all means in your power to see that it accurately creates the lists mentioned in my June 23 telegram.

In the same mailing I have included a sufficient quantity of printed individual declaration forms so that all the French and Foreign Jews in your department can fill out the declaration form required by the law.

It is your responsibility to send out immediately these printed declaration forms to your communes according to the approximate number of Jews known to reside therein.

Here are the conditions under which the operations pursuant to the law of June 2, 1941 are to be implemented.

I. Administrative procedures the Mayors must follow:

You will instruct your mayors to enforce strictly the requirement that all Jews in their districts will deliver their completed

---

83   Ibid. Marked 635.

individual declaration form to the Mayor's office before July 31, 1941.

Formal notification of these requirements for the Jews to follow should appear in all forms of publicity available: press, radio, billboard posters, et cetera ... in small communes the official directive will be distributed by sounding horns or drums.

May I bring to your attention that those Jews who cannot come to pick up their declaration forms (for example those in the military, young men attached to the *Chantiers de la Jeunesse*, defendants or condemned prisoners, incarcerated persons, internees or persons under administrative lodging) the method of declaration distribution will be as follows: the mayors will deliver to competent service heads the necessary number of declaration forms, which when filled out will be retransmitted by the service heads back to the mayor's office.

After checking the finished declarations submitted prior to consolidating them to the lists provided, the mayors will check that:

1) The forms are properly completed

2) Create a list of names and addresses of the Jews who have not submitted their declarations.

II. Administrative procedures the Jews must follow:

All adult Jews, whether French or foreign, are compelled to fill out a declaration or be included in such a declaration in the time limit that the above mentioned municipal order has indicated.

The declaration must be filled out by the husband for any non-separated wife and by the legal representative for minors or people under restrictions.

It should be expressly noted that the declaration required by law will only be fulfilled when the printed form that must be completed by the interested parties has been personally delivered and received, or sent by registered mail, to the mayoral office of their residence. Any prior declaration received in a format different from the imposition of these new regulations is null and void. Thus offenders will be exposed who would not have filled out the printed form to the penalties prescribed by the law of

June 2, 1941: imprisonment ranging from one month to a year, a fine between 100 to 10,000 francs.

III. Administrative procedures the prefects must follow:

You must carefully save the duly completed declarations that the mayors have returned to you, and only send to me, for the moment, a copy of the list of Jews known to you which has been derived from properly registered declarations in your possession.

I am sending with this mailing to your address 6,500 individual printed blank declaration forms.

I will shortly forward to you index cards for different categories that will be established for use by your services in connection with the individual declarations made. When these index cards will be sent, they will be accompanied by complete instructions for use.

Please acknowledge receipt of this letter and send me a copy of your instructions to the mayors of your department.

For the Admiral of the Fleet
Minister of the Interior
State Councilor
Secretary General of the Police
Henry Chavin[84]

The Gard bureaucracy went to work following the detailed instructions sent down from the Vichy government, publicizing the procedures those categorized as Jews, according to the Vichy Jewish Statutes, had to observe. The index form cards[85] were made available to the Jewish population and made their way to the Château of Montfrin, from which Robert Schreiber was absent; they were duly filled out by someone undetermined for Jean-Claude and Suzanne, and not signed by them, as was stipulated that the declaration be done in the Gard under the law of June 2, 1941. Their individual index cards were later stamped "subject to the stipulations of the law of December 11, 1942." [86] Suzanne's card listed her as Schreiber, no given name listed, born 29/8/1895 (August 29, not

---

84   Ibid. Marked 708-711.
85   Ibid. Unmarked but stamped "for the law of June 2, 1941 and subject to the stipulations of the law of December 11, 1942."
86   *Vichy France and the Jews.* Ibid., 291. According to Marrus and Paxton, the last bit of basic anti-Jewish legislation enacted by Vichy was the law of December

Suzanne and Jean-Claude Schreiber's initial identity cards issued for French Jews. Mme. Schreiber had the functionary indicate that she was a member of the Catholic community in Montfrin.

the correct date of June 29) in Paris, of Fernand and Sol Aghion (her maiden name, Crémieux, was not listed), French by birth, married in the Catholic religious community, housewife, at Montfrin. Under other information it was written that she arrived in Montfrin in 1925 and currently resided in Marseille. For Jean-Claude Schreiber it indicated his birth date as 11/4/1918 (April 11), in Paris, French citizen, with an address at Montfrin and a profession of farmer [there was no mention of the Servan name addition]. The two Schreibers, mother and son, were subsequently transposed to larger ledger lists for all Jews in the Gard; the first one was handwritten and included mostly law-observant Jews who resided in Nîmes. On this list, a correction had been made for Suzanne to reflect the known fact that she had been born "Crémieux, and her

---

11, 1942, which required that any and all Jewish documentation be stamped *Juif* or *Juive*. This is undoubtedly why these index cards were so stamped after the fact.

birth date was correctly registered thereon." The second ledger had been transposed from the handwritten one to a typewritten format, which reflected the corrected information. The typewritten format allowed for a few more names to be included on the ledger page, but again, except for Montfrin and Anduze addresses (one each), all the Jews listed lived in Nîmes.[87]

One further list was generated in the Gard for Vichy's perusal per the various stipulations of the overlapping Jewish census laws. This tabulation from July 1941 included numbers for both French and foreign Jews, the later by nationality of origin, and was further broken down by gender and children under the age of fifteen. This last statistic for foreign Jewish children would figure tragically about one year later, when Pierre Laval proposed that those children of age sixteen and under accompany their parents on the deportation trains bound for the east, a category of deportee not initially requested by the German authorities instituting the Final Solution in France. The Gard list reflecting French Jews consisted of 501 males, 345 females, and 115 children under the age of fifteen, thereby totaling 961 individuals of French citizenship. The Foreigners list consisted of 970 males, 583 females, and 146 young children, totaling 1,699 foreign Jews, from twenty-one countries or being categorized as stateless. The foreign Jews were from Germany, South America, Belgium, Great Britain, Cuba, Egypt, Spain, Greece, Hungary, Italy, Luxembourg, Latvia, Palestine, Poland, Rumania, Russia, Switzerland, Czechoslovakia, Turkey, Austria, and Morocco (protected French), or were classified as stateless. The Poles were the most numerous, with the combination of Germans and ex-Austrians following closely behind.[88]

---

87 ADG. 1 W 138. Ibid. Marked 41. ADG. 1 W 140. Unmarked, except for Gard archive stamp. On both these ledger lists all the people enumerated were of French birth and their last names commenced with the letter "S."

88 ADG. 1 W 138. Ibid. Marked 640. *Vichy France and the Jews.* Ibid., 263, and note 180. Adolph Eichmann's deputy in charge of the deportation program in France in June 1942 was Theodor Dannecker. Initially, he did not want to have the deportation convoys encumbered with children, only adult Jews between the ages of sixteen and forty. Laval had become familiar with German planning after Eichmann's visit to France on July 1 and made known his feelings relative to including children to Dannecker shortly thereafter. Paxton and Marrus quote Dannecker's report of July 6 to Eichmann in Berlin: "President Laval proposed that, in the deportation of Jewish families from the Unoccupied Zone, children under sixteen can also be taken. The question of the Jewish children remaining behind in

Another example of the Jewish census was sent handwritten on July 11, 1941, to the prefecture, which was "the declaration of belongings attributable to a Mr. Charles Cremy, known as Crémieux, a French Israelite, former President of the Industrial Tribunal, former President of the Departmental Labor Commission, former member of the High Labor Commission, and a member of the Legion of Honor." There followed a list of the shares he owned in six corporations, a property he owned in the Goudes suburb of Marseille that was rented out as a restaurant, and notation of 160,390 francs in his bank account at 1 Grand Temple Place in Nîmes. It was signed Crémieux. [89]

This person may or may not have been a relative of Suzanne's. Had he been related and had she been informed of its nature, it would only have added to the malaise she felt, which caused her to write an eight-page letter at the end of 1941, which she put in an envelope and whereon she wrote, "My wishes, for my children after my death. Immediately after." She sealed the letter and placed it in a desk drawer in her Marseille apartment. These were her words: "My dear children, I must today, due to the new laws which so cruelly target us, change the provisions of my will. In what concerns your father, he will inherit what the law will confer on him and that will be just. He has always done for me, and for you, all that he had to do and all that he could do. I loved him for a very long time, and you must know that I have never betrayed him. Influence within his family and other elements turned him against me, and away from our hearth. I have suffered terribly. When I ceased to love him deeply you know that I could have dazzled society. But it was not my maternal duty alone which prevented me from pursuing that course; I have never loved anyone enough to risk bringing shame to you about my conduct.

"I have suffered much, I have worked very hard for you, to raise you and to see you assimilated even more so into our country's culture if that is possible. I have been a true believer, much more than you have ever supposed; perhaps only Jean-Claude understood that. For me our

the Occupied Zone does not interest him." Dannecker kept asking Berlin to make a decision regarding the children issue. His replacement, Heinz Röthke, noted that in his contacts with the French police they repeatedly "expressed their desire to see the children also deported to the Reich with their parents." It was not until July 20 that Eichmann telephoned his consent.

89   ADG. 1 W 138. Ibid. Marked 720.

baptism was an infinite joy. I desire to receive the church's sacraments and be buried in a religious ceremony. I implore you to marry according to your heart's desire, but I would prefer that you marry someone of the Christian faith. I would also prefer that they not be foreigners. I ask you to practice your religion. That idea alone gives me the hope and patience to endure our martyrdom.

"Tomorrow is Marie-Geneviève's First Communion. It is a great day for me, for if, like you, Jean-Claude, she commits and holds herself before God and before all men, I will be proud of her. Guard my decorations, my treasure [meaning Jean-Claude], but put me in my coffin alongside your citations. You are a brave little Frenchman. Promise me that you will always be an ardent patriot, deeply nationalistic, and that you will never be drawn into revolutionary extremism. You have the mud of France on your shoes.

"I want to be buried in the cemetery of Montfrin near my parents, near my brother André [mistakenly written[90]]. Moreover, I do not allow your father to attend my funeral, and I only wish that my true, intimate friends are there. I wish that afterwards sometime, you three will come to pray alone on my tomb, while I promise to adore you for ever and hold dear your memories eternally. I bless you and I love you. Maman

"If you discover amongst my books the novel *Tristan and Isolde* that your father gave me for our engagement, give it back to him. He will understand. Could he feel some remorse?"[91]

In January 1942, three policemen, charged with monitoring food supply, knocked on the chalet door of Nanouk and asked Robert about a shipment of four hundred liters of wine that had arrived from Montfrin. Robert showed them his letter to his tenant farmer requesting the shipment, but the wine was confiscated for the use of a sanatorium after they admonished him "to remember that everything which isn't authorized is forbidden." In February, Suzanne sent him a letter via Marie-Claire in which she urged him to return to Montfrin in order to protect it from being assigned a provisional administrator by the CGQJ. However, she added a comment that by making this suggestion she felt it

---

90 Suzanne was buried in the Montfrin city cemetery alongside her father, mother, sister and **brother-in-law**, in their family plot, when she died in 1976. I have photos of the headstone, which is located just to the left of the main entryway.
91 *La Saga Servan-Schreiber*. Ibid., 463–464.

The final wishes of Suzanne Cremieux were observed. Photo of the Cremieux family tombstone in the Montfrin cemetery.

would be grounds for him to oppose it. He did not choose to depart for Montfrin. On March 12, a letter arrived from a cousin in America for the brothers in Mégève, as the United States, although now at war with Japan, Germany, and Italy, was still a neutral nation in its relationship vis-à-vis the Vichy government. The American cousin urged his French ones to leave for the United States as soon as possible, but Emile replied that it was too soon. Emile went on to give his thoughts about future options in light of the World War: "It seems we have to choose between four dominations: Germany, Russia, Japan (the yellow race), and the Anglo/Americans. I scarcely believe in an Anglo-American victory for they are too far behind the others in war preparation and their ability to sacrifice is inferior to that of the other three. Russia is the more likely victor and 1942 will determine that result. If that is the case, why bother to leave, as Communism won't delay in taking over America too. It's better for us to adapt to that situation here rather than over where you live."[92]

Winter gave way to spring and spring to summer, during which time the snow melted in Mégève and Laval succeeded Darlan. In Russia, Hitler launched his Army Group B southward in his ill-fated Caucasus campaign, which had initial success in capturing the Crimea by July 2. Eleven days earlier, Rommel's Afrika Corps had captured Tobruk, so on the surface things looked positive for Germany. Around this time, Jean-Claude informed his father that he had been summoned to the Gard prefecture by a Mr. d'Ornano, the departmental commissioner for Jewish affairs. On July 10, the good news was received that no provisional administrator would yet be appointed for Montfrin, as Jean-Claude offered witnesses' affidavits that he was working the château's lands. The fact that he had also served in the same army unit with the commissioner in November 1940 certainly did not hurt his cause. He additionally had shown a letter he had written to his father, which outlined the progress of the various crops he planned to harvest, as proof that he was actively working the land. It covered in detail the vineyards, fruits, vegetables, potatoes, beans, garlic, lambs and goats, chickens and eggs, and the weather. Emile and his son, Jean-Jacques Servan-Schreiber, were in downtown Lyon on the July 14 holiday and witnessed the anti-Laval and anti-German demonstrations there. Laval had become even

---

92   Ibid., 465, 467, 472.

more unpopular after his appalling speech of June 22, wherein he had openly said he desired Germany's victory and advocated continued collaboration with France's Occupier. Reputedly, the two Schreibers had heard demonstrators cry out for Laval to be hanged.[93]

Of course, it was in this time period that the infamous *Vél' d'Hiv* roundup took place in Paris. The action's code name was *Vent printanier*, and the German authorities expected that as many as twenty-eight thousand Jews would be swept up by the French police who planned and led the operation. The municipal chief of police in Paris, M. Hennequin, drew up the orders for the nine thousand French policemen involved, who started to knock on doors early in the morning of July 16, 1942. German uniformed personnel were scarcely to be seen. The operation continued for forty-eight hours and yielded a disappointing (for the Germans) 12,884 Jewish men, women, and children, of whom nearly six thousand, mostly male adults, were interned at the Drancy transit camp located in a northeastern suburb of Paris. The remainder of nearly seven thousand, of whom four thousand were children and the balance women, were stuffed into the velodrome. This location was totally lacking in adequate water, food, bedding, sanitary, and medical facilities, which caused horrifying conditions during a confinement that lasted five days.

Minister of Interior Bousquet had agreed to a similar operation for the Unoccupied Zone, as long as it was totally French-led and focused on foreign and stateless Jews. The main operation occurred on August 26–28 and ultimately yielded about 7,100 Jews, again a deception for the Germans, who believed that there had been a pool of forty thousand Jews from which to draw. The French people of the Midi, who witnessed the Jews being crammed into cattle-like cars at the various railway stations, were disgusted and appalled by what they observed. Public opinion was negatively aroused for the moment. The first deportation train had left from Drancy for "the east" in March 1942, and these new roundups in July and August increased the flow of Jews from France to what turned out to be Auschwitz in Poland. From the onset, French police and railroad employees manned the cattle-car freight trains which were crammed with suffering Jews, whom they turned over to the Germans at the border crossing with Germany at Noveant.

---

93   Ibid., 476–478; *France: The Dark Years.* Ibid., 277.

By the end of September, when the convoys were temporarily suspended, some 42,500 Jews had been dispatched from France to meet their terrible fate.[94] The Schreiber brothers in Mégève heard word that twenty thousand Jews, mostly foreigners, had been arrested in Paris and sent on "to an unknown destination," and another ten thousand were being delivered to the Germans from the Unoccupied Zone. This worried them so much that Emile fabricated a Russian certificate stating that their mother had been an issue of a Lutheran marriage. News of a devastating nature reached Robert in an August 31 letter from Suzanne, wherein she recounted the story of one of her Jewish friends, who had committed suicide as a result of the pressure exacted by Vichy's anti-Semitism. She ended the letter speaking to the truth as she saw it regarding the fate of foreign Jews in France: "The American responsibility is heavy in this matter, having refused for two years to send boats to extricate these foreign Jews [from France]. Since 1933 we welcomed them while they [the American government] have refused them since 1940." There was more than a grain of truth to this cry from the heart. [95]

On September 12, word was received in Mégève about the fate of a cousin, Trude Apfel. She had written a note that was found along a railroad track near Paris, indicating that she was being deported to somewhere in Poland. Since she was actually transported sometime in August, she most likely had slipped the note through an opening in the freight car that left as part of a convoy that month from Drancy, hoping that it would be found. Robert received a registered letter on September 17, which contained the news he was dreading: it announced that a provisional administrator had been appointed for his Montfrin estate. He left immediately for Vichy to see if he could get the order countermanded, but it was a fool's errand, and he returned empty-handed. In Vichy's Official Journal of September 23, 1942, on page 3247, the following extract appeared from the CGQJ concerning provisional administrators:

Under the provisions of Article 1 of the law of July 22, 1941, relative to businesses, possessions, and assets belonging to Jews, it is ordered:
Article I-The decree of August 29, 1942, naming M. Vial

---

94 *Vichy France and the Jews.* Ibid., 250–252, 256–261.
95 *La Saga Servan-Schreiber.* Ibid., 481, 483.

(Albert) 16 Cours Pierre-Puget, Marseille, as provisional administrator for all the buildings and in particular the property known as the "Château of Montfrin and Vallabrègues (Gard)" belonging to Mr. Schreiber (Robert), residing at Mégève, Haute-Savoie, Château Lanouk [sic].

Article II- All buildings, rights to property or rights to any rental leases, and in particular the property known as "Château Montfrin and Vallabrègues (Gard)" belonging to Mr. Schreiber (Robert) residing in Mégève, Haute-Savoie, Château Lanouk [Nanouk].

Provisional Administrator: M. Paulet, 9 rue Château Fadaise, Nîmes. (Dossier 2721).[96]

On September 2, M. Paulet presented himself unannounced to Jean-Claude at the château, a few days after the grape crop of sixty-four tons had been picked. He made the point to Jean-Claude that he had not rushed there and did not want to be a bother, as long as he could apply the law. According to Jean-Claude, he would allow him, Jean-Claude, to prepare a typewritten inventory for M. Paulet to endorse, but that all future financial transactions must pass through the office of a local notary he had appointed. An agreement apparently was worked out that for a small percentage of the monthly receipts, M. Paulet, who maintained he was not compensated for his function, would leave Jean-Claude pretty much alone. Or so it went according to *The Saga*. But provisional administrators came and went, as did heads of the CGQJ. Darquier de Pellepoix had replaced Vallat in April 1942, with the result that bribery and financial scandal became more rampant in the administration of Jewish property acquired by the Vichy state.[97]

Emile Schreiber had prepared documentation on his family's Aryanization for submission to the office of Darquier de Pellepoix in Vichy. He felt he had an influential acquaintance there in the person of M. Villard, who was a Vichy staff member in the Hotel du Parc. Emile's Jewish status precluded his entry into Darquier's office, and although his dossier seemingly was passed on, it was most likely ignored. However,

---

96 ADG. 1 W 136. Ibid. Marked 232.
97 *La Saga Servan-Schreiber.* Ibid., 486–487; *Vichy France.* Ibid., 180; *Vichy France and the Jews.* Ibid., 294–295.

Villard reputedly obtained permission from Prefect Chiappe's office for Robert to make a brief trip to Montfrin. The fact that Emile could travel back and forth from Mégève to Vichy indicates that former contacts could still open doors for some French Jews who had the financial wherewithal to travel on excursions that were normally dangerous for people categorized as Jewish.[98]

On Sunday, November 8, 1942, BBC broadcasts had been heard by Robert, Suzanne, and Jean-Claude, who were respectively in Mégève, Marseille, and Montfrin, concerning the American landings in French North Africa. Suzanne rang Robert, worried that the Germans would certainly occupy the Mediterranean coastline of France. At 5 AM on November 11, Jean-Claude heard a familiar sound signaling a military approach to the chateau's main entrance. Armored tracked vehicle treads were chewing up the pavement, which he confirmed by looking out his window. A German column had arrived, being led on foot by a local gendarme sergeant. Quickly, he and his girlfriend, Sabine Worsmer, dressed, took their already packed baggage, and slipped out a lower door into the town, to take the next bus bound for anywhere. The Schreiber clan in Mégève was reassured for the moment when they heard on November 15 that the Italians had been assigned responsibility by Hitler for southeastern France, now including the Haute-Savoie, where Mégève was located. Meanwhile, Jean-Claude managed to join his mother in Marseille, where she had found him a job with a friend, Gabriel Montagne, who was a large wine producer with fields in the department adjoining the Spanish frontier close to Barcelona. This allowed him to slip over the Pyrénées from Perpignan into Spain on the night of November 26, while his mother entertained at dinner in her apartment members of the Italian Armistice Commission. His ever-adventurous eldest sister, Marie-Claire, visited Montfrin Château, where the German Luftwaffe general commanding the base at Courbessac had chosen to billet himself and his staff. The general allowed her to lock up certain valuable possessions in a room, after which she returned to her job in Marseille.[99]

In spite of being in the Italian Zone, Robert and Emile fled Mégève for a remote mountain farm, when they heard that the Germans had

---

98   *La Saga Servan-Schreiber.* Ibid., 488.
99   Ibid., 490-491.

threatened the French fleet at Toulon on November 27 in Operation "Lila." This threat resulted in Vichy ordering the scuttling of the fleet, which was anchored in the harbor. The two brothers returned to Nanouk when they felt things were safe again, only to hear on the radio on December 9 that all French Jews now would be obligated to have their identity cards stamped "*Juif.*" As footnoted earlier, this new law of December 11, 1942, would apply to stamping the word "Jew" prominently not only on identify cards for both foreign and French Jews but also on ration cards. On January 11, the three Schreiber brothers submitted to this procedure so that they would not be accused of breaking a Vichy law. By the way, Marrus and Paxton have pointed out the key administrative and enforcement roles the CGQJ and the French police played in helping round up Jews in France for the Germans: "As SS General Oberg wrote to French Police Chief Bousquet on July 29, 1942, as the two police services solidified their agreement to work together: 'I am happy to confirm, moreover, that the French police has up to now performed in a manner worthy of appreciation.'"[100]

Rumors continued to circulate that Jews were going to be rounded up in Mégève, so the brothers considered trying to flee to Switzerland. They decided against attempting to take this step, as life was much more expensive there, and they felt they could not afford it. They had done a calculation on what it had cost them to stay in Emile's chalet in Mégève per year and arrived at a figure of five hundred thousand French francs. Their figures revealed that 60 percent of the total went for food, and now they could no longer count on anything to be sent to them from provisions produced at Montfrin. To cheer themselves up, they decided on February 14, 1943, to invite some acquaintances to join the family for dinner to celebrate the latest Allied victory. Some twenty-four guests dined on warm salmon pate prepared by the cook, but some felt a bit queasy over having to fete a Russian victory over the Germans at Rostov on the Don River. They were also troubled that January 22–27, 1943, had marked a large joint operation in Marseille by some ten thousand French police and several thousand Germans in the Old Port. Its purpose was to eliminate a center of "opposition and crime" there and it was razed, with some twenty-two thousand people forcibly moved elsewhere. Suzanne and Marie-Claire must have witnessed some of these

---

100   Ibid., 492–493; *Vichy France and the Jews.* Ibid., 369–370 and note 76.

maneuvers. On March 29, Marie-Claire telephoned Robert to inform him that the Gestapo had been trying to find Suzanne to arrest her, and that she and her mother were going into hiding and were sending young Marie-Geneviève to join him in Mégève.[101]

Earlier in this chapter, documentation has been cited concerning moving all foreign Jews thirty kilometers away from the Mediterranean coast, affixing the word "Jew" now onto all ration cards, and the increasing German interest and influence (like SS Oberscharführer u. Stellvertr's) in monitoring the whereabouts of all Jews. Suzanne Crémieux-Schreiber and her daughter, Marie-Claire Servan-Schreiber, had reason to fear all these additional pressures on Jews.

On April 3, Marie-Claire telephoned her father again in Mégève to tell him that when she had visited her mother's apartment the day before to check the mail, the Germans had almost apprehended her. She was frightened enough to promise never to visit the apartment again, to quit her job at Savon Brothers and to stay hidden with her mother at her friends' home in nearby Meyragues. On April 18, Suzanne left for Sainte-Maxime to visit Jeanne Reynaud, the ex-premier's wife, so Marie-Claire was alone the next day in Meyragues, giving a bath to her hosts' two young children, when there was a knock on the door. She opened the door and was asked if she was Madame Crémieux. She detected a slight German accent in the French spoken and said she was only the governess, giving her name as Marie-Claire Servan, as indicated on her papers. Regardless, she was taken away, reputedly threatened by her abductors with revolvers en route to Marseille, where by nightfall she was deposited at the Gestapo's premises on rue Paradis.

The next day she was taken in the company of a young female collaborator to the apartment on rue Dragon to see if the maid would recognize Marie-Claire as a Schreiber or Crémieux. Marie-Claire knocked on the door and as soon as the maid opened it she shouted out, "Does Madame Crémieux live here?" The maid, Marguerite, astutely answered immediately that no one was in and that she did not know where she was. By the evening, Marie-Claire was back to the Mainguys' home in Meyragues, where one could imagine that everybody breathed a collective sigh of relief. By early May, Jean-Claude had succeeded in crossing from Spain into Algeria, where he planned to join a Free French tank

---

101   Ibid., 307; *La Saga Servan-Schreiber.* Ibid., 497, 500.

unit. At the same time, Robert noticed an ominous sign placed near the park benches in central Mégève, which was still under Italian control: "Forbidden to Jews, municipal order of May 1, 1943."[102] Robert undoubtedly had suffered additional stress when he learned in March that a new provisional administrator had been appointed by Darquier de Pellepoix to replace M. Paulet, nearly four months after Jean-Claude had left town. On page 689 of the Official Journal of the CGQJ of March 10, 1943, it was noted that M. Rey, 15 rue de la Servie, Nîmes, had taken over responsibility for the ex-Schreiber holdings in Montfrin. [103]

In reference to Jews of Italian origin, there were two telegrams from police officials in Vichy that Prefect Chiappe received in late March, which touched upon the Italian nationality. At this time, the Italian government was still technically—and in fact—a German ally. The telex of March 20 asked the prefect to investigate urgently if any free Italian Jews wanted to be repatriated to Italy. Those individuals were to be placed on a list that was to be submitted to Vichy. The second telegram, dated March 23, listed seven or eight other Jewish nationalities and requested lists of any interned from those specific countries and whether any of the various nationals listed had requested to be repatriated. A handwritten draft was composed on March 24 by Prefect Chiappe, in which he referenced the telegram number and replied that he had no interned Jews in his department, and that no one of the nationalities mentioned wished to be repatriated except for one Mr. Jose Bessudo, a Spaniard. The telegram went on to reference the telex of March 20 and instructed that anything that might have been ordered for any Italians should be delayed. On March 29, the Italian vice consul in Nîmes, Roberto De Cardona, wrote Prefect Chiappe the following letter:

"Dear Mr. Prefect: In the Nîmes newspapers of today, March 29, I read that, among others, Israelites of Italian nationality are required urgently to go in person to the Central Commission for Foreigners at the mayor's office. I am obliged to ask you, Mr. Prefect, what is the motive for this summons? Sincerely yours, the Italian vice consul, Roberto De Cardona."

The protest might have made some impression on the prefect, but the only data found subsequent to Consul Cardona's letter was a

---

102 *La Saga Servan-Schreiber.* Ibid., 502–503.
103 ADG. 1 W 136. Ibid. Marked 519.

list of foreign-born Jews by nationality, at the bottom of which were two Italians, a married couple, Maurice and Rachel Rosenthal, both of whom were born in Constantinople in the early 1880s. They were residing in Remoulins in 1943, where Mr. Rosenthal was employed. His wife's maiden name was given as Donsaft. [104] The consul's implied objection was part of an Italian effort to be "humane" toward the Jews, in response to a German threat to the Italian government to repatriate all Italian Jews in France to Italy. All this maneuvering would end right after September 8, when the Allies unexpectedly announced an armistice with Italy, which had capitulated on August 8, 1943.

However, prior to that date during 1943, as Robert Paxton points out, Jews in the Vichy zone were pawns in the negotiations between the Germans in charge of Jewish policy and their French counterparts, more on the basis of rich versus poor than foreign versus French. The poor were in camps, where they could easily be rounded up, now directly by the Nazis, while the rich could use their means to seek alternative methods of escape or evasion. And the Italians in their occupation zone around Nice acted to obstruct the French relative to foreign Jews. In June 1943, the Italian police head in their zone of France, Inspector General Guido Lospinosa, saved seven thousand foreign Jews from being arrested by the French in Mégève. However, when the Germans took over the former Italian Zone, no Jew was safe, rich or poor, foreign or French.

One of the tens of thousands of Jews, who found his life threatened by the Germans was fifteen-year-old Stanley Hoffmann, who lived in Nice along with his Austrian mother. For a few months, they used their wits and help from friendly neighbors to escape German searches. But they became desperate to get out of Nice, as the situation became more and more perilous for all Jews who remained. Thanks to assistance from Hoffmann's courageous history teacher, who forged false French Aryan documents for both of them, they were able to travel west to an inland spa resort in Languedoc, Lamalou-les-Bains, where they successfully waited out the end of the war. Stanley Hoffmann later became (and still is) an eminent political scientist at Harvard who has written extensively on twentieth-century France.

Lamalou-les-Bains remains to this day a place where the French go to "take the waters," but when I stopped there in summer 2009,

---

104   ADG. 1 W 143. Ibid. Marked 269, 270, 271, 272, 273, and 286.

the person in charge of the Visitors Center was totally unfamiliar with Stanley Hoffmann. What Professor Hoffmann's message was after he saw Max Ophüls's image of France during the dark years of occupation in the *Sorrow and the Pity* is worth quoting (thanks to Julian Jackson). "In my memory, the schoolteacher … who taught me French history, gave me hope in the worst days, dried my tears when my best friend was deported along with his mother, and gave false papers to me and my mother so that we could flee a Gestapo-infested city in which complicity of friends and neighbors was no longer a guarantee of safety—this man wipes out all the bad moments, and the humiliations, and the terrors. He and his wife were not Resistance heroes, but if there was an average Frenchman, it was this man."[105]

On June 11, Suzanne stopped briefly at Nanouk on her way to Aix-les-Bains, which was also in the Italian Zone, and where she judged she would be safer than in Marseille. She related additional details of the story of Marie-Claire's Gestapo scare and the adventures Jean-Claude experienced during his six-month trip from France to Spain and finally to Algiers. On June 15, some friends in Mégève heard Jean-Claude participate in a Radio Algiers broadcast concerning his joining the Free French forces, where his unit turned out to be the Fifth RCA. Jean-Jacques Servan-Schreiber also wished to join his cousin Jean-Claude in the Free French forces in North Africa. He decided to cross over into Spain with his father after his oral exams were completed for admission to one of the top-tier universities in Paris. Robert decided not to accompany them when he heard on July 29 that M. Rey, the current provisional administrator, had decided to sell Montfrin after the wine harvest was concluded in September. He planned to contest this in some to-be-determined fashion.

With Italy's surrender anticipated, rumors were abounding that the

---

105   *Vichy France.* Ibid., 182–183; *Vichy France and the Jews.* Ibid., 315–321. Marrus and Paxton open their section, *The Italian Interlude,* with this quotation: "According to Bousquet, [the Italian officer] Lospinosa declared: the Germans are very severe in carrying out measures against the Jews; the French are more severe than the Italians; while the Italians strive for a humane solution to the Jewish problem." Note 121: from Oberg to Himmler and Kaltenbrunner, July 1, 1943, found in the German archives relative to their occupation of France. *France: The Dark Years.* Ibid., 378, note 100; Stanley Hoffman. *Decline or Renewal? France since the 1930s* (1974), 60.

Germans would arrive soon to replace the Italians. Jean-Jacques arrived in Mégève after passing his exams, but word came that he would be called up to join the *Chantiers de la Jeunesse*, if not the STO, by October 1. The time had come to flee Mégève, and Emile purchased train tickets for Toulouse for himself and Jean-Jacques, with a departure scheduled for September 9. Robert bade them farewell, and the father and son, accompanied by their Aryan wife/mother Dénise, boarded a train that arrived in Toulouse early in the morning of September 10. They all left the next morning for Saint-Girons to rendezvous with a guide, who was contracted to lead the two men up the Pyrénées into Spain. On the night of September 11/12, the husband and son bid adieu to Dénise, and they made the eight-kilometer march with the guide to cross over the border.[106]

Robert Schreiber felt extremely embittered toward Vichy due to its actions against his commercial and residential properties. He committed the following to his diary while he contemplated the increased danger he faced through the Germans taking over all of France, now that they were replacing and disarming the Italians. "Other misfortunes had come pelting down on me; if I had to accept without complaint what the Germans had done to me like occupying my château of Montfrin in November 1942 along with its farms, I feel more ashamed for my country to have the CGQJ assign a provisional administrator for the same estate. Thus my country had no respect for the services I had rendered it during the war of 1914–1918, or for those of my son during the war of 1939–1940. It is not because I was personally affected that I raise my protest but because France disowned and rejected the Jews, just like it had cast out the Protestants. These unworthy measures, by punishing Jewish interests, lifted the Jews up morally, but they debased France, my beloved country, to the level of a Hitlerian Germany."[107]

But the thought of danger to his person persisted, and he knew he had to act soon in order to protect his life. Toward the end of September, he slipped away to lie low in a more remote ski station, Fayet, nearer to Chamonix. It was just as well that he was out of the Gard, as the search for Jews continued even when they changed residences, as the following archival record indicates. The police commissioner of the city of Saint-

---

106   *La Saga Servan-Schreiber.* Ibid., 505–506, 510–513.
107   *Journal.* Ibid., 458–459.

Gilles responded as follows on January 31, 1943, to an inquiry from Prefect Chiappe:

> In observation of your instructions of December 4, 1942, relative to any changes of residence for French or foreign Israelites, it is my pleasure to answer that no new Jewish resident arrived in Saint-Gilles during the month of January 1943, and no current Jewish resident left the city.
>
> However, the French Jew Meyer, Emmanuel, born August 26, 1870, in Marmontiers (Bas-Rhin), who has been residing in our commune since July 1940, had been arrested by officials of the Gestapo on January 22, 1943, and taken away to an unknown destination.

Perhaps this nondescript French citizen, Mr. Meyer, was one of the forty-nine thousand Jews that Heinz Röthke, Dannecker's successor, estimated had been shipped from France eastward to that "unknown destination" by his accounting dated March 6, 1943. Of course, as we know, this total was very disappointing to the Germans charged with contributing to the Final Solution in occupied France.[108]

Rustenholz and Treiner picked up the balance of their story of the Schreiber family after September 11, 1943, in volume 2 of *La Saga Servan-Schreiber: Le Temps des Initiales*, where the remainder of the war years was covered briefly in the first sixty pages or so. Much of the rest of 1943 concerned Emile after he arrived in Algiers, where he heard from Jean-Claude on October 21 that he was commanding a French unit of five Sherman tanks. This was also the day that the Crémieux decree was reinstated by the Free French representatives, giving back the protection of the law to Algerian Jews, which Vichy had annulled in 1940. Evidently, Suzanne and Marie-Claire had traveled by early November to Paris, where they stayed with one of Suzanne's friends in an apartment on the Champs-de-Mars. Supposedly, Marie-Claire found employment in an aviation factory that had been a Felix Amiot enterprise. On February

---

108   ADG. 1 W 142 Ibid. No.90 marked 626. *Vichy France and the Jews.* Ibid., 307–308, note 92. Marrus and Paxton comment on the increased presence and tempo of arrests of Jews by the Gestapo in the Midi during April–May 1943. Nîmes was an initial target, as were Aix-en-Provence, Avignon, Carpentras, and Marseille.

10, 1944, Emile's son, Jean-Jacques, left Morocco for Alabama in the United States for pilot training. About this same time, Robert had quit Fayet for Paris, where he lunched with Emile's wife, Dénise, and saw his youngest daughter, Marie-Geneviève. No mention was made of seeing Suzanne, who had had a writ issued on December 15, 1943, requesting a divorce from Robert, who evidently refused to grant it on January 4, 1944. Robert had also received word in Paris that the current provisional administrator for Montfrin had put it up for liquidation for a sum of 3,500,000 francs. However, at the same time, he heard rumors that when France was freed, the original proprietors would have first rights to reacquire property confiscated by Vichy. Tragic news reached Emile around March 18 that their cousin Franz Schreiber, his wife, Charlotte, and thirteen-year-old daughter, Vera, had been deported east. They were never heard of again. Emile wrote when he received this news that: "It is well recognized that atrocities such as this happen, but you only fully comprehend them when they happen to a member of your family. I have become a member, pure and simple, of those wishing for the extermination of the Germans."[109]

The Schreiber-Crémieux Marriage Officially Terminated

For some time, Robert and Suzanne had not only drifted apart but also had been at cross-purposes in many aspects of their relationship. While he was in Paris, Robert decided to join a resistance movement in some capacity. The authors claim that when no post was offered to him, he blamed it on Suzanne. He left Paris and arrived in the Cantal near Mauriac, where he had secured an administrative position as of May 1, 1944, working on the Aigle dam near the middle section of the Dordogne River. By D-Day he was able to join a partisan group of the FTP (*Franc-tireurs et partisans*) to act as a lookout for German activity near the Marèges hydroelectric dam in the adjoining Corrèze department. The wealthy capitalist entrepreneur had become a laborer associated with the Communists!

The pace of events quickened after the Allies broke out of Normandy on July 31 and set their sights on Paris. Jean-Claude participated in Operation Anvil, the extremely successful Allied invasion along the Mediter-

---

109   *La Saga Servan-Schreiber 2-Le temps des initiales* (Paris: Seuil, 1993), 21–22, 25, 34, 37–39.

ranean coast, which included seven French divisions from North Africa, and took place on August 15. Apparently on August 31, he managed to advance with four tanks from Avignon to "liberate" Montfrin village, where he was greeted by, among others, Antoine Joffre, the watchman of Montfrin Château. Robert, meanwhile, had quit the FTP to make his way to liberated Montfrin, intent on taking up his residence there again and assuming his old position of mayor. Rustenholz and Treiner maintain that he was able to "touch" five hundred thousand francs in a safe deposit box that remained hidden in Montfrin. Emile joined him there briefly around mid-September, on his way to Paris. Marie-Claire returned from Paris during the fall and carried news to her father that his divorce with Suzanne had been finalized on April 28, with an effective date of July 18, 1944. This was a far different form of divorce from what was going on in post-liberation France between accused Vichy collaborators and "resistant" France in this time of rabid *épuration*, known in English as the purge.[110]

Nearly two years later, on May 22, 1946, a French divorce court appraised the community property valuation of the Schreiber-Cremieux estate as follows:

- Montfrin Château along with 72.5 hectares of farm land— 3,650,000 francs

- Montfrin Château furnishings and artworks—350,000 francs

- Paris apartments (2) furnishings—100,000 francs

- Liquidity—410,000 francs

- Securities—240,000 francs

- Total Marriage Estate—4,750,000 francs

Due to the fact that at the time of their formal engagement in 1916, Robert contributed far more to the marriage contract than had Suzanne, his 1946 settlement amounted to more than 4,000,000 francs, and hers was estimated at 50 percent of the Paris furniture valuation, plus 360,000 francs in cash. But we are moving slightly ahead of our story.[111]

---

110 Ibid., 41–43, 45–53; *France: The Dark Years.* 368, 554–555.

111 *La Saga Servan-Schreiber*, vol. 2, 64–66.

When Robert returned to a liberated Gard in the summer of 1944, his primary aim was to regain control of all that he had lost to the machinations of the Vichy state against their French Jewish citizens under their laws of spoliation. De Gaulle's provisional government which ruled France from August 1944 through October 1945, when initial postwar national elections were held, instructed their newly appointed prefects to aid in this process. By the way, Suzanne Crémieux might have lost a battle in her personal war with Robert Schreiber over their monetary divorce settlement, but she finally won the right to vote, along with all her adult French sisters. Female suffrage was promulgated on April 21, 1944, through an edict of the French Committee of National Liberation.[112]

A press release had been issued in the Gard by the office responsible for Jewish Interests in September 1944, which instructed newspapers to make certain information public. Its subject was "Protection of Possessions Belonging to Jews" and its initial paragraph stated: "A decree dated September 27, 1944, issued by the office of the Commissioner of the Republic for Languedoc-Roussillon, stipulates that everyone having acquired or taken possession of furnishings (movables) or real estate (immovables) subsequent to June 26, 1940, belonging to people classified as Jews by German ordinances or terms of the defacto Vichy government's issued laws characterized as racial in nature, is bound within fifteen days of the publication of said order, to make a declaration at the prefecture or sub-prefecture.

"In observation of said decree, the prefect invites the people so designated above, to make their declaration at the prefecture's Fourth Division, Departmental Office for Jewish Affairs, before the 12th of October, 1944."[113]

On October 24, 1944, Robert Schreiber addressed the following handwritten letter to M. Joseph Ducart, the 4th Division's Departmental Secretary for Jewish Interests in the Gard Prefecture:

---

112 *France: The Dark Years*. Ibid., 594–595. Ironically, just before Suzanne Crémieux could cast her first vote in May 1945, her companion on the *Massilia*, Pierre Mendès France, who ultimately would become her son-in-law, resigned from de Gaulle's government in a battle over economic policy with René Pleven, as discussed by Julian Jackson.
113 ADG. 1 W 136. Marked 9.

Dear Sir,

Subsequent to our telephone conversation of today, I would appreciate very much your urgent attention to make all necessary arrangements concerning my postal checking account: No. 254-41 in Limoges, administered by M. Pierre Clauzel, provisional administrator, so that it can be unblocked as soon as possible. Please accept my deepest thanks,

Robert Schreiber, President of the Municipal Delegation in Montfrin

On October 31, the following letter was sent from the prefecture in Nîmes to the person in charge of handling postal checking accounts in Limoges, Haut-Vienne: "I have attached to the letter a copy of my order of October 30, 1944, by which I have authorized M. Robert Schreiber, property owner in Montfrin, and holder of CP account 254.41 Limoges, to draw upon funds that were deposited to this account subsequent to September 22, 1944. I will be obliged to you for bringing this instruction to the attention of any interested parties in your administration." It was signed on behalf of M. Ducart. [114]

On June 26, 1944, M. Ducart had issued an internal prefectural memo that addressed an associated subject in the following fashion: "The Prefect of the Gard, in conformity with the instructions outlined in the decree of September 22, 1944, of the Commissioner of the Republic in Montpellier, authorizes M. Robert Schreiber, mayor of Montfrin, to collect from M. Clauzel, former insurance agent, rue de la Tresorerie, Nîmes, the complete dossier and documentation relating to all his personal possessions."

On October 30, the newly appointed prefect of the Gard, M. D. Paganelle, had issued the following order to his administrators, including the section related to Jewish Interests:

Having duly noted the ordinance of August 9, 1944, relative to the restoration of the Republican Legality on French continental territory, and Article 3 of said ordinance which annulled all acts which established or applied any sort of discrimination founded on a Jewish quality, and the order of September 27,

---

114   Ibid. Marked 368, and 365.

1944 from the Commissioner of the Republic for Languedoc-Roussillon, be it so ordered,

Article 1—M. Clauzel, insurance agent in Nîmes, provisional administrator of the possessions of M. Robert Schreiber, property owner in Montfrin, is discharged from his functions.

Article 2—M. Robert Schreiber is authorized to have at his disposal all sums deposited to his account CP 254-41, Limoges, subsequent to September 22, 1944.

Article 3—The Secretary General of the Prefecture is responsible for executing this present order."[115]

The procedures Robert Schreiber went through in either submitting to Vichy's Jewish Statutes or reestablishing ownership of his possessions that had been placed in the hands of various provisional administrators did not occur in a vacuum. Other Jewish families in the Gard who survived the war experienced similar administrative abasements and travails. Earlier in this chapter the experiences of the Berr family of Mas Devèze near Nîmes were chronicled concerning expropriation and reacquisition. There were coincidences in the Berr-Schreiber cases and those twists of fate did not stop with 1941 or 1942. M. André Carcassonne, the uncle of Marcel Berr, wrote Prefect Paganelle on August 31, 1944, to inform him of certain facts, including that when Mas Devèze had been appropriated by the CGQJ, M. Pierre Clauzel had been appointed its provisional administrator or trustee. Paul Clauzel features very prominently in the Schreiber story in the same capacity.

Now we return to the Suzanne Crémieux and Robert Schreiber family narrative for the time period from late 1944 through the end of the war in Europe and beyond. By February 1945, Suzanne had returned to her rue du Boccador apartment in Paris. Jean-Claude advanced with French military forces into Germany, seeing his last action near Baden-Baden in April. This was the same month in which his father returned to Paris to reassume the reins at *Les Echos*, as his brother, Emile, having been appointed an economic advisor to Georges Bidault, was on temporary duty with de Gaulle's delegation to the San Francisco UN conference. Robert soon thereafter adjusted the journal's ownership to a 50/50 basis between him and Emile, and hired Marie-Claire to work in the

---

115   Ibid. Marked 204 and 366.

subscription department. When Jean-Claude separated from military service in March of 1946, he also joined the firm, living with his father in Paris while he worked there.

In the meantime, Marie-Claire had made the acquaintance of a handsome, ne'er-do-well French gentleman of distinguished noble background, Count Jacques Claret de Fleurieu, whom she married. She had a daughter, Nathalie, with him in 1946 but returned to work soon thereafter at *Les Echos*, to continue what turned out to be a long and distinguished career in journalistic publicity. She later had a son, Jean-René, who was born on December 31, 1950, after which date her husband departed as a volunteer to fight in Korea. Basically, the wife and husband lived apart until the count died of a heart attack in London in late 1965. During 1957, Marie-Claire entered into a relationship with Pierre Mendès France, the French premier, whom her cousin Jean-Jacques Servan-Schreiber, the founder of *L'Express*, christened PMF in homage to how his American friend, John Kennedy, was referred to as JFK. Marie-Claire had played with Mendès France's young children on the *Massilia* and would marry him in Montfrin Château in a modest ceremony on January 2, 1971.[116]

But we must return for a moment to 1945 and the continuing efforts by what would become France's Fourth Republic to make amends for what Vichy and the CGQJ had done to the French Jews. It is worth repeating that on April 22, 1945, there appeared Ordinance No. 45-770 in the French Republic's Official Journal "which announced the second enforcement measure of the Ordinance of November 12, 1943, on the rescinding of the despoilment of possessions made by the enemy or those under its control and enacting the restitution of their possessions to the victims of those actions which had been the object of such stipulations." Even though the word Jew or Israelite was not used in the body of the copy of the reinforcement of this ordinance, it was obvious to whom this measure applied. On August 4, 1945, the head of the Restitution Department in the Finance Ministry of the French Republic's Provisional Government in Paris, M. Perroisse, wrote the prefect in Nîmes, instructing him to publicize specific information about how one could recover personal papers obtained through the spoliation process.

---

116 *La Saga Servan-Schreiber*, vol. 2. 55–64, 122–126, 437.

This document was very specific concerning whom and what it touched upon: Jews and documentation taken from them. It stated:

> Under the Vichy regime the ex-Commissioner General for Jewish Questions was conducting inquiries for determining the Ayranization of property whose owners were presumed to be Israelites.
>
> It frequently happened that before appointing a provisional administrator or giving an order to sell or liquidate a property, the owners were required to hand over certain civil documents which established their origins. These documents have remained in the archives of the ex-CGQJ.
>
> A good number of these credentials could be of very great interest to those who had been demanded to furnish them and who had not returned at the time to pick them up. The Restitution Service, which has these records in its possession, would be pleased to return them quickly to their original owners.
>
> Consequently, so that our service can proceed to give back these civil documents to the interested parties, I request that you distribute to the general public through the press and radio services of your department, the following text [the headline, as handwritten by the prefect; author's italics] *Restitution of Civil Documents to Israelites*: The Restitution Service is in possession of a number of important civil documents coming from the Commissioner General of Jewish Questions, relating to possessions it was charged to take over for administration. The interested parties may apply to recover their documents. They only have to request their return via the proper proofs of identity, at the Restitution Service, 1 rue de la Banque, Paris 2e.

Peace had come to Europe on VE Day, May 8, 1945, when the Allied powers accepted the unconditional surrender of the German armed forces. Robert Schreiber had started publishing *Les Echos* again on the prior November 15 and in the postwar period, it would become France's foremost economic daily. We already are aware of the fact that many of his and Emile's children commenced their journalistic careers working there. Emile's eldest son, Jean-Jacques Servan-Schreiber, was able to use the platform of *Les Echos* to publish his approved French model of *Time* magazine, *L'Express*. Its first issue appeared on May 14, 1953, and featured a famous interview with Pierre Mendès France about the war in Indochina, which was going badly, titled "France Can Accept the Truth." From that time on a philosophical and political split developed between Robert's son Jean-Claude and Jean-Jacques, which led to a rather complete breakdown in relations in the early 1960s. At that time a battle erupted over the ownership of *Les Echos*, which resulted in its sale to the Beytout family, owners of Roussel Laboratories. This troubled Robert, to see the enterprise he had formed fifty-five years earlier disappear over a spat between the Schreiber families' eldest sons. His failing health had caused him to withdraw from the business, and he died from a heart attack on April 21, 1966. Four days later, he was buried on top of a hillside overlooking Montfrin Château, with no Christian or Jewish inscriptions on his casket or the rough-hewn monolith that marked his gravesite, situated amongst the cypress trees.[117]

Suzanne Crémieux, Robert's ex-wife, returned to her former passion in the postwar era, politics. Now she could not only vote but also stand for election as a candidate in France for the Fourth Republic's Parliament. Like her famous uncle, Adolphe Crémieux, and her father, Fernand, she became a Radical Party senator representing the Gard department from 1948 to 1953, and again from 1959 until her death on July 11, 1976. She had been interested in feminist politics all her life, and undoubtedly had taken pride in the passage on January 17, 1975, of the Loi Weil (named after Simone Weil), which finally allowed abortion in France under certain closely defined conditions. Her daughter, Marie-Claire Mendès France, who had been quite a daredevil herself during the German occupation, wrote that her mother had not been fully aware of the dangers she had courted: "Contrary to what my mother wished to believe, the Crémieux family, although they were of old French stock, were as threatened as any Polish immigrants [under the anti-Jewish laws of Vichy]. It was necessary to outsmart the authorities." Even though Suzanne penned her final wishes around the time the Germans were occupying Marseille in late 1942, she survived

---

117 *La Saga Servan*-Schreiber, vol. 2, 126–130, 388–389 ; *Journal.* 238, 476–477. http://afmeg.info/squelettes/dicofemmesjuives/pagesnotice/cremieux.htm. Marie-Claire Mendès France, *L'esprit de liberté, Paris, de la renaissance* (1992), 343.

the war and was eighty-one years old when she passed on. One primary wish from 1942 was certainly honored: she was buried in the family crypt in Montfrin cemetery, alongside her parents and siblings. The headstone reads:

Fernand Crémieux Family;
Fernand Crémieux, Gard Senator, 1857–1928
Sol Crémieux born Aghion, 1865–1940
André Alphandery, son-in-law, 1870–1938
Esther Alphandery, born Crémieux, 1884–1959
Suzanne Crémieux, Gard senator, 1895–1976[118]

A Final Accounting

When war was declared in 1939, there were approximately three hundred thousand Jewish people in France. Approximately 110,000 were foreigners who had sought refuge there during the 1920s and 1930s, and the balance of some 190,000 were of French citizenship. The number of foreign Jews increased by more than twenty thousand in 1940 due to an influx of Dutch and Belgian Jews, plus some Germans. These Jewish refugees fled their countries and joined the Exodus in May/June, forcibly joined by the 6,500 German Jews that Hitler expelled from his own country into France. We have seen documentary evidence of how Robert Schreiber and his immediate family members attempted to follow the letter of the anti-Jewish laws that were imposed on them by Marshal Pétain and his Vichy government. Hope for better days to come in late 1940 sprang eternal for most Jews, French or foreign, especially for those living in Unoccupied France

Between the time of the initial German demanded registration of September 27, 1940, for Jews in Occupied France, and the first Vichy-

---

118   *La Saga Servan-Schreiber*, vol. 2. 459. http://www.senat.fr/sen4Rfic/cremieux_suzanne000769.htlm.

Marie-Claire Mendès France. *L'esprit de liberté* (Paris: Presses de la Renaissance, 1992), 343. Marie-Claire Mendès France died in 2004. She spent many of her last years at Montfrin Château with her son, Jean-René. Her husband, Pierre Mendès France, passed away in Paris on October 18, 1982. According to an e-mail the author received from Jean René de Fleurieu on March 6, 2011, his mother had requested that her ashes be spread near the monolith under which her father was buried.

mandated census of Jews in the free zone nine months later, 287,962 Jews registered. This figure amounted to roughly 90 percent of all the Jews in France, the western European country in which the largest number of Jews were to be found. These catalogued registrations of specific names with residential addresses were momentous steps in the direction of making it much easier for the French or German authorities to make arrests when the time came to do so. The facts concerning Hitler's murderous feelings toward the Jews and how he had treated them in Germany since his assumption of power were well known and documented. Without wishing to lay any blame, it seems fair to say that on the initial choice to show some manner of resistance to the edicts imposed only about 10 percent of the Jews in France chose to do so. Of course, this path of compliance probably made more sense to upper-class French citizens like Robert Schreiber, who had become categorized as a Jew by the state. However, his actions were in stark contrast to retired general André Boris in Nîmes, who had written Prefect Chiappe on June 26, 1941, his objections to having to register as an Israelite. Amazingly, in September 1940, the French Rabbinical Council drafted a statement wherein they expressed loyalty to Marshall Pétain and adherence to the tenets of his National Revolution. [119]

The number of Jewish people deported from France for extermination during the Holocaust has been precisely calculated at 75,721. Approximately two-thirds of this gross number were foreign Jews and the balance were French citizens. Therefore, the percentage of Jews rounded up by the French police, and transported in French cattle-car trains by the SCNF to be handed over to the Germans at the border was about 24 percent of all the Jews in France (76,000/320,000). Only about 2,500 of the Jewish deportees survived that horrific experience (3.3 percent). France's hexagon represents a fairly large geographical area, which is approximately 20 percent smaller, by comparison, with the American state of Texas. However, the French topography is much different, featuring a diversity that ranges from mountainous areas to rolling plains, all traversed by a multiplicity of rivers that flow through and separate valleys and communities. Its prewar population of forty-

---

119   *France: The Dark Years.* Ibid., 363–367; ADG. 1 W 138. Ibid., dated June 26, 1941, marked 156.

two million people was very spread out over the country, in spite of the importance of Paris as a metropolitan center.

France's topographical area also features a significant contrast with the much smaller geographical, highly urbanized countries of the Netherlands and Belgium, both of which had sizeable Jewish populations in 1939. For example, nearly two-thirds of the 140,000 Jews in Holland were living like Anne Frank's family in Amsterdam. Both of these countries were fully occupied by the Germans. On the one hand, the Dutch government and its Queen Wilhelmina had crossed the North Sea and taken refuge in England. Belgium's King Leopold III stayed in his country retreat after having capitulated to the Germans on May 27, 1940, an act deemed unconstitutional by his ministers. The deportation rates of the prewar Jewish citizens in these two countries just to the north of France are another area of stark contrast. About 78 percent of all Dutch Jews were shipped east to the Nazi death camps, while close to 45 percent of all Belgian Jews suffered a similar fate. Again, very few survived the Holocaust.

One could say that the survival rate of all Jews in France was paradoxically high. But one should also ask the question of how much higher it could/would have been if Marshall Pétain, his interior ministry, their police, and all the other collaborationist enablers had refused to cooperate in doing the dirty work for the relatively few Germans available for such a task in France, 1940–1944. The answer to this can only be sought by examining a complete cross-section of French civil society during this dark period and checking their various reactions to what they thought or actually knew to be transpiring under Vichy and the German occupation.[120]

Although worried, the great majority of French Jews exhibited a high degree of complacency after the debacle of 1940, in spite of the Jewish Statutes imposed by Vichy, at least up until the Vél d'Hiv roundups of summer 1942. French Jewish organizations like the Central Consistory and the UGIF (General Union of Israelites of France) were very ambivalent toward any foreign Jews. The former's leader, Jacques Helbronner, an acquaintance of Pétain since 1917, was used by Vichy's head of state and was contemptuously called "the marshal's Jew" by Jewish refugees.

---

120   *France: The Dark Years.* Ibid., 362–363; *Vichy France and the Jews.* Ibid., 356–372.

The UGIF, set up reluctantly by Vallat late in 1941, was administered by Vichy for both zones, and naively felt it could protect French Jews while letting the foreign ones take the brunt of the Nazis' plans for Jewry. Part of their charge was to protect Jewish orphan children, but their record-keeping actually made it easier for all the unfortunates, and specifically those children, to be rounded up.

Robert Paxton quotes Edith Thomas, a writer, Resistance member, and future conservator of the National Archives, on what she witnessed in the former Italian Zone in July 1943: "I saw a train pass. In front, a car containing French police and German soldiers. Then came cattle cars, sealed. The thin arms of children clasped the grating. A hand waved outside like a leaf in a storm. When the train slowed down, the voices cried 'Mama!' And nothing answered except the squeaking of the springs. ... The truth: stars worn on breasts, children torn from mothers, men shot every day, the methodical degradation of an entire people. The truth is censored. We must cry it from the rooftops." [121] This was written in 1943, when much more was known by some people about where the sealed cattle-car trains were heading. In 1940–1941, the immigrant Jews already had some personal experience with harsh discrimination, yet still not enough to risk noncompliance with the French or German racial dictates.

The *rafles* of July 1942 in Paris removed blinders from many Jewish eyes, especially foreign ones, and they started to take evasive steps. Julian Jackson quotes what fifteen-year-old Annie Kriegel, the future French historian, witnessed on July 16 in her Jewish neighborhood on rue de Turenne: "I saw a policeman in uniform who was carrying a suitcase in each hand and crying. I distinctly remember those tears running down a rugged, rather reddish face because you would agree that it is rare to see a policeman cry in public. He walked down the street, followed by a small group of children and old people carrying little bundles ... It was the roundup ... I continued on my way when at the crossroads ... I heard screams rising to the heavens: not cries and squawks such as you hear in noisy and excited crowds, but the sort of screams you hear in hospital delivery rooms." She was so traumatized that all she could do was pause to sit on a park bench. Later on, she reflected that it was on that tragic day she lost her childhood innocence.[122]

---

121 *Vichy France.* Ibid., 183–184; *France: The Dark Years.* Ibid., 357, 363–365.
122 Ibid., 366–367.

Many Jews joined armed resistance groups, and most prominent among such organizations was the Immigrant Workers Movement (MOI), a Communist affiliate, whose most stunning coup was the assassination of Fritz Sauckel's STO deputy in France, Julius Ritter. This feat was engineered by Armenian-born Missak Manouchian and described earlier. Some historians argue that this Parisian band of brothers and sisters (Annie Kriegel joined one of their elements after her parents escaped south) was more loyal to Communist interests than to caring about the fate of their Jewish brethren. There are two reasons to infer otherwise. The first is that they were willing to put their lives on the line in order to kill those whom they deemed the real enemies of France: Germans and French collaborators. Second, their organizations were at the forefront of the effort to publicize information they had gleaned from their sources about the fate awaiting any Jews being deported eastward. They recommended that Jews go into hiding just before the July roundups, and later on were among the first to publish articles about the German use of Zyklon B gas in their extermination chambers. Saving actual lives was more complicated, and although a Jewish Children's Relief Organization (OSE) in the Unoccupied Zone helped save several thousand children, any real effort to succeed on a large scale needed the risky cooperation of French society, which was not necessarily committed to any resistance camp.[123]

When the First Jewish Statute was published in October 1940, it created very few waves amongst the non-Jewish French population. The vast majority of people were mostly unresponsive, as their concerns were largely centered on how to cope in ordinary life under the tough conditions existent in the Occupied and Unoccupied Zones of a France under Hitler's heel. Prefect reports, as Pierre Laborie had indicated, reflected the initial lack of outrage to the racial discriminatory laws of 1940 and 1941.[124] That the Vichy government had created the Jewish exclusions

---

123   Ibid., 368-370.
124   *L'Opinion Française Sous Vichy.* Ibid., 273–276. Laborie properly cites Michael R. Marrus and Robert O. Paxton for uncovering the prefect reports in this regard. Only fourteen of forty-two Vichy prefects reported public reaction to the First Jewish Statute, nine of which were favorable and one mixed. Only twelve made mention that there was any public comment whatsoever concerning the second statute of mid-1941 and they were equally split between favorable and mixed. *Vichy France and the Jews.* Ibid., 181–182.

had a great import over time. Important elements of French society, like lawyers, for example, actively contributed valuable input as to which Jews were actually to be excluded, in the form of the numerus clausus quotas imposed. It is probably fair to say that anti-Jewish feelings were stronger in the south, which includes the Gard, because many foreign and French Jewish refugees were concentrated there after the Exodus, and they were resented as strangers in some rural communities, or competitors for limited food supplies in major urban areas.[125] After all, French Vichy—not the Germans—had initiated the discriminatory racial legislation against the Jews. One Jew, R. Poznanski, caught precisely the initial mood in the Free Zone: "Here we can still move around freely and don't fear arrest at any moment. But as for the attitude of the French, one feels more at home in the Occupied Zone."

In Nîmes, however, there was a major exception to this unsympathetic feeling in the person of Pastor Marc Boegner, who took a strong moral stand in private letters he wrote to Admiral Darlan and the Grand Rabbi of France when the creation of the CGQJ was announced. The letter to the Grand Rabbi of March 26, 1941, was not meant to be made public but a copy was obtained and published by a Parisian collaborationist journal, *Au Pilori*. Pastor Boegner expressed his long-held conviction that the Vichy anti-Jewish statutes were racist and unfair, and affirmed that the Protestant Church: "which has known the suffering of persecution, feels a sharp sympathy for [the Jewish people]." The fact that at the time he mainly pleaded for French Jews does not diminish his courage to speak out on an unpopular subject, and is in great contrast to the silence from his local Catholic counterpart. On October 31, 1941, the pastor of Marrakesh in Morocco wrote Pastor Boegner about his fears that Pope Pius was going to sign a Vatican Accord with Hitler. His lengthy letter concluded: "It is not an Anglophile who speaks to you as it is somewhat against my nature to see the Anglo-Saxons fight with the Moujiks [the Russians] at their side. But to see the French in Russia in German uniforms!" The letter was marked by the SCT "Surveillance

---

125 Marrus and Paxton comment on a climax of popular anti-Semitism (or scapegoat assignment) in a quotation from an SCT report of August 1942: "The Jews excite a violent antipathy in the Free Zone. Their insolent attitude, the luxury that they indulge in shamelessly, the black market that they help support, make them hated." Ibid., 181, note 7. This was written just before the August roundups occurred in the south.

575/SCCT-380-T of November 5, 1941" with usual SCT bureaucratic efficiency, as Pastor Boegner and his correspondence were closely watched all the time.[126]

Events in June and July 1942 brought the French, at least temporarily, out of their torpor vis-à-vis the inhuman treatment of Jewish people in their country. The first action was the German edict that Marshal Pétain would refuse to implement in the Free Zone, which dictated that all Jews in the Occupied Zone, foreign or French, above the age of six, had to wear a stitched or sewn yellow Star of David on the exterior of their clothes.[127] Jean Guéhenno wrote in his diary on June 16 that "for the last eight days the Jews have had to wear the yellow star in order to bring public contempt upon them. Never have the people been so kind to them. As Nietzsche knew, 'Spare the man any shame.'" He quoted a German philosopher to harpoon Hitler's henchmen, and at that moment many Frenchmen felt as he did. Of course, the real turning point was the roundups in July and August. We have referenced the heartrending experiences of Edith Thomas and Annie Kriegel. Catholic hierarchy in the Unoccupied Zone joined in the chorus of condemnation from the pulpits of Toulouse, and then Montauban, Lyon, Marseille, and Albi. Archbishop Saliège's pastoral message of August 23 in Toulouse was clear in its denunciation of the arrests of the Jews, whom he labeled as "our brothers." These messages stirred up publicity on a subject about which even the resistance press had heretofore been largely circumspect. Although other concerns like STO arose to divert French attention, beneath the surface large segments of the French civil population were stirred by this dreadful treatment of all Jews, and many of them would become unsung heroes for aiding significant numbers of Jews in France to escape the Nazi grim reaper machine in the east.[128]

It is these ordinary French citizens from all classes and walks of life who must be credited in large part with the 76 percent survival rate of the Jews in France during the Holocaust. We have witnessed some advantages that wealth gave to a family like the Schreibers, but even their family members were the beneficiaries of help from friends, neighbors,

---

126   *Nimes at War.* Ibid., 119 and note 128; ADG. 1 W 42. Marked 590. *France: The Dark Years.* Ibid., 370–373.
127   *L'Opinion Française Sous Vichy.* Ibid., 263.
128   Ibid., 374–376. *Journal des Années Noires*; Ibid., 266.

or employees in avoiding the Vichy and German nets. An area like the Cévennes mountains, the southern limit of the Massif Central, is in the Gard as well as crossing over into the adjacent departments of Hérault, Aveyron, Lozère, and Ardèche. That area was rich with stories of the concealment and saving of Jewish people, dating certainly from 1942. We have already described the story of Stanley Hoffmann and his mother, and how they were helped to escape the Germans in Nice and hide out for the rest of the war in Lamalou-les-Bains, which is in the Hérault. Robert Zaretsky relates how Pastor Boegner gathered sixty-seven fellow Protestant pastors in September 1942 in the Musée du desert in Mas Soubeyran, the home of an ancient Camisard rebellion leader, where he used their ancient experiences of persecution, exile, and death in order to inspire them to help the Jews. Later on, he reflected how this moment in time was the investiture of "the ministry that, up until France's liberation, helped thousands of French and foreign Jews escape from the French and German police."[129]

Mas Soubeyran, not very far from the Gardon River, lists itself on its website as a point near the end of the famous Robert Louis Stevenson Trail. Further northwest about thirty-three kilometers is another village definitely on the Stevenson Trail, Saint-Germain-de-Calberte. In summer 2008, I drove the narrow, curving roads, with fearful precipitous drops to avoid, through mountain pine forests into that village, where I saw Parisian vacationer families still hiking the Stevenson trail while leading their rented pack donkeys. Times were very different in 1943–44 in this lovely but remote Cévènol village in the Lozère. Julian Jackson recounts that eight foreign Jewish families—including Greeks, Hungarians, Poles, and Russians—were hidden in the hotel, while another five Jews were concealed by the village schoolteacher. The local village post office did its own unauthorized interception of a letter that a "French Aryan" hotel guest wrote denouncing the presence of these Jewish families. The letter was never forwarded. Escape networks, including Catholic ones, existed and did yeomen work in helping Jews escape French or German snares, but it is the unsung and often nameless individuals who handled a few Jews at a time who probably made the numbers of those saved so significant.

Jackson also gives an account of another French Jewish historian,

---

129   *Nimes at War*. Ibid., 121 and note 138; 122.

Pierre Vidal-Naquet, saved along with his brothers and a sister by his schoolteacher. His parents were not so lucky and perished in Auschwitz, while the four children were taken to hide out in Sainte-Agrève in northwest Ardèche in the home of an old Protestant lady. The reasons for survival were numerous and varied from department to department. Irène Nemirovsky or her husband Michel Epstein certainly did not benefit from their high Vichy or important German contacts. However, their two daughters were saved, amazingly, by a sympathetic German officer who had a blonde daughter whom Dénise Epstein resembled. He gave the two girls forty-eight hours to disappear. *Suite Française* was also saved, as their father gave them the valise containing the first two chapters and notes of their mother, the author. She might have survived if she had sneaked into the Italian Zone, which was the safest area until the Germans occupied that section of France in late 1943.[130]

Yet when the Germans occupied southern France in late 1942 after the invasion of North Africa or took possession of the Italian Zone one year later, almost all Jewish people were aware that bad things could happen to them if a knock came on their door in the middle of the night. Most Jewish people had begun to react differently from the time of the Vel' d'Hiv roundup, when they were surprised in Paris by the French police's coordinated actions against their community. Several additional factors were at work to help save them. The majority of French people had become anti-German and anti-Vichy certainly by 1943. The Germans did attempt to step up their arrests of Jews, but their troops had other priorities in anticipation of any Allied invasion. The numbers of the Gestapo were few, and the French police were no longer as cooperative as they had been in the big roundups of 1942. Ordinary citizens were willing to supplement the maturing Jewish evasion networks, and as we saw in the story of Jean-Claude Servan-Schreiber, people could succeed in crossing the Pyrénées into neutral Spain or Switzerland, which many thousands of Jews did.

But in a geographically diverse France, the essential element in this process to aid the Jews was the increasing willingness of average French citizens, although fearful of France becoming a battleground again, to

---

130 *France: The Dark Years.* Ibid., 377–378; Olivier Philipponnat and Patrick Lienhardt. *La Vie d'Irène Nemirovsky* (Paris : Editions Grasset Denoel, 2007), 417–423, and note 17, letter from Dénise Epstein to Myriam Anissimov.

put their safety on the line because they had become more revolted by Vichy and German actions and racial policies. Vercors's splendid novel, *Le Silence de la mer*, published secretly in France in February 1942, in which an old man and his daughter "resist" by refusing to converse with a cultured German officer billeted with them, was famously criticized by Arthur Koestler in London for being an inadequate form of resistance. To the contrary, Jean Bruller's (Vercors was understandably a *nom de plume*) important act of resistance was to publish and distribute this novel clandestinely under the German occupation, in what became the first volume of the *Editions de Minuit*. A great debate broke out in France over what constituted real resistance and real collaboration, which still is going on today. My point is that what thousands of ordinary French citizens did, independently or as part of established networks, to help feed, clothe, and conceal Jews from the authorities in the latter half of the Occupation, if not earlier, was indeed the choice they made individually *to resist*.[131]

---

131   *France: The Dark Years.* Ibid., 380-381, 442; *Vichy France.* Ibid., 38 ; *De Munich a la Libération.* Ibid., 256–257, note 1.

Afterword

"Complaints about food supplies are numerous. The cost of living is very high. The ninety cent per hour wage increase gives no satisfaction. The queues in front of the stores are lengthy and particularly at the time of wine delivery. The allotment of this drink will be clearly insufficient: one-half liter per day."[1]

"For example, during the first day of demonstrations at Alès about two hundred women, with their 'little nippers' in tow, formed outside the sub-prefecture and chanted 'Bread! Bread!' Having received no answer from the officials, the women returned the following day with a catchier slogan: 'Death to the sub-prefect. We want bread to eat.'"[2]

"For there can be no salvation where there is not some sacrifice, no national liberty in the fullest sense unless we have ourselves worked to bring it about, ... Whatever form the final triumph may take, it will be many years before the stain of 1940 can be effaced." —Marc Bloch[3]

"I am not a hero. I was just an ordinary housewife and secretary." —Miep Gies, who helped hide Anne Frank and preserved her diary[4]

---

1   ADG. 1 W 42. Survey summary for Alès, July 17, 1941, marked 363.
2   *Nîmes at War*. Ibid., 180, letter dated February 21, 1942.
3   *Strange Defeat*. Ibid., xii.
4   *New York Times*. January 13, 2010, in an editorial memorializing the death of

"France was at times an accomplice in this shame [the Holo-caust]. She is bound forever by the debt she has incurred."[5]

"A crime committed in France by France. ... We owe to the Jewish martyrs ... the truth concerning what happened."
—President François Hollande [6]

M uch of the material in this book consists of translation of archival documents, particularly, but not only, in the chapters devoted to public opinion in the years from 1940 through 1944. My intent has been to translate these documents in a literal fashion, so that the words speak for themselves. I have tried to refrain as much as possible from voicing my own opinion about from whence these expressions of concerns or difficulties came. However, I have on occasion given a warning to readers that some portions, especially some summary report commentary, might have been written to please the boss, so to speak. Perhaps this warning is especially applicable to several of the hundred-plus Gardois documents that are cited in chapter 6, just after the primary war concern statistics given for Montpellier, Toulouse, and the Gard. For example, the many references to the Silhol assassination could be interpreted to favor his political affiliation and the Milice, at the time when Vichy's world was falling apart. With the primary exception of this section, where possibly it is better often to read against the grain to maintain proper perspective, I believe the major concerns of the people are expressed in a clear, direct fashion.[7]

Miep Gies, age 100. The piece ended by saying of the Franks' protectors: "Their collective story is an enduring reminder that human beings always have a choice, even when millions were acceding to unspeakable evil."

5   *Postwar: A History of Europe Since 1945*, 819–820. Statement by Jacques Chirac's Prime Minister, Jean-Pierre Raffarin, on March 15, 2005, at the Holocaust Museum in Jerusalem.

6   *Le Figaro*, July 23, 2012. *"Vél d'Hiv: Hollande rompt avec Mitterrand. »* Discourse given by French President Hollande on the occasion marking the seventieth anniversary of the Vél d'Hiv roundup.

7   H. R. Kedward. *In Search of the Maquis: Rural Resistance in Southern France 1942–1944.* (Oxford, UK: Oxford University Press, 1993), 112–113. Kedward mentions that as early as 1942, some citizens in the Unoccupied Zone sensed that there was a chance that private mail was being intercepted and read by Vichy. There were examples where certain SCT officials were lax in observing the many

The penury associated with daily life was the predominant concern in the minds of the Gardois citizenry. Some of this destitution was caused by the huge demands forced upon the French economy by Hitler's rapacious administrators. The German war machine imposed voracious needs on all France in food supplies, primary materials for industrial production, finished military equipment, and labor, in addition to the money to pay for the German army to occupy France. In turn, Pétain and his various Vichy governments had to respond with administrative restrictions to cope with such German impositions, which took the form of individual rationing cards and tickets for the allocation of basic foodstuffs. From the unfiltered complaints registered in the Gard we know that great deficiencies frequently existed for what the French would consider essential staples: bread, milk, meat, and even wine. This situation was aggravated in a department like the Gard where a monoculture based on wine existed.

Prior to the war, the Gard's economy[8] was greatly dependent on the delivery of basic foodstuffs that came from other departments within France. The war's effect was draconian on the availability of essential food supplies. In December 1943, some seventy tons of meat were required weekly to provision the Gard adequately and the department could only produce five or six tons. One can imagine where that meat mostly stayed: in the countryside where it was produced. In 1942, the weekly requirement for potatoes was fifteen thousand tons, and the Gard produced only three thousand tons, if it was lucky. We have seen how

---

admonitions formally issued them to keep the contents of SCT interceptions and reports secret. Awareness of the depth and breadth of the SCT program was relatively limited, however. We know from Vichy circulars we examined in chapter 1 that efforts were made by various interior ministry officials, including Réné Bousquet, to limit the frequency of reporting and the actual number of copies distributed. Perhaps this worked to some degree but, for instance, the January 1944 summary report of Inspector Piquet (see chapter 6) was distributed to officials in Vichy, Marseille, and the Gard (the prefect's office and the Archives). It is more likely that the relatively limited number of people who were truly active in any Resistance efforts had the common sense to be very circumspect in their private communications. Kedward's point about the frequency with which collaborators put their opinions in writing toward the end of the war is reaffirmed also in the many letters quoted at the end of chapter 6. ADG. 1 W 42. Contrôle Technique of Nîmes Report for January 1944, marked No.135/A, 35.

8   ADG. 1 W 40. Marked 45 and 225.

the SCT kept close watch on M. Lufiacre's conversations in 1940–1941 when he was the man in charge of potato distribution. The geographical areas of the Gard most drastically affected by short rations were the southern viniculture plains which included Nîmes, and the Alèsian coal-mining basin. The vast majority of the Gard's population was included in these agricultural and primary materials areas critical to the Gard's economic well-being. Of course, when the German occupation troops arrived in the Gard, which coincided with the fear of Allied bombing raids and/or invasion, living conditions became even more difficult.[9]

Claude Emerique gives a precise description of the ascending level of difficulties in food resupply experienced in the Gard. Rationing was imposed as early as July 1, 1940, when cards were issued for obtaining bread. New categories added August 1 were for sugar, coffee, pasta, rice, fats, and soap. In September, meat was rationed, and then milk, cheese, and potatoes in the final quarter of 1940. At first people felt rationing would place a fair burden on everyone, but as the general penury expanded, people began to complain of favoritism in the issuance of cards and tickets that were doled out by the local mayors. Different standards were applied for rural and urban areas, with the latter issued larger allocations of vegetables and meats, as the authorities thought the rural peasants could use their own resources for these food categories. The situation that evolved was far from perfect, due to the fact that the irregularity of food-supply delivery from sources outside the Gard worsened as time passed.

Rations were specific for eight age groups or work-related categories, and the cards were stamped with the appropriate alphabetical code:

- E: children under 3 years

- J1: children between 3 and 6 years

- J2: children from 6 to 13 years

- J3: children from 13 to 21 years

- A: adults from 21 to 70

- V: people over 70 and ill people

---

9   *La Résistance dans le Gard.* DVD. File://E:_xml\fiches\30978.htm. Fabrice Sugier, 17/06/2009.

- T: laborers

- C: agricultural workers

Only men were issued tobacco rations; supplemental categories were added later for women who were pregnant and mothers who were breast-feeding, as well as for laborers doing hard work that required maintaining strength, and sick children.

Bread being such a French staple, it is instructive that as of January 26, 1941, its ration was cut 25 percent to 75 grams a day for young children (E), 150 grams for children aged 3–6 and old people (J1 and V), 225 grams for children over 6 through all adults (J2–J3 and A), and 300 grams per day for laborers (T and C). If the laborer in fact received his daily bread allowance, this translated into just one French baguette per day. Of course we already know how many Gardois complained bitterly about the poor delivery of food supplies that were insufficient in quantity anyway. Producers protested equally that they could not charge enough for what they did deliver, and both segments of the population raged over the chaos created by bureaucratic restrictions. We already have read much about the lack of tobacco, fatty materials, and even wine. The pleasures deprived workers in this regard made them more sullen. Another example given that could make a miner's work extra gruesome was the lack of soap. A miner supposedly was issued 125 grams of soap per month. That amount would suffice to clean the grimy coal off a miner's body for only three consecutive days of work in the mines, and they worked six days a week during the war years.

Forming lines became a conditioned reflex for women during 1940–1944 and a fact of life necessary for survival, if one were lucky. Queuing was a necessity every day, whether it was to obtain the requisite food-rationing cards or tickets at the mayor's office, or to get in the lines at multiple stores. In France at this time, no supermarkets existed, so there were only specialty stores like the baker, the butcher, the vegetable/fruit seller, the fish monger, etc. These lines consumed hours of the home-makers' time and some started to form very early in the morning, well before the approved queue-up time of 6 AM. The lines naturally took on a social milieu of their own, where rumors and frustrations with the regime were propagated, that did not bode well for the future of Pétain's national renewal efforts. Some people had to resort to fraudulent ways to gain their ration cards or tickets, and we have read instances where *réfractaires*, for example, robbed or pillaged banks and administrative offices in the Gard to secure these paper necessities for survival. The black market thrived during the war years, especially in the Gard's rural areas. Whether people were wealthy, or bank robbers, or plain thrifty folks, they all participated in the *marché noir* from time to time, with the exception of the working poor undoubtedly. But this illegal entity thrived because the concerted efforts of the state failed to provide for even the reduced level of necessities that were needed to sustain their average citizens. Neither rationing, nor alternate food substitutes, nor efforts to control pricing satisfied the people, and these botched efforts just added to their high level of dissatisfaction.[10]

Louis Begley named a chapter is his recent book, *Why the Dreyfus Affair Matters*, after a famous quotation by William Faulkner: "The Past Is Never Dead."[11] Begley goes on to state: "The erratic and lawless actions of successive French ministers of war and high-ranking officers in the course of the Dreyfus Affair can similarly be traced to a defining national Trauma: the humiliating defeat suffered by the French army in the Franco-Prussian War of 1870."[12] In spite of the ultimate exoneration and reinstatement of Captain Alfred Dreyfus, that past affair lived on within the French psyche. Its anti-Semitic effect expanded exponentially during the 1930s and it certainly maintained its impact after the even greater trauma for the French army and nation, the debacle they suffered again at the hands of the Germans in May–June 1940. It influenced the formation of Pétain's Vichy government along with its National Revolution agenda.

President Jacques Chirac wrote about the tragic events surrounding the descendants of Captain Dreyfus and Emile Zola, one hundred years after their occurrence. He affirmed that the injustice revealed and then rectified "spoke with a strong voice to our hearts" and that Zola's words

---

10   Ibid. file://E_xml\fiches\30978.htm Claude Emerique.
11   William Faulkner. *Requiem for a Nun* (New York: Random House, 1951). The full quotation is "The past is never dead. It's not even past." Albert Camus adapted Faulkner's novel for the stage in 1956 as *Requiem pour une nonne*, and Barack Obama quoted Faulkner's phrase in his March 18, 2008, "A More Perfect Union" speech on race in America.
12   Louis Begley. *Why the Dreyfus Affair Matters*. (New Haven: Yale University Press, 2009). Kindle edition location 480-484.

written to another French president "have remained in our collective memory as a great moment of human conscience." He went on to warn his citizens that "a half-century after Vichy, we know that the dark forces of intolerance and injustice can penetrate right to the heights of the state." Eight years later, on July 12, 2006, President Chirac spoke again about this racist episode, this time to those assembled at the Military School in Paris. He exhorted the people "to rebuff racism and anti-Semitism, defend the rights of man, the primacy of justice: all those values which today are part of our heritage. They can seem to have been fully established. But it is necessary for us to always maintain extreme vigilance: the fight against forces of darkness, injustice, intolerance, and hate are never definitively won."[13]

In chapter 8 and elsewhere, I have covered extensively how certain Jewish people were treated by the Vichy government in both the Gard and elsewhere in France during its Dark Years, 1940–1944. The Schreiber-Crémieux alliance created a family of privileged people, thanks to the business acumen and financial success of Robert and the political connections and social prowess of Suzanne. That they were rich did not alter the basic fact that they were in the crosshair sights of the Vichy authorities due to their racial composition. The Germans added to the pressure once they occupied all of France. Like the vast majority of French Jews, the Schreibers followed the rules set down by Vichy under the various anti-Jewish statutes. From time to time, it might have seemed that various connections they had from the past benefited them, but they really didn't in the long run. What they and their immediate family members did enjoy was some good luck in time and space, along with some active help from average people. Robert, Suzanne, and especially Marie-Claire seem to have experienced some chancy situations. Jean-Claude also ran risks, both in the Gard and when he was in the active military fighting against the German invaders. He suffered three wounds participating in campaigns at the beginning and the end of the war. The youngest daughter must have encountered perils as well. Some Schreiber cousins of German birth reputedly were rounded up and placed on one of the Auschwitz-bound convoys from France, never to be heard from

---

13 http://www.cahiers-naturalistes.com/chirac.htm   4/6/2011.   http://fr.wikisource.org/wiki/Allocution_de_M._Jacques_Chirac_%C3%A0_propos_d'Alfred_Dreyfus_en_2006

again. Robert Schreiber and Suzanne Crémieux lived to see both of their last wishes honored by their children. Under the circumstances, they could consider themselves lucky indeed to have survived the war.

We have read multitudinous examples in which French functionaries went about doing their work diligently under Vichy, which aided that state in its overt policies of collaboration. These bureaucrats must share, in choosing to do their jobs, some degree of collusion in the achievement of Vichy's mission, of which the anti-Jewish activities were the most egregious. As Robert Paxton writes in his conclusion of *Vichy France*, "Even Frenchmen of the best intentions, faced with the harsh alternative of doing one's job, whose risks were moral and abstract, or practicing civil disobedience, whose risks were material and immediate, went on doing their job." However, we who did not live through such circumstances cannot afford to cast stones and be tempted to say we would have acted otherwise. The France of 1940–1944 was a time in mankind's dark history when some relatively few courageous French men and women did choose to "save a nation's deepest values" (as Jacques Chirac referenced above) by refusing to obey the state.[14]

On January 25, 2011, Guillaume Pepy, the chairman of the Société Nationale des Chemins de Fer Français (SNCF), made the company's first formal public apology directly to Holocaust victims. At a ceremony conducted in the railroad station at Bobigny, a Paris suburb, from where some twenty thousand Jews had been shipped mostly during 1943 and 1944 to Nazi death camps, he proclaimed: "In the name of the SNCF, I bow down before the victims, the survivors, the children of those deported, and before the suffering that still lives." The *New York Times* reported that "Mr. Pepy was responding to years of litigation brought by lawmakers, survivors, their descendants and some American Jewish organizations. They say the company never formally apologized for shipping seventy-six thousand European Jews (including French ones) to the Franco-German border in seventy-six rail cars originally designed to transport cattle, between 1941 and 1944. (German trains then took the deportees to Nazi death camps)." The article went on to state that some French historians, including Arno Klarsfeld, the son of Serge and Beate Klarsfeld, and the CGT union, felt the speech

---

14 *Vichy France*. Ibid., 382–283.

criticized the SNCF and its wartime members unfairly.[15] Articles on the subject of responsibility for the French deportation of foreign and French Jews during World War II, as well as litigation seeking compensation by some of the living victims, had appeared in the French and American press in the past. In February 2009, the French Council of State, which has the final say on civil law matters, ruled on the subject and called for "solemn recognition of the responsibility of the state." It endorsed what president Jacques Chirac had proclaimed in 1995, that France was "responsible for damages caused by actions which did not result from the occupiers' direct orders but facilitated deportation from France of people who were victims of anti-Semitic persecution." But the French court went on to rule that "Jewish war victims have had enough compensation." I suppose any living relatives of the Jewish man taken away by the Gestapo in Saint-Gilles we read about might take exception to this statement.[16]

"French Château's Owners Enter a Thicket of Intrigue" was the headline in The *New York Times* on March 2, 2010. It related the story of a château property of 1,940 acres near Orleans, which had been purchased by a Parisian Jew, Emile Akar, in 1936. He had fled in the exodus to Marseille, where he died of natural causes in November 1940. The property had been seized by the CGQJ, and the appointed provisional administrator had sold it in a contract dated November 27, 1941, to a M. Fernand Plee, "of French nationality, non-Israelite." Much confusion currently reigns about this matter, as in 1945 no one in the Plee family notified the new French government of this transaction and it was a forgotten incident until 2006, when the Plee descendants contested a zoning change in court, which initiated a property search. The article neared its interesting end by stating: "And yet, this much is certain: in a note dated September 25, 1941, a departmental prefect informed the General Authority for Jewish Questions of the existence of the Château de l'Ecluse, 'a Jewish property' belonging to M. Emile Akar; on October 24, the General Authority named Bernard Guilpin its administrator. And on November 27 Mr. Guilpin sold the estate—he would collect

---

15   The *New York Times*, January 26, 2011, article by Maia de la Baume, published on January 25: "French Railway Formally Apologizes to Holocaust Victims."

16   The *New York Times*, February 17, 2009, article by Charles Bremner in Paris: "Jewish War Victims have had enough Compensation, French Court says." Also in Le Figaro:fr, *L'Etat français reconnu responsable dans la déportation des Juifs.*

a fee of 13,238 francs for his services, more than $6,500 in modern terms—to M. Fernand Plee." A modern-day descendant of M. Akar, Jean-Francois Akar, gave the final quotation in the article: "Our forgiveness is granted for whoever asks it." None of the Plee descendants has asked for it. Perhaps some secrets like that rest dormant in the property registrars' files in Remoulins.[17]

Early in October 2010, headlines appeared within France when Serge Klarsfeld "announced the discovery of an original draft of the law that first established discriminatory practices aimed at Jews under the Vichy government of France." The *New York Times* reported on October 6 that the document in question reputedly "includes handwritten annotations made by Marshal Pétain, France's chief of state from July 1940 until August 1944." At the time of these sensational headlines, no independent handwriting expert apparently had been consulted. However, Jean-Pierre Azéma did tell the daily newspaper *Le Parisien*: "We used to say that Pétain himself had never truly participated in the policy of state anti-Semitism, exclusion, and discrimination. Until now (Mr. Azéma said), historians had no decisive proof that the marshal, cherished by the French at the time, had participated in the writing of the law." If proven true, this could add to quite a bit of revisionism. Whether Pétain did this or not, these laws were rigorously applied by his functionaries, led in the Gard by Prefect Angelo Chiappe.[18]

On March 10, 2011, the *Times* published an article on Stephane Hessel, a hero of the French Resistance who had been tortured by the Gestapo. M. Hessel, who is half-Jewish, has written, at age ninety-three, a four-thousand-word book called *Time for Outrage* (*Indignez-Vous!*), which has sold about 1.5 million copies in France. It now is published in English and many other languages, and "protests France's treatment of illegal immigrants, the influence on the media of the rich, cuts to the social welfare system, French educational reforms, and, most strongly, Israel's treatment of the Palestinians." The book has received its share of criticism from politicians and French intellectuals, especially for its criti-

---

17   The *New York Times*, March 2, 2010, article by Scott Sayare: "French Château's Owners Enter a Thicket of Intrigue."

18   The *New York Times*, October 6, 2010, article by Maia de la Baume: "Vichy Leader Said to Widen Anti-Jewish law. Vichy France and the Jews." Ibid., 16–18 gives some background concerning Pétain and how he conducted himself vis-à-vis Jewish people in public and private.

cism of Israel. M. Hessel counters such accusations by saying, "I know what it is to be a Jew. ...I am myself of Jewish origin, and therefore I can only be fully in support of the idea that the Jews, after all they have suffered, need a country where they are at home ... But I want it to be an honest country." He and his wife did visit Gaza in 2009 and described it as "an open-sky prison for a million and a half Palestinians" and said that "for Jews themselves to perpetuate war crimes is intolerable."[19]

"The past is never dead. It's not even past."

However, as Shakespeare put it, "Wherefore what's past is prologue; what to come, in yours and my discharge."[20]

In September 2009, my wife and I were invited to lunch by Jean-René de Fleurieu at Montfrin Château, where he prepared a delicious informal meal in the ex-chapel kitchen, in the midst of grape harvest time on the property. It was a delightful visit, topped off by a tour of the interior of the château and coffee and conversation in the salon. After our visit we trekked up to Robert Schreiber's final resting spot overlooking the property. Later by happenstance, we ran into Jean-René in one of his wine fields, from which he took us on a tour of his modern and pristine *Moulin des Ombres*, where he produces fine virgin olive oil. We left with three bottles in hand, a most kind gift from the Frenchman to his foreign guests. Only later when I did a search on the de Fleurieu name did I realize what these acts of kindness done to American strangers presaged. An ancestor, Charles Pierre Claret de Fleurieu (1738–1810), had entered the French navy at age thirteen. He undoubtedly came to the attention of King Louis XVI because of his work in 1766 with the engineer Louis Berthoud on the marine watch or chronometer, in the search for fixing longitude. De Fleurieu conducted important experiments with that device during his voyage to the Caribbean in 1768–1769, when he commanded the frigate *Isis*. In 1776, he was appointed inspector general of all ports and navy yards in France (*L'intendant* in French), and from 1778 through 1783 he was placed in charge of all naval war plans against England during the War for American Independence. His strategic planning contributed to dispatching Admiral de

---

19   The *New York Times*, March 10, 2011, article by Elaine Sciolino, "A Resistance Hero Fires Up the French."

20   *The Works of William Shakespeare* (New York: Oxford University Press, 1938). *The Tempest*. Act II, Scene I, 215–251.

Grasse and his fleet to American waters from Brest on March 22, 1781.
Generals Washington and Rochambeau had decided in May to consoli-
date their American and French troops against the British forces based
on New York City, where the British enjoyed naval superiority. However,
in August, when Washington learned that de Grasse's fleet of twenty-
nine ships of the line and more than three thousand additional French
troops was bound for the Chesapeake, where Cornwallis was vulnerably
encamped at Yorktown, he decided the better opportunity for combined
operations was in Virginia. On September 5, de Grasse fought the
British fleet to a draw off the Chesapeake, and by mid-September, Washington's forces arrived to start investing the British defenses at Yorktown.
Washington convinced a nervous de Grasse to keep maneuvering at sea,
blockading the York River estuary. We know the result: Washington's
superior armies attacked on September 28, never letting up the pressure,
and on October 19, 1781, General Cornwallis surrendered his British
army. The world had turned "upside down," and in effect, American
independence had been won. So it could be said that our often forgotten American indebtedness to the French nation at our beginning also
includes some personal indebtedness to the de Fleurieu ancestry for the
role played by Charles Pierre Claret, Comte de Fleurieu.[21]

The title page of this book references the roots of coincidence. The
Comte survived the terror of the French Revolution and was actually
appointed by Napoleon I to many positions of importance, starting in
1797. He abetted American expansion through being minister plenipo-
tentiary for Napoleon during the negotiations attendant to the Louisi-
ana Purchase. Upon his death in 1810, Napoleon ordered a state funeral
and instructed that de Fleurieu's body be interred in the Panthéon. It
is often written and spoken that in the twentieth century, the United
States of America twice came to the rescue of the Allies, including especially the French, in the two World Wars. A case most certainly can
be made that although these efforts might not have been totally altru-
istic in nature, they could be construed as repayments for what the
French nation did from similar motivations to gain the United States
its freedom and independence. Regarding the Schreiber-Crémieux clan,
the American-led invasion on D-Day, *Jour-J*, was certainly an instru-

21   Robert Middlekauff. *The Glorious Cause: The American Revolution, 1763–1789* (New York: Oxford University Press, 1982), 562–570.

mental step to putting an end to the Vichy policies of collaboration with Hitler and his Nazi policies, which had imperiled characteristics so intrinsic to the French persona, such as the rights of man, or liberty, equality, and fraternity.[22]

---

22 http://fr.wikipedia.org/wiki/Charles_Pierre_Claret_de_Fleurieu. Also, Edited Appletons Encylopedia, Copyright 2001 Virtualology.

Select Bibliography

Primary Sources

Archives départementales du Gard (ADG)
Etat Provisoire
Versements de la Préfecture: Cabinet du Préfet, 1940–1945

1 W 29 Contrôle postale. Acheminement du courrier, réglementation, 1940–1944

1 W 30 Transcription du courrier interzone. Registre et bordereaux de transmission
1941–1942

1 W 31 Rapports de synthèses des contrôles de communication du Préfet 1941–1944

1 W 32 Interceptions téléphone 1940–1943

1 W 33 Interceptions téléphone, télégraphe 1944–1945

1 W 34 Téléphone, poste. Enquêtes suite une interception postale ou téléphonique 1942

1 W 35 Interceptions: circulaires et instructions, statistiques, textes, et rapports. Courrier interzone, contrôle PTT dossiers 1940–1945

1 W 36 Interceptions postales 1941

1 W 37 Interceptions postales 1941–1942

1 W 38 Interceptions postales 1944

1 W 39 Interceptions postales 1944

1 W 40 Interceptions postales 1940

1 W 41 Interceptions PTT et rapports 1940
1 W 42 Interceptions PTT et rapports 1941–1944
1 W 132-1 W 143 les Juifs: enquêtes, recensements, questions juives (12 dossiers)

Secondary Sources

Rick Atkinson. *An Army at Dawn*. New York: Henry Holt, 2002.

———. *The Day of Battle*. New York: Henry Holt, 2007.

Roger Austin. *Surveillance and Intelligence Under the Vichy Regime : The Service de Contrôle Technique, 1939–45*. Intelligence and National Security, 1/1, 1986.

Jean-Pierre Azéma. *De Munich a la Libération 1938–1944*. Paris: Seuil, 2002.

Jean-Pierre Azéma, François Bédarida, Daniel Cordier, editors. *Jean Moulin Face à l'Histoire*. Manchecourt, France: Flammarion, 2003 (2000).

Louis Begley. *Why the Dreyfus Affair Matters*. New Haven: Yale University Press, 2009.

Marc Bloch. *Strange Defeat: A Statement of Evidence Written in 1940*. New York:
W.W.Norton, 1968.

René de Chambrun Papers, 1914–1995. Stanford University, Hoover Institute Archives.

William Faulkner. *Requiem for a Nun*. New York: Random House, 1951.

Philippe Burrin. *La France a L'Heure Allemande 1940–1944*. Paris: Seuil, 1995.

Sarah Fishman, Laura Lee Downs, Ioannis Sinanoglou, Leonard V. Smith, Robert Zaretsky, editors. *France at War: Vichy and the Historians*. New York: Berg, 2000.

Eric Foner. *The Fiery Debate: Abraham Lincoln and American Slavery*. New York:
W. W. Norton, 2010.

Douglas Southall Freeman. *Lee's Lieutenants: A Study in Command*. New York: Charles Scribner's Sons, 1943.

Ernest B. Furgurson. *Chancellorsville 1863: The Souls of the Brave*. New York: Vintage Books, 1993.

Pierre Giolitto. *Histoire de la Jeunesse sous Vichy*. Paris: Perrin, 1991.

Jean Guéhenno. *Journal des Années Noires 1940–1944*. Paris: Gallimard, 2002.

Alistair Horne. *To Lose a Battle: France 1940.* New York: Penguin Book, 1979.

Agnès Humbert. *Notre Guerre. Résistance: A Woman's Journal of Struggle and Defiance in Occupied France.* Paris: Editions Emile-Paul Frères, 1946. English Translation by Barbara Mellor. New York: Bloomsbury, 2008.

Institut d'histoire du temps présent. *L'œil et l'oreille de la Resistance.* Toulouse: Eres, 1986.

Julian Jackson. *France: The Dark Years 1940–1944.* Oxford: Oxford University Press, 2003

Tony Judt. *Postwar: A History of Europe since 1945.* New York: Penguin Press, 2005.

Alice Kaplan. *The Collaborator: The Trial and Execution of Robert Brasillach.* Chicago: University of Chicago Press, 2000.

H. R. Kedward. *In Search of the Maquis: Rural Resistance in Southern France 1942–1944.* Oxford, UK: Oxford University Press, 2003 (1993).

Serge Klarsfeld. *Le Mémorial de la déportation des Juifs de France.* Paris, 1978.

Pierre Laborie. *L'Opinion Française sous Vichy.* Paris : Seuil, 1990.

———. *Les Mots de '39–'45.* Toulouse: Presses Universaires du Mirail, 2006.

E. B. Long with Barbara Long. *The Civil War Day by Day: An Almanac 1861–1865.* Garden City: Doubleday & Company, Inc., 1971.

Geert Mak. *In Europe: Travels through the Twentieth Century.* New York: Vintage Books, 2008.

Michael R. Marrus and Robert O. Paxton. *Vichy France and the Jews.* Stanford: Stanford University Press, 1995 (1981).

James M. McPherson. *Ordeal by Fire: The Civil War and Reconstruction.* New York: McGraw-Hill Companies Inc. 2001.

Marie-Claire Mendès France. *L'esprit de liberté.* Paris: Presses de la Renaissance, 1992.

Robert Middlekauff. *The Glorious Cause: The American Revolution 1963–1789.* New York: Oxford University Press, 1982.

Irène Némirovsky. *Suite Française.* Paris: Denoël, 2004.

Robert O. Paxton. *Vichy France: Old Guard and New Order 1940–1944.* New York: Columbia University Press, 2001 (1972).

Olivier Philipponnat & Patrick Lienhardt. *La Vie d'Irène Némirovsky.* Paris: Grasset-Denoël, 2007.

Denis Peschanski, editor. *Vichy 1940–1944 Archives de guerre d'Angelo Tasca.* Paris: Fondazione Giangiacomo Feltrinelli, 1986, Editions du CNRS.

Henry Rousso. *The Vichy Syndrome: History and Memory in France since 1944*. Cambridge, MA: Harvard University Press, 1991.

Alain Rustenholz and Sandrine Treiner. *La Saga Servan-Schreiber: Une Famille dans la Siècle*. Paris: Seuil, 1993.

————. Volume 2, *Le Temps des Initiales*. Paris: Seuil, 1999.

Robert Servan-Schreiber. *Journal*. Paris: Editions Leo Scheer, 2009.

The Works of William Shakespeare. *The Tempest*. New York: Oxford University Press, 1938.

William L. Shirer. *The Nightmare Years 1930–1940*. New York: Bantam, 1985.

John F. Sweets. *Choices in Vichy France*. New York: Oxford University Press, 1986.

Richard Vinen. *The Unfree French: Life under the Occupation*. New Haven: Yale University Press, 2006.

Leon Werth. *33 Jours*. Paris: Seuil, 1988.

Robert Zaretsky. *Nimes at War: Religion, Politics, and Public Opinion in the Gard 1938–1944*. University Park, PA: Pennsylvania State University Press, 1995.

Index

9 781604 948837